PUBLICATIONS ON ETHNICITY AND NATIONALITY
OF THE
SCHOOL OF INTERNATIONAL STUDIES
UNIVERSITY OF WASHINGTON

Volume 2

This book is sponsored by Comparative Studies
in Ethnicity and Nationality
of the School of International Studies
of the University of Washington

5LC

Ethnic Change

EDITED BY

CHARLES F. KEYES

SEATTLE • UNIVERSITY OF WASHINGTON PRESS • LONDON

$S\text{-}r, 20.00 \mid 10.00 \mid 12/28/81$

Library of Congress Cataloging in Publication Data
Main entry under title:

Ethnic change.

    (Publications on ethnicity and nationality of the
School of International Studies, University of Washing-
ton ; v. 2)
    1. Ethnicity—Addresses, essays, lectures.
2. Ethnology—Addresses, essays, lectures. 3. Cross-
cultural studies—Addresses, essays, lectures.
I. Keyes, Charles F. II. Series: Washington (State).
University. School of International Studies. Publica-
tions on ethnicity and nationality of the School of
International Studies, University of Washington ; v. 2.
GN495.6.E86   305.8   80-54426
ISBN 0-295-95812-X   AACR1

Contents

v

Foreword

SINCE the fall of 1972, the program in Comparative Studies in Ethnicity and Nationality (CSEN) in the School of International Studies
at the University of Washington has conducted an annual seminar,
usually focusing on a theme relating to the rise and decline of ethnic
identities among diverse peoples around the world. The program
and the seminar, from its inception, have been interdisciplinary in
scope and have also drawn from specialists in most major regions of
the world, including both developing and postindustrial societies, for
papers and presentations. The program and the seminar also have provided a framework in which faculty and advanced graduate students
with a common interest in the subject of ethnicity and nationalism can
interact in a more lively and meaningful manner than is customary in
classroom and advisory settings. Several graduate students who have
participated in the CSEN program have gone to various parts of the
world to carry out dissertation research on ethnic issues.

The quality of the papers presented at the seminars and the dis-
sertations and other research done by graduate students in the program
has been so consistently high that it seemed worth-while to develop a
regular outlet for publication of the best results of the program-spon-

sored research. An initial selection of papers was published in a special issue of the journal *Ethnicity* in September 1976.[1] In 1979, the University of Washington Press launched a publication series on Ethnicity and Nationality, in which this volume is the second number.[2]

This volume, *Ethnic Change,* developed out of the CSEN seminar coordinated on the same topic in 1977 by Charles F. Keyes. The idea behind the seminar and the volume was that some of the most fundamental and controversial issues in the study of ethnicity might be examined most profitably in situations where ethnic groups are forced to adjust to radical changes in their environment such as are produced by migration, state expansion and penetration into outlying areas, and revolutionary changes in economy and society. In conformity with the traditions of the CSEN program, Professor Keyes selected his participants from several disciplines and from specialists working in different parts of the globe, so that anthropologists, sociologists, political scientists, and economists contributed papers on North America, Great Britain, Southeast Asia, the Middle East and North Africa, and Sierra Leone in sub-Saharan Africa. Finally, it deserves especially to be noted that two of the papers were contributed by graduate students who received training in and contributed to the development of our program, Carter Bentley and Richard Trottier.

Two major issues are explored in depth in the contributions to this book. The first is the debate between "primordialists" and "instrumentalists" or "circumstantialists" concerning the relative weights to be assigned to cultural and situational factors, to ties of sentiment and interest in the formation, persistence, and decline in ethnic identities in different contexts and at different times. The second, closely related, issue concerns the degree and types of variability to which ethnic identities are subject in different contexts and times.

On these issues, the papers in this volume provide fresh and original approaches and insights that take the primordialist-instrumentalist debate out of the realm of generalities into confrontations with concrete cases. The contributions and issues are framed by the introductory essay of Keyes and the concluding essay of Cohen and by two metaphors, which reflect the range of difference still remaining on this issue. The metaphor of the gyroscope, mentioned by Keyes, conveys the idea that the content, form, and the boundaries of ethnic groups may oscillate widely while still maintaining a central core or point. Cohen

1. Paul R. Brass and Pierre L. van den Berghe, *Ethnicity and Nationalism in World Perspective, Ethnicity* 3, no. 3 (September 1976): 197-303.

2. The first was M. Nazif Mohib Shahrani, *The Kirghiz and Wakhi of Afghanistan: Adaptation to Closed Frontiers* (Seattle: University of Washington Press, 1979).

refers in his essay to Barth's metaphor of ethnicity as a vessel that is always there, but argues that the vessel itself may vary and even disappear. If we return to the metaphor of the gyroscope, Cohen's imagery suggests that there may sometimes be no central point or core that persists through time, but that every aspect of an ethnic group's culture and the definition of the group itself may be subject to change beyond recognition.

Although, therefore, there remain some differences among the contributors concerning the relative weight to be assigned to cultural and social structural factors in ethnicity, the principal value of this collection of papers lies in the presentation by the several authors of original ways of examining variability in ethnicity and its limits, if any, and in the precision of the arguments. The papers by Banton, Light, and Nagata make clear that it is important to distinguish precisely the relevant interacting groups and the cultural practices and behaviors that may or may not be changed, that the ethnic boundaries of a group may be defined in local/regional or national terms, and that conflicting definitions of ethnic categories and their boundaries usually persist and may be used for different purposes in different contexts. The contributions by Bentley, Tessler, and Fox et al. show how specific factors, such as the introduction of cultural criteria to reinforce the boundaries between ranked status groups, the urban or rural residential status of persons from the same ethnic groups, and the pace of penetration of the state into the lives of ethnic minorities or geographically peripheral peoples may affect the boundaries between ethnic groups, their attitudes toward assimilation or differentiation in a host society, or the timing of the rise of ethnic nationalism. The papers by Trosper and Trottier suggest the conditions under which and the purposes for which panethnic identities are formed and panethnic movements succeed or fail. Altogether, these papers add up to a major contribution to specifying the components of culture and behavior that are subject to change, the range of "vessels" that can be used by different ethnic groups to promote their interests and preserve their identities, and the conditions that influence change in the content and salience of ethnic identities.

This book would not have been written were it not for the support provided to the CSEN program and to the Seminar on Ethnic Change by several agencies and individuals. The Seminar on Ethnic Change was funded as part of a grant to the CSEN program to develop problem and topic-oriented programs in International Studies at the graduate level by the United States Office of Education. Support for the research assistants who assisted in the coordination of the seminar and in the preparation of the volume was provided by the Graduate School of the University of Washington. Administrative and secretarial support for the CSEN program that made it possible to get the manuscript typed were provided by the College of Arts and Sciences. Professors Herbert Ellison and Kenneth Pyle, past and current directors of the School of International Studies, provided material and moral support for the CSEN program during this period and were instrumental in securing approval for the publication series. This second volume in our series goes far to repay these debts.

PAUL R. BRASS
Chairman
COMPARATIVE STUDIES IN
ETHNICITY AND NATIONALITY

Preface

FOR a number of years the program in Comparative Studies in Ethnicity and Nationality at the School of International Studies, University of Washington, has sponsored a research seminar to which outside speakers have been invited to present papers. Since 1976, specific themes have been chosen by the coordinators of the seminar as foci for papers and discussion for each academic year. In 1977 I was asked to coordinate the seminar for the year and I chose as my theme the subject of "Ethnic Change."

In inviting people to participate in the seminar, I attempted to seek out scholars who had done research in quite different contexts, including in both nonindustrialized and industrialized societies. I also sought people of different disciplinary backgrounds. That anthropology is rather overrepresented is a function not only of my own disciplinary orientation but also of the tendency of anthropologists more than others to be involved in the study of ethnic group relations in non-Western societies. I was also guided by my desire to invite scholars who would be able to confront in significant ways the fundamental problems that have emerged in the study of ethnicity. While the papers resulting from the seminar and now included in this volume cannot be claimed to represent anything more than themselves, I do feel that the seminar succeeded in stimulating the thinking of those who, at the University of Washington, have been involved in the study of ethnicity for many years. I can only hope that this collection will succeed to the same degree for others interested in the field.

One of the fortunate side benefits of the seminar was the opportunity it afforded to invite Professor Abner Cohen to spend several months at the University of Washington. Not only did Professor Cohen present the preliminary version of the paper included in this volume, but he also gave a series of lectures on ethnicity that were very well attended by both students and faculty. Both these lectures and my private discussions with Professor Cohen served to advance my own understanding of the subject of ethnicity.

I am indebted to Carter Bentley and Richard Trottier (both of whom have contributed to this volume) for their help as research assistants in the organization of the seminar. The seminar also benefited from a presentation made by Professor T. G. McGee who was, unfortunately, unable to prepare a paper to be included here. Professor Paul Brass, the director of the Program in Comparative Studies in Ethnicity and Nationality, provided the administrative support that made the seminar possible. Finally, I am grateful to Ms. Wendy Cavanaugh who was secretary of the program at the time and who provided invaluable assistance in my efforts to bring the seminar program into existence.

CHARLES F. KEYES

ETHNIC CHANGE

In this paper, Keyes proposes a theoretical approach to the study of ethnic change that takes into account both the cultural interpretation of ethnicity as a primordial characteristic of identity and the social manipulation of ethnicity in the pursuit of objective interests. Ethnic change, it is argued, is a dialectical process that begins when people experience a radical shift in their social circumstances (when they migrate to a new society or are incorporated into a new political order). As people evolve new patterns of social adaptation to their changed circumstances, they begin to reassess the saliency of the cultural basis of their ethnic identities. And, as new cultural meanings are given to their identities, they also develop social patterns in accord with the premises of their identities. Examples in Keyes's paper are drawn mainly from the other papers in the volume.

CHARLES F. KEYES

The Dialectics of Ethnic Change

THE study of ethnicity has reached something of a theoretical impasse. Neither the approach that conceives of ethnicity primarily as implying a cultural heritage shared by a group nor the approach that views ethnicity as a form of social organization that functions to achieve certain common ends of a group of people are wholly adequate for interpreting the large and growing number of cases that attest to the persistence of ethnicity as a factor in social relations. In this paper I will attempt to develop an approach that takes both the cultural and social dimensions of ethnicity into account. The significance of both dimensions can best be assessed in changes in which radical alterations of circumstances render problematical both modes of cultural identity and modes of social adaptation. Given this position, I asked those who participated in a research seminar that I organized in 1976-1977 under the auspices of the Program in Comparative Studies in

I have benefited in writing this paper from discussions with Paul Brass and Pierre van den Berghe as well as with the participants in the seminar whose papers appear here.

Ethnicity and Nationality of the School of International Studies, University of Washington, to make ethnic change a focal theme of their presentations. While not all of those who participated in the seminar would agree with my argument, their papers, here included, have all contributed to my own efforts to fashion a dialectical approach to the study of ethnicity.

The theoretical position I take in this paper is not restricted in its application to efforts to understand ethnicity; it is fundamental to the whole range of problems explored in the social sciences. However, I think that problems that have emerged in the efforts to interpret ethnicity, together with problems related to the study of kinship, are particularly critical for focusing attention on fundamental assumptions underlying social science theory.

ETHNICITY AS CULTURAL IDENTITY

In a previous paper (Keyes 1976), I contended that ethnic identities implicate a "primordial" relationship between people. According to Geertz, a primordial attachment between people is "one that stems from the 'givens'— or, more precisely, as culture is inevitably involved in such matters, the assumed 'givens' of social existence" (Geertz 1963, p. 109). Such givens, I have argued, are assumed to be determined at birth. The givens at birth that have been subject to cultural elaboration in many different societies include sex, locality and time of birth, physiological features that are recognized as marks of biological inheritance, and social descent or links with forebears. Ethnicity, I maintain, derives from a cultural interpretation of descent.

People are differentiated with reference to descent by virtue of assumptions made about the cultural legacy one gains from one's parents and through one or both of them from one's ancestors. As anthropological literature demonstrates, it is not necessary for the purposes of reckoning descent that one be the biological child of another; rather, descent presupposes a socially validated parent/child connection (cf. Schneider 1967, p. 65). I believe that it is important to distinguish between social descent and genetic descent, the latter consisting of biological characteristics transmitted through genetic inheritance. While knowledge of or visible manifestations of genetic descent have sometimes been used in construing the attributes of social descent, there are many cases where genetic and social descent are not linked.

My argument regarding ethnicity as being a cultural construal of descent is convergent with the argument advanced by E. K. Francis (1976; see, for example, p. 39), although my approach was developed before I became aware of Francis's work. In a recent paper, van den Berghe (1978) has sought grounding for the primordialist position in sociobiological theory. He argues (1978, p. 403) that "both ethnicity and 'race' (in the social sense) are, in fact, extensions of the idiom of kinship, and that, therefore, ethnic and race sentiments are to be understood as an extended form of kin selection." While I am persuaded that kin selection provides the underlying motivation that leads human beings to seek solidarity with those whom they recognize as being "of the same people" or as "sharing descent," such recognition, I would emphasize, is predicated upon the cultural construal of what characteristics indicate that others do or do not belong to the same people as oneself. Man is an "incomplete animal" who completes himself, as Geertz reminds us (1973, p. 49), through culture that he himself has created and, moreover, "not through culture in general but through highly particular forms of it." Thus, while ethnicity may rest on a universal predilection of humans to select positively in favor of their own kinsmen, it also is variable because of the diverse cultural meanings that people in different historical circumstances have drawn upon in interpreting and in action upon this predilection.

While, according to my argument, ethnicity is a form of kinship reckoning, it is one in which connections with forebears or with those with whom one believes one shares descent are not traced along precisely genealogical lines. Americans, for example, predicate their national identity upon connections with the "Pilgrim Fathers" and with the forefathers "who brought forth upon this continent a new nation" even though few Americans could actually trace genealogical connections with members of the Plymouth community or with those who wrote the Constitution or fought in the Revolutionary War.[1] Since descent can be posited with different "ancestors" who lived at different times in the past and can be traced through either or both parents, it is possible for a person to belong to more than one ethnic group just as he or she might belong to more than one descent-defined kin group. And despite such potentialities, it is also possible and often the case that an individual belongs to no ethnic group.[2] The potentiali-

1. In fact, those who have been able to trace actual genealogical connections to ancestors who fought (on the American side) in the Revolutionary War have sometimes attempted to set themselves apart from other Americans, as in organizations like the Daughters of the American Revolution.

2. In this paper I will be only tangentially concerned with individual uses of ethnic identity or with changes in identity by individuals as distinct from groups. I am here concerned primarily with the cultural sources of ethnic identities and with the social uses that groups make of these identities.

ties for group formation that the tracing of descent makes possible are only realized insofar as group identities based on descent are formulated culturally and given social functions.

Since what constitutes one's ethnic heritage is not determined genetically, it must be learned. And it can be learned only if among the meanings to which one is exposed certain of these are marked as being intrinsic elements of one's heritage acquired from one's forebears through one's (socially defined) parents. Such cultural markers of ethnicity, like those marking genealogical descent, constitute a system of classification that permits one to distinguish different categories of people. The basis of ethnic classification appears universally to be predicated upon the perception of real cultural differences between peoples who live in proximity to one another (see, in this connection, Schwartz 1975). A culturally homogeneous group of people that is isolated from other groups can be internally divided into descent groups, as in the manner of Australian aboriginals who maintain distinctions between descent groups through the totemic links they make between groups and different natural phenomena, but it could not constitute an ethnic group. Such cultural isolates are extremely rare, however, and most of the world's peoples, past and present, have been exposed to cultural differences.

There is no invariable pattern as to which cultural differences will be seized upon by groups as emblematic of their ethnic differences. Language is often a diagnostic feature of ethnicity, but not all ethnic groups speak a distinctive language. There are some cases, like that of the Acadians of New Brunswick discussed in the paper by Fox, Aull, and Cimino (pp. 221-32, infra), where objective patterns in speech communication are different from those of neighboring groups. In other cases, like that of the Welsh discussed in the same paper, "ethnicity is . . . related more to the symbol of a separate language than to its actual use by all members of a group" (DeVos 1975, p. 15). In other cases, such as Jinghpaw and some Lisu speakers in Northern Burma (Leach 1954), speakers of quite distinctive languages may consider themselves and be considered by others as members of the same ethnic group. Finally, there are other cases, such as English settlers in Australia, who are distinguished ethnically despite the absence of linguistic differences to make the distinction.

As with language, so too with religion, another cultural feature that is often taken as being an essential element of the cultural heritage of an ethnic group. Tessler in his paper points to the continuing salience of religion as a basis of ethnic identity among Jews and Arabs in North Africa and Israel. Nagata and Bentley also show how adherence to Islam is an important element of ethnic identity among peoples in

Malaysia and the southern Philippines. Yet both of these writers also show how ethnic distinctions are made between coreligionists in these two areas. Despite the insistence of the Bajau of the southern Philippines that they follow Muslim practices, the dominant Tausug insist that the Bajau practices are not Muslim but pagan and thereby reject any commonality between themselves and the Bajau. Malay Muslims, who, as Nagata shows, are internally differentiated into ethnic subgroups, distinguish themselves from fellow Muslims living in the country who are of Arab, Indian, Chinese, or mixed Malay and Indian descent. In another context, I have discussed how Karen peoples living in the border areas between Thailand and Burma maintain that they belong to a single ethnic group (albeit differentiated into a number of subgroups) despite being divided in their religious adherence between traditional Karen animists, Protestant and Catholic Christians, Buddhists, and followers of a number of syncretic religions (Keyes 1979).

What cultural characteristics are marked as emblematic of ethnic identity depends upon the interpretations of the experiences and actions of mythical ancestors and/or historical forebears. These interpretations are often presented in the form of myths or legends in which historical events have been accorded symbolic significance. Origin myths often tell how ancestors of a people became associated with a locality that is thereby identified as an ethnic homeland. For example, origin myths of the Lao tell of a founding ruler, descendant of the King of Heaven, who first came to earth near present-day Dien Bien Phu in North Vietnam and then moved to establish himself in northern Laos at Luang Prabang. Here he had to claim the land at the expense of the Kha, the autochthonous people of the area. This myth, told in many versions and dramatized in rituals carried out until quite recently, provided a charter for Lao ethnicity not only in terms of a particular territory but also with reference to autochthonous inhabitants who became subject to Lao authority (Archaimbault 1973, pp. 73-130). Migrations figure prominently in many of the charter myths of ethnicity. For example, Bentley, in his paper, quotes a myth from the Bajau people of the southern Philippines that relates how the ancestors of the Bajau had come from Johore in the Malay Peninsula and had become a boat people dispersed throughout the Sulu Archipelago.

The conversion of a people to an historic religion, such as Buddhism, Christianity, or Islam, often becomes mythologized and marked as a defining cultural characteristic of an ethnic identity. In Sri Lanka, for example, Singhalese identity is embedded in myths and legends that tell of the conversion of their ancestors to Buddhism, the creation of a sacred topography on the island, and the defense of the religion against alien invaders (Obeyesekere 1975). Similarly, the identities of Malays in Malaya and of the Tausugs in the Philippines, discussed in the papers by Nagata and Bentley, draw upon myths and legends of the conversion of the ancestors to Islam.

Intense suffering experienced by ancestors of a people have also been subject to symbolic interpretations and made the foundations of ethnic identities. The experiences of slavery inflicted upon Blacks in America have been given extensive interpretation in songs and stories; Alex Haley's *Roots,* both as a book and as a TV dramatization, is but a recent, albeit widely acclaimed, construal of Black identity with reference to the experience of slavery. The recurrent pogroms and persecutions and particularly the massive killings in the Holocaust have provided powerful themes for the formulation of Jewish identity, even for many who have rejected Judaism as a religion. The experiences of resettlement on reservations, of battles with Whites, and of struggles for access to traditional lands and treaty rights endured by Indian tribes in America have been forged together in legend and myth as the basis for a pan-Indian identity (see, for example, the papers by Trottier and Trosper in this volume).

The formulation of the mythical and legendary charters of ethnic identity can be found in a variety of forms: stories, both oral and written, songs, artistic depictions, dramatizations, and rituals. However formulated and presented, the symbols of ethnic identity must be appropriated and internalized by individuals before they can serve as the basis for orienting people to social action. DeVos, who has concerned himself with the psychological dimension of ethnicity, has argued that the communication of an ethnic identity is often carried out in rituals in which people confront intense emotional crises: "A major source of ethnic identity is found in the cultural traditions related to crises in the life cycle, such as coming of age, marriage, divorce, illness, or death. It is particularly in rites of passage that one finds highly emotional symbolic reinforcement of ethnic patterns" (DeVos 1975, p. 26).

The symbols of ethnicity, communicated in such contexts as when a mother tells a child of the fortitude of their ancestors to strengthen the child's resolve to endure some pain or criticism of others, serve to establish for an individual a sense of survival, a sense linked to the continuity of the group of which he or she is a member by descent: "Ethnicity . . . is in its narrowest sense a feeling of continuity with the past, a feeling that is maintained as an essential part of one's self-definition. Ethnicity is also intimately related to the individual need for collective continuity. . . . Ethnicity in its deepest psychological level is a sense of survival. If one's group survives, one is assured of survival, even if not in a personal sense" (ibid., p. 17).[3]

An ethnic identity thus becomes a personal identity after an individual appropriates it from a cultural source, that is, from the public display and traffic in symbols. An individual may be faced with several alternative versions of the same identity from which he or she must choose. For example, Japanese-Americans are today confronted with at least two quite different versions of Japanese-American identity, the one that stresses the success that previous generations of Japanese-Americans have had in realizing the material benefits of the "American Dream" and the other that emphasizes the second-class status of Japanese-Americans, particularly as epitomized in the movement of Japanese-Americans to relocation camps during World War II. Nagata gives another example from Malaya where Muslims of Indian descent oscillate between Malay and Indian identities. Individuals may also be constrained in certain contexts to choose between several identities that are subsumed one within the other. In Malaya, in one context one may identify as a "Malay" in contrast to Chinese or Indian, while in another context one may identify as "Minangkabau," thus marking one's descent from people who migrated from the Minangkabau area of Sumatra, in contrast to other Malay-speaking Muslims of the Peninsula.

The choice of identities in terms of the context of social interactions shows that ethnicity is salient only insofar as it serves to orient people in the pursuit of their interests vis-à-vis other people who are seen as holding contrastive ethnic identities. While cultural formulations that serve to define the heritage assumed to have been determined by virtue of one's descent from mythical ancestors or historical forebears are essential to the establishment of ethnic identities, they are not sufficient in and of themselves to make ethnicity a factor in social relations. In addition, ethnic identities must also be seen as delimiting specific types of social action in the context of intergroup relations. Ethnicity has a social as well as a cultural dimension.

ETHNICITY AND THE STRUCTURE OF SOCIAL ACTION

I maintain that ethnicity is a variable in social action only if

3. For further discussion of the psychological mechanisms whereby ethnic identities are internalized see the papers in the volume edited by DeVos and Romanucci-Ross (1975). The psychocultural dimension of ethnicity was the topic of the research seminar held in 1977-1978 at the University of Washington, organized by Professor Simon Ottenberg under the auspices of the Program in Comparative Studies in Ethnicity and Nationality.

access to the means of production, means of expropriation of the products of labor, or means of exchange between groups are determined by membership in groups defined in terms of nongenealogical descent. It must be stressed that the relationships between groups is not undertaken because they adhere to culturally validated differences of presumed descent but because of their interests in obtaining spouses, resources, labor, produce, wealth, or information through production, expropriation, and exchange.[4]

Much of the recent literature on ethnicity has been concerned with the structure of ethnic group relations. I will not attempt to review all of this large literature, but will attempt only to identify the basic points made in it regarding the structure of ethnic group relations.[5] Cohen, in a paper published in another context (Cohen 1974), has summarized the argument regarding the linking of the pursuit of interests with ethnic distinctions:

In the course of the organization of economic production, exchange, and distribution, and more particularly through the processes of the division of labour and the competition for greater shares of income between men, a variety of interest groups emerge, whose members have some interests in common. To operate successfully an interest group has to develop basic organizational functions: distinctiveness (some writers call it boundary); communication; authority structure; decision-making procedure; ideology; and socialization. . . . But even in the advanced liberal industrial societies there are some structural conditions under which an interest group cannot organize itself on formal lines. . . . The members of interest groups who cannot organize themselves formally will thus tend to make use, though largely unconsciously, of whatever cultural mechanisms are available in order to articulate the organization of their grouping. And it is here, in such situations, that political ethnicity comes into being. [Ibid., pp. xvi–xviii]

I would modify this argument to take into account those cases where ethnic groups acting as interest groups persist or even re-emerge in contexts in which it is possible for such interests to be pursued by formal organization. Ethnic groups may persist because they have long been associated with the relatively effective pursuit of certain interests even when, from an outsider's viewpoint, a formal organization may appear likely to be even more effective. Moreover, ethnic

---

4. A number of colleagues have noted that in my paper on "Towards a New Formulation of the Concept of Ethnic Group" that I did not give sufficient attention to political relationships between groups. This point is well taken and in the present paper I have attempted to view ethnic group relationships as taking place within the total political-economy of societies.

5. For reference to this literature, see the excellent comprehensive bibliography, with annotations and a coded index, recently compiled by Bentley (in press).

groups persist or re-emerge in reaction to efforts to rationalize interests with reference to organizations in which one has only objective interests in common with fellow members. In other words, ethnicity is a factor in some social contexts because it is perceived by people as a means to overcome the alienation brought about by the increased bureaucratic rationalization of their lives. In short, while ethnic groups may exist in some societies because in those societies particular interests can be pursued only through such groups, the increased organization of society along rationalized bureaucratic lines does not inevitably lead to the decline or demise of ethnic groups.

At least two major types of social structure can be recognized as obtaining between ethnic groups that within a particular society function to promote certain objective interests of their members. Perhaps the most common type is one that Barth has termed "symbiotic": "The positive bond that connects several ethnic groups in an encompassing social system depends on the complementarity of the groups with respect to some of their characteristic cultural features. Such complementarity can give rise to interdependence or symbiosis, and constitutes the area of articulation" (Barth 1969, p. 18).

In such situations, different ethnic groups carry out different political-economic functions that collectively make possible the persistence of the total society. In such an ethnic division of labor certain groups usually have greater access to wealth and power than do other groups.

Many of the studies undertaken by social scientists on ethnic group relations have attempted for particular societies to identify the characteristics of the ethnic division of labor, to assess the rigidity of boundaries between constituent ethnic groups, and to determine the extent to which the groups are fixed in specific strata of the society. The variations in these several factors have led some social scientists to distinguish subtypes of societies having an ethnic division of labor along a continuum between "plural societies" and "pluralistic societies." In a plural society, most objective interests are pursued by people in the context of ethnic groups, boundaries between groups are quite rigid, and each group has a fixed place in the stratification. In pluralistic societies, in contrast, social life is much more open.

[Ethnic groups in a pluralistic society] differ in wealth, power, occupation, values, but in effect an open society prevails for individuals and for groups. Over a time substantial and rough equalization of wealth and power can be hoped for even if not attained, and each group participates sufficiently in the goods and values of social life of a common society so that all can accept the common society as good and fair. There is competition between groups, as between individuals, but it is muted, and groups compete not through violence but through effectiveness in organization and achievement. Groups and individuals participate in a common society. Individual choice, not law or rigid custom, determines the degree to which any person participates, if at all, in the life of an ethnic group, and assimilation and acculturation proceed at a rate determined in large part by individuals. [Glazer and Moynihan 1970, pp. xxiii-xxiv]

South Africa and Malaysia have often been noted as examples of plural societies, although there is some evidence that Malaysia, at least, is becoming a more open society (Nagata 1975). On the other hand, the north of the United States has been characterized as a pluralistic society, albeit with some reservations noted in recent years (see Glazer and Moynihan 1970; Gordon 1964; 1978).

A second major type of social structure that obtains between ethnic groups within a single society is one in which minority groups maintain almost a totally separate existence. Again, Barth has provided a characterization of this type: "In some social systems, ethnic groups co-reside though no major aspect of structure is based on ethnic inter-relations. These are generally referred to as societies with minorities, and the analysis of the minority situation involves a special variant of inter-ethnic relations" (Barth 1969, p. 30). Tessler (see infra pp. 155-97) has provided examples of such situations in his discussion of the "nonassimilating minorities" of Jews in Tunisia and Morocco and Arabs in Israel. "Ethnic enclaves," as I prefer to call such minorities (since the term minority has such ambiguous meanings) can also be found in many societies: for example, certain American Indian groups in the United States, particularly among those in the Southwest, Jews in East European ghettos and rural communities prior to World War I, and tribal communities in many traditional societies in Asia and Africa.

If the members of a nonassimilating ethnic enclave are of sufficient number, they may seek to separate themselves from the society in which they are located and to organize themselves into separate political entities. The term *nation* has come to be used for those ethnic groups that succeed in attaining or aspire to separate political status (cf. DeVos 1975, p. 11). Ethnic groups that have previously been a part of an ethnic division of labor have sometimes attempted to redefine their ethnicity in separatist terms and to seek enclave status or even political independence. Such has been the ambition of Black nationalist groups in the United States and Black liberation movements in southern Africa. On the other hand, previously autonomous groups, such as certain American Indian groups, have exchanged enclave status for that of being an ethnic group within a plural or pluralistic society.

At this point I have begun to introduce some consideration of dynamic factors in the relationships between ethnic groups. Before I turn to consider the processes of ethnic change more fully, I should like to stress once again that any adequate theory of ethnicity must take into account not only the functions of ethnicity in the pursuit of social interests but also the cultural formulations of descent from which people derive their ethnic identities. Much confusion in theoretical discussions regarding ethnicity stems, I maintain, from confounding the cultural and social dimensions of ethnicity. A theory of ethnicity that can be used to interpret the variety of cases in which ethnicity is a factor must take into account, and yet distinguish between, both of these dimensions.

ETHNIC CHANGE

I begin with the fundamental premise that a tension obtains between cultural meanings that people construct to differentiate their primordial identities from those of others and the patterns that emerge in social interactions as individuals and groups seek to pursue their interests. In New York City, for example, Blacks and Puerto Ricans are clearly distinguished (by themselves as well as by others) as culturally defined ethnic categories; yet, given the social similarities of many Blacks and Puerto Ricans in the urban economy, they have developed patterns of acting in concert to achieve certain economic ends. Such tension between the cultural and social dimensions of ethnicity leads people to assess the applicability of their ethnic identities for orienting themselves towards social action and in determining the social boundaries that, if consistently breached, would threaten their identities.

In relatively stable situations the cultural and social dimensions of ethnicity may be kept in relatively close accord through the imposition of sanctions on those who act inappropriately. Many groups refuse to recognize as members the offspring of those from the group who have married someone from another group. For example, the premise that a child of a Jewish man and Gentile mother is not a Jew still serves in some Jewish communities to discourage the outmarriage of Jewish males. Disinheritance or excommunication (if religion is an essential attribute of ethnicity) may also be used as sanctions. However, when people find themselves faced with fundamental changes in the political-economy in which they engage in social relations, the mechanisms that have previously been used to resolve the tension between cultural identities and social patterns may no longer work. In such changed circumstances, the salience of pre-existing ethnic identities may become highly problematic.

I maintain that the process of ethnic change, set in tow by a radical shift in the social situation in which people act, is a dialectical one. In radically changed circumstances, pre-existing patterns of social action often prove to be no longer viable. New patterns are then evolved and these, in turn, stimulate, either consciously or unconsciously, a reassessment of the appropriateness of the functions of ethnic group identities upon which these affiliations are predicated. Concomitant with the necessary changes in social patterns, those living in new circumstances may also have to adopt new cultural meanings and practices. The experiences of change themselves may be subjected to cultural interpretation and both these formulations and the newly adopted cultural characteristics may be utilized in the reassessment of ethnic identities. Whatever is involved in the assessment of the salience of ethnicity for social action, it is carried out in the context of public engagement with cultural meanings such as are presented in formal schooling or in such other activities as rituals, ceremonies, club meetings, political rallies, periodical and book publication, and so on. After a period of time—a period that is highly variable but is rarely, if ever, less than a single generation—new ethnic identities are formed, or old identities are invested with new meanings. As ethnic groups begin to be mobilized in terms of these reformulated or new ethnic identities, yet other social patterns may be altered. Eventually, unless the situation continues to undergo further radical change, ethnic groups achieve a degree of equilibrium within whichever type of social structure obtains in the society (plural, pluralistic, separatist) and a relatively stable tension between cultural identity and social patterns is established.

The classic case of changed circumstances that precipitate ethnic crises is that in which peoples of different ethnic backgrounds come into contact following the migration of one or the other group. The literature on ethnicity is full of the studies of peasants who have migrated to cities, of settlers on a frontier who are now in contact with the aboriginal inhabitants, of the poor of one country who have moved to a richer country, or of those who have fled for political reasons from their home country to find a haven in another. The essays by Banton and Light in this volume both take up the question of what types of changes follow after peoples have migrated from one social context to settle in a very different one. Banton draws on recent studies of immigrants to the United Kingdom from Commonwealth countries in the West Indies, Africa, and the Indian subcontinent in his reconsideration of models of assimilation of migrants from less developed to industrialized societies. Banton shows that in the cases considered, as in many other cases described in other studies, "total assimilation" in which the migrant group or the descendants of migrants disappear into the larger society and lose their ethnic distinctiveness does not occur.

Immigrants to a heterogeneous industrial society cannot assimilate to the total society. They join the ethnic groups and social strata that are closest to them in the situation in which they find themselves, and a lot will depend upon the kinds of occupation they are able to secure. Assimilation is then a two- or three-step process. The immigrant joins a local group that is in opposition to other local groups but has interests in common with them in opposition to large sections of the total population. In the process, ethnic identities are sometimes changed. [Banton, infra, p. 43]

Assimilation, Banton argues, "is better seen as the reduction of cultural distance between specified groups with respect to particular aspects of behavior" (p. 50). Assimilation is necessary if migrants, or their descendants, are to succeed in adapting to their new contexts; however, since their situations in a complex industrialized society vary, different migrants—even perhaps from the same background—may choose different adaptive strategies.

But reduction of cultural distance is not only a function of the adaptation that migrants or their descendants make to their new land. Assimilation is also conditioned "by the extent to which members of the [migrant] group are disposed to adopt the values of the receiving society, or hold to those of the society from which they have come" (p. 37). In other words, premigration identities can be an independent variable affecting the process of assimilation. Banton points out that West Indian migrants have been more willing "to conform to the expectations of the receiving society than [have] the Asians" who have also migrated to the United Kingdom. Assimilation is also conditioned by the degree to which groups native to the receiving society are willing to allow migrants to identify with them. In the United Kingdom, most native groups are not very receptive to migrants.

In Britain ethnicity is legitimate only in the restricted sense that individuals are accepted as being Scottish, Welsh, and Irish as well as British. These are not hyphenated Britons, but members of ancient nations inhabiting the territory they occupied before the United Kingdon was formed. The suggestion that there could be Indian-Britons as there are Irish-Americans is something new, and would probably not be generally accepted by the White British population, members of which would be inclined to argue that if people want to be Indian they should live in India. [Ibid., p. 41]

In contrast to the United States, then, migrants to the United Kingdom have been forced to remain aliens, sometimes being restricted to ethnic enclaves or else permitted to assume only certain positions in the ethnic division of labor. Many migrants from the Indian subcontinent have not been unwilling to accept such a status, viewing themselves as temporary sojourners who will, one day, return "home." On the other hand, West Indian migrants have not happily accepted confinement to enclaves and treatment as racially distinctive aliens. The tension that remains has revolutionary potential: "Disappointed by the discrimination that seems so pervasive and unyielding in the majority society, many of them are less inclined to conform to its expectations and look towards a future society different from both the sending and receiving societies" (ibid., p. 41).

Light has also concerned himself with the implications of migration and has focused his attention on the utility of the model that has posited that new ethnic groups in an urban center in a capitalist society would replace previously established ethnic groups in the lowest economic occupations in the urban economy. With successive migration of new ethnic groups, older groups would be replaced through a process of "ethnic succession" at the lowest levels and eventually the process resulted in the full assimilation of the descendants of earlier migrant groups. Light argues that this pattern of "ethnic succession" is a special case that is by no means applicable to all newly arrived ethnic groups. "Ethnic succession as defined is a special case that arises when, in a labor shortage, the interests of old-ethnic labor, capital, and newcomer ethnics briefly coincide" (Light, infra, p. 68). Light identifies several other patterns of adaptation to the new situation that migrant groups might follow: a new group might "leapfrog" older groups and find occupations higher in the economic system than those followed by existing groups; they may displace an older group without the latter assuming a higher position in the economy; or they may improve the value (monetary, prestige, or both) of work they previously engaged in and that they monopolize in their new environment (this pattern Light calls "situs-enhancement").

All of these patterns of adaptation depend upon a migrant group retaining the distinctive identity (what he calls "ethnic consciousness") with which they arrived. This situation simply does not hold in many cases. Light deals with one type of change in ethnic identity that may occur in the migrant situation—a change in what he calls "ethnic scope," referring to the "boundaries of an ethnic group." Thus, an ethnic identity may come to be held by peoples who previously held distinctive identities, the new identity deriving from a recognition of higher order commonalities than those previously utilized as markers of identity. "For simplicity's sake, we can distinguish continental, regional, national, and local scope. A continental scope defines a continent-wide ethnic identity: for example, Asian, European, Latin American. A national scope embraces a national ethnic identity, for example, Italian, Irish, Chinese. A regional scope indicates a regional ethnic identity, for example, Calabrian or Cantonese. Local scope means same place origin, that is, a 'Landsmann' or 'paisano' " (p. 71).

Implicit in Light's discussion is the recognition that descent in ethnicity as in kinship can be traced to more remote or more proximate ancestors and forebears depending upon the type and size of group that is to be mobilized for specific social functions. Light suggests that competition for economic benefits is an important factor in stimulating changes in ethnic scope. He hypothesizes that "Intergroup competition generally expands the scope of ethnic identities and increases their intensity" (p. 79; also see pp. 73-74). Light also recognizes that ethnic identities of migrant groups can undergo changes in addition to those of scope. However, he does not attempt to analyze the nature of such changes, concluding only that "the trend and tendency of change is an empirical problem" (p. 72).

I maintain that it is possible to identify some patterns of change in ethnic identity that characterize the adaptation of migrant groups to new societies. Students of kinship have long recognized that new descent groups come into existence when some members of a kin group split off and establish themselves at a different location. While the descendants of the group that split off can still trace descent to focal ancestors they share with those who did not split, for some purposes they may also trace descent only to those ancestors who effected the fissioning of the kin group. So, too, migrants, whether they left their homes for political or economic reasons, have split with those who remain behind. Descendants of migrants can still trace descent to ancestors who lived and died in the homeland, but they can also trace descent to those who migrated. Tales of ancestors who migrated to a frontier to carve out new homes, of ancestors who were constrained to work in low-paying and demeaning jobs to keep alive in a hostile urban community in which they had settled, of ancestors who were ridiculed or persecuted because they insisted on wearing "strange" clothing, spoke with "foreign" accents, adhered to "alien" religions, or had different skin colors have all become for one group or another the sources for the symbols of new identities.

The migration of new groups to a society may lead to ethnic change not only for the migrant groups who are constrained to adapt to a new social situation but also to the existing groups whose social context has been significantly altered by the arrival of migrants. Nagata has given an extended example of such a case in her discussion of the continuing reformulation of "Malay" identity as indigenous Malay-speaking peoples have accommodated themselves to the migration of small numbers of highly prestigious Arabs, to massive numbers of Chinese, to significant numbers of Indians, some of whom were adherents of Islam, and to migrations of related but culturally distinctive peoples such as the Minangkabau. In addition to adapting to a society in which migrants have brought about major changes in social patterns, indigenous Malay-speaking peoples have also had to adapt themselves to significant alterations in their cultural patterns, including their conversion to Islam several centuries ago and more recent adoption of Westernized law and education. Moreover, the society of Malaya has been restructured at the state level, first under British rule and, since 1957, under governments of an independent Malaya (now Malaysia).

Both the radical changes in the social system found in the Malayan Peninsula and in the cultural practices followed by Malay-speaking peoples have stimulated concerns, in recent years consciously expressed, as to "What is a Malay?" While certain cultural emblems of Malay identity, notably adherence to Islam and knowledge of the Malay language, have remained as essential attributes of Malay identity for centuries, these attributes are not shared by Malays alone. Moreover, some cultural characteristics, once thought intrinsic to Malay identity (e.g., patterns of dress and of diet) are no longer shared by many people who are still considered (and still consider themselves) to be Malay. Not only has the cultural dimension of Malay identity altered through time, but the social interests that Malays, as Malays, pursue have also changed. Whereas during the colonial period there had been a marked ethnic division of labor in Malaya, in recent years the Malay government has sought through legal and educational means to promote the entrance of Malays into occupations previously held mainly by Chinese or Indians. Yet, despite the shifting cultural and social aspects of Malay identity, a common element of that identity has remained. That element is a sense of shared descent, of belonging to the same *bangsa*. "The term *bangsa* conveys the double ideas of a people sharing both a common origin and a common culture. . . . [I]t has a primordial quality, for it implies that the cultural traits are inalienably and inextricably associated with a particular people, that is, carried by a community whose ultimate unity derives from a single origin" (Nagata, infra, p. 98). Appeals to this identity, in terms of the cultural characteristics that are currently assumed to constitute the Malay ethnic heritage—for example, Islam, Malay language, indigenous as distinct from migrant—continue to have major implications for politics, intergroup, and even interpersonal relations in Malaysia today.

Migration is not the only process whereby ethnic change is initiated. Ethnic change may also result from the radical alteration, brought about by force or administrative action, in the structure of intergroup relations in the political economy of a social system. Bentley has described, in his paper, how the Tausug, a people who from historical records appear to have been migrants to the Sulu Archipelago of the Philippines, succeeded in becoming the dominant ethnic group in the region both politically and economically. Subsequently, the mythical charters of the ethnic identities of the major groups in the region—the Bajau and Samal as well as the Tausug—have been formulated so that they "do not reflect this process of ethnogenesis but instead mirror current relations between the groups" (Bentley, infra, p. 147). Tausug myths now stress that they are of local origin and link them to Islamic origin themes. Samal, who were probably the aboriginal inhabitants of the region, are characterized in Tausug mythology as poor Muslims who are therefore morally inferior to the Tausug. Finally, the Bajau are relegated to a pariah pagan status in Tausug mythology and both Tausug and their own myths point to an origin outside the archipelago and migration into the region later than the Tausug although historically they probably preceded the Tausug.

Arabs in Israel and Jews in North Africa, discussed in Tessler's paper, found that their social worlds were radically reshaped following the creation of the state of Israel in 1948 and the independence of Tunisia and Morocco in 1956. Jewish enclaves were left in Morocco and Tunisia after most Jews in these countries migrated either to Israel or to France. Similarly, some Arabs remained in enclave communities in Israel when many of their fellow Arabs left to become part of the Palestinian diaspora. In the years that have followed, members of these ethnic enclave communities have, for the most part, adopted new patterns of adaptation and, in the process, have altered their ethnic status. Because certain cultural attributes, particularly religion, have been assumed to be an inherent aspect of the ethnic heritages of both Jews and Arabs and because the states of Israel, Morocco, and Tunisia have been inextricably linked to one ethnic heritage, there has been almost an absolute barrier to total assimilation on the part of members of either group vis-à-vis the other. It is for this reason that Tessler has characterized these ethnic enclave communities as "nonassimilating minorities."

This characterization notwithstanding, there has been some assimilation of some North African Jews to the dominant culture. Djerban Jews in Tunisia, Tessler points out, have, in contrast to most other Jews in North Africa, increasingly oriented themselves to Tunisian Arab civilization. While their adherence to Judaism remains an ultimate barrier against total assimilation, Tessler still feels that there has been increasing assimilation of Djerban Jews into Tunisian society and that "the ethnic identity of Djerban Jews is changing and the Tunisian component of that identity is growing rather than diminishing in importance" (Tessler, infra, p. 176). Assimilation of another type has also taken place among Jews in North Africa who have left Morocco or Tunisia not for Israel, but for France, the country that had previously controlled these societies. In France, North African Jews have often exchanged their Jewish identities for that of a French identity, this assimilation having been made possible by their French education while still in North Africa. Tessler presents evidence that a similar process has also affected the character of ethnic change among many Jews remaining in Morocco and Tunisia.

[In these instances,] ethnic change involves movement away from communal consciousness and toward identification on an individual basis with European society, a pattern we have characterized as "diasporization." Its members increasingly think of themselves as belonging to a more diffuse cultural tradition whose population and political centers are outside their homeland. [Ibid., p. 178]

North African Jews are not the only peoples to have oriented themselves towards France and eventually to have assimilated to French culture. During the colonial period, France pursued from time to time a policy of "assimilation" toward colonial populations, and implemented this policy by the establishment of schools in which a small number of people in all French colonial dependencies were given the same education as were Frenchmen in the metropolitan homeland. Today, France includes peoples of Vietnamese, Goanese, Algerian, and Senegalese origin—indeed, peoples from all former French colonies—who are culturally indistinguishable from native-born Frenchmen. Racial differences have not been barriers in France, as in the United Kingdom, to the assimilation of those who were not born Frenchmen. On the other hand, Frenchmen have not been very receptive to those settlers in France who seek to perpetuate their ethnic distinctiveness.

Tessler has also identified a third type of ethnic change among nonassimilating minorities. In his research among Arabs in Israel he found that "among nonurban Arabs there is growing communal solidarity coupled with improving relations with the dominant majority and its political system" (ibid., p. 180). These Arabs would, thus, appear to be following patterns recognized in the United States, as well as in a number of multiethnic Third World countries in which members of an ethnic group accept the basic premises of the political order and seek to realize their objective interests in nonviolent competition with those of other ethnic groups. In fact, change in this direction is likely to be aborted for nonurban Arabs in Israel. For one thing, Israel is prevented from being a truly pluralistic society owing to a fusion of Jewish identity and the state. Moreover, leadership of Arabs in Israel comes mainly from urban Arabs who reject any type of assimilation to the dominant culture of Israel. One must question, as in fact Tessler does, whether "Israeli Arab" is a very stable or perduring identity.

The more likely pattern of ethnic change among Arabs in Israel is that already followed by many urban Arabs. For them, the most reasonable strategy involves neither assimilation to Israeli culture nor even accommodation and integration into Israeli society, except as a temporary measure. Tessler found that urban Arabs in Israel were experiencing "increasing communal solidarity, political consciousness and identification with the nationalism of a neighboring people" (ibid., p. 178), that is, with Palestinian nationalism. Thus many Arabs in Israel use their ethnic identity to orient themselves towards expressions of separatist nationalism and irredentism.

The emergence of ethnic nationalism among Arabs in Israel has been stimulated by the radically changed political situation in the Middle East following the creation of Israel and the political independence of neighboring Arab countries. Fox, Aull, and Cimino have identified yet another set of factors that have prompted the emergence of ethnic nationalism. For them, these factors are not historically particular, as appears to be the case for Arab ethnic nationalism in Israel. Rather, Fox, Aull, and Cimino have argued that there is a type of ethnic nationalism, exemplified in their paper by movements in Wales, New Brunswick, and South India, that develops as "a means for (or attempts at) political mobilization under specific conditions of state organization, summed up in the term *welfare state*" (Fox, Aull, and Cimino, infra, p. 201). They argue that for the purposes of their analysis, colonial states and Western welfare states have considerable similarity. "Because the colonial state is an introduced form and therefore has no indigenous competitors and because the economic system is preindustrial and of low productivity, the colonial administration becomes the major source of power and economic preferment" (ibid., p. 239). In welfare states, the bureaucracy is also often "the major source of power and economic preferment," particularly in less developed areas of the state. In situations in which a welfare state bureaucracy or a colonial administration has increasingly intruded into the social life of peoples, conditions may be created in which ethnic nationalism, promoted by self-conscious elites, will develop. "As the evolving Western industrial state and, later, welfare state increasingly intrudes into locality and community life and increasingly co-opts the older class bases of political opposition, it gives impetus for local or regional counterelites to utilize inchoate ethnic sentiments for political goals" (ibid., p. 206).

Fox, Aull, and Cimino do not attempt to analyze how people come to have "inchoate ethnic sentiments" but assume that these sentiments are present and can be mobilized by local counterelites who seek to unite people, divided by local, class, and other differences, to meet a common threat posed by an intrusive bureaucracy. Welsh and Acadian ethnic identities are actually discussed in specific terms, not as inchoate sentiments, at some length in the body of the paper. The Welsh have a history of cultural distinctiveness that has long been seen as part of the heritage of those born in Wales. This heritage has been linked to stories of former independence and to the actions of such cultural heroes as Owain Glyn Dwr, who lived in the fifteenth century. Today, Welsh identity is symbolized by adherence to non-conformist Protestant sects, by a distinctive Celtic language (which few people actually speak), and by a national cultural festival, the Eisteddfod. Communication of these symbols in familial activities, in chapel sermons, in school instruction, in songs, poetry, and other artistic forms performed at the Eisteddfod and at other times have all served to provide a basis for the ethnic sentiments that have been recently mobilized by Welsh nationalist leaders.

Acadian ethnic identity has its basis in the creation of a new society in the New Brunswick wilderness by the ancestors of the present-day Acadians. The formation of Acadian identity has been given mythological (what Fox, Aull, and Cimino call ideological) formulation (see ibid., p. 224). This formulation, together with recent experiences of conflict with government and ecclesiastical officials (who have been for some time mainly of Irish descent), particularly over education, have provided the basis for the ethnic sentiments mobilized in contemporary Acadian nationalism.

The case of the non-Brahmans of South India discussed by Fox, Aull, and Cimino points to an issue that they do not raise, but is implicit in their discussion. This issue—to what extent Indian caste can be equated with ethnicity—has been debated from time to time in the literature on ethnicity. Some scholars like DeVos and Wagatsuma (1970) not only make this equation, but also see "caste" as a particular type of ethnic group found in societies other than India; specifically, they characterize the Eta of Japan as a caste. Many Indianists, in contrast, have insisted that caste in India is a unique historical phenomenon and should not be identified with any more general social type. Clearly, caste, as the name *jati* indicates, is an identity that, like ethnicity, is assumed to be given at birth; it is also assumed to be determined by descent. Moreover, castes, again like ethnic identities, are associated with distinctive cultural emblems and with distinctive values (caste dharma) that serve to orient their members towards social action. Yet Indian castes also belong to a system of social relations that, while having some similarities to other systems based on stratification of ethnic groups, still have some highly significant particular features that would be eclipsed by assimilating them to a more universal social type. The point is that for some purposes Indian castes can be seen as being a type of ethnic group, while for other purposes they cannot. Although it is not argued in these terms, such an assumption can be seen to be implicit in the position Fox, Aull, and Cimino take, that non-Brahman political movements entailing the mobilization of people from a number of non-Brahman castes in South India are an example of ethnic nationalist movements.[6]

6. After reading these comments, Fox wrote to me, taking issue with my interpretation:

You say that we equate caste and ethnicity (in relation to the non-Brahman movement), at least for some purposes. That is decidedly *not* what we do. We show the emergence of a new political movement in reaction to British colonial intrusion—a movement that brings together separate castes or caste clusters for altogether novel (political) purposes and within an altogether novel (political) framework that has little continuity with traditional caste organization. I do not really concern myself with whether caste is equivalent to ethnicity. All I am saying is that the non-Brahman movement has a similar genesis and development to movements found in Wales and Acadia, and there is use of ascriptive diacritica of one sort or another in all of them. You may wish to say that there are similar characteristics or attributes involved in ethnicity and traditional South Asian caste, but we neither entertain this question nor does the non-Brahman material as presented (since we do not treat it as an outcome of traditional caste, but as a modern reaction) serve as a basis for our taking a position in this matter.

To this I responded:

I am afraid that I am not persuaded by your assertion that the non-Brahman movement has nothing to do with caste. While I have no problem whatsoever with your argument that similar forces gave rise to the non-Brahman movement as gave rise to the other movements you and your coauthors discuss in your paper, I am hard put to find any *ethnic* ascriptive diacritics being utilized in this case. Indeed, the term you chose as a label—"*non-Brahman* movement"—evokes a caste factor even though the use of caste here is nontraditional.

Whatever one makes of the non-Brahman case, the cases of the Welsh and the Acadians both appear to be examples of that type of ethnic change in which pre-existing ethnic identities have been utilized in new ways to realize objective goals vis-à-vis powerful bureaucratic agencies of the state. A similar situation has obtained in the case of the American Indians, as can be seen from the discussion in the papers by Trosper and Trottier. The migration and settlement of non-Indians in the United States led to successive contacts between non-Indians and various Indian tribes. As non-Indian populations grew at a much faster rate than did Indian populations in the United States and because non-Indians had considerably greater administrative and physical force, Indian tribes were constrained to accept the structure of relationships imposed upon them by non-Indians. As Trosper shows, there were significant similarities in the experiences of Indians in their relationships with non-Indians even though the Indians themselves came from many different cultural and social backgrounds.

Since the 1930s Indians in the United States have been subjected to the same types of intrusions into their lives of a welfare state bureaucracy as were experienced by the Welsh in the United Kingdom and the Acadians in Nova Scotia. In response, American Indians have, again in a comparable way to the Welsh and Acadians, attempted to mobilize groups defined in ethnic terms to confront the agencies of the state and to seek to establish some autonomy and local control over their lives. However, unlike the Welsh and the Acadians, American Indians did not have a single cultural heritage to draw upon in the formation of their ethnic nationalism. By claiming common interests (whether, in fact, reservation and nonreservation Indians share the same common interests vis-à-vis the state is somewhat problematic), however, a number of American Indian leaders have attempted to forge a pan-Indian ethnic identity through the symbolic reinterpretation of the history of Indians of the whole country. In this case, ethnic change has involved not only the assertion of new interests to be pursued by those who share the same ethnic heritage but also the assertion of a new ethnic identity.

Both Trosper and Trottier point to the symbolic actions associated with the occupation of the island of Alcatraz in the late 1960s as an important example of the efforts on the part of Indian leaders to formulate a pan-Indian identity. Drawing upon the experiences of the occupation of Alcatraz and the subsequent forcible eviction of those involved, Indian writers and speakers have invested formulations of Indian identity with an emotional quality that echoes other emotional experiences in the history of Indian relations with non-Indians.

Trottier has summarized the symbolic content of the pan-Indian identity formulated by those involved with the occupation of Alcatraz: "The distinctiveness of Indian identity is expressed partly through stereotypical symbols that refer to no single tribe, though many are of Plains Indian origin: the Great Spirit, a peace pipe ceremony, tipis, feathers . . . , sacred healing ceremonies, and 'the universal eagle symbol' " (Trottier, infra, p. 289).

Indian leaders have had some success in mobilizing people to pursue political goals as a group united by a common pan-Indian identity. This success has been particularly marked, as Trosper shows, among those Indians who have realized that they do share objective interests that stem from treaty relationships instituted between the United States government and various tribal groups in the past. However, some Indian tribes, such as the Navajos, who have maintained relative autonomy as ethnic enclaves, have been little attracted to the pan-Indian movement.

Trottier discusses another effort to create a new ethnic identity that would serve to unite peoples previously holding quite distinctive identities. Some people of various Asian backgrounds have attempted to forge a pan-Asian-American identity that could be utilized to mobilize people against a claimed common threat of racist attitudes of Whites towards Asians (ibid., pp. 293-94). Racism is claimed to result in an economically disadvantaged position of Asians today as was the case in the past. In addition to a response to racism, one also wonders whether efforts to create a pan-Asian-American movement are not also related to the increasing encroachment of the state on the lives of the peoples of Asian descent.

While the leaders of the pan-Asian-American movement have not had an equivalent of the Alcatraz experience of the Indians that could be used as a basis for formulating a new Asian-American identity, there have been a number of efforts to give public expression to what is asserted to be the common heritage of all Asian-Americans. Among the symbolic themes that have figured prominently in these formulations are those of persecutions of the Asian migrants who first settled in America, of the exploitation of Asian labor, and of coming from ancient civilizations. However, given the very different backgrounds from which peoples of Asian descent come, given the continuing salience of such identities as Chinese-American, Japanese-American, and so on up to and including the new Korean-American and emerging Vietnamese-American identities, and particularly given the very different interest situations in which people of Asian descent find themselves, an Asian-American identity is still embryonic, at best.

When new identities do become established, as appears to have occurred in the case of American Indians—or, at least, for some American Indians—then the process of ethnic change has come full circle. This circular, or, more properly, dialectical, process is well illustrated in Cohen's paper with which this volume concludes. The ancestors of the people who became the Creoles of Sierra Leone were originally of diverse cultural and social backgrounds: some were poor Blacks from England, others were ex-slaves who were liberated in Africa, and yet others were native Africans who had been captured and were destined to become slaves, but had been recaptured and set free. Despite this diversity of background, by the mid-nineteenth century descendants of these peoples had begun to emerge as a distinctive group within Sierra Leone society and had begun to take on the identity of "Black Englishmen," thereby indicating their cultural similarity to the British as opposed to the indigenous groups in the country. This new common identity, later labeled *Creole,* has subsequently served to orient those who hold it to particular ways of acting within Sierra Leone society. But, these social patterns have not remained constant as Creoles have been constrained to accommodate themselves to changing circumstances as Sierra Leone changed from a colonial to an independent state and as power passed from British rule to a government dominated by non-Creoles. These changing circumstances have also led Creoles to alter the cultural characteristics that they take to be associated with their identity. Yet, Creoles have continued to constitute a distinctive ethnic group within Sierra Leone society, albeit now less identifiable in terms of ethnicity than in terms of other symbolic interpretations of primordiality (kinship and amity, for example), which are more acceptable today as Creoles continue to seek to maintain their control over sectors of the Sierra Leone bureaucracy and economy.

As all of the papers in this volume taken collectively illustrate, ethnicity, as one type of primordial assumption about the nature of human identity, can be found in all types of societies, industrial as well as nonindustrial. Yet, because ethnicity is not genetically determined, it is a variable factor in social relations. Both the cultural attributes that are presumed to be associated with an ethnic identity and the social uses for which groups are mobilized with reference to their ethnic identity can vary through time. Changes in ethnicity, in both cultural and social dimensions, are precipitated, I have argued, by radical changes in the political-economic contexts in which people live. The papers included in this volume have identified such radical changes as occurring as a function of the process of migration, of the expansion of the boundaries of a state, of institution of new administrative programs that are designed to provide benefits for or to inflict demands upon peoples, or of revolutionary change in the basic structure of a society. People often respond to these changes in terms of their established ethnic identities, but find that these identities, either in their cultural content or because of the assumptions about who shares the same identities, are not appropriate in the new situation. In adapting to the new situation, new identities may be evolved. Yet, once evolved, these new identities are assumed to define for people who they truly are as descendants of their ancestors or forebears. Primordial identities continue to serve as gyroscopes for those buffeted by uncertainties as to the best way to pursue their interests or for those alienated by the dehumanized agencies designed to organize the ordering of social ends in a rational way.

REFERENCES

Archaimbault, Charles
    1973 *Structures Religieuses Lao (Rites et Mythes)*. Vientiane: Vithagna.
Barth, Fredrik
    1969 "Introduction." In *Ethnic Groups and Boundaries*, ed. Fredrik Barth, pp. 9-38. Boston: Little, Brown.
Bentley, G. Carter
    In Press *Studies in Ethnicity and Nationality: An Annotated Bibliography*. Seattle: University of Washington Press.
Cohen, Abner
    1974 "Introduction: The Lesson of Ethnicity." In *Urban Ethnicity*, ed. Abner Cohen, pp. ix-xxiv. A. S. A. Monographs, no. 12. London: Tavistock Publications.

DeVos, George

    1975 "Ethnic Pluralism: Conflict and Accommodation." In *Ethnic Identity: Cultural Continuities and Change,* ed. George DeVos and Lola Romanucci-Ross. Palo Alto, Calif.: Mayfield Publishing.

DeVos, George, and Romanucci-Ross, Lola, eds.

    1975 *Ethnic Identity: Cultural Continuities and Change.* Palo Alto, Calif.: Mayfield Publishing.

DeVos, George, and Wagatsuma, Hiroshi

    1967 *Japan's Invisible Race: Caste and Culture in Personality.* Berkeley: University of California Press.

Francis, E. K.

    1978 *Interethnic Relations.* New York: Elsevier.

Geertz, Clifford

    1963 "The Integrative Revolution: Primordial Sentiments and Civil Politics in the New States." In *Old Societies and New States: The Quest for Modernity in Asia and Africa,* ed. Clifford Geertz, pp. 105-57. New York: Free Press.

    1973 *The Interpretation of Cultures.* New York: Basic Books.

Glazer, Nathan, and Moynihan, Daniel P.

    1970 *Beyond the Melting Pot: The Negroes, Puerto Ricans, Jews, Italians, and Irish of New York City.* 2nd ed. Cambridge, Mass.: Massachusetts Institute of Technology Press.

Gordon, Milton M.

    1964 *Assimilation in American Life: The Role of Race, Religion and National Origins.* New York: Oxford University Press.

    1978 *Human Nature, Class and Ethnicity.* New York: Oxford University Press.

Keyes, Charles F.

    1975 "Towards a New Formulation of the Concept of Ethnic Group." *Ethnicity* 3: 202-13.

    1979 "Introduction." In *Ethnic Adaptation and Identity: The Karen on the Thai Frontier with Burma,* ed. Charles F. Keyes. Philadelphia: Institute for the Study of Human Issues.

Leach, E. R.

    1954 *Political Systems of Highland Burma.* Cambridge, Mass.: Harvard University Press.

Nagata, Judith, ed.

    1975 *Pluralism in Malaysia: Myth and Reality.* Leiden: E. J. Brill.

Obeyesekere, Gananath

    1975 "Sinhalese-Buddhist Identity in Ceylon." In *Ethnic Identity: Cultural Continuities and Change,* ed. George DeVos and

Lola Romanucci-Ross, pp. 231-58. Palo Alto, Calif.: Mayfield Publishing.

Schneider, David M.
    1967 "Kinship and Culture: Descent and Filiation as Cultural Constructs." *Southwestern Journal of Anthropology* 23: 65-73.

Schwartz, Theodore
    1975 "Cultural Totemism: Ethnic Identity Primitive and Modern." In *Ethnic Identity: Cultural Continuities and Change*, ed. George DeVos and Lola Romanucci-Ross, pp. 106-31. Palo Alto, Calif.: Mayfield Publishing.

van den Berghe, Pierre L.
    1978 "Race and Ethnicity: A Sociobiological Perspective." *Ethnic and Racial Studies* 1: 401-11.

In this paper, Banton reconsiders a classic concept used in the study of ethnic change, "assimilation." He challenges the conventional concept as being a unitary process that applies only to groups and not to individuals. Banton proposes a revision of the concept in light of a model of social behavior as an exchange or transaction, a model elaborated upon to a considerable extent in recent social science theory. He argues that assimilation might best be seen as the reduction of cultural distance between specified groups with respect to some particular aspects of their behavior. The opposite process, called differentiation, is one whereby groups increase the cultural distance between them, again with respect to some aspects of their behavior. Drawing upon examples from analyses of minority-majority relations in Great Britain and the United States, Banton argues that assimilation is a more complex process than previously thought. While groups may be assimilating in some ways, they may also be differentiating themselves in others. Assimilation often takes place not on a group level, but on an individual basis. Finally, assimilation does not necessarily lead to a group's achieving an accepted place within a society.

MICHAEL BANTON

The Direction and Speed

of Ethnic Change

THE entry in the *Dictionary of Social Science* on "assimilation" begins "the term literally means the process of becoming 'alike' or 'more alike'"; but it has good reason for continuing "as used in sociology, it denotes (a) the process whereby a group, generally a minority or an immigrant group, is through contact absorbed into the culture of another group or groups; (b) the result of such absorption." Sociologists now use the word in a narrower sense than they did before World War I, but the restriction in the signification of the concept has never been intellectually justified. It results from the kind of social theory that was current earlier in the century and from the preoccupation of sociologists with the problems arising from the immigration into the United States of White ethnic populations. The process (a) listed in the *Dictionary* is an example of one kind of assimilation, and not the only kind. This essay contends that it is more rewarding to regard

The author wishes to thank his colleague, Robert Miles, for helpful comments upon an earlier draft of this essay.

assimilation as a process of great generality, one whereby cultural differences are reduced, and to pair it with the opposing process of differentiation, whereby cultural differences are increased. It sees both processes as resulting from the choices of individuals when faced with alternatives generated by social structures and situations (Banton 1977).

THE WARNER MODEL

The simplest exemplification of the definition found in the *Dictionary* is presented in W. Lloyd Warner's studies of White ethnic groups in his well-known works on *Yankee City*. Some of the implicit features of this concept become explicit if it is represented by a diagram of the kind suggested in figure 1, which shows two groups, *A* (the majority and *B* (the minority), with a cultural difference that is scored as 10 points along the horizontal axis. After one hundred years group *B* has been completely absorbed by *A*, which has continued along precisely the course it would have followed had *B* not appeared upon the scene. The zero point from which group *A* starts is put a little distance to the right of the vertical axis, so that the line representing its course is not confused with the axis showing the passing of time. This diagram brings out three features of the Warner conception. First, time: some groups are assimilated more quickly than others; second, the difference between the two groups is cultural; and, third, the process of assimilation operates upon the totality of the minority's culture.

But it is a matter of common observation that cultural change among immigrants proceeds more rapidly among immigrants in behavior that helps them earn a living, like learning a language, than in their private domestic lives. The implication of a uniform process of change is misleading, as is the failure to acknowledge that the receiving group undergoes change in absorbing the other. A more helpful diagram would be of the kind provided in figure 2. This preserves the time dimension, the dotted lines representing the courses that groups *A* and *B* would follow if there were no cultural change whatsoever, but it separates the speed and direction of change. The lines running up to points *C, D,* and *E* might, for example, represent change in language, cuisine, and a particular sporting activity. *C* indicates that the minority has found it convenient to adopt the language of the majority, but at the same time has contributed some words and expressions to the common speech, so that *A* has come one-tenth of the way towards meeting *B,* while after sixty years the two groups can no longer be distinguished linguistically. In cuisine, change is more

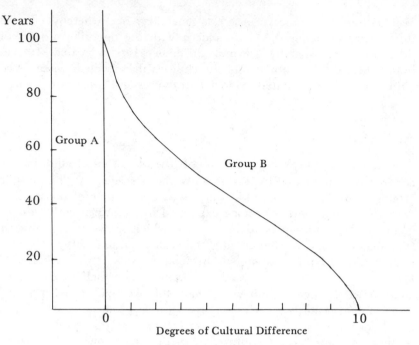

Fig. 1. The Warner Model of Assimilation

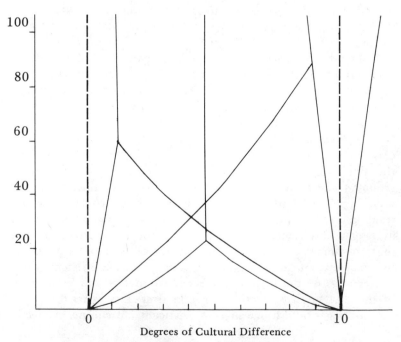

Fig. 2. Process of Cultural Change

evenly balanced and more rapid, each group adopting some of the dishes favored by the other, but because the foodstuffs of the native group are cheaper, B adopts more from A than A does from B. It is easier to try a new dish than to try a language, and people rarely lose status by trying new foodstuffs, so assimilation proceeds more rapidly in this field than in some others, and after twenty-five years the groups are no longer distinguishable in this area. In both these instances the minority changes in the direction of the majority, but sometimes it is the other way round. This may happen when the minority brings a cultural feature particularly suited to the receiving country, as Swedish settlers brought the log cabin to the United States. Majority changes in the direction of the minority are, however, more likely in the expressive than the instrumental realm. Minorities bring dances, costumes, and sports, which, like football, may soon lose their ethnic identification, or, like judo and karate, may become both ethnic and international. The line leading to E represents a situation in which after ninety years a minority sport has been generally adopted in a slightly modified form.

The weaknesses of the Warner model are well known. It is now widely accepted that a conception of assimilation as a unitary process is misleading. The B group moves towards A at different speeds in different areas of life and the A group usually moves itself. Stages in processes of change have occasionally been discerned but they are restricted to particular circumstances. The adoption by immigrants of majority practices may give an appearance of change but underlying values may not have altered. Moreover, the majority society itself is divided by socioeconomic status, regions, life styles, and perhaps by ethnicity. Social life in the different sectors of work, schooling, home, and religion, may be compartmentalized so it becomes difficult to identify the group or practices in the majority society to which the minority may be expected to assimilate. It is customary to ask to what extent a minority is assimilated, but the question can also be asked of the majority. Yet a criticism as serious as any of these is that the Warner model fails to recognize that group membership is itself problematic. Ethnic identities are not primordial characteristics programmed into individuals, but have continually to be established from the actions of people as they choose to align themselves in one way or another and make use of shared notions about who belongs in what social category. It is not just that some members forsake the immigrant minority group, or pull it in a different direction, but that members of the majority are engaged in changing their group, too.

Many of these conceptual lacunae exist because assimilation

has been discussed almost exclusively with reference to immigration. Yet minorities are not necessarily immigrants, nor are majorities necessarily indigenous. Minorities may be subjected to a pressure to change that is implicit in the political and economic superiority of an expanding group—as White influence has spread in Amerindian regions in the United States, or English influence in other parts of the United Kingdom. Assimilation can be said to have occurred in Brazil, where a clear division between Europeans and Africans (and to some extent between them and Amerindians) has given way to a continuous gradation without one group's having absorbed another. Moreover, ethnic change at the local level may, in the short term and in certain features of behavior, run in a direction opposite to that of change at the national level. A group that is a numerical minority in the state may be in a majority locally, so that people belonging to the national majority may be under pressure to change towards the group that is the local majority even if it is a national minority. For example, in parts of British cities where there are substantial numbers of Black children it is not uncommon for White and Asian children to interest themselves in Black music and adopt Black speech patterns.

Among the weaknesses in Warner's analysis was his failure to acknowledge that the process he studied was but one variety of assimilation among many, and that change could follow a different course when power relations between the groups were less unbalanced. Another oversimplification was his representation of assimilation as occurring on the group level. From the illustrations he gave, for example, of conflicts between parents and children, it is clear that he saw individual actions as building up to create the process, but because his focus was on the group he took account only of those individual actions that could be fitted into his model and ignored those that could have pointed to the limitations stemming from his assumptions.

To measure cultural changes it is necessary to specify which feature of culture is being examined and to delimit the populations (groups A and B) precisely. Any reduction in cultural difference, regardless of which group moves most, and for what reasons, is then seen as a process of assimilation. A movement in the contrary direction (to position F in fig. 2) is then regarded as a process of differentiation. A group that is assimilating to the minority in certain respects may increase its differentiation in others. For example, a forthcoming study of a Sikh community in England reports that an increasing proportion of young men are wearing the turban. This is the result in part of growing pressure for conformity within the ethnic colony and in part of a reassertion of ethnic pride in the face of White rejection (Ballard, R. & C., 1977, p. 47). Other groups differentiate themselves on account of shared beliefs (like the avoidance of pork by Black Muslims), so that the increase in cultural difference is an unintended consequence of their actions. These processes are not limited to ethnic groupings. The history of social stratification is replete with examples of upwardly mobile groups trying to assimilate to groups higher on the scale, and of these groups trying to prevent this by sumptuary legislation or by adopting new social styles. There is no fundamental sociological difference between the two kinds of change, but it is convenient to distinguish ethnic change as cultural change identified with ethnic groups.

GROUP ORIENTATION

Warner described a situation in which the rewards offered by the majority (or receiving society) for conforming behavior by members of the immigrant group were so much greater than the rewards an immigrant could receive for loyalty to his traditional culture that cultural change was overwhelmingly on the part of the minority moving towards the majority's expectations. Change is rarely that simple, and though it is not possible to attempt a classification here of all the various relations between majority and minority, it is desirable to identify, as one of the most relevant dimensions, the relative attractiveness to the immigrant of the cultures of the sending and receiving societies.

The disposition on the part of an immigrant group to maintain or reduce cultural differences, that is, its social orientation, will be affected by the extent to which members of the group are disposed to adopt the values of the receiving society, or hold to those of the society from which they have come. This is represented in figure 3. The vertical axis measures the attractive power of the receiving society, the horizontal axis that of the sending society. The intersection creates four quadrants or "boxes." The circumstances defined by the boxes below the line (2 and 3) result in minority groups with relatively strong boundaries; those defined by the boxes above the line (1 and 4) result in groups with very weak boundaries because the members of them respond as individuals to the relative attractions of the two societies.

Box 1, the upper left-hand quadrant, is the place for immigrants strongly attracted to the receiving society and willing or eager to conform to its expectations. Box 2 contains immigrant groups who have left their original country not to join another, but to be on their own. Many religious communities, like the Hutterites, the Amish,

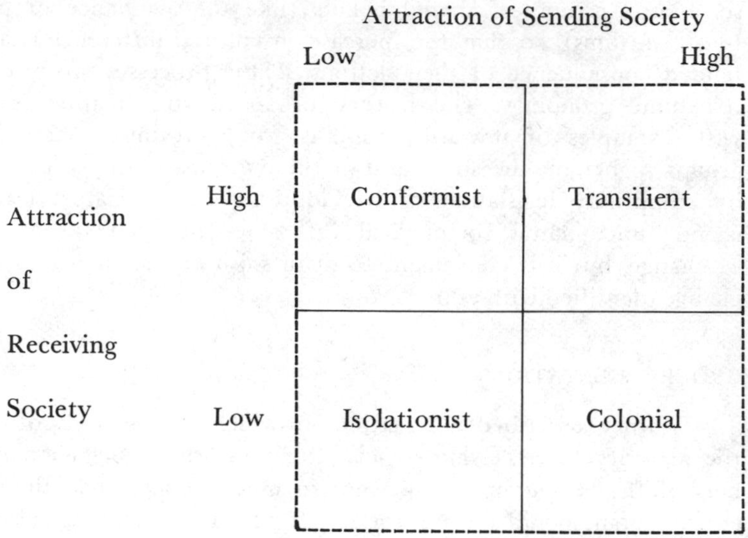

Attraction of Sending Society
Low
High
Attraction of Receiving Society
High
Low
Conformist
Transilient
Isolationist
Colonial

Fig. 3. The Orientation of Immigrant Groups

Ukrainian
Ukrainian
Polish
Romanian
Russian
Yugoslav

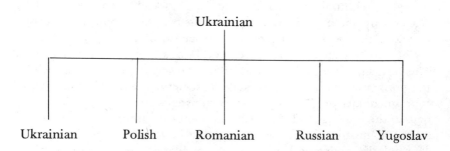

Fig. 4. Ethnic Categorization in a Northwestern Ontario Town (After Stymeist 1975, p. 50)

and the Dukhobors, have left Europe for North America to live a separate existence, conceding only minimally to the demands their new state makes upon those who would be its citizens. Box 3 includes migrant workers who are in the receiving society but not of it. Their group life may be maintained by the rotation of personnel, usually male, with new migrants coming to take the place of "target workers" who have saved the capital they want and are returning to their home country. A special category of migrant workers, which could well be called migrant rulers, has been made up of European administrators employed by imperial countries to administer the affairs of countries they have conquered or taken into protection. Being richer, the administrators can afford to bring out their families and to send their children back to the sending society for schooling. There are also groups who settle new territory intending to create an outpost of their home country, and these, like the British in New Zealand, may eventually become independent societies. Since the original sense of the word *colony* is that of a settlement of people residing in a foreign country, and there is no convenient alternative word, the adjective *colonial* is the most suitable designation for the outlook of a group oriented towards the society of its origin. (Since World War II the critics of imperialism have often referred to it as "colonialism"; they have been concerned about circumstances in which colonization has been accompanied by the subordination of the local population, but this is more truly a characteristic of imperialism.) The groups in boxes 2 and 3 seek to resist the attractions of the receiving society by strengthening group boundaries and employing a strategy known as incapsulation. Box 4 encloses migrants equally attracted by both societies. Some Europeans who settle in North America decide after a while that they would be happier in the countries of their birth but when they return there they compare them unfavorably with North America. They have difficulty settling in either society because they become so conscious of the attractions of the other. Since they are ready to move between them they may appropriately be called transilient (cf. Richmond 1967, p. 252).

The situation described by Warner in *Yankee City* belongs in Box 1, beginning towards the bottom left-hand corner of the box and moving up towards the upper left as the disposition to conform to the New England pattern of life increases with the passage of time. The immigrants might retain a sentimental attachment to the sending society but it was little more than that because their new society could provide them with a much higher standard of living than the one they had left. The United States was a land of great opportunity and could demand a corresponding commitment. Because almost all the inhabitants of the United States were immigrants, the bulk having arrived towards the end of a four-hundred-year period, all of them could claim a connection with one or more sending societies. It was legitimate and proper for a United States citizen to claim an ethnic identity associated with a sending society at the same time that he claimed to be a true American. Indeed, in parts of the United States and Canada, men and women have been expected to have the attribute of ethnicity as well as that of citizenship, so that it has been said that there are no unhyphenated Americans.

In recent years the word *immigrant* has for many people in the United Kingdom signified a person whose ancestors were natives of a "colored' Commonwealth country: the West Indies, Africa, or the Indian subcontinent. Members of the Asian and African minorities can be located in Box 3 of the diagram. Comparing their position to that of European ethnics in New England, it should be noted that the cultural gap between the sending and receiving societies is greater, and that the Asians are tied tightly by religion and moral outlook to their homeland culture; the Asians have come to Britain as migrant workers intending to return with the capital they have accumulated; because of the great improvement in communications they are able to keep in touch with their homelands more easily, more cheaply, and more immediately than has been possible for intercontinental migrants in earlier periods; the material rewards available to workers in Britain are not so much higher than those Asians can obtain in their own countries that the attractions of life in Britain should be beyond question. Moreover, the social climate has changed so that among Europeans there is now a greater appreciation of cultural diversity and less confidence in the superiority of European ways. These and similar considerations tend to strengthen the migrants' orientation towards the sending society at the expense of the receiving society, but they reinforce the conception of Asians as migrant workers rather than immigrants.

Americans have for a long time seen theirs as a country of immigration. The indigenous natives, the North American Indians, do not have the power to enforce a claim to ownership of the territory, and since the other groups are themselves immigrant they cannot justify any claim to pre-eminence on such grounds. They could, and have, exerted great pressure upon immigrants to conform to established social patterns, but there was no charter for permanently allocating people to categories with different rights and obligations. The rights and obligations of citizenship were fundamental. Different patterns can be seen in countries in which there was a substantial population prior to immigration, and which have not seen themselves as countries of immigration. Malays believe that as sons of the soil they have rights in Malaysia that the Chinese do not. Even if the Chinese are dutiful citizens and beat the Malays in fair competition they may not be allowed to acquire pre-eminence. Similar feelings have been an element in the restriction of the rights of Asians in East Africa and their expulsion from Uganda, and they are reflected in British sentiments about recent immigration. In Britain ethnicity is legitimate only in the restricted sense that individuals are accepted as being Scottish, Welsh, and Irish as well as British. These are not hyphenated Britons, but members of ancient nations inhabiting the territory they occupied before the United Kingdom was formed. The suggestion that there could be Indian-Britons as there are Irish-Americans is something new, and would probably not be generally accepted by the White British population, members of which would be inclined to argue that if people want to be Indian they should live in India.

The position in Britain of persons of West Indian descent is less straightforward. Their ties with the sending societies are less strong than the Asians' and the cultural gap is smaller. Economic opportunities in their homelands are severely restricted and the balance of advantage is more firmly in favor of their settling permanently in Britain. They came with a greater willingness to conform to the expectations of the receiving society than did the Asians, so that to begin with they could have been placed in Box 1 of figure 3 but towards the center of the figure. Disappointed by the discrimination that seems so pervasive and unyielding in the majority society, many of them are less inclined to conform to its expectations and look towards a future society different from both the sending and the receiving societies. This cannot be represented in figure 3 and is more like a move towards position F in figure 2.

The process whereby members of a group change their orientation and, possibly, move from one "box" to another, can be seen as the outcome of a bargaining process. The history of American Indians in the southern states shows that in the late eighteenth and early nineteenth centuries some groups were adopting many elements of White culture, but with the establishment of the slave regime the rewards of participation in the new states were outweighed by the costs of their being forced into a servile status, so they withdrew from interaction with Whites so far as possible, returning to closer relations only when the balance of rewards shifted (Peterson 1971). If, in figure 3, the sending society is replaced by traditional Indian society and the receiving society by White American society, this would mean that in the eighteenth and early nineteenth centuries the Choctaw could be located on the right-hand side of Box 1, moving under the slavery period to the left side of Box 3 and then back again in more recent times. These changes have been largely a response to the sort of rewards they were offered for participating in the majority culture, but a diagram like figure 3 is unable to reflect the changes that the two cultures have undergone over time.

The rise of elites that press new strategies upon fellow members of their groups can also be seen as a feature of intergroup bargaining. In certain respects the Black Power movement has been an attempt to increase the differentiation of Blacks from Whites in the United States (as by moving to position F in figure 2). Its tendency has been to restrict the kinds of relations with Whites that Blacks were prepared to enter, and to bargain for better terms of trade. The position of such an elite resembles that of trade-union leaders in that it needs first to establish control over its group, to make sure that every prac-titioner is a dues-paying member. Mere recognition of a shared interest is not sufficient, for if the union can get a pay rise, everyone in the trade or work unit will benefit irrespective of whether he is a member. To use the colloquial expression, he can take "a free ride." The cost to the individual of joining is almost certainly greater than benefit stemming from the probability that one more member will affect the outcome of the negotiations (Olson 1965). The union leadership, or the minority group leadership, therefore, has to do more than appeal to self-interest; it has to prevent people taking free rides if it is to mobilize its potential power and thereby change its relations with other groups.

SOCIAL DIVISIONS

The Pilgrim Fathers came to America because they believed that their religion was a private affair that should be free of state regulation. Many other groups followed them for similar reasons and modern American sociologists may be unaware that they take for granted the separation of church and state. This may help explain Warner's otherwise surprising failure to discuss religion in connection with assimilation. The immigrant was expected to change much, but he was never expected to change his faith. Catholics and Jews were not to be assimilated to Protestants. In religious affairs there has been a triple melting pot with assimilation occurring in each of the three divisions. The practice of each religion has become more American so that, for example, American Catholicism has differentiated itself from Italian Catholicism; as each of the three faiths has become more American in mode of expression and practice so they have become more similar. Cultural change has been simultaneously assimilating and differentiating according to the standpoint from which it is seen.

The same model is applicable to ethnic groupings. Immigrants to a heterogeneous industrial society cannot assimilate to the total society. They join the ethnic groups and social strata that are closest to them in the situation in which they find themselves, and a lot will depend upon the kinds of occupation they are able to secure. Assimilation is then a two- or a three-step process. The immigrant joins a local group that is in opposition to other local groups but has interests in common with them in opposition to larger sections of the total population. In the process, ethnic identities are sometimes changed. This has been observed by anthropologists for twenty years or more. For example, it has been said "from the point of view of the African on the Copperbelt all tribes other than those from his particular home area tend to be reduced into three or four categories bearing the label of those tribes who, at the coming of the Europeans, were the more powerful and dominant in the region." In these circumstances a category of "Nyasa," including all immigrants from what was then Nyasaland developed as if it were a "tribal" category comparable to a cultural unit like "Bemba" (Mitchell 1956, pp. 28-30). A similar process has been noted in a Northwestern Ontario town where the category "Ukrainian" comprehends Polish, Romanian, Russian, and Yugoslav (see fig. 4), apparently because the Ukrainians are the most numerous representatives of what appears to others as one ethnic unit. The anthropologist heard someone called a "Uke" and inquired if he were a Ukrainian. The answer was "yes," but when asked from what part of the Ukraine his family came, the man replied, "They didn't. They came from Poland. I'm a Polack." He chose to present himself as a Ukrainian because in the receiving society ethnic identities had been redefined (Stymeist 1975, p. 50).

Any attempt to predict the direction of cultural change amongst West Indians and Asian immigrants in Britain must first confront the question of which social divisions in British society are likely to have the strongest influence. It has been suggested that there are in principle three main strategies within orthodox political channels by which colored people could seek to improve their position in British society; by promoting class solidarity, ethnic group solidarity, or Black solidarity (Lawrence 1974, p. 156; Phizacklea and Miles 1977). There are powerful reasons for doubting whether any of these processes will occur, at any rate, in so simple a manner. Tensions between White workers and colored are strong, as are tensions between Asians and West Indians. Ethnic group solidarity may for a time be a significant feature of Asian political activity because of its roots in the homelands, but it is unlikely to meet the needs of British-born Asian young people who expect to spend their lives in the receiving society. Quite possibly most of the new generation will feel that they cannot improve their position by orthodox political means since their numbers are small and they have difficulty effecting coalitions with majority pressure groups. In any case processes of cultural change are affected by relations in spheres other than that of politics, and people are often motivated more strongly by considerations of social status than of shared class interest. It seems more likely that the development of minority relations in Britain will include some of the features of a multiple melting-pot structure; Christian, Jewish, Muslim, Sikh, and Hindu, with the various ethnic groups being ranked within each division. As in the United States, differences of religion constitute a culturally legitimate basis for a distinctive identity in private relations, while the culture of the receiving society will influence the practice of each religion. In public spheres, primarily those of work and schooling, assimilation will proceed directly, but in the private spheres of family life and recreation it will be a two-step process in which differences between coreligionists are first reduced.

CHANGING GOALS

Migrant workers who are initially but little attracted towards the receiving society's values and practices may change their goals when they are faced with new choices. This is brought out in a study of Pakistanis (both Muslim and Christian) who have left towns in Pakistan to live in Bristol. The author of the study shows that the alternatives with which they are confronted do not constitute a simple choice between Pakistani and English ways. In the first place, Pakistani culture itself is changing, and though it is difficult to classify the modes of change, it does not seem unfair to distinguish two particular processes. One is that of ashrafization, derived from the Arabic word for noble. In the villages and urban areas the newly wealthy seek to become "noble" by imitating ashraf families, and by displaying their orthodoxy as Muslims. People from families that have been wealthy for a longer period are more inclined to adopt Western styles. Men or women who dress in particular ways will be called "modern" (using the English word) and notions of love matches, companionate marriages, and the like, will be identified in the same way. Muslim migrants come to Britain with the intention of returning to Pakistan, and as their income increases they adopt a combination of the ways of behaving that confer status back home (Jeffery 1976).

Yet in pursuit of their objectives they make unanticipated

decisions that lead them to modify their goals and that in the end increase the probability of their remaining in England. They begin as target workers, choosing the kinds of work and residence that will enable them to save, and remit home, as much money as possible. They can do this most easily if they migrate on their own, leaving their wives and children to live in the country with the lower cost of living (though, of course, there are additional reasons for such an arrangement). After a while, some wives find this unsatisfactory, and they come to Britain, perhaps bringing other young male members of the family so that they in turn can be established as migrant workers. The pattern of migrant living in Britain then changes from the male dormitory to the family house. The men at work and the children at school have to operate within English institutions, but in family life, recreation, and religion the migrant group tries to isolate itself and resists assimilation. The migrants value an English education but they fear that their children may grow away from them and that the girls may be corrupted by a way of life that offers too little protection not only to the girls themselves but to the reputation of families, which will suffer dishonor if their daughters do not contract marriages of the approved kind. For this reason the girls may be sent or taken back to Pakistan.

The cultural change described in this study is of a limited kind. Some of it is change toward modern styles in Pakistani cities rather than toward British culture. Some of it is an adaptation of homeland values such as is displayed when a rather distant kinsman is able, because of the smallness of the kinship network in Britain, to consider his female relative a "sister" and she can without impropriety receive him without a chaperone. The men perform work they do not like because "pay overrides the disadvantages"; that is, they do not change their evaluations of types of work but value the money because of what it can secure them in their own culture. In the home there were few conflicts between girls and their parents (ibid., pp. 122, 106, 5). Nevertheless, there is every reason to believe that after a time the parents will be faced with the more difficult problem of deciding whether their future lies in Pakistan or in England and, if the latter, it will be less easy to avoid some testing choices about their ethnic identity. Sikh and Hindu migrants from India, who immigrated earlier and have not kept quite such close contact with their home villages, have probably moved further along this path (Ballard, R. and C. 1977, pp. 22, 34).

So too have West Indians. The author of a study of immigrants from Monserrat states that though almost all the migrants talk and act as if they will return he suspects that no more than one in five will ever do so. Opportunities in the homeland are very restricted and many migrants will be tied to their children who will wish to remain (Philpott 1973, pp. 178-80). Though many West Indians in Britain feel a need for political solidarity in dealings with the English, they are divided by rivalries between the sending societies; these give rise to a ranking by prestige, which though disputed and less clear cut than among the Pakistanis, is sometimes significant. Thus in one London borough there was an expectation that Barbadians would outrank Trinidadians who in turn would outrank Jamaicans. Because the Barbadians were expected to take the leading positions in any West Indian organizations, and the Trinidadians to take the secondary offices, willingness to form voluntary associations on a Caribbean basis was reduced (Pollard 1972, pp. 375-77).

A study of Jamaicans in another British city is of interest for its description of differentiation within the ethnic minority (Pryce 1974). Some migrants change towards British expectations, some away from them, showing certain similarities to the patterns reported for a Black neighborhood in Washington (Hannerz 1969). There is room for argument about how many life styles should be distinguished among the first generation, and what names should be given to them, and this account differs in several ways from that given by the research worker. One life style conforms closely to English expectations: those who follow it seek many of the goals that bring status in English society. It is the style of the "mainstreamers" or "mainliners," and its upper reaches may be distinguished as the local West Indian elite. Also on the conforming side are the "saints," or members of West Indian Pentecostal churches who look to the next world for true satisfaction but are respectful of the conventional values that the mainstreamers share with the English. On the opposite side are the Black nationalists, or people who would be considered politically "conscious" of the wrongs done to Blacks. This category is not at present a large or coherent one, perhaps in part because the logic of a truly nationalist outlook would dictate that they should return to the West Indies to take part in the political life of societies in which Blacks constitute the majority. In between the mainstreamers and the nationalists come the "hustlers" who make a living by disreputable means (such as earnings from prostitution). These life styles are the reference points in the social field within which immigrants make their choices about the kinds of social career they wish to follow.

Earlier it was remarked that group membership is itself problematic. Children do not have to adopt the social identities of their parents, and they are likely to do so only to the extent that the rewards outweigh the costs. In the Asian minorities the parental generation can at present offer much greater rewards to children who follow in their footsteps than can the corresponding generation of West Indian parents. The extended kinship network of the Asian groups can offer their young people significant emotional support and material assistance of the greatest importance in such matters as house purchase, which is dependent upon capital accumulation. The parents go to great lengths to assist their children and are willing to compromise to maintain family unity. One anthropologist writes "Parents are acutely conscious of their powerlessness in the fact of their children. They say that if they give in to their children's demands for the same degree of freedom as their English friends receive, then the children will be lost; if they are oppressive and authoritarian their children . . . will take th first opportunity to rebel. . . . I have met fathers who will wait for their sons to return home before making quite a minor decision, so that they can have their say." The same account continues, "Children have enormous respect for their parents and are usually unwilling to precipitate inevitable shame on their parents by acting in a way that will be condemned by others." To marry without parental consent would result in expulsion from the family group. Many of the young men who have behaved in a rather English manner as, for example, in striking up liaisons with girls, change radically when faced with the responsibilities to their kinsfolk that are embodied in marriage; some of them insist that their marriages must be arranged in completely traditional style and say that they do not want to meet their bride before the ceremony (Ballard 1973, pp. 18, 22-23). Another author who confirms this interpretation remarks on the young men who are sent back to the Punjab to visit their kinsfolk where they are received lovingly and generously as long-lost sons of the family. It reinforces their tendency to define themselves as Asian (Thompson 1974, p. 246). Many of the young people in England emphasize that they obtain much enjoyment from being Asian in culture and associate themselves with Asian criticisms of contemporary English life.

West Indian parents in England cannot offer their children the same emotional or material rewards for identifying themselves with the elder generation's view of how people should lead their lives. Because of the circumstances in the inner city areas in which so many have made their homes, and the lack of the group supports that are so important to any understanding of Asians' position, a great deal of the deprivation suffered by the first generation of West Indian settlers is transmitted to the next. Unemployment levels are high. Cultural change among the Asians is likely to occur within an Asian framework with a desire for modernity used to select from and reinterpret the traditional heritage. Among the West Indians that heritage is much less distinctive and is a less extensive resource for those who are under pressure in a very competitive environment. Like their fathers, the young men have to choose between three basic life styles, those of the mainstreamer, the hustler, and that which I have called, rather hesitantly, the Black nationalist. Some young men will show features of more than one life style. Many of the hustlers have adopted a mode of dress, language, and musical expression that symbolizes revolt against both White society and the outlook of mainstream parents, and it is sometimes identified as Rastafarian although the young men in question probably do not subscribe to the religious beliefs that characterize the Rastafarian group in Jamaica. Sociologically, the main significance of Rastafarianism is its search for a culture that is distinctively "Black" and different from both English culture and the colonial culture of the West Indies. Political consciousness may therefore be significant in the hustler's rejection of White values. That the life styles in question cannot be sharply differentiated, and that no one has yet identified corresponding styles among the girls, may not be important. The hypothesis is that ethnic change among the Black minority in Britain will be an outcome of choice between alternative models of conduct representing different combinations of elements from several cultures. In may therefore be helpful to look for emerging alternative life styles.

MINORITY AND MAJORITY

Asian young people frequently say that they are both Asian and British and wish to be accepted by everyone as having dual social identities (Ballard, C., forthcoming). Young people of West Indian parentage similarly wish to be recognized both a Black and as having the same civil rights as other British people. Whatever the justification for such a view, there is some doubt about whether a dual identity is one of the options open to them. Maurice Freedman testified that to be an Englishman and a Jew is probably the aim of a very large proportion of Jews born in England, and, in view of their less distinctive appearance and their longer period of residence, it ought to be easier for Jews to establish a dual identity than Asians or West Indians. Yet Freedman doubted whether Jews had in fact reached such a position. There was resistance from non-Jews that hindered their acceptance as simply another religious community, even within a predominantly secular society, while orthodox believers could not accept an interpretation of their religion that allowed Jews to behave in public and private just like the English (Freedman 1955, pp. 227-28). The English-born Jew was under pressure to choose between being a Jew resident in England, or a Jewish Englishman (whose faith had been politically domesticated), or an Englishman of Jewish extraction (who had only a sentimental identification with other Jews). For the Jew resident in England, his faith has implications for conduct in a wide range of situations and for the roles he may enter, so it gives rise to a basic role. For the Jewish Englishman (and even more the Englishman of Jewish extraction) Judaism has relatively few social implications and, in so far as it gives rise to any role at all, it is to an independent role (Banton 1965, pp. 33-34).

There are strands in English opinion that suggest that the extent to which second-generation settlers wish to be Asians or Blacks, to that extent they can be less than fully English (or Scottish or Welsh). It is difficult to identify the nature of the resistance since, though much has been written about minority relations in Britain, there have been so few attempts to ascertain and interpret White attitudes about color in relation to social contexts. Mr. Enoch Powell has several times articulated this resistance since his Eastbourne speech of 16 November 1968 in which he maintained that the "West Indian or Asian does not, by being born in England become an Englishman." In law he becomes a United Kingdom citizen but if he grew up in a community of people from the same culture "he will by the very nature of things have lost one country without gaining another, lost one nationality without acquiring a new one." For English people, a dark skin has traditionally been a sign that the person in question comes from overseas, perhaps from one of the dependent territories in the empire, and that he has no permanent place in Britain. White Anglo-Saxon Protestants looked with disapproving eyes upon many of the later immigrants to the United States, but the balance of power between ethnic groups in that country was very different from that in Britain. Those Englishmen who think like Mr. Powell would say that Britain does not have to become a multiracial society. Immigrants should either work their passage to the eventual acceptance of their descendants into English society, or they should return to the society in which they can be themselves without changing their ways.

The second-generation settlers will contest this. Some of the forces with which they must struggle are those with which ethnic minorities in the United States have had to contend: scapegoating, ethnocentrism, economic interest, competition for social status, and so on, but there are respects in which the British social system is different. Possibly there is a stronger pressure in the political field to locate disputed issues on the left-right dimension since (until recently) the British two-party structure has not been cross-cut by regional differences as much as in the United States. American political parties have accommodated themselves to ethnic variation and compose a slate with a suitable distribution of ethnic names. British parties cannot do this; the single successful candidate is supposed to represent the interests of all his constituents. Jews have been active in all the British parties and the newer immigrant groups will have to follow them if they are to have any political influence. They will be unable to do so if being Asian or Black is as important to them as being English. Whereas it used to be the West Indians who most readily attracted English prejudice (while the Asians made themselves less conspicuous) in recent years is has increasingly seemed as if more hostility was being directed towards the Asians because they maintained their distinctiveness. The tacit question "Why can't they be like us?" seemed to touch upon doubts concerning the loyalties of minority members. If people wish to be Asian or Black as well as English will the social implications be any more extensive than with the citizen who attends a synagogue instead of a church? Will they claim representation as a minority, and if so, can they accept any collective responsibilities to balance the rights they claim? Is color to be a sign of a role relevant only in the private domain? To combat White prejudice the minority members need to organize collectively, yet in so doing they can increase the hostility towards themselves. The direction of cultural change among the minority will be affected by such considerations and by the kind of bargain struck with the majority about the relative rewards to be obtained from different strategies.

CONCLUSION

"Assimilation" means different things to different people. Yet if it is understood in its basic sense of increasing similarity there can be no question that it is one of the most fundamental of social processes. The conventional conception of it as a unitary process operating on the group level distracts attention from the underlying motive force, that of individuals responding to what they believe to be the direction of their interests. Assimilation is better seen as the reduction of cultural distance between specified groups with respect to particular aspects of behavior. A weaker group may in some fields assimilate rapidly to the stronger, in some change but slowly, and in others differentiate itself further, while the course of change will be channeled by social divisions within the majority. Frequently there is a two-step process whereby an immigrant group reduces the cultural distance between itself and one of the divisions of the majority society and in this way acquires a place in the wider structure. Sometimes it is not possible for minority members to find an acceptable place for themselves; they have difficulty getting their claims to a distinctive social identity legitimated since such an innovation depends upon action by both majority and minority.

REFERENCES

Ballard, Catherine
In press "Culture Conflict and Young Asians in Britain." In *Support and Stress,* ed. Delroy M. Loudon and Verity Saifullah Khan.
Ballard, Roger
1973 "Family Organization Among the Sikhs in Britain." *New Community* 2: 1-13.
Ballard, Roger and Catherine
1977 "The Sikhs: The Development of South Asian Settlements in Britain." In *Between Two Cultures: Migrants and Minorities in Britain,* ed. James Watson, pp. 21-56. Oxford: Blackwell.
Banton, Michael
1965 *Roles: An Introduction to the Study of Social Relations.* London: Tavistock Publications.
1977 *Rational Choice: A Theory of Racial and Ethnic Relations.* Bristol: Social Science Research Council, Research Unit of Ethnic Relations (Working Papers, no. 8).
Freedman, Maurice
1955 *A Minority in Britain: Social Studies of the Anglo-Jewish Community.* London: Valentine Mitchell.
Gould, Julius and Kolb, William L.
1964 *A Dictionary of the Social Sciences.* London: Tavistock Publications.
Hannerz, Ulf
1969 *Soulside: Inquiries into Ghetto Culture and Community.* New York: Columbia University Press.
Jeffery, Patricia
1976 *Migrants and Refugees: Muslim and Christian Pakistani Families in Bristol.* Cambridge: At the University Press.

Lawrence, Daniel
1974 *Black Migrants, White Natives: A Study of Race Relations in Nottingham.* Cambridge: At the University Press.
Mitchell, J. Clyde
1956 *The Kalela Dance: Aspects of Social Relationship Among Urban Africans in Northern Rhodesia.* Manchester: Manchester University Press.
Olson, Mancur
1965 *The Logic of Collective Action: Public Goods and the Theory of Groups.* Cambridge, Mass.: Harvard University Press.
Peterson, John H.
1971 "The Indian in the Old South." In *Red, White and Black: Symposium on Indians in the Old South,* ed. Charles M. Hudson, pp. 116-33. Southern Anthropological Society Proceedings, no. 5. Athens: University of Georgia Press.
Philpott, Stuart B.
1973 *West Indian Migration: The Montserrat Case.* London: Athlone Press.
Phizacklea, Anne-Marie and Miles, Robert
1977 "Class, Race, Ethnicity and Political Action." In *Political Studies,* forthcoming.
Pollard, Paul
1972 "Jamaicans and Trinidadians in North London." *New Community* 1: 370-77.
Pryce, Kenneth N.
1974 "West Indian Life Styles in Bristol." Ph. D. dissertation, University of Bristol.
Richmond, Anthony H.
1967 *Post-War Immigrants in Canada.* Toronto: Toronto University Press.
Stymeist, David H.
1975 *Ethnics and Indians: Social Relationships in a Northwestern Ontario Town.* Toronto: Peter Martin Associates.
Thompson, Marcus
1974 "The Second Generation—Punjabi or English?" *New Community* 3: 242-48.
Warner, W. Lloyd and Srole, Leo
1945 *The Social Systems of American Ethnic Groups.* New Haven, Conn.: Yale University Press.

Many studies of migrant groups to cities, particularly in the United States, have employed a model of ethnic succession that holds that immigrant minorities assume the poorest jobs and housing on first arrival, have occupied this lowly niche for a generation or more, and have then moved upward in the social hierarchy as other ethnic newcomers arrived to replace them on the bottom. Light argues in this paper that ethnic succession is a special case that arises in periods of labor scarcity. He distinguishes ethnic succession from four other modes of ethnic rank changing: displacement, leapfrogging, situs enhancement, and situs deterioration. Since these five processes may be compound as well as simple, concurrent as well as seriatim, the process of ethnic rank changing is much more complex than the older model of ethnic succession indicated. Moreover, each of the five modalities encourages differential emphases in intensity and/or scope of ethnic identity. Ethnic groups contain people who engage in various rank-changing processes and whose ethnic identities correspond to their divergent experiences. Hence, ethnic groups in modern societies are normally dynamic and heterogeneous conglomerates whose members do not agree about ethnic identity or programmatic priorities.

IVAN LIGHT

Ethnic Succession

UNTIL recently, treatment of ethnicity began with the premise that ethnic cohesion was sentimental: people form ethnic groups because they are, they regard themselves, or they are regarded as "bound together by common ties of race, of nationality, or culture" (Morris 1968, p. 167; see also Schermerhorn 1970, p. 12; Ware 1931, p. 607). Since common ties originated in the primordial past, sentimental approaches to ethnicity ("primordialism") looked to the past for the source, intensity, and boundaries of contemporary ethnic groups. Corresponding to the claims ethnic groups make about themselves, primordialism has intuitive appeal. Additionally, primordialism properly limits ethnic self-definition to only those who can make a persuasive claim to a common heritage.

Nonetheless, in the last decade research in ethnicity has turned away from simple primordialism, for three reasons. First, research has indicated that ethnic boundaries are flexible and responsive to social conditions in the present. Ethnic boundaries cannot, therefore, be regarded as inexorably cast in primordial molds by deceased ancestors (Wallerstein 1960, p. 13; Brass and van den Berghe 1976, p. 198;

Barth 1969; Lyman and Douglass 1973). Second, the resurgence of ethnicity around the globe in the last decade has called into question the hitherto prevailing assumption that ethnicity is an archaic survival that tapers into oblivion in the course of modernization (Bell 1975, p. 141; Hechter 1975, 1971; Bates 1974; Kornblum 1974, pp. 208-9). Primordialism cannot readily account for historical variation in the intensity of ethnicity nor for its resurgence in the modern world. As in the case of ethnic boundaries, these variations in intensity of ethnic awareness indicate that living people are making a lot or a little of their "primordial" ties according to present convenience. Primordial ties do not impose themselves upon the living.

Finally, ethnic groups, it is increasingly realized, are not just sentimental associations of persons sharing a primordial tie. They are also interest groups. The evidence supporting this reconsideration is the pronounced occupational and industrial specialization of ethnic groups in the modern world as well as in antiquity (Glazer and Moynihan 1970; Barth 1969, pp. 19-20). This specialization Hechter (1976) has aptly labeled the "cultural division of labor." Because ethnic groups occupy special industrial and occupational sectors, they assume the special political-economic interests their specializations impose. For example, when an ethnic group specializes in the long-distance cattle trade, as do the Hausa in Yorubaland (see Cohen 1969), then the welfare of the cattle industry is synonymous with the welfare of the ethnic group. Thus approached, ethnicity looks like a special ideology whose function is the promotion of political-economic interests of ascriptive subgroups (van den Berghe 1976, p. 250). Cohen (1969, p. 4) even defined ethnicity as an emergent from intergroup strife "in the course of which people stress their identity and exclusiveness." As always, the latent purpose of stressing identity and exclusiveness is to prevent outgroups from impinging successfully upon "the profit span" (Weber 1968, p. 341) or, when the situation is reversed, to enhance the predation of the ingroup. Therefore, the sense of ethnicity waxes in periods of intergroup competition for scarce rewards and wanes in periods of accommodation.

The emerging interest-group conception of ethnicity is difficult to define. Obviously, it need not exclude any sentimental and primordial component. In fact, groups are strongest and most unambiguously ethnic when they do draw upon sentimental as well as interest attachments. Without primordial ties, an ethnic group is only an interest group; without interest attachments, on the other hand, primordial sentiments do not yield a lively, self-conscious group life. Interest needs to be a part of our conception of ethnicity because interest is empirically a part and because, without acknowledgment of interest, observed changes in ethnic boundaries or intensity are impossible to explain. This inclusive formula (ethnicity=primordial ties+interests) cannot, of course, sweep away the problem of how to draw a firm line between interest and primordial components. Here as elsewhere in social theory, thorny issues of circularity arise: same interests because same ethnic, same ethnic because same interests, or both? (See Bonacich 1975, p. 111). This problem is too difficult for a priori resolution, and there is, moreover, no compelling need to impose a deductive strait-jacket upon research. For the moment, all that is necessary is to explore the limits of interest to test and expand our enhanced but still changing understanding of ethnicity and interest.

GAPS IN THEORY

As matters stand, the interest-group conception of ethnicity faces two problems. One is the general relationship between interest and the boundaries of ethnic groups: under what circumstances do ethnic boundaries expand or contract? The second and more serious is the lack of framework for assessing the structure of intergroup relations in sequence of development. One such framework now available is Hechter's (1971,1975) "reactive theory of ethnic change." This framework fits the case in which other-ethnic capitalists impose their political-economic system by conquest upon indigenous peoples. Although a promising beginning, Hechter's (1976, p. 221) reactive theory ignores precapitalist and noncapitalist imperialism so gaps in coverage appear here. Moreover, even when most generously assessed, Hechter's formulation only encompasses situations in which immigrants impose themselves upon indigenous people as superordinates. But Lieberson (1972) has distinguished a second framework: immigrants are subordinate and natives are superordinate. An example is rural-urban migration of uprooted peasantry. In the industrial sectors of the world, immigrant subordination is the prevailing type (Francis 1976, p. 252). Since the reactive theory of ethnic change does not encompass this modal situation, the interest-group conception of ethnicity lacks a framework of analysis in the central case.

THE SPLIT LABOR MARKET

A possible framework for the immigrant-subordinate, modal case is the "split labor market" (SLM) theory of ethnic antagonism (Bonacich 1972, 1976). The central hypothesis defining this approach is the presumption that "ethnic antagonism first germinates in a labor market split along ethnic lines" (ibid., 1972, p. 549). Under this circumstance high-priced labor takes protective action to prevent scabbing and wage cutting by low-priced, other-ethnic labor. Victory for more expensive labor takes the form of exclusion of low-priced other-ethnic labor from the territory, or caste exclusion of low-priced workers from high-wage sectors. Victory for cheap labor displaces high-wage workers from their industries or occupations (ibid., 1976, p. 41). Bonacich's formulation fits the immigrant-subordinate case because subordinate newcomers do typically enter the labor force as cheap labor. As such, they pose a threat to higher priced, old-ethnic labor, and situations of ethnic antagonism occur.

Nonetheless, several objections limit SLM theory as a general framework for ethnic relations in situations of immigrant subordination. First, a split labor market is neither a necessary nor a sufficient condition for ethnic antagonism. Using Swiss data, Walliman (1974) has pointed out that even when new ethnic laborers are as costly as old ethnic laborers—hence no split labor market exists—the mere appearance of additional labor undermines the psychological and economic position of old labor. This deterioration produces ethnic antagonism in the absence of a split labor market. Conversely Hilton (1977) has noted that California Whites did not object to Chinese cheap labor in periods of labor shortage. In this California case, a split labor market existed but ethnic antagonism did not result. Parallels to the California experience are the prompt reaction of European workers to *Gastarbeiters* when the recession of 1974-75 produced labor surplus instead of labor shortage. Since the split labor force can exist with or without ethnic antagonism, and vice versa, the case for the split labor etiology is in doubt.

Second, the split labor market theory treats the simple case when costly labor meets cheap labor. But SLM theory offers no guidance to complex historical situations that arise when still cheaper labor appears on the scene. That is, if costly group 1 has encapsulated low-priced group 2 in segregated occupations, what happens when group 3 then appears? This has occurred in North American industrialization as successive waves of immigration have appeared. The split labor force formulation cannot realistically ignore this temporal dimension. What is evidently required is a historical framework capable of accommodating increasing complexity resulting from sequential migration.

ETHNIC SUCCESSION

The familiar concept of "ethnic succession" seems to offer a suitably historical framework to fill these gaps. As an empirical generation, ethnic succession has already proven of immense value in ordering the data of more than a century of ethnic change in the United States and Canada. Indeed, the idea has more or less bestraddled North American thought so that efforts to discuss ethnic change begin with this implicit image, if only as a point for critical departure. Stripped to essentials, the working model of ethnic succession holds that immigrant minorities have assumed the poorest jobs and housing (Aldrich 1975), occupied this lowly niche for a generation or more, then moved upward in the social hierarchy as other ethnic newcomers arrived to replace them on the bottom (Shibutani and Kwan 1965, p. 121). Of course, those who move up still rank behind predecessor minorities they displace because the predecessors also rise in the socioeconomic hierarchy. This simple model leads to the conception of a hierarchical ethnic ladder with each immigrant minority occupying a rung corresponding to its time of arrival in the host society. The oldest settlers rank highest; the newest rank lowest; and intermediate groups fall between. This is the "rank-sequence rule" of ethnic succession: all earlier immigrants rank above all later immigrants.

The sequential pyramids in figure 1 illustrate the model. At time one, group 1 is all alone, and its members are upper, middle, and lower status. At time two, group 2 people begin to arrive. They take the lower positions so that group 1 people now occupy only middle and upper status positions. At time three, group 3 people, a newcomer ethnic minority, finally appear. They take over the lowest level positions in the occupational system and housing realm. Group 2 people move up to the middle-status level, and group 1 becomes at last homogeneously upper status in character. The system grows in over-all size because of migration; the expansion of the system creates room at the top; old-ethnics move upward in social rank when newcomers arrive.

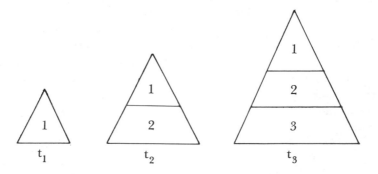

Figure 1

This is simple ethnic succession because all later immigrants rank below all earlier immigrants. Rank sequence is inviolate.

CRITIQUE OF SUCCESSION MODEL

The succession model has obvious appeal because North American societies do evidence a rough empirical correspondence to it (Smelser 1976, p. 87; Shibutani and Kwan 1965, p. 121; Banton 1967, p. 337; Baltzell 1958, p. 223; Koenig 1943). Over successive generations, White American and Canadian ethnic groups have moved up the social ladder from starting places near the bottom. As they moved, newcomers replaced them in abandoned jobs and housing. This glacial process has given rise to a rough correspondence, in industrial regions at least, between social rank of a White minority and its time of arrival. Outside North America, other illustrations of the same or similar processes also appear in Australia (Inglis 1975; Shibutani and Kwan 1965, p. 121). In Europe today "guest workers" occupy the poorest jobs and worst housing (Castles and Kosack 1973; Walliman 1974). Hardly any Swedes work on Volvo production lines; those jobs belong to Turks and Greeks (Oberg 1974). The Swedes are managers and white-collar workers. However, a close look at the guest workers also indicates that those who have been the longest in the host countries now hold better jobs than those who have most recently arrived. This is lifetime occupational mobility within the guest worker population. The phenomenon points toward a future date when below the old-stock native-born on the top, European societies will contain subordinate layers of middle and lower status ethnics. Status position in European societies will then demonstrate a rough correspondence with time of immigration with those whose forebears came earlier ranking higher than those whose forebears came later.

This risky prediction offers an excellent opportunity for airing obvious difficulties. Sometimes immigrants begin as subordinates but thereafter ascend the social hierarchy faster than some old-ethnics; hence violations of rank sequence appear (Thernstrom 1973, pp. 142-43). Sometimes newcomer ethnics enter the status hierarchy in the middle ranks, above some old-ethnics but below the elite. The "middleman minority" characteristically occupies this position (Bonacich 1973). Finally, some newcomers may move up the status hierarchy faster than others and some may not move up at all. These three exceptions do not exhaust the range of empirical possibilities. But they demonstrate that ethnic succession is only a tendency, not an iron law.

Unfortunately, North American users of succession imagery have been too little aware of these pitfalls. As a result, ethnic succession became the center of an ideological debate. The popular succession framework casts Blacks and Hispanics as "the newest immigrants" (Handlin 1959, p. 42; see also O'Kane, 1969; Kristol 1970; Sowell 1975, p. 149; Banton 1967, p. 337). White old-ethnics (Irish, Italian, Jewish) outrank them because they came earlier, but the White ethnics still rank below their Anglo-Saxon predecessors. The succession framework also organizes the orthodox explanation for criminality among Blacks. For example, in his national television series ("The Age of Uncertainty") John K. Galbraith told Americans in 1977 that misbehaving Blacks and Puerto Ricans in the slums are no worse than had been their now respectable White predecessors. This optimistic view identifies the stage of rapine and riot as the natural precursor of decent respectability attendant upon social ascent in due and inevitable course (see also Sowell 1975, p. 63); The most fervent affirmation of this doctrine appears in Banfield (1974), a conservative polemic. Banfield (1974) portrayed rural-urban migration as a process of resocialization in the course of which improvident and ignorant rural migrants acquire middle-class standards and foresight, and thus earn a higher social position. A Marxist version is Szymanski (1976) who understands ethnic succession as a process whereby capitalists import docile labor to replace workers who learned how to organize. Indeed, Szymanski's data show that Blacks are no longer on the bottom: Latin American immigrants now have lower incomes than Blacks.

In general, however, radicals have rejected the succession and assimilation framework for non-Whites, without, for the most part, disputing its applicability to White old-ethnics. Their view has received overpowering support from Thernstrom's (1973, pp. 176-91) historical research in comparative ethnic mobility. "Split labor force" (Bonacich 1972, 1976) and "dual labor market" writers (see Ng 1977; Gordon 1972, pp. 43-52; Flanagan 1973, pp. 253-73) have emphasized the institutional barriers that prevent contemporary Asians, Blacks, and Hispanics from penetrating the high wage sectors of the American economy, the obvious first step in any succession process. The reaction against the succession framework is sharpest in Blauner (1972, pp. 51-81) who argues that color prejudice locked non-Whites into ghettos. "Internal colonialism" is Blauner's (ibid., p. 52) characterization of this situation: "Racial groups in America are . . . colonized peoples; therefore their social realities cannot be understood in the framework of immigration and assimilation that is applied to European ethnic groups."

All the empirical objections to the succession model reduce to the observation that numerous violations of rank sequence occur. These

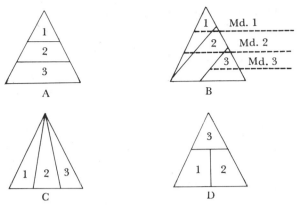

Figure 2

violations are of two sorts: some groups rank higher than they ought on the basis of ordinal sequence; other groups rank lower. Figure 2 illustrates some of the deviations that can arise from violations of rank sequence. Pyramid A displays perfect conformity to rank sequence. However, in Pyramid B some threes outrank some twos, and some twos outrank some ones. These are violations of rank sequence, but the illustration offers no basis for deciding whether the violations arise from groups moving ahead too fast, too slow, or both. Despite the violations of rank sequence, the influence of ethnic succession still appears in the median status level of the three groups. The median level of 1 outranks the median of 2, and the median of 2 outranks the median of 3. In this complex situation, succession explains some but not all of the hierarchical position of the three groups. On the other hand, pyramid C displays a status relationship in which the influence of succession is nil. Groups 1, 2, and 3 are equally represented at every level of the social hierarchy, and the median status level of all groups is identical. Of course, a sequential passage from pyramid A to C would involve gross violations of rank sequence, and, these violations would accrue to the benefit of group 3 at the expense of the rank of groups 1 and 2. One must presume that these violations would only succeed despite the opposition of the adversely affected groups (1, 2); indeed, this opposition is the principal source from which the rank-sequence rule derives its "authority."[1] The same observation applies to the radical *bouleversement* of ethnic groups in pyramid D. There status position is inversely related to sequence of arrival, a

1. The Bible (Deut. 28:43) lays this curse on unobservant Jews: "The alien who lives with you will raise himself higher and higher, and you will sink lower and lower."

patent violation of rank sequence adversely affecting the status rank of groups 1 and 2.

In sum, self-interested enforcement of rank sequence is what guarantees ethnic succession, and violations of this rule undermine it. Rank sequence depends, first of all, upon norms. "We were here first so we should rank higher" is the basic norm. Its corollary is: "Don't push ahead." When subordinate ethnics do not accept this norm, they push into power conflict with higher ranking ethnics who do. When the higher ranking ethnics prevail, rank sequence remains inviolate.[2] When a subordinate ethnic group does accept this norm, it legitimizes its social inferiority. This is "rank concession" in Orrans's (1971, p. 90) terminology. The consequences he traced (p. 92 ff.) are social emulation of the superordinate group, power-incorporative borrowing, and deterioration in subordinate ethnic solidarity. In the North American context, these predictions turn into cultural and structural assimilation based on Anglo-conformity, and pretty neatly correspond to the sequence of developments described by North American sociologists. What was missing in their early formulations was, however, an appreciation of the role of power, norms, and norm-enforcement in propping up the hierarchical arrangement. What they described as invariant natural sequence was in reality an adjustment to intergroup power disparities in particular historical circumstances.

SUCCESSION IN SOCIOLOGICAL THEORY

The intellectual sources of confusion about power and conflict in ethnic succession are deeply rooted in the history of sociology. As an empirical generalization, ethnic succession is very familiar in North American literature since the 1930s, but systematic analysis of the concept has been remarkably missing except in urban ecology (see Aldrich 1975). For example, recent textbooks of ethnic and race relations do not list ethnic succession in their index (see Francis 1976; Schermerhorn 1970; Blalock 1967). True, Shibutani and Kwan (1965, p. 121) index the concept, but their treatment is strictly de-

2. This situation resembles a waiting line: those at the head of the line assume responsibility for preventing latecomers from pushing ahead, and rank in line depends upon their success in enforcing their "right of priority." This analogy suggests the "queue theory of the labor force" (see Hodge 1973), and these are points of comparison. However, the queue theory assumes intergroup differences in employability as given, and overlooks normative and power bargaining. For example, the minimum wage affects the employability of low-ranking labor—and the minimum wage is a political issue. For this reason, the queue theory is more descriptive than analytic of intergroup differences in employability.

scriptive—not analytical. For this reason, Park's (1936) discussion must still be the starting place for critical review. The purpose of this review is to increase the precision of terminology, to bring out the conceptual ambiguities and errors in Park's germinal concept, and thus prepare for empirical studies of the succession process.

Park (1936) defined succession as "any orderly and irreversible series of events." This series develops in "increments." "The effect of each succeeding increment of change reinforces and carries forward the effects of the preceding." Change proceeded in stages. Hawley (1971, p. 99) explains the stages as an alternation of periods of growth and equilibrium. Following this usage, urban sociologists conventionally distinguish phases of invasion and succession in land use. Invasion is the intrusion of a new usage; succession its consolidation.

The major difficulty in Park's writing concerns the possibility of uncontested as well as contested succession. The alternation of phases of conflict and accommodation is unambiguous in the writing of Park (1950, p. 150) and his students. Indeed, Park (1936, p. 176) believed that "the function and effect of competition" was precisely to accomplish "a division of labor which has diminished competition." This emphasis leaves no doubt that Park never considered uncontested succession. This oversight caused serious confusion because early studies of ethnic succession in industry reported uncontested succession. In their analysis of Newburyport, Massachusetts, Warner and Srole (1945, p. 63) described in detail the process of ethnic succession. "The workers of the newly arrived groups started at the very bottom of the occupational hierarchy and through the generations climbed out of it and moved to jobs with higher pay and increased prestige. Each new ethnic group tended to repeat the occupational history of the preceding ones." However, Warner and Srole (ibid., p. 65) treated the process of succession as an "infiltration" rather than a stampede. Change was evenly rather than unevenly distributed in time. Additionally, they concluded that ethnics moved into "occupations abandoned by middle class natives." The natives, they also insisted, did not leave "because the ethnics with their lower wage demands" had "forced them out." Rather, "ethnics *replaced* natives" (ibid., italics in original).

Another case of uncontested succession turned up in Lind's study of ethnic groups in Hawaii. Lind (1938, pp. 248-49) observed that immigrant laborers "first swell the occupational pyramid at the bottom" where they are "free to compete for status" with outgroups. "Under the influence of pecuniary motives the immigrant invariably deserts the unskilled-labor ranks as rapidly as possible and pushes up into the places left vacant by his predecessors or into those created by the expanding character of the economy. Every immigrant group tends to follow certain well-marked paths of social and economic advancement."

The language indicates that Lind was concerned with intergroup conflicts because groups "compete" and "push up." Yet, ethnic succession in Hawaii actually involved uncontested occupancy of industrial vacanies rather than displacement of predecessors. This Hawaiian case did not justify the optimistic conclusion that "every immigrant group" must invariably receive its reward in sequence, the basic fallacy of succession theorists.

Another familiar example is the labor migration of Blacks in the 1930s and 1940s. In the Depression years, northerly migration of southern Blacks slowed to a trickle. After all, there were few jobs in the depressed North, and every opening had numerous White claimants. But in 1942 war production produced a labor shortage. Whites grabbed the best jobs. Blacks then moved northward in great numbers to fill lower ranking vacant positions—and the newcomers encountered no opposition (Thernstrom 1973, pp. 198, 215; Handlin 1959, pp. 48-49).[3] Here again, the massive succession of Blacks to lower ranking jobs occurred without contest because they occupied vacancies.

These simple distinctions indicate that "ethnic succession" is a deceptively simple idea. There are contested and uncontested succession. Contested successions involve social conflicts between newcomers and incumbent old-ethnics. Conflict arises because newcomers are reducing or threatening to reduce the quality of work or housing incumbents occupy or might occupy. On the other hand, when newcomers fill in low-ranking vacancies, succession proceeds without conflict (Thernstrom 1973, pp. 43-44). But the rate and timing of succession is also significant. Abrupt and rapid succession may occur without conflicts when newcomers are only filling vacancies. Conversely, a slow and continuous succession may transpire in an atmosphere of crisis when entrenched ethnics draw sharp lines between themselves and newcomers. These cases prove that rate or timing of ethnic change is in principle compatible with either contested or uncontested succession.

3. Bonacich (1976) argues that Franklin Roosevelt's National Industrial Recovery Act created a "radical coalition" of Black and White workers during the great Depression. This interethnic coalition formed because of the NRA prohibition of cheap labor. That prohibition eliminated intergroup wage competition and, therewith, intergroup antagonism. Her observation correctly underscores the effects of regulatory legislation upon intergroup wage competition and social relations. But the specific effect of the NRA ended in 1939 when the Supreme Court declared the act unconstitutional. Hence, the NRA cannot account for interethnic labor harmony during World War II.

Nonetheless, the presence or absence of manifest social conflict in a succession sequence depends upon how rapidly and in what rhythm succession is proceeding. When, for example, newcomers crowd into limited vacancies, they rapidly exhaust unoccupied work or housing. Saturation achieved, supernumerary newcomers threaten to compete with old-ethnics for jobs and housing. The phase of succession without conflict has ended. The new conflict-ridden situation is likely to resemble a split labor market in which newcomer ethnics form a cheap labor threat to incumbent old-ethnics. Of course, the crucial issue is not the absolute rate of succession. The issue is, rather, the rate of newcomer influx relative to the rate of old-ethnic social ascent. If incumbent old-ethnics are moving up rapidly to better jobs and housing, then low-ranking vacancies rapidly proliferate, and newcomers can occupy them as rapidly. If, however, the influx of newcomers is more rapid than the upward mobility of incumbent ethnics, then supernumerary newcomers unavoidably come into potential competition with incumbents for work and housing.

ETHNIC SUCCESSION DEFINED

The balance between the egress of old-ethnics and the influx of newcomers provides the basis for clarifying distinctions. We shall hereafter restrict the term "ethnic succession" to the occupation by newcomers of low-ranking vacancies. Specifically, ethnic succession occurs when newcomer ethnics occupy inferior vacancies in housing and jobs, usually in the wake of upwardly mobile old-ethnics. Thus defined, succession is always uncontested, and never produces any violations of rank sequence. The absence of conflict in ethnic succession is the result of, first of all, the absence of intergroup competition for low-ranking vacancies. Second, higher ranking, upward mobile old-ethnics have an interest in the recruitment of new ethnics to perform low-ranking work. The performance of such work is, after all, the key to their own mobility, and to local prosperity. For example, the shortage of Swedish workers, a result of Swedish prosperity, necessitates the importation of foreign workers to perform manual jobs on Swedish assembly lines. Were these workers unavailable, Swedish industry would be crippled, and its prosperity curtailed. In this sense, Swedish workers want and need non-Swedish labor to perform the manual jobs that support their own supervisory status as well as the Swedish economy. Therefore, in times of prosperity and labor shortage, Swedish workers welcome and encourage the importation of non-Swedish labor. When labor surpluses later appear, the attitude of Swedish labor toward foreigners becomes exclusive.

Since ethnic succession as defined never causes intergroup conflict or violations of rank sequence, the presence of both requires an explanation. What mechanisms can eventuate in slower-than-expected social ascent or faster-than-expected social ascent? This question implies the contrast of two, mutually repugnant sets of social mechanisms: mechanisms of exclusion/retardation, and mechanisms of integration/acceleration. The mechanisms of exclusion/retardation are basically ones Bonacich (1973, 1976) described in her victory-of-expensive labor theory in a split labor market. When this victory is total (and it hardly ever is), high-wage, old-ethnic labor is totally successful in its self-interested effort to forestall and frustrate an invasion of their industries or occupations by newcomers. The exclusionary mechanisms include, first of all, political exclusion of newcomers from the territory, and, therefore, from the labor market. When territorial exclusion fails, exclusion from the labor market serves the same function. Against those who cannot be excluded from the labor market altogether, protective barriers may yet prevent penetration of high-wage sectors already occupied by old-ethnic labor. Devices to assure labor market exclusion include: child and woman labor restrictions, mandatory education provisions, minimum wage and working standards legislation, and public welfare programs to care for the unemployed. Welfare makes it possible to survive without working; the other restrictions make working at subsistence wages impossible and unemployment more common. Together the measures create a survival program for the permanently unemployed. Devices to protect high-wage, old-ethnic industries include: caste segregation of occupations and industries, nepotistic or racially exclusive hiring practices, educational credentialism, civil service tenure, seniority systems, occupational licensure requirements, and "fair trade" laws. These measures neutralize the chief advantage of newcomer ethnics: a desperate willingness to work long hours for low wages under inferior working conditions. Unable to penetrate these defensive perimeters, newcomers in the labor market cannot displace incumbents in violation of rank sequence. They do, however, occupy those occupations and industries in which protective barriers against entry are minimal or absent. Old-ethnic labor abandons these sectors in favor of those in which protective barriers do exist. The over-all result is a dual labor market in which old-ethnics work in regulated sectors while substandard working conditions, low wages, and laissez-faire prevails in newcomer-dominated industries and occupations.

What are typical mechanisms of integration/acceleration? Bonacich's (1973, 1976) treatment of this victory-of-capital situation is perfunctory, and requires some elucidation. Of course, as in the previous illustration, these mechanisms are totally effective only when capital is totally victorious, an eventuality that rarely occurs. Bonacich (1976, p. 41) has covered this entire tendency with the concept of "displacement" by which she means the actual substitution of cheap labor for high-wage labor. With the first displacement, newcomer ethnics enter the labor market despite the opposition of incumbent old-ethnics; with subsequent displacements, they move up the job hierarchy, possibly pushing ahead of old-ethnics in violation of rank sequence.

Important as it is, displacement does not exhaust the economic mechanisms for integration/acceleration available to newcomers. Violations of rank sequence can occur without displacement. One occasion is leapfrogging. Leapfrogging arises when newcomers occupy middle or higher ranking vacancies. The vacancies may reflect new opportunities caused by the development of the expanding economy, or the egress of upward mobile old-ethnics, or both. When the economy is expanding, vacancies often require entrepreneurship to locate and develop. The vacancies do not, in this case, resemble empty slots newcomers just occupy. Newcomers must mobilize entrepreneuerial resources to find and develop the opportunity (Light 1979). When vacancies develop because of old-ethnic egress, on the other hand, filling them is simple ethnic succession, provided that the vacancies newcomers occupy had no old-ethnic claimants. That situation might arise when (fig. 1) the ascent of group 1 ethnics leaves vacancies. If filled by group 2, the vacancy-filling is ethnic succession. If filled by group 3, the process is leapfrogging. In any case, newcomer leap-frogging displaces no one since newcomers only occupy vacancies and there need be no cost-of-labor disparity between leapfrogging newcomers and old-ethnic aspirants. However, leapfrogging newcomers block old-ethnic succession in violation of rank sequence. Therefore, the potential for intergroup antagonism is obvious.

Situs enhancement offers an additional mechanism for violations of rank sequence without displacement. Situs enhancement occurs when newcomers improve the value (monetary, prestige, or both) of work they occupy. The basic technique is monopolization of an industry or occupation in the interest of high prices and profits (Weber 1968, pp. 43-46; see also Cohen 1969). Unions and trade associations share this objective. Radical enhancement of a situs can change the rank order of ethnic groups in the society, even permitting violations of rank sequence. For example, Irish-Americans and Italo-Americans in New York City and Scandinavians in Portland (Pilcher 1972) entered the longshore industry as casual labor under extremely unfavorable working conditions. They organized this industry into monopolistic trade unions, admission to which was virtually closed to outgroups. These unions improved the economic status of newcomer ethnics.

Finally, newcomer ethnics gain access to political power by means of which they can level or reduce barriers that forestall invasion of high-wage sectors already occupied by old-ethnic labor. The split labor model altogether ignores the political power of newcomers. Naturally, the extent and type of newcomer political power is variable. In the United States, Canada, Australia, and Great Britain, newcomer ethnics have had prompt access to the franchise; labor-importing nations of continental Europe have not accorded the same privileges to guest workers. The franchise permits newcomer ethnics to rescind laws or practices (minimum wage, licensure, discriminatory hiring, etc.) that restrict their access to high-wage sectors, and even to sponsor legislation intended to expedite their penetration. Examples of the latter include: headstart programs for disadvantaged kindergartners, multicultural education, and vocational training programs. Even when no institutionalized political power is available to newcomer ethnics, riot or insurrection or threat always confers extra-institutional political power. The intervention of labor-exporting governments on behalf of overseas nationals is yet another source of political power frequently but not always available to newcomer ethnics. In forwarding integrationist objectives, the newcomers deploy their institutional and extra-institutional political power as allies of capital in its continuing struggle with high-wage labor.

ETHNIC SUCCESSION IN PERSPECTIVE

The sequential arrival of ethnic minorities is the typical model of economic development under capitalism. In general, this process involves a social conflict between big capital and newcomer ethnics on one side, and high-wage old-ethnics on the other. In this struggle, economic threats are neutralized by political countermoves and vice versa. Capital, newcomers, and old-ethnic labor have access to political power as well as to economic power. In parliamentary democracies, capital is weaker in political than in economic power; and labor is stronger in political than in economic power. For this reason, capital prefers weak and noninterventionist governments that neutralize the political preponderance of labor whereas labor prefers interventionist governments that restrict the freedom of action of capital. Ethnic succession as defined is a special case that arises when, in a labor shortage, the interests of old-ethnic labor, capital, and newcomer ethnics briefly coincide. Under these circumstances, old-ethnic labor withdraws its usual objections to the immigration of newcomers, and their penetration of local labor markets. When, in the course of the business cycle, labor surplus appears again, the three-sided political-economic struggle also resumes. Violations of rank sequence reflect the varying outcomes of this seesaw struggle.

Nonetheless, succession is a crucial step in the model sequence because high-priced labor, under this special circumstance, waives its politically preponderant opposition to penetration of "its" territory and labor markets by newcomer ethnics. This transitory waiver sets in motion a chain of consequences. First, newcomer ethnics arrive to occupy inferior jobs and housing left behind by upward mobile old-ethnics. This is ethnic succession. Second, old-ethnics develop protective barriers that exclude newcomers from high-wage sectors already occupied. These protective barriers reflect the preponderant political power of the old-ethnics. Third, newcomer ethnics acquire countervailing political power of their own. In alliance with capital, they employ this political power to reduce or eliminate the barriers that protect old-ethnics against their competition. Violations of rank sequence then appear as a result of the political/economic influence of newcomer ethnics. Fourth, these violations set in motion political/economic countermobilizations of old-ethnics. When old-ethnics prevail, rank sequence is protected; when newcomers prevail, rank-sequence irregularities appear. The deadlock is broken when and if a labor shortage compels all ethnics to withdraw normal objections to the introduction of still more recent migrants from heretofore untapped regions of the globe.

ETHNIC CONSEQUENCES OF ETHNIC SUCCESSION

What are the ethnic consequences of the chain of events set in motion by ethnic succession? That is, what happens to the definition and intensity of ethnicity at every stage of this process? Assimilation theorists (see Falk 1973) have argued that a unilinear, continuous diminution of ethnic consciousness accompanies succession. Assimilation purportedly supports succession as cause and effect. For example, learning the host society's language is an obvious prerequisite to full participation in its economy, and the learning of the new language exposes the immigrant family to the higher status culture of the host society (Gordon 1964, pp. 77-78). In the same sense, prevailing theorists have believed that a lively sense of ethnicity poses problems for economic integration so that efforts to make an economic adjustment compel immigrants to move away from ethnic consciousness in favor of functional bases (class, occupation, industry) of solidarity (Ware 1931, p. 612). In this belief, immigration theorists have simply reflected the prevailing view of ethnicity as an archaic solidarity that tapers into oblivion in the course of modernization.

True, there have been dissenters. Proponents of value congruence theories have claimed that some immigrants present cultural values congruent with the host societies that recruit them. For example, the remarkable social ascent of Japanese in North America has commonly been attributed to the immigrants' affirmation of hard work, discipline, and self-reliance, values resonant with the Anglo-American mainstream (Kitano 1969; Petersen 1972). In this case, social ascent transpired because of (not despite) alien values, institutions, and clannishness (see Light 1972, 1978; Bonacich 1975). The famous "race relations cycle" of Robert Park (1950, p. 150) proposed another dissent. Arguing that the main drift of ethnicity in the modern world was toward obliteration in favor of functional bases of solidarity, Park nevertheless maintained that the main drift proceeded in a repetitive cycle of contact, competition, accommodation, and assimilation. In this view, ethnic consciousness waxed and waned even as ethnicity proceeded toward obliteration.

Empirical evidence has not confirmed the simple succession-assimilation model. Gordon (1964) has noted that assimilation proceeds in the cultural sphere as expected, but that structural assimilation has not followed. The much noted revival of ethnicity in North America has has also called into question the old-fashioned expectation of unilinear and continuous decline in intensity of ethnic consciousness. The source of these difficulties has been the unexamined model of ethnic succession analysts naïvely employed. In reality, uncontested ethnic successions are transitory moments in immigration sequences. The moment ended, fissures in the labor market promptly emerge, and newcomer ethnics disadvantageously located in the Balkanized labor market mobilize economic and political power to seek access to high-wage sectors in violation of rank sequence. This mobilization encourages a counter-mobilization also along ethnic lines, during which a long-slumbering ethnic consciousness reawakens. The alternation of hard times and flush times engenders a parallel cycle of ethnic intensity in the labor force. Entrepreneurial ethnic groups need ethnic solidarity to support their economic structure so their ethnic consciousness is, as a result, independent of the reciprocal pressures that mold it in the labor force. However, entrepreneurial leapfrogging can produce a malign and reactive ethnic consciousness among those left behind in violation of rank sequence.

ETHNIC SCOPE

Common to virtually all treatments of succession-assimilation, dissenting or mainstream, has been the presumption that the scope of ethnic consciousness remains the same, although the intensity of ethnic consciousness changes. Thus, "Italians" or "Irish" or "Jews" are said to have improved their status position, and experienced an accompanying change—usually decline—in ethnic consciousness, but the units still remain in principle what they were before: Irish, Italians, or Jews. As Nahirny and Fishman (1965, p. 312) have observed, this "dubious assumption . . . ignores the central fact" that generations differ among themselves in "the nature of their identification with ethnicity" as well as the intensity of identification. An empirical illustration is Barton's (1975, p. 169) research into intermarriage among Italians, Romanians, and Slovaks in Cleveland. For the immigrant generation, the salient boundaries of endogamy were locality of origin and dialect. Later, the boundary expanded to encompass conationals. Finally, White Catholics had become the endogamous boundary. These changes are qualitative transformations of what constitutes ethnicity—who is in the group—not merely changes in intensity of ethnic consciousness.

Ethnic scope refers to the boundaries of an ethnic group. It is roughly congruent with group size, although discontinuous and capricious rather than formal or logical in character. For simplicity's sake, we can distinguish continental, regional, national, and local scope. A continental scope defines a continent-wide ethnic identity: for example, Asian, European, Latin American. A national scope embraces a national ethnic identity, for example, Italian, Irish, Chinese. A regional scope indicates a regional ethnic identity, for example, Calabrian or Cantonese. Local scope means same place origin, for example, a Landsmann or paisano. These four do not exhaust the possibilities. Keyes (1976) treats ethnicity as comparably "nested" segments of kinship relationship. "Ethnic groups, unlike races, are not mutually exclusive but are structured in segmentary hierarchies with each more exclusive segment subsuming ethnic groups which were contrastive at another level." What is crucial in this view is not the contrast of race and ethnicity, but the acknowledgment that ethnic identity is a qualitative phenomenon as well as a quantitative (intensity) one, and that multiple levels coexist.

The nested segments that make up ethnic consciousness need not exclude one another and typically do not. For example, a person's ethnic identity simultaneously encompasses being European, Italian, Tuscan, and paisano, although one or the other normally predominates in a given role. Since intensity and scope are in principle independent, the possibilities of ethnic change are more complex than social scientists who ignore scope suppose: each level may increase in intensity, decrease in intensity, or remain unchanged over time. Therefore, "ethnic consciousness" rarely changes as a unitary whole, each segment increasing or decreasing in exact proportion to all the others. Usually, some segments are changing faster than others so that the qualitative profile of ethnic identity is changing in addition to the intensity of ethnic consciousness. For example, in North America, the foreign born and their posterity have passed through three phases of ethnic consciousness in this century. In the first phase (1880-1924) regional consciousness and local consciousness (both initially high) declined in intensity while national ethnic consciousness (initially low) increased (Nahirny and Fishman 1965; Barton 1975). In the second phase, national ethnic consciousness began to decline while regional and local ethnic consciousness continued to decline or remained stable but submerged. This was the era (1924-45) of Americanism and Anglo-conformity (Krickus 1976, pp. 354-58). This third and most recent (1946-   ) involves the resurgence of national ethnic identity without an accompanying resurgence of regional ethnic identities, which remain below the threshold of visibility (Nelson 1976). Has "ethnic consciousness" in North America increased or declined? The question is impossible to answer. All one can conclude is that the profile of ethnic consciousness has changed; local and regional levels have receded, and the national level has declined and resurged.

A world-wide view of ethnicity confirms this multidimensional scope of ethnic consciousness. In Africa, van den Berghe (1971, p. 511) observes a "general growth in the scale of relevant ethnicity" occasioned by processes of "sub-ethnic fusion." The ethnic consciousness of Europeans is changing too. In the nineteenth century, "Germany" and "Italy" were geographical expressions. The politics of central European diplomacy in the nineteenth century involved regional rivalries that pitted Austrian against Prussian and Piedmontese against Tuscan. Nationalism triumphed in 1914 and 1939. However, regional identities in Western Europe have receded since World War II, and supranational (European) consciousness has risen to challenge triumphant nationalism. The Common Market and North Atlantic Treaty Organization are two reflections of a more inclusive level of ethnic awareness in Western Europe. To characterize the ethnic consciousness of any European, Asian, or African individual, one would need to acknowledge the coexistence of multiple categories, some more inclusive than others. These categories change over time in relation to one another. The trend and tendency of change is an empirical problem, but one may assert in general that no people can produce a changeless historic profile of ethnic consciousness. Even the Bible (Num. 1-4) distinguishes twelve tribes of Israel, but tribal identity hardly exists among modern Jews, adherents of the world's oldest religion, so "Jewish" identity is qualitatively different even if unchanged in intensity.

SUCCESSION AND DISPLACEMENT IN INDUSTRY

Of the writers who have treated ethnic succession, only Kornblum (1974) has specifically addressed the changing scope of ethnic identity in the process. Others have proceeded on the contrary-to-fact supposition that ethnic boundaries persist but diminish in intensity. Kornblum examined succession in the government of the Chicago steelworkers' union. In this setting, newcomer ethnics (Blacks and Mexicans) confront White old-ethnics, chiefly Italians and Slavs. As the newcomers enter the union, they naturally seek to augment their political influence in it in proportion to their augmented representation in the membership. What was the consequence for ethnic identity? Kornblum (ibid., p. 159) found that steelworkers adjusted the scope of their ethnic identities to the exigencies of power competition in union policies. "Among themselves the Mexicans, or the Poles, or the South Slavs may say, 'We are in this for us. We've got to get our share.' But ethnic solidarities are continually redefined in the process. The Serbians and the Croatians learn to view themselves as 'Hunkies,' and to see their common cause; the Mexicans must make peace between the competing territorial segments of their group in the ward."

To overcome the political preponderance of their predecessors, newcomer ethnics had to bring together scattered and mutually competing subgroups in the interest of all-ethnic solidarity. Only unity yields the political strength that permits a newcomer group to achieve power, prestige, and jobs in the steelworkers' union. Therefore, concludes Kornblum (ibid., pp. 161-82, 215) the ability to build national ethnic solidarity is the test that succession imposes upon newcomers. Reaching a similar conclusion, Trottier (this volume) declares that "the unifying function is of major importance" in the expansion of ethnic identities. This expansion is actually a form of structural and cultural assimilation among subgroups whose fusion creates the enlarged ethnic group.

This conclusion suggests a hypothesis: In immigrant-subordinate situations, intergroup competition expands the scope of ethnic identity. Bell (1975, pp. 158-59) claims that people choose a level of ethnic consciousness "in relation to an adversary." Referring similarly to "shifting levels of ethnicity," van den Berghe (1971, p. 512) has called attention to the propensity of people to activate the level most favorable to themselves. The result is "a continuous process of fission and fusion . . . with ever shifting patterns of alliance between groups and subgroups." In this context, a regional or local scope of ethnic identity corresponds to a competition among subgroups within a national ethnic group. The adversary is the extra-regional, extra-local conational. When, however, regional or local coethnics initiate competition with extra-national nonethnics, they break into a more demanding sphere of competition. In this sphere, local and regional chauvinism is self-defeating because conationals confront a powerful external threat. The adversary having changed, national ethnic solidarity grows while regional and local ethnic solidarity become inactive. The changing scope of ethnic consciousness represents a special case of Coser's (1956) theory: external threats reduce the salience of intragroup ethnic identities and increase the intensity of expanded, higher level ethnic identities.

This hypothesis fits Kornblum's findings in the Chicago steelworkers union, but refined terminology refines his analysis. Replacing White old-ethnic union officials with Mexican or Black is simple succession so long as the influx of newcomers only equals the egress of upward mobile old-ethnics. But the empirical case immediately identifies two situational difficulties. First, the pressure of newcomers on old-ethnic officialdom threatens to become a displacement or displacement with succession, and only the reactive pressure of incumbent old-ethnics can prevent the rate of influx from exceeding the rate of egress. Second, Black and Mexican union officials "represent" newcomer ethnic groups that "deserve" augmented representation in proportion to their augmented influence in the steel industry labor force. Newcomers wish to acquire political power in the union. On the other hand, the elevation of Black and Mexican newcomers to positions of influence within the steelworkers' union violates rank sequence because newcomer officials then outrank old-ethnic rank and file. For example, a Mexican newcomer has an important union job whereas a Slav with thirty years of on-the-job seniority is still a rank-and-file worker. From the point of view of the old-ethnics' rearguard, the elevation of new ethnics violates legitimate rank expectations: some newcomers rank higher than some old-ethnics. Taken together, both complications create an atmosphere of displacement, leapfrogging, and social conflict. The result is the expansion of ethnic scope among newcomers and old-ethnics alike in the interest of mobilization around the issues of this conflict.

ILLEGAL ENTERPRISE

The theme of ethnic succession has been nowhere livelier than in the literature on organized crime. In a classic essay, Bell (1960, p. 141) described the sequence of Irish, Jewish, and Italian preponderance in organized crime as "part of the inevitable process of ethnic succession." Echoing this theme, Glazer and Moynihan (1970, p. 210) pointed out that "each ethnic group trying to achieve wealth and recognition . . . has in sequence produced underworld figures." However, Glazer and Moynihan (ibid., pp. 210-11; see also Cloward and Ohlin 1960, pp. 199-202) called attention to tensions between established Italian racketeers and Black and Puerto Rican newcomers, exclaiming over the retarded pace of ethnic succession. Lately, Ianni (1974) has concluded that Black and Hispanic minorities are at last replacing Italians in some sectors of organized crime. "Ethnic groups move in and out of organized crime," writes Ianni (ibid., p. 14), "and their time in control comes and goes."

Recent historical studies of organized crime have, however, challenged the long-prevailing generalizations about ethnic succession in the rackets. Haller (1972, p. 217) declared the succession model "obscures more than it illuminates," and Block (1978, p. 471) criticized Bell's "crude generalizations" about ethnic succession. This empirical critique actually reflects the general malaise of succession models in social science as much as their uncritical employment in the specific area of organized crime. Nonetheless, the case histories of ethnic groups in illicit industries offer an opportunity to test, amplify, and refine the model of ethnic change thus far developed. Does ethnic succession in the rackets reflect the changes in ethnic scope that Blum found in the steelworkers' union? A synoptic history of Black, Chinese, and Italian racketeering turns up numerous points of contiguity with other research in ethnic change and also illustrates the utility of the refinements in terminology developed in this essay. However, close examination of three case histories also indicates numerous shortcomings in prevailing literature. The most serious is the paltry role of ethnic succession in the rackets. Leapfrogging, displacment, and situs enhancement were actually the modal processes of ethnic change; succession played little role.

Italians

Prior to 1919, Italian racketeering in America involved the competition of local-origin gangs of immigrants for the exploitation of illegal opportunities within the Italian colonies. This competition reflected and encouraged regional and local chauvinism in scope of ethnic identity. Gangs recruited membership from particular localities in southern Italy, and formed into rival blocs of Sicilians and Neapolitans (Nelli, 1976, pp. 69-100). Prohibition (1919-1933) changed this relationship by permitting Italian gangs to penetrate the general (i.e., non-Italian) economy. However, this penetration brought them into competition with Jewish and Irish racketeers who had, theretofore, outranked Italians in illegal enterprise (Haller 1972, p. 219). The career of Al Capone (Light 1974b) illustrates the interstitial phase of conflict that ensued. Of Neapolitan origin, Capone recruited followers from all regions and localities of Italy as well as among talented non-Italians. The heterogeneous Capone aggregation actually came into conflict with regionally exclusive and nepotistic Sicilian gangs based in Chicago's Little Sicily. Of course, Capone's mob was also in competition with non-Italian racketeers. During Prohibition-era beer wars, the Capone mob defeated its Sicilian and non-Italian rivals, and ultimately achieved hegemonic domination of Chicago underworld. In New York City, a parallel broadening of national solidarity was in progress among racketeers of Calabrian, Neapolitan, and Sicilian origin. These byzantine intrigues came to a head in the Maranzano-Masseria and subsequent Maranzano-Luciano conflicts (see Block 1978). Each succeeding conflict reflected a widening of ethnic horizons among racketeers, and the ultimate victor, Luciano, actually owed his triumph to alliances with non-Italian criminals (Nelli 1976, p. 210).

The upshot of these processes was general abandonment in the mid-1930s of regional identities in Italian organized crime. At the same time, the consolidation of Italian hegemony reduced the necessity of alliance with non-Italian criminals so the mixed-ethnic aggregations of the Prohibition era gave way to ethnically homogeneous "all-Italian" mobs. The new Italo-American crime families awarded memberships to persons of Italian descent regardless of provincial or local origins, and the conference of Italo-American gangs (the Mafia or Cosa Nostra) became permissively Italian in scope. This it still remains.

The ascension to rackets hegemony of Italo-Americans in the 1930s has been recurrently cited as the key example of ethnic succession in illegal enterprise. Does the case justify this label? In a loose sense, it does. Italians did become rackets overlords while theretofore equiprominent other-ethnics abandoned illegal industries, retired, or accepted coordination. This process was also accompanied by a broadening of ethnic identity among the Italians who ceased to emphasize regional identities and began to emphasize national ethnic identity. On the other hand, Italians did not simply move up into vacancies others left behind (cf. Hannerz 1974, pp. 49-50). The Volstead Act created the industry, and entrepreneurial Italians joined the scramble to make money in this open-to-all illegal market (Haller 1972, p. 219). In this many-sided scramble, Italians leapfrogged and displaced other-ethnic rivals (ibid.). Their hegemony achieved, Italians then shifted into an ethnically restrictive policy of all-Italian solidarity in the interest of situs enhancement. To describe these slippery and self-reversing sequences as "ethnic succession" is to gloss over the micro-dynamics of a complex process in the interest of an imperfectly fitting, unexamined generalization. The history of Italians in rackets is by no means a simple and well-fitting example of ethnic succession in American life. Additionally, the Italian case history offers no support for any mechanical or unilinear model of succession and assimilation. Ethnic consciousness among Italian racketeers increased and decreased in scope, and waxed and waned in intensity according to the vicissitudes of the industrial situation they confronted. The much-vaunted ethnic exclusiveness of the Cosa Nostra is the normal and predictable self-protection of situs-enhanced industrial monopolizers confronting the adverse possibilities of other-ethnic competition.

Chinese

Lodges of the Triad society originated in South China (ca. 1640) as anti-Manchu political groupings, and membership was, in principle, available to anyone (even non-Chinese) who subscribed to the fraternal ideology. This universalistic tradition persisted in Triad derivatives in the United States. However, late nineteenth- and early twentieth-century Chinese racketeering in America always remained encapsulated in Chinatown. Unlike the Italians, the Chinese did not move out of their enclave into the mainstream of illegal business during the Prohibition era. As a result, Chinese tongs competed only with one another. Internal competition reinforced regional identities. Despite the formal universalism of Triad lodges, the leading Hip Sing Tong and On Leong Tong developed respectively as four-districts and three-districts dialectal communities (Lyman 1974). When the economic development of Chinese-American communities moved beyond illegal enterprise (Light 1974b) the growing legal sectors coincided with an enlarged all-Chinese ethnic consciousness. Indeed, the most advanced sectors of Chinese-American labor have by now embraced an "Asian-American" level of ethnic consciousness in the interest of political solidarity with other Asian minorities. However, the Chinese-operated illegal economy lagged behind the expanded scope of ethnic consciousness characteristic of the legal sector. Regional rivalries and regional consciousness continued to reinforce one another. Since 1965, the immigration of Hong Kong Chinese has created new, China-born competitors for illegal opportunities in American Chinatowns (Light and Wong 1975). As a result, a reorientation of ethnic identities is now occurring in their illegal sector: Hong Kong-born, Cantonese-born, native-born.

The continued encapsulation of Cantonese racketeers in the China-town economy is a violation of rank-sequence: Italians entered the illegal mainstream and now outrank Cantonese (not Hong Kong-born, who are recent immigrants) in this industry even though Italian immigration began three decades after Cantonese. The case indicates that industrial succession is not an automatic or mechanical process that relentlessly proceeds. Cantonese did not break out of the ghetto in crime, and regional identities have persisted to this day in illegal markets of Chinatown. Succession of Cantonese actually occurred in the expanding professions, notably engineering and pharmacy; in legal sectors old-fashioned regional identities have waned in favor of supranational and national ethnic identities. As a result, Chinatowns' non-mobile rearguard industries continue to operate on the plane of locality and regional chauvinism whereas the Chinese advance guard has developed broader definitions of ethnic identity.

Blacks

Prior to the mid-1930s, the best developed illegal business of urban Blacks was policy gambling (Light 1977b). A variant of this lottery is number gambling, introduced in this country in the mid-1920s by Caribbean Blacks. Although the historical record is sketchy, native-Caribbean rivalries in lottery gambling seem to have accompanied native-Caribbean ethnic consciousness in New York City, where virtually all the West Indians lived. In other American cities, lottery gambling among Blacks involved the competition of rival cliques—but these sanguinary competitions did not eventuate in ethnic rivalry or awareness. A Jewish racketeer, Arthur ("Dutch Schultz") Flegenheimer, forced himself in on Black-owned number gambling in 1933. After Flegenheimer's assassination in 1935, Italians claimed headship of the Harlem number industry as well as lottery gambling in other metropolitan Black districts (Nelli 1976, pp. 225-29). The accession of Italians to number supremacy involved a critical accentuation of "Black consciousness," usually in the wake of the Mafia's assassination of prominent Black gamblers. The accession of Italians to racketeering prominence in Harlem also produced a surge of "Black consciousness" that combined native and West Indian migrants into an all-Black solidarity front against White intruders.

The contrast of the Black and Chinese cases is instructive (Light 1977a). Neither minority moved into the illegal mainstream on schedule. But unlike the Chinese, Blacks actually lost control of their leading illegal industry, numbers gambling, as the result of an alien invasion. This invasion reflected the vertical and horizontal expansion of Italian-controlled illegal firms. The predatory expansion of Italian crime hegemonies augmented the power and social rank of Italian racketeers. Yet, this effect depended upon the subordination of "kings and queens" of policy in the Black ghetto who quit the business or became salaried administrators for Italian enterprises. Italian accession was in no sense a filling up of vacancies; on the contrary, the accession of Italians in numbers gambling depended upon situs enhancement of their hegemonic position in non-Black rackets, and displacement of Black vanguards.

SUMMARY AND CONCLUSION

Sequential immigration is the typical process of economic development under capitalism. The time sequence of immigration crucially frames the intergroup competition that results. Ethnic succession is a special case involving the linked upward mobility of ethnic groups located at different levels in the social hierarchy. Succession occasions no conflict because labor shortages have caused high-wage, old-ethnic labor to withdraw its usual objection to immigration of newcomer ethnics. Succession also occasions no disturbance in the rank order of ethnic groups relative to one another. The rank-sequence rule measures this condition: groups must rank in strict order of arrival.

Violations of rank sequence occur when groups move ahead more slowly than sequence requires or faster than sequence permits. Mechanisms of exclusion/retardation tend to produce slow-down violations; mechanisms of inclusion/acceleration tend to produce speed-up violations. In general, exclusion/retardation depends upon the preponderant political/economic power of high-priced labor acting to protect its industries and occupations from invasion by newcomers. Inclusion/ acceleration reflects the economic and political preponderance of capital and newcomer labor in alliance. The objective of this alliance is to break up the Balkanized labor markets that protect high-wage, old-ethnic labor fom direct competition with newcomers.

Intergroup competition generally expands the scope of ethnic identities and increases their intensity. Encapsulation in parochial loyalties collapses because movement into the mainstream initiates competition with other-ethnics, thus necessitating a broadened scope of ethnic identity in the interest of enhanced power. The exception is situs enhancement, which implies an exclusive strategy since the welfare of the ingroup then depends upon limiting the number of competitors, including same-ethnic competitors. It is unclear what effect, if any, simple ethnic succession produces on ethnic identity. Since the process transpires without competition, simple ethnic succession might in principle occur without any accompanying expansion in scope or intensity of ethnic consciousness. On the other hand, even simple successions raise the threat of intergroup competition, thus compelling rearguard old-ethnics to mobilize for self-protection.The result is multilateral mobilizations that both intensify and expand ethnic identities.

Social rank refers to the wealth, power, or prestige of a group. Occupations and industries are the building blocks of social rank. Since ethnic groups are differentially located in the economy, they tend to have distinctive profiles of ethnic-dominated industries and occupations. Succession, displacement, leapfrogging, and so forth, occur in specific industrial and occupational contexts. Therefore, industries dominated by a particular ethnic group may be simultaneously undergoing different changes, some in succession, some displacement, some enhancement. In this circumstance, all ethnics have primordial ties in common, but they confront different occupational vistas. These vistas induce some ethnics to call for restrictive, others for expansive boundaries, and some for a defensive and some for an aggressive posture. The predictable consequence is a plurality of voices in the ethnic community. The alignment of these voices is precisely where the interest component of ethnicity can make a contribution to microanalysis.

In a simple case, all ethnics are identified with a common industry or occupation (see Cohen 1969; Light and Wong 1975). In this case, interest and ethnicity entirely overlap, and the two are difficult to distinguish. But simple cases are empirically unusual, especially in complex societies. For the most part, ethnics participate in many industries and these industries are changing. The industrial mix produces a babble of mutually contradictory rhetoric within the ethnic community— except when the same threats beset all the industries. An example might be a split labor market in which all old-ethnics (whatever their industry) confront a massive threat of displacement because of cheap labor competition. This threat brings an abrupt unanimity of interest to a situation that is normally a bewildering array of conflicting subinterests. These watershed events may have massive political and institutional consequences. However, the passage of time is likely to erode unanimity because industries change in different ways—some flourishing, others languishing. When this happens, people who used to be unanimous begin to disagree.

This analysis suggests that ethnicity is not simply a sentimental survival in the modern world. On the contrary, the ability to expand or contract ethnic identities provides a buffer for large and threatening changes in the society. The deployment of this power builds ethnicity into the societal division of labor, thus renewing its utility into the next generation. Because ethnic boundaries are flexible, people can adjust them to meet situational needs. Because ethnic solidarity confers power, people have a motive to make the adjustments necessary.

REFERENCES

Aldrich, Howard
    1975 "Ecological Succession in Racially Changing Neighborhoods: A Review of the Literature." *Urban Affairs Quarterly* 10: 327-45.
Baltzell, E. Digby
    1958 *Philadelphia Gentlemen.* Chicago: Quadrangle Books.
Banfield, Edward C.
    1974 *The Unheavenly City Revisited.* Boston and Toronto: Little, Brown.
Banton, Michael
    1967 *Race Relations.* New York: Basic Books.
Barth, Fredrik, ed.
    1969 *Ethnic Groups and Boundaries.* Oslo: Scandinavian University Books.
Barton, Josef J.
    1975 *Peasants and Strangers.* Cambridge, Mass.: Harvard University Press.
Bates, Robert H.
    1974 "Ethnic Competition and Modernization in Contemporary Africa." *Comparative Political Studies* 6: 457-84.
Bell, Daniel
    1960 *The End of Ideology.* Rev. ed. New York: Free Press.
    1975 "Ethnicity and Social Change." In *Ethnicity,* ed. Nathan Glazer and Daniel Moynihan, pp. 141-74. Cambridge, Mass.: Harvard University Press.
Blalock, Hubert M., Jr.
    1967 *Toward a Theory of Minority Group Relations.* New York: John Wiley and Sons.
Blauner, Robert
    1972 *Racial Oppression in America.* New York: Harper and Row.

Block, Alan A.
    1978 "History and the Study of Organized Crime." *Urban Life*
        6: 455-74.
Bonacich, Edna
    1972 "A Theory of Ethnic Antagonism: The Split Labor Market."
        American Sociological Review 37: 547-59.
    1973 "A Theory of Middleman Minorities." *American Sociological
        Review* 38: 583-94.
    1975 "Small Business and Japanese American Ethnic Solidarity."
        Amerasia Journal 3: 96-112.
    1976 "Advanced Capitalism and Black-White Race Relations
        in the United States: A Split Labor Market Interpretation."
        American Sociological Review 41: 34-51.
Brass, Paul and van den Berghe, Pierre L.
    1976 "Ethnicity and Nationalism in World Perspective." *Ethnicity*
        3: 197-201.
Castles, Stephen and Kosack, Godula
    1973 *Immigrant Workers and Class Structure in Western Europe.*
        London: Oxford University Press.
Cloward, Richard and Ohlin, Lloyd E.
    1960 *Delinquency and Opportunity.* Glencoe, Ill.: Free Press.
Cohen, Abner
    1969 *Custom and Politics in Urban Africa.* Berkeley and Los
        Angeles: University of California Press.
Coser, Lewis A.
    1956 *The Functions of Social Conflict.* Glencoe, Ill.: Free Press.
Falk, Gerhard
    1973 "The Assimilation Process in America." *International
        Behavioural Scientist* 5: 70-80.
Flanagan, Robert J.
    1973 "Sequential Market Theories and Racial Discrimination."
        Industrial Relations 12: 253-73.
Francis, E. K.
    1976 *Interethnic Relations.* New York: Elsevier.
Glazer, Nathan, and Moynihan, Daniel Patrick
    1970 *Beyond the Melting Pot.* 2nd ed. Cambridge, Mass.: Massa-
        chusetts Institute of Technology Press.
Gordon, David M.
    1972 *Theories of Poverty and Unemployment.* Lexington, Mass.:
        D. C. Heath.
Gordon, Milton M.
    1964 *Assimilation in American Life.* New York: Oxford University
        Press.

Haller, Mark H.
    1972 "Organized Crime in Urban Society: Chicago in the Twentieth Century." *Journal of Social History* 5: 210-34.
    1974 "Bootlegging in Chicago: The Structure of an Illegal Enterprise." Paper presented at the Annual Meeting of the American Historical Association, Chicago.
Handlin, Oscar
    1959 *The Newcomers: Negroes and Puerto Ricans in a Changing Metropolis.* Cambridge, Mass.: Harvard University Press.
Hannerz, Ulf
    1974 "Ethnicity and Opportunity in Urban America." In *Urban Ethnicity,* ed. Abner Cohen, pp. 37-76. London: Tavistock Publications.
Hawley, Amos H.
    1971 *Urban Society.* New York: Ronald Press.
Hechter, Michael
    1971 "Towards a Theory of Ethnic Change." *Politics and Society* 2: 21-45.
    1975 *Internal Colonialism: The Celtic Fringe in British National Development, 1536-1966.* Berkeley and Los Angeles: University of California Press.
    1976 "Ethnicity and Industrialization: On Proliferation of the Cultural Division of Labor." *Ethnicity* 3: 214-24.
Hilton, Mike
    1977 "The Split Labor Market and Chinese Immigration, 1848-1882." Paper presented at the Annual Meeting of the American Sociological Association, Chicago.
Hodge, Robert W.
    1973 "Toward a Theory of Racial Differences in Employment." *Social Forces* 52. 16-30.
Ianni, Francis A. J.
    1974 *Black Mafia: Ethnic Succession in Organized Crime.* New York: Simon and Schuster.
Inglis, Christine
    1975 "Some Recent Australian Writing on Immigration and Assimilation." *International Migration Review* 9: 335-44.
Keyes, Charles
    1976 "Towards a New Formulation of the Concept of Ethnic Group." *Ethnicity* 3: 202-13.
Kitano, Harry H. L.
    1969 *Japanese Americans: The Evolution of a Subculture.* Englewood, Cliffs, N. J.: Prentice-Hall.

Koenig, Samuel
1943 "Ethnic Factors in the Economic Life of Urban Connecticut."
American Sociological Review 8: 193-97.
Kornblum, William
1974 *Blue Collar Community*. Chicago: University of Chicago Press.
Krickus, Richard
1976 *Pursuing the American Dream*. Garden City, N. Y.: Double-
day.
Kristol, Irving
1970 "The Negro Today is Like the Immigrant Yesterday." In
Cities in Trouble, ed. Nathan Glazer, pp. 139-57. Chicago:
Quadrangle Books.
Leiberson, Stanley
1972 "A Societal Theory of Race and Ethnic Relations." In
Intergroup Relations: Sociological Perspectives, ed. Pierre
L. van den Berghe, pp. 38-51. New York: Basic Books.
Light, Ivan
1972 *Ethnic Enterprise in America*. Berkeley and Los Angeles:
University of California Press.
1974a "From Vice District to Tourist Attraction: The Moral
Career of American Chinatowns, 1880-1940." *Pacific Historical Review* 43: 367-94.
1974b "The Career of Al Capone." Paper presented at the Annual
Meeting of the American Sociological Association, Montreal.
1977a "Numbers Gambling Among Blacks: A Financial Institution." *American Sociological Review* 42: 892-904.
1977b "The Ethnic Vice District, 1880-1944." *American Sociological Review* 77: 464-79.
1979 "Asian Enterprise in America: Chinese, Koreans and Japanese
in Small Business." In *Self-Help in America: Patterns of
Minority Economic Development,* ed. Scott Cummings.
Port Royal, N. Y.: Kennikat Press.
—— and Wong, Charles Choy
1975 "Protest or Work: Dilemmas of the Tourist Industry in
American Chinatowns." *American Journal of Sociology*
80: 1342-68.
Lind, Andrew
1938 *An Island Community: Ecological Succession in Hawaii.*
Chicago: University of Chicago Press.
Lyman, Stanford M.
1974 *Chinese Americans*. New York: Random House.
Lyman, Stanford M., and Douglass, William A.
1973 "Ethnicity: Strategies of Collective and Individual Impression

Management." *Social Research* 40: 344-65.

Morris, H. S.
    1968 "Ethnic groups." In *International Encyclopedia of the Social Sciences* 5: 167-72.

Nahirny, Vladimir, and Fishman, Joshua A.
    1965 "American Immigrant Groups: Ethnic Identification and the Problem of Generations." *Sociological Review* 13: 311-26.

Nelli, Humbert S.
    1976 *The Business of Crime.* New York: Oxford University Press.

Nelson, Bryce
    1976 "Feeling of Ethnic Pride on the Rise." *Los Angeles Times,* April 30, sec. 1, p. 1.

Ng, Wing-Cheung
    1977 "An Evaluation of the Labor Market Status of Chinese-Americans." *Amerasia* 4: 101-22.

Oberg, Kjell
    1974 "Treatment of Immigrant Workers in Sweden." *International Labour Review* 110 (July-December): 1-16.

O'Kane, James M.
    1969 "Ethnic Mobility and the Lower Income Negro: A Socio-historical Perspective." *Social Problems* 16: 302-11.

Orrans, Martin
    1971 "Caste and Race Conflict in Cross-Cultural Perspective." In *Race, Change, and Urban Society,* ed. Peter Orleans and William Russell Ellis, Jr., pp. 82-150. Beverly Hills, Calif.: Sage Publications.

Park, Robert
    1936 "Succession: An Ecological Concept." *American Sociological Review* 1: 171-79.
    1950 *Race and Culture.* Glencoe, Ill.: Free Press.

Petersen, William
    1972 *Japanese Americans.* New York: Random House.

Pilcher, William
    1972 *The Portland Longshoremen.* New York: Holt, Rinehart, and Winston.

Schermerhorn, R. A.
    1970 *Comparative Ethnic Relations: A Framework for Theory and Research.* New York: Random House.

Shibutani, Tamotsu, and Kwan, Kian
    1965 *Ethnic Stratification.* New York: Macmillan.

Simpson, Ida Harper and Simpson, Richard L.
    1977 "Occupational Permeability and Labor Force Cohort Stability." Paper presented at the Annual Meeting of the American

Sociological Association, Chicago.

Smelser, Neil J.
 1976 *The Sociology of Economic Life.* 2nd ed. Englewood Cliffs,
   N. J.: Prentice-Hall.

Sowell, Thomas
 1975 *Race and Economics.* New York: David McKay.

Szymanski, Albert
 1976 "Latin Workers in the United States." Paper presented at the
   Annual Meeting of the Pacific Sociological Association,
   Anaheim, Ca.

Thernstrom, Stephan
 1973 *The Other Bostonians.* Cambridge, Mass.: Harvard University
   Press.

van den Berghe, Pierre L.
 1971 "Ethnicity: The African Experience." *International Social
   Science Journal* 23: 507-18.
 1976 "Ethnic Pluralism in Industrial Societies: A Special Case."
   Ethnicity 3: 242-55.

Villemerz, Wayne J. and Rowe, Allan R.
 1973 "Black Economic Gains in the Sixties: A Methodological
   Critique and Reassessment." *Social Forces* 54: 131-93.

Wallerstein, I.
 1960 "Ethnicity and National Integration in West Africa." *Cahiers
   d'études Africaines* 3: 9-139.

Walliman, Isidor
 1974 "Toward a Theoretical Understanding of Ethnic Antagonism:
   The Case of Foreign Workers in Switzerland." *Zeitschrift
   für Sociologie* 3: 84-94.

Ware, Caroline
 1931 "Ethnic Communities." In *Encyclopaedia of the Social
   Sciences* 5: 607-13.

Warner, W. Lloyd and Srole, Leo
 1945 *The Social Systems of American Ethnic Groups.* New Haven:
   Conn.: Yale University Press.

Weber, Max
 1968 *Economy and Society.* 3 vols. New York: Bedminster Press.

In this paper, Nagata first reviews competing "primordialist" and "circumstantialist" theories of ethnicity, and concludes that an adequate theory must combine both approaches. She argues that the primordial basis of ethnicity entails the acceptance by a people of particular attributes or behavior as being products of biological inheritance and acquired only by birth. These primordial attributes become the basis of ethnicity when expressed in a charter of identity and a myth of origin. Whether such charters and myths are made the basis for the formation of ethnic categories or groups depends on if, in the pursuit of given interests, persons are mobilized with reference to these charters and myths in opposition to other categories or groups that are mobilized around comparable charters and myths. Such mobilization can be rather diffuse or it can take the form of highly organized movements; variation in form depends on the particular social circumstances that obtain. Utilizing her approach, Nagata then considers the ethnicity of Malays on the Malay Peninsula. She begins by showing how her affiliation with Islam came to be seen as a primordial characteristic of Malay identity. She then examines how in modern times Malays have distinguished themselves (and been distinguished by others) from other comparable ethnic groups on the Malay Peninsula, including groups that are also Muslims.

JUDITH NAGATA

In Defense of Ethnic Boundaries:
The Changing Myths and Charters
of Malay Identity

INTRODUCTION

In a kaleidoscopic world of shifting identities, there is one that appears to be emerging with a new effect. Loyalties to class, occupation, and state, often claimed to be the hallmarks of "modernism" and rationality, are suddenly being challenged by a supposedly atavistic loyalty, a survival from a more traditional, even primitive, past. This is the ethnic factor, which poses problems simultaneously for administrators and academicians alike. The peculiar "problems" of ethnicity stem from three of its principal characteristics: its potential for mobilizing interest groups; its appeal to sentiments of common origin and shared basic identity, often labeled the "primordial," which are capable of generating considerable emotion; and the problem of the relationship between ethnic identity and culture.

It is important to examine all of these characteristics in some detail, if only because there is no general consensus as to the role played by each in the genesis and perpetuation of ethnicity. Indeed, two major schools of thought are already discernible among social scientists, each one giving primacy to a different factor. Following Glazer and Moynihan (1975), we may provisionally refer to the two approaches by the rather crude labels of "circumstantialists" and "primordialists," which essentially parallel the older terminology of Shils (1957), who wrote of "primordial" and "ideological" *Bünde*. The first approach regards ethnicity as a dependent variable, created and controlled by a broad combination of external interests and strategies, which invest it with a potential for action and mobilization. The second reverses the order, and sees ethnicity emanating out of a corpus of basic, elemental, and irreducible ("primordial") loyalties, with a power and determinism uniquely their own (cf. Geertz 1963; Isaacs 1974). The latter viewpoint leaves some social scientists academically uneasy, for they feel poorly equipped to handle such loyalties and sentiments, which seem to slip dangerously out of the world of tangible interests and groups into a half-world of emotion and unreason. It is in the domain of the primordial that value judgments are most commonly found, and it is probably this factor that has triggered the frequent association of ethnicity with anachronistic, undesirable, and retrogressive tendencies (cf. Eisenstadt 1979; Inkeles 1969). However, it has never been entirely clear in the writings of the primordialists whether primordiality and ethnicity are in fact two ways of saying the same thing, whether primordiality is merely one among several aspects of ethnicity, and just how essential it is to ethnic identity.

The circumstantialists, by contrast, treat ethnic phenomena as "reactive" (cf. Wallerstein 1972; Hechter 1976), and derive them from other conditions of the social environment. Thus various observers of the ethnic scene have concluded that ethnicity is dependent on ecological (Leach 1954; Barth 1970; Haaland 1970), economic (Cohen 1969; Foster 1974), political (Hechter 1976), and even class factors (Stavenhagen 1975; Wallerstein 1972; Patterson 1975). It follows from this line of thought that ethnic identity, and particularly ethnic mobilization, are relatively flexible and amenable to change as dictated by external exigencies. Far from being fixed categories or groups rooted in an immutable (primordial) base, ethnic attachments are merely elaborations or symbolic expressions of more fundamental relationships, even of the infrastructure itself. By this same token, individual ethnic affiliations should also be open to maneuver according to interest, and unconstrained by any prior imperative status.

Each of these two "polar" approaches (circumstantialist and primordialist) has to contend with a common third problem; this concerns the role of "culture." Many of the earlier, more naïve approaches to the ethnic puzzle assumed the primacy, or at least prominence, of cultural attributes in defining ethnic character and boundaries (cf. Naroll 1964; Gordon 1964; Mitchell 1956; Epstein 1958). In a slightly different tradition, since the time of Furnivall, it has been a basic axiom of all "pluralists" that cultural differences, as manifested in institutional and organizational form, lie at the root of the deep and pervasive ethnic cleavages by which the plural society is distinguished. Absence of value consensus or cultural difference at its broadest creates lines of opposition between the constituent segments of society, reflecting differences in "core" beliefs, practices, and institutions, all of which are basically cultural in origin (Smith 1965, p. 62). Based on this premise, the degree of social separateness and incompatibility varies directly with the degree of cultural pluralism.

Although a collaborator with Smith in some writings (e.g., 1969), and himself associated with the pluralist tradition, Kuper was among the first to question to the a priori dependency relationship between cultural and other forms of social and political grouping, including the racial and the ethnic (1969, p. 16). This view was developed even more explicitly by Barth (1970, pp. 14-15) in his assertion that there is no necessary continuity or congruence, in time or space, between social (including ethnic) groups and cultural practice. By way of logical conclusion to a long line of developmental thought on this issue, Glazer and Moynihan (1975) have also made the point that a "cultural" definition of, say, the Irish in the 1970s would diverge strikingly from a cultural description of the same group two or more generations previous. This analytical separation between ethnicity per se and culture is now becoming accepted by most social scientists as a matter of course (e.g., Hechter 1976; Brass 1976). The present tendency is now to regard culture as a mere epiphenomenon of ethnicity, dependent on more basic organizational and strategic factors. This view of the role of culture is developed in its most extreme form by the "circumstantialist" school of writers, to the point where culture is relegated to a very secondary position in the ethnic scheme of things, as a series of symbols that justify the existence of particular (ethnic) interest groups. According to this view, embodied for example in Cohen's idea of "retribalization" (1969), cultural markers can even be manipulated to rationalize the identity and organization of the ethnic group.

For writers associated with the primordial school of ethnicity on the other hand, culture is usually conceived to be more integrally connected with the process and being of ethnic identity, although even they recognize that some behaviors and emblems may change independently of basic identity. It is at this point that we are faced with the knotty problem that presumably confronted the primordialists: are some cultural attributes more central or core elements to identity and group differentiation than others? For example, are beliefs and behaviors associated with kinship, religion, and language more basic and deterministic of social boundaries? That is, some aspects of culture may be both sufficient and necessary to the maintenance of an ethnic identity, whereas others are not even necessary. If we close in on the latter statement, then we can raise the possibility that certain parts of culture play a special, even unique, role in ethnogenesis and the perpetuation of ethnic boundaries, while others are merely incidental attributes of ethnic status. A crucial question therefore is how such cultural elements can be isolated from one another and their various roles assessed.

Another issue, which has borne heavily in the past on the primordial approach, is the pervasive positivism within the social science tradition. This has led to an evaluation, implicitly at least, of ethnicity as regressive, an anachronism, or more significantly as a nonrational and even undesirable form of attachment (e.g., Eisenstadt 1970; Geertz 1963; Inkeles 1969; DeVos 1975; Porter 1975). It is often used by political scientists and sociologists as the polar opposite to such notions as "modernity," political development, and national integration, and by implication, of progress itself. Among the assumptions made are that universalistic ties are "better" than particularistic and affective ones, and that allegiance to class, or indeed to any ideological as opposed to primordial ties, is intrinsically more advanced and functional for society than ethnic loyalties and sentiments. It is necessary to balance this heritage therefore by paying attention to another tradition arising from social philosophy that is concerned with the problem of "meaning." In the context of ethnicity, the meaning of an identity or loyalty to those involved should be just as legitimate a subject of investigation as the more tangible social conditions in which it is embedded.

At present, the weak status of "ethnicity" as an "etic" or social scientific concept, and the equally poorly defined role of the primordial, cultural, and organizational factors in ethnic behavior, make it difficult even to phrase meaningful questions about the relationship between them, save in the most general terms. What we need to know is how these factors co-vary: for example, is primordiality an essential component of ethnicity, and how does it accommodate to changing social conditions? What provides the symbolic focus and meaning of social action that goes beyond the purely instrumental? In the attempt to answer these questions, we shall try to draw the issues together in such a way as to suggest a definition of ethnicity that will apply across cultures.

It is my contention that the distinctiveness of ethnicity and that which separates it from other types of social identity and organization lies in the unique way in which elements of primordiality and other (nonprimordial) cultural attributes and awareness of strategic interests (the *für sich* quality) are combined and used. To phrase it somewhat more epigrammatically, it could be asked, when and why is a cultural attribute a primordial attribute?

First, we must clarify the meaning and uses of the term *primordial* and how far such attachments are truly irreducible and "given." At first sight, there appears to be little problem in identifying the attachments most commonly said to be primordial: kinship, descent, birthplace, territory of origin, and race. But two other attributes frequently appended to this list, religion and language, do not appear to share quite the same qualities as the first group. By doing a sort of componential analysis, we can say that religion and language do not conventionally convey the notion of the blood relationship, common descent, unity through inheritance of shared territory, that is conveyed by the other attributes (cf. Keyes 1976). Empirical evidence seems to suggest, however, that under certain conditions religion and language may play a primordial role, whereas in others they are quite clearly only incidental attributes of ethnic identity and may be abandoned or changed without detriment to the preservation of ethnic status (for example, religion is irrelevant to the status of being a German). When used primordially, however, religion becomes an essential component of ethnic identity and membership. This entails a belief (or the kind of behavior that predicates a belief) in the acquisition of religious affiliation through descent alone, at least in the local world view ("emic" or folk concept). Shared religion is associated with a myth of biological relatedness that thereby invests it with a deeper level and intensity of meaning. Thus Judaism is popularly used primordially as an essential marker of Jewish identity. The stress on descent through the mother and the questionable status (as "real" Jews) of converts or inmarried spouses, attests to the inherited, primordial quality attributed to religion in folk usage. Likewise the Chinese Muslims of Taiwan (Hui) speak as though Islam is such an integral part of Hui identity that it is "carried in the blood," even of those who are not religious (Pillsbury 1976). A similar case might be made for the Old Order Amish who do not permit in-group conversion, such that the only access to religious membership is by birth, and those who reject the faith are, as in the case of Orthodox Jews, considered "dead" to the group. Religious affiliation can be gained only through descent and no other access is possible. Individuals incorporated into a group by adoption are probably in a position similar to that of those who marry in, and only their progeny will have full status by descent.

It may now be seen that one logical extension of the primordial use of religion is its use as a charter, two roles it may perform simultaneously, although strictly they are analytically separate. Its function here is both a definition of the ethnic boundary and the provision of a myth to explain and justify the group's distinctiveness.

Language, like religion, can assume a primordial quality, largely, I suspect, because of its strong association with the earliest and most intimate stages of socialization that normally take place within the family or descent group, and hence can easily become blurred with other inherited qualities. Language is more likely to be used primordially in connection with such groups as Basques, Welsh, inhabitants of some regions of India or China, where its distinctiveness is inextricably interwoven with a fairly exclusive, closed, and endogamous population. As a charter alone, of course, language is a common symbol of unity and marker of other kinds of boundaries, for example, those of class. Although the primordial and charter roles of a trait are often fused, the two must not be confused, analytically at least. It is only when they do coincide that they are distinctively ethnic. Provisionally, we may say that religion and language are sometimes primordial qualities, but not invariably so.

Race is another primordial attribute whose function as an ethnic charter is variable. It is well known among social scientists that in some situations the role of race or physical features may be subordinate to other social considerations, hence not a charter of ethnic identity. Whereas in the United States, blackness of skin is used as a primordial charter of a particular ethnic status, and as a myth explaining assorted characteristics of the Black population, there are other societies where blackness can be ignored or redefined in favor of other charters, allowing entry into other ethnic categories. The Black Jamaican Chinese are a case in point. Even after several generations of intermarriage with the local population, and in apparent contravention of the physically obvious, Black Chinese are still regarded as "Chinese," for the focus here has shifted to the carefully preserved myths of patrilineal descent, which provide the charter for their identity (Patterson 1975).

Returning to the original list of primordial traits, we may now take a further look at the very wellspring of primordiality, ties of descent and blood, and their malleability as ethnic charters. If ethnic status depends on putative bonds of blood and descent, then it must be subject to the same manipulations and modifications that descent groups may undergo. As anthropologists are well aware, the genealogies that "prove" the authenticity of rights to membership in a kin group (and whose mythical charter role provides the added dimension of antiquity that lends further compulsion to the relationship), are themselves amenable to modification in appropriate circumstances. Proving one's origins by recourse to pedigrees (or negatively, rejection thereof), through selection of the genealogy conferring the greatest advantage (and without also unduly straining credibility), is a practice adopted by many immigrants to new places. Thus Indians in Spanish America must generally move out of their natal community before credibly claiming mestizo or Ladino status for, otherwise, the known genealogical connection would make the shift in (ethnic) identity incongruous and insupportable. Sometimes a sufficient passage of time and a trust in the fickleness of the social memory is enough for a revamping of genealogy and ethnicity to be attempted. Thus some "Malays" who have been overseas for a number of years, have returned with the new titles of *Shah* or *Khan* that demonstrate descent from a Middle Eastern lineage or *qu'om*. This is translated into Malay as *kaum,* and has a comparable meaning of "lineage" or a "people" but with a definite implication of shared descent. The point about fictive genealogies, of course, is that in the most successful cases of modification there is by definition no evidence of the switch, hence its charter function cannot be challenged.

Finally, following the same line of argument, birthplace and territorial origins can be primordialized, for it is not difficult to associate these with common descent, and as such they can assume an etiological function. The separation of indigenes from immigrants indeed is one of the most basic "ethnic" distinctions of all. Provisionally, it may be suggested that once a cultural attribute or behavior is accepted (by its bearers) to be carried by biological inheritance and to be acquired only by birth, it is primordialized. Thus many aspects of culture may play either role, depending upon the circumstances. Conversely, it is difficult to claim for any attribute a universal or invariable primordial quality, for reasons just provided. What also emerges is that the status of cultural characteristics as primordial or nonprimordial can even vary for the same people in different situations (as will be shown with the Malay material), so that different boundaries rise and fall, and different oppositions are created as needed. Primordiality then seems to be partly a matter of usage as much as an inherent property of specific traits that exist sui generis. The ethnic significance of culture appears to lie in the way in which it is primordialized, and secondly whether it is used as a charter of identity and myth of origin.

It is at this point that the other side of the ethnic coin, the circumstantialist mode, comes in. It is in this domain that we must seek the interests and issues that create, activate, sustain, and perpetuate the loyalties and sentiments that are subsequently rationalized by a primordial charter. To this end, existing identities may be selected or resurrected, or new ones generated. The social category or group that is salient for a given interest will be identified by those primordial(ized) characteristics that most effectively differentiate them from the significant oppositional categories in connection with that particular issue. This may occur as a means of differentiating subgroups within larger, more inclusive groups or entirely separate groups one from another. Thus, Malays can subdivide into "lesser" Javanese and Minangkabau, and so forth, invoking place of origin of those particular groups as charter, or expand to incorporate Indian Muslims and Arabs into Malay identity, and use Islam as a primordial charter. Another switch to "race" may then be made to filter out any "unwanted" Chinese Muslims. The social situation is thus a critical variable that provides the setting in which primordiality is defined and is meaningful.

We may now revert to the basic question of the nature of ethnicity from a more objective or etic perspective. Ethnic categories and groups share many features with other social groups. With social classes they share the strategic, *für sich* potential (though not necessarily actualized) for mobilization and even conflict, and a tendency to identify on the basis of opposition to like or parallel groups. Purely cultural markers characterize both ethnic and other special interest asssociations in varying degrees of formal organization, for example, the students of a university, members of voluntary associations, or of certain professions. Even the primordial charter is shared with (not specifically ethnic) kinship organization. While we may accept that kinship constitutes a near-essential vehicle of ethnic membership, we recognize that they are not entirely the same thing, and that there must be a way of distinguishing them etically. (In the same vein, the sex-based primordiality and potential activism of women's movements, together with their associated package of cultural symbols and boundaries, could also qualify as ethnic.) How then are kinship and sex groups different from ethnic ones? The final factor seems to lie in the institutional self-sufficiency and self-reproducing capacity of the ethnic community, in its ability to cater to the needs of both sexes, all ages and stages of the life cycle, which makes them potential "candidates for nationhood," as Geertz terms it. Hence the common association, on the political level at least, with irredentism, secession, and threats to national integration. Other social groups, including classes and kinship units, are unable to replicate this. Classes are by definition part of a wider totality—one class presupposes other (even a sytem of) classes, with a division of function between them. Kinship units likewise cannot be institutionally self-sustaining or self-reproducing without contravening the laws of incest.

Our etic summary of ethnicity as a distinctive social phenomenon runs as follows: a category or group with some perception of shared culture, one or more aspects of which will be used primordially as a charter for membership (and for excluding specific nonmembers). It has the capacity for an institutionally self-supporting and self-sustaining existence. Consciousness, mobilization, and formal organization may vary from the diffuse identity of a mere category to the militant activism of a political movement, and this will be determined by the external social circumstances.

One qualification should be added at this point. There are some societies and some social situations in which ethnic affiliation may coincide emically with other types of social interest group or collectivity. An example of this would be the fusing of (objective) class interests and identities with ethnic commitments, when ethnic idioms are substituted for class ones, as they are in Malaysia. This even extends to the use of primordial charters to justify "ideological" or "class" interests (cf. Nagata 1975; 1976).

What I seek to do in this paper is to use the approach to ethnicity issues outlined above as a starting point for an examination of a particular case of ethnogenesis and identity formation. Using both historical and contemporary materials, I shall present a diachronic account of how the Malays of the Malay peninsula (now West Malaysia) have, over a period of several hundred years, defined their own boundaries and established their identity. I shall also try to ascertain who have been the significant others, the "non-Malays," by way of opposition. What is also important, in the light of the introductory remarks, is to discover to what extent these perceptions are shaped by external conditions and strategic interests, including identity ascription by others (e.g., colonial authorities), and where the primordial factor comes into play. It also remains to be demonstrated what role is played by cultural attributes, and how far their importance to ethnicity is dependent on either primordiality or changes in the social environment.

HOW THE MALAYS CAME TO BE:
THE GENESIS OF AN ETHNIC COMMUNITY

In 1511, the Portuguese first established a foothold in Malacca, a west coast port on the Malay Peninsula with a cosmopolitan Asian population, but it was not until over two hundred years later, in 1786, that the British, through the East India Company, first laid a formal claim to Penang Island. This was followed in 1819 by the British presence in Singapore (under Raffles), and it was to be the end of the nineteenth century before any formal treaties were made between the British and the sultans on the mainland, beginning with the Treaty of Pangkor in 1874.

The relative lateness of intensive European settlement leaves us with a lengthy period in which ethnic definition and interaction between local populations were largely uninfluenced by western colonialism. In this paper I shall be dealing with both the broad picture—that is, the general ethnic tendencies in the peninsula at large, particularly in the historical period—and with more specific community-level interactions. Most of the community-specific data are derived from personal field work, hence limited in scope and application. I will try to be as precise as possible as to the range of applicability of my statements on Malay ethnicity in time and place, and as to the situations by which they appear to have been determined.

Prior to the fourteenth century, and at the time of the first Islamization of the Malacca ruling house, the Malay Peninsula, the coastal strip of North Borneo, and most of the archipelago of what is now Indonesia, were a constellation of somewhat unstable segmentary states with shifting boundaries, each under its own monarch, usually some sort of quasi-divine king. Although it is difficult to document the original use of the term "Malay" with certainty, the Malays seem to be associated with most of the early states of the western archipelago of the Malay Peninsula and Sumatra, and at least as early as the kingdom of Srivijaya or Palembang from the seventh century A.D. While politically fragmented, with territorial affiliations to such states as Tumasik (Singapore), Malacca, Pahang, Kedah, and so forth, the populations of these polities were broadly identified as "Malays." Other political states were associated with the Javanese (Majapahit), the Acehnese (Pase), the Minangkabau (the state of the same name), and to the north were various Siamaese (Thai) states. Before the advent of Islam in the fifteenth and sixteenth centuries, all these Malays were Hindu in religion and Indic in custom.[1]

The inland Malays were mainly rice cultivators, while their coastal confrères followed a variety of occupations, including fishing, trading, and piracy. Economically, the entire life of the area was extremely

---

1. Since the early Christian era, this part of Southeast Asia was subject to the deep and pervasive influence of India, largely as a result of trade, and the local culture consequently absorbed much Indian custom and religious practices.

cosmopolitan and commercially active during this period, accompanied by considerable movements of people and ideas. It was a crucible, therefore, for a number of lively ethnic mixtures and interactions, of which the Malays were but one element.

Although history does not provide all the details we would like for this study, it is doubtful if the epithet "Malay," as applied to the widely dispersed, free-roaming communities of several political states at this time ever referred to more than a category of people, having in common just a language and certain nonprimordial characteristics of culture *(adat)* (cf. Schrieke 1966; Van Leur 1967). Given that one of their principal affiliations was to their states or monarchs, that they shared the Hindu religion with other local populations, and that effective politicization and mobilization of interests and populations beyond that level was difficult, the question of a primordial charter may not have been a pressing one, and was probably expressed only in terms of *bangsa.* The term *bangsa* conveys the double ideas of a people sharing both a common origin and a common culture. Etymologically, it is derived from the Sanskrit *vaṃsa,* "line of descent." Emically, it has a primordial quality, for it implies that the cultural traits are inalienably and inextricably associated with a particular people, that is, carried by a community whose ultimate unity derives from a single origin. In this respect, they resembled many transnational communities, such as the modern Anglo-Saxons of the British Commonwealth. At this time the majority of the Malays were Hindu by religion, although the gradual encroachment of Islam, beginning with the kingdom of Srivijaya in Sumatra, was already being felt, mainly through the influence of Indian Muslim merchants. Initially, it must be supposed, religion was a mere cultural attribute, incidental but not central to, Malay identity. For some time Hinduism and Islam probably coexisted much as do Roman Catholicism and Protestantism in the German community. As Van Leur (1967, p. 115) and Schrieke (1966, pp. 28, 38) point out, however, the spread of Islam soon acquired a strong economic and political significance. Conversion to the new faith became an expression of strategic interests, varying from valuable trading contacts with (Muslim) Gujarati merchants, to emulation and favor of the ruling classes. Among the rulers themselves it became crucial to political alliances with other Muslim states. Islam was also being used politically as a banner of opposition to the incoming Portuguese and Spaniards, for whom political confrontations and defense of economic interests, cloaked in a religious charter for a crusade against the infidel was nothing new. Islam thus became a potential and actual basis of mobilization, and a justification of unity between some peoples and opposition to others. As the interests of the local

Malay populations, regardless of immediate political affiliation, co-alesced against the alien European (and against the remaining Hindu kingdoms), the oppositional aspect gained in importance and the positive identity of the *bangsa* grew sharper. At this stage Islam was equated with membership in local Malay communities, and on the way to becoming an intrinsic element of Malayness, such that in Malay areas it could be said that to enter Islam *(masok Islam)* was the same as to become a Malay *(masok Melayu)*. In theory at least, by this religious charter any Muslim convert could, in the local context, claim Malay identity. In what way then can it be argued that Islam was becoming primordialized? In Southeast Asia, any *kafir* (non-Muslim) inmarrying spouse of a Muslim must also convert to the new faith, so it is likely, as Van Leur points out (1967, p. 113), that within a generation or two the effect would be one of apparent inheritance of religious affiliation. As with Judaism, it was probable that the initial convert did not entirely shake off the status of an outsider, that is, an ideological as opposed to a primordial member, but the children would be full-status members of the community. Thus members of Muslim ruling families in Malacca and Sumatra were marrying into the families of their Hindu Javanese *shahbandar* (mayors) and Indian *mantris* (ministers), and the offspring, if not the inmarried parent, were considered full Malays. What began as just an attribute therefore gradually became integral to Malayness, and eventually no non-Muslim could claim Malay status, and simultaneously the association of religion and birth grew stronger.[2]

The new faith did not succeed in any great measure in changing other aspects of local Malay culture, which remained in many respects solidly Indic (ibid.). Although important to Malay status, these traits of culture did not rival Islam as a charter of ethnic identity.

When it was necessary for a Malay to differentiate himself from a Muslim Javanese or Acehnese, the usual resort would be to that of a separate *bangsa,* that is, all those descended from a different (putative) social line. While the concept of *bangsa,* as noted above, also has overtones of shared culture, this is secondary in the emic view to the solidarity acquired through common descent or origin, and the actual content of that culture, Indian or other, received less attention than religion and the Malay language. These distinctions would have been most important in such polyethnic places as Malacca, where

2. A similar inference is made by Obeyesekere (1975) when he claims that a modern "true" Sinhala can only be identified in terms of Buddhism, in opposition to the Christians who stand for alien economic and political interests, and hence lose their essential Sinhalese identity. A further implication is that Buddhism in Sri Lanka is acquired only through Sinhalese descent and vice versa.

Gujaratis, Bengalis, Bugis, Javanese, Arabs, Chinese, and others all resided within the confines of the city. Affirmations of the validity of *masok Melayu* notwithstanding, it was (and certainly is today) probably true that in differentiating Malay Muslims from other Muslims, whether from the Middle East or China, the secondary elaboration of *bangsa* was raised, such that, among other things, the credibility involved in a primordial claim of shared descent could be maintained. Thus selection of the appropriate charter is determined partly by who you are not, or who you do not wish to be. On a world-wide basis, Islam is not primordialized.

We turn now to the better documented nineteenth century in the Malay Peninsula, and examine how Malay identity was expressed, who belonged to this category, and under what conditions. In direct continuity with an old historical pattern of physical mobility and free-roaming traders and adventurers, the peninsula was economically and demographically in many ways still a frontier or pioneer territory and subject to the immigration and settlement of numerous non-Malay Southeast Asians, in addition to East and South Asians and a growing number of Europeans. Under British colonial influence, further immigration of other Asians, principally Chinese and Indians, was actively encouraged. Chinese from the overpopulated southeastern provinces of Kwangtung and Fukien were recruited for mining, urban, laboring, and commercial occupations, while the majority of the Indians was imported from Tamilnad in South India as indentured labor for the rubber plantations. Neither of these immigration policies, however, made much impact until the early twentieth century. Prior to this, small numbers of independent Chinese and Indians, largely traders, had long mingled with the other Southeast Asian immigrants in Malaya, and as we shall see, had even intermarried with the local Malay population.

Probably the best way to illustrate the effects of the intermingling of these various peoples and the processes of creation, crystallization, and shifting of ethnic identities and charters, is by means of an extended case study of one settlement, for which detailed descriptive and statistical data are available. The example to be taken is that of one of the Straits Settlements,[3] George Town, the principal city of Penang Island, first founded by the British East India Company

3. Before the formation of the Federation of Malaya in 1948, the three Straits Settlements, Penang, Malacca, and Singapore, were crown colonies, originally ruled directly from the metropolitan center. The nine sultanates that made up the peninsula of Malaya were administered by various forms of indirect rule during colonial times.

in 1786, and subsequently incorporated into the Federation of Malaya. It is now the second largest city of the country, exceeded by only the capital, Kuala Lumpur. Although it cannot be claimed that Penang is representative of all communities in the Malay peninsula, it does provide sufficient material from which to extrapolate some ideas as to the generation and maintenance of ethnicity.

In Penang, we start with an ethnic *tabula rasa*. At the time of its takeover by the East India Company, only a few small enclaves of fishermen and refugee pirates were present on the island (Macalister 1803; Vaughan 1857, p. 409; Clodd 1948), hence ethnogenesis and ethnic change can be observed in every stage.

As early as 1794, a letter from the representative of the East India Company to the governor general of India mentions a variety of immigrants in George Town: Malays from the neighboring state of Kedah and from Sumatra, Javanese, "Buggesses" (Bugis from Borneo and Sulawesi), Chulias (South Indian Muslims), Siamese, and Burmese. By 1805, another colonial official reports the addition to the local population of Chinese and of Parsees from Bombay, and by 1835 of Acehnese, Battas (Batak), Bengalis, Arabs, Armenians, Caffrees (Africans); and a category labeled "Native Christians" had been added to the roster (Low 1972, pp. 125-26). In 1881, the first official census showed, in addition to the above, Boyanese (islanders from Bawean, near Java), Manilamen, Singhalese, Persians, and a new category, the Jawi Peranakan. The origin of the Jawi Peranakan lay in the unions of Indian Muslim males and Malay women, and resulted in a hybrid category that extended beyond the initial generation to subsequent unions of hybrid with hybrid (cf., the mestizo or mulatto). Literally, the term means "born in the land of the Jawi (Malays)," with the added implication of descent from a Jawi also. Sometimes this was transmuted into Jawi Pekan ("Jawi of the town"), which emphasizes the predominantly urban residence of this population, due to their mercantile occupation. The other variant sometimes found, Jawi Bukan, implies "not a Jawi at all," that it, an implied opposition to the "true Malay" *(Melayu jati)*. The term Jawi Peranakan continued to be used in censuses until 1911, after which time it no longer had formal administrative significance, although it has continued to enjoy popular currency until the present day. This will be discussed below.

Finally, the enormous influx of new Chinese and Indian settlers in the early part of the twentieth century added a new dimension to the social composition of Penang, and changed its relative proportions substantially. As a result, the population of the city of George Town in 1970 consisted of 71.5 percent Chinese and 13.3 percent Indians, compared with 13.8 percent Malay and 1.4 percent other, such that the non-Malays in this city numerically (and also economically) eclipsed the "host" community (Department of Statistics 1972, p. 248).

Although not listed separately in any census, one more category common in popular usage and in the local world view is that of the Baba Chinese. The Baba were originally, like the Jawi Peranakan, offspring of mixed unions, this time between Chinese males and Malay females. In this case, neither the father nor the offspring embraced Islam, hence were not incorporated into the Malay community. On the other hand, they were not regarded (by self or by other Chinese), as true "Chinese," but as a distinct, self-perpetuating hybrid community. Babas adopted much of Malay culture, including dress, language, and foods, and in many cases even "forgot" the Chinese language altogether. Their attachment to the patrilineage and its ancestors, however, provided the primordial charter by which they preserved their distinctiveness from the Malays. From the other (non-Baba) Chinese on the other hand, the charter invoked was one of birth (Malaya versus China), which had primordial implications and was the basis of the separate identity of the Baba. The massive immigration of large numbers of Chinese to Malaya in the early twentieth century eventually gave rise to a substantial Malaya-born Chinese population, with the result that the charter of opposition is now phrased in terms of language (Baba Malay versus a dialect of Chinese), and this is primordialized in the sense that it can only be acquired through birth in the appropriate community.[4]

Most Chinese, Baba and non-Baba, practice one of the traditional Chinese religions (Buddhism, Taoism, Confucianism), but a small minority belong to Islam. Some are descended from original Chinese Muslims from China (Hui), others are converts, in some cases for the economic advantages to be gained thereby.[5] Yet as will be seen, save in some cases of intermarriage, the old principle of the equivalence of *masok Islam* and *masok Melayu* does not apply within the local Malaysian community. That is, whereas there is some quasi-legal mechanism (formal profession of Islam) capable of conferring a change

4. Baba Malay (the language of the Baba Chinese) is a peculiar version of Malay, with a basic Chinese structure, grammar, and idiom, but with many Malay loanwords and turns of phrase.

5. In some parts of Malaysia, including Penang, a convert to Islam qualifies as a "Malay" for purposes of access to certain resources such as taxi licenses and scholarships, normally set aside for Malays as part of their "special position." This is not universally true in other parts of the federation, for example, Kelantan, nor does it mean that Chinese Muslims are socially (emically) accepted as Malays in the local community.

in ethnic status, the blatant absence of any primordialism in this (legal) charter apparently deprives it of effective impact on the informal social level.

The modern term "Malay," used in its grossest form in opposition to "non-Malay" (usually Chinese and Indian), obscures a whole host of internal differentiations arising from their history. For the category of Malay has been built up by a gradual series of aggregations from a variety of other peoples who still sometimes assert their separate identity. We turn now to an examination of the factors that appear to have contributed to the various ethnic labels and clusters listed first in the censuses, and second in everyday interaction.

The first set of labels are administratively generated ones, hence externally imposed categories that do not always coincide with, and may even conflict with, popular categories. Although early accounts and censuses recognize the separate identity of such communities as Javanese, Bugis, Boyanes, Acehnese, and so forth, before 1911, only the first three were regarded by the colonial authorities as the true "Malay races." It is probable that the Acehnese were excluded for political reasons (a circumstantialist explanation), in view of the long and exhausting Acehnese wars of the late nineteenth century, and their depredation of Penang shipping and trade. By the 1947 and 1957 censuses, the term "Malaysian" had been substituted for the 1911 term, "Malay races," and was applied to all those of Indonesian origin, including the Acehnese. Since 1963 "Malaysian" came to assume a political, contractual significance, referring to any citizen of that state, and the term "Malay" has re-entered the census once more. Officially, "Malay" now may include, besides the Indonesians, Indian Muslims and Arabs, if they wish to so identify. From the official point of view, therefore, there has been a gradual accretion or "census assimilation" of certain lesser categories (probably for administrative convenience), based on what appeared to be similarity of culture, and on favorable political relations with their parent communities outside the federation. These classifications, however, reflect only the broad framework within which popular categories and charters are created.

One early official ethnic taxonomy may have helped to set the pattern for (or at least did not contradict) one of the major ethnic divisions of today. This was based on religion. In early nineteenth-century Penang, a mini-system of indirect rule administered the local population through local representatives known as Kapitans ("captains"). Thus the Kapitan China represented the Chinese (who were all presumed to have their own religion), the Kapitan Kling the Hindus, and a third Kapitan represented the "Mussulmans," which included, besides all the "Malay races," the Indian Muslims and Arabs. The artificiality of this taxonomy is revealed, for example, by the resistance expressed by some Arabs to their new confrères. Finally, in this taxonomy, too, "Native Christians" were seen as a separate category, and ranked alongside other "ethnic" groups. The role of religion in defining ethnic boundaries on the emic level will be discussed below.

For the first forty years of census-keeping from 1881 to 1921, the Arabs were accorded a separate identity on the strength of their claim to separate descent lines, claims they began in the days of the Kapitans. Annotations to these censuses, however, suggest that even within this forty-year period, the recorders were dubious as to the validity of these claims: "It is extremely doubtful whether those who so describe themselves . . . have any real claim to be considered members of that race," since few spoke Arabic or had even one parent born in Arabia (Census Department 1911, p. 91). After 1921, therefore, Arabs were forced to choose between Malay and "other" identity, and this may have been among the many factors that precipitated a major crisis of identity for the Arabs in the 1920s and 1930s. During this period, a time of religious (Islamic) reform and of political self-examination, the banner of Islam was used to justify anticolonial activism. As a result, the two elements of identity, religious and political, became fused, and religion gradually assumed a primordial quality, such that Arabs and other non-Malay Muslims began to change their ethnic status, that is, to become Malay (cf. Roff 1967) and the *masok Islam/masok Melayu* equation was resurrected once more. From that time on, in political contexts at least, Arabs have widely claimed Malay identity, although in more interpersonal, local contexts they reassert their Arabness under the prestigious charter of connection with the Holy Land. Even where status is determined by social circumstances, a primordial charter is always sought, although the degree to which it is officially accepted varies. So far as Arab identity is concerned, culture is a two-edged sword. As I have described elsewhere, the *same* aspects of culture may be used in different contexts to assert first Arab, then Malay, identity. Whether the aspect in question is assigned to the Arab or Malay side will be determined by the primordial charter behind it.

While official classifications probably played a part in shaping some categories, for example, the major threefold division of Malaysian society into Indian, Malay, and Chinese, and the use of religion as an ethnic boundary marker, they frequently conflicted with popular views, and the emic situation provides a somewhat different configuration of identities. There are still several ambiguous ethnic statuses on the periphery of Malayness, and I have described elsewhere (Nagata 1974) cases of oscillation, from Malay to something else.

Whatever the census definition, local recognition of different types of "Malays" persists. The most extreme case is that of the Boyanese, who maintain separate communal houses *(pondok)* and practice endogamy, which provides the necessary genealogical charter of their ethnic exclusiveness. In most other cases, where there is greater interaction, the sub-Malay populations adjust their primordial claims and charters according to the needs of the occasion. It comes as no surprise to learn that Javanese, Bugis, and so forth do not hesitate to identify as Malays, which they justify on the basis of common *bangsa,* when certain political economic privileges are at stake (ibid.). The primordial dimension of the *bangsa* concept is sometimes made even more explicit when both Indonesian and other Malays will speak of cementing their strength even further by intermarriage and the unity of *darah dan daging* (flesh and blood). Internal divisions involve the lesser (but equally primordial) distinctions of more immediate territorial origin and descent *(sukubangsa)* or smaller segment of a *bangsa.*

One other internal Malay distinction deserves attention here. Minangkabau, who also originate from west central Sumatra in Indonesia, established a separate and solid community in the Malaysian state of Negri Sembilan several centuries ago. Minangkabau custom is substantially different in a number of important respects from that of the other Malays, and this has implications for their "ethnic" status. The central feature of Minangkabau custom (known as *adat perpateh,* as opposed to the *adat temenggong* of the other Malays), is its matrilineal descent[6] and social organization based on matriclans *(suku).* Minangkabau identity therefore depends upon membership in a *suku,* which is clearly the basis for a primordial distinction where this is required, and differentiation of the Malays into separate *sukubangsa.* The two can, of course, coalesce against other non-Malay communities in the name of a common broader *bangsa* when necessary. In such cases the *adat* differences lose their explicit association with birth and become a mere incidental cultural attribute for the while.

The Arabs likewise have long validated their oft-changing status and ethnic claims over the past century by manipulating their charters, and investing them with the appropriate primordial content. In claiming Malayness, they acknowledge their several generations of intermarriage with local women and the fact that they have "drunk the milk" of the country, thus invoking the right of descent, but they can alternatively

6. In Indonesia, where the original Minangkabau still live, the opposition between Minangkabau and other communities has become legendary, and has provided the material from which a number of popular novels (for example, *Hamka*), have been written, in which the dominant theme is one of conflict between the two types of *adat* and the effects of descent rules upon inter-*sukubangsa* relations.

play up their separate patrilineages or *qu'om* (Malay *kaum*), originating from the Middle East, and claim a distinct identity. This last may even be reinforced by claims of descent from the Prophet Mohammed, symbolized by the use of titles exclusive to these lineages (*Syed* for males, *Sharifah* for females).

So far as the authorities were concerned, the Jawi Peranakan existed only between 1881 and 1911, but in the popular vocabulary and paradigm of ethnicity, they still persist. Initially, as noted above, the Jawi Peranakan were a hybrid category, Indo-Malay, and this was stressed in such graphic descriptions of Jawi Peranakan character as a mixture of "Malay courage and Indian cunning" (Vaughan 1857). Clearly, in view of their genealogy, there is no problem in establishing a primordial basis for Malay identity where desired, and in the present day this is frequently done. Indeed, the principal obstacle to a permanent ethnic change (true assimilation) by the Jawi Peranakan to Malayness lies in exclusion by the Malays who point to the non-Malay strands in their ancestry by way of justification. The Malays consider the Jawi Peranakan socially inferior, and when they wish to make a status distinction will claim different *sukubangsa* membership. Pejorative epithets suggestive of this separate *sukubangsa,* for example, *mamak Kling* (descended from Indians) are sometimes used as verbal weapons to insult alleged Jawi Peranakan. This same distinction has also long been used in micropolitical conflicts where primordial criteria are used to justify other differences. Thus in the politically restive 1920s and 1930s, the Jawi Peranakan, like the Arabs of the same period, had to sort out their ethnic identity amidst the various political, religious, and social issues of the day. This was a time when, as a result of the Malay "consciousness-raising" referred to above, a great debate was held on the subject of "what is a Malay?" in the schools, in voluntary associations, in the press, and public fora generally. The debate represented part of a concern with political mobilization against aliens, and of course the first problem was to identify the "aliens." The alien could be equated with either the Europeans or anyone who was not a *Melayu jati.* This debate is still carried on today, in connection with such activities as a recently formed Malay Petty Traders' Association, in which a major division occurred along lines of *Melayu jati* and "other Malays," principally the Jawi Peranakan. With its status connotations, the latter identity is usually imposed from the outside, and rarely used spontaneously in self-assignation, except in jest.

There is little in the way of objective cultural difference to distinguish "pure" Malays from Jawi Peranakan, and the latter have consciously tried to abandon any vestiges of non-Malay practice, for example, certain naming procedures, items of dress, and wedding ritual. As with the Arabs, too, many cultural practices can be manipulated to justify either identity, as the case may be. Indian customs can thus be used by Malays to distinguish themselves from the Jawi Peranakan, or to express solidarity of identity, by stressing the common Indian origin of much of Malay custom. What is important, however, is the use of ideas of primordiality and charter myths in varying combinations in different situations. The very term Jawi Peranakan is an ambivalent one, for on the one hand it underscores a difference in origin, although born in Jawi territory and of at least part Jawi (Malay) ancestry. The importance of primordial ethnic claims through the genealogical charter is vividly illustrated by an allegedly common practice whereby Indian Muslims from Tamilnad or other South Indian regions will endeavor to marry higher status North Indian girls, and hope that in the succeeding generation, a marriage with a "pure Malay" can be arranged. This is probably as much an idealized myth to explain both the ethnic status hierarchy and the frequent identity switching as calculated strategy or actual occurrence. It does attest, however, to the importance of a primordial charter as a basis for claims to ethnic status. Finally, the conditions in which the various identities are operative depend largely on the interests stemming from the broader social, economic, and political environment. In matters of commerce and business, it is still often advantageous to cultivate non-Malay status and networks (in view of the popular stereotypes of Malay entrepreneurial incompetence), while for political and prestige reasons, Malay identity is usually more desirable.

Like the Jawi Peranakan, Indian Muslims are increasingly oscillating between Indian and Malay status. The social, political, and economic pressures are similar to those that influence the Jawi Peranakan, but the claim to common identity usually resides in the domain of religion. Here, Islam is perceived to create a *Gemeinschaft* community with primary grouplike ties, at least within the local context, if not on a world-wide basis. This is then reinforced by a common place of birth, Malaya. In the folk view, Islam becomes one of the facts of birth, inextricably bound up with family and lineage. Here, the emphasis is placed on its association with socialization and intimate, domestic relationships.

The latter associations promote the inclusion, where desired, of all those in Malaysia of Islamic heritage, for example, Indians, Arabs, and Indonesians, but with the significant exception of the Chinese. It can only be concluded that the exclusion of the Chinese is to be sought in their economic dominance in the country at large, which alienates them from the rest of the Muslim community. Their status as converts (often extended also to Chinese Muslims by descent, the

Hui), as members of an ideological rather than a primordial *Bund,* is underscored by referring to them as *saudara baru* ("new associates"), and organizationally by relegating them to a separate branch of the Muslim community, the Chinese Muslim Association. Finally, the Chinese are regarded as a totally different *bangsa,* and referred to as the *bangsa Cina.*

Most of the above analysis is based on the Penang situation. Much of it would apply at least to other urban areas, although it should be noted that Jawi Peranakan are less numerous in other parts of the peninsula, with the possible exceptions of Kuala Lumpur and Singapore. Baba Chinese, on the other hand, are most numerous in Malacca. In some states, however, there is less flexibility in manipulation of ethnic boundaries. In Kelantan, for instance, no Indian Muslim or even an Arab may claim Malay status so long as his genealogy is known, or even suspect, and this is true both emically and legally. Among the factors responsible for these regional differences would be relative proportions of the major categories in the population and the occupational division of labor. Another factor is probably the colonial one, and the effect of some of the administrative classifications established by fiat. In Kelantan, for example, the numerical and economic dominance of the "pure Malays," the low pressure of immigration, and the negligible impact of the colonial presence all played a role in maintaining clearer and less ambiguous boundaries between Malays and non-Malays, hence reducing the need for alternative charters and primordial rationales.

Today, at the state level, we have another administrative classification, embodied in the official constitutional definition of a "Malay." This definition is a purely cultural one: any person who speaks Malay, follows Islam, and practices Malay custom *(adat).* As in the foregoing examples, this must be measured against emic or actual usages. Literally interpreted, almost any resident of the Federation of Malaysia could qualify, or train themselves to become "Malay," particularly as practice of *adat* is never seriously assessed. Although official policies carry weight in the allocation of resources and privileges when ethnicity is a condition of eligibility, in most cases the interpretation of eligibility is left to the personal determination of local government agents, usually in keeping with usage in the area.

By way of supplement to the original constitutional definition is a newer, administratively created ethnic category, the Bumiputera, literally "sons of the soil." This category uses as its charter the quality of indigenousness, a bond by virtue of birth on the same soil, which simultaneously conveys some notion of antiquity and of residence from time immemorial. This places together in a single category both the Malays (including the "marginal" Malays, as described) and the non-Muslim tribal peoples (*orang asli*) in both West and East Malaysia. Since the word *asli* also means "original" there was a half-hearted attempt to generate a term *Melayu asli* (in place of *Melayu jati*), as another oppositional epithet to the marginal or oscillating variety of Malay.

The Bumiputera category is opposed to the equally new (and administratively coined) term *kaum pendatang* (immigrant community), which is applied to the Chinese and Indians collectively. The circumstances stimulating this new classification are both demographic and economic. The population of Malaysia, alone among Southeast Asian countries, is divided almost equally between the "majority" Malays and the several "minorities." That the latter collectively comprise almost 50 percent of the total is politically and psychologically threatening to the Malays. Without including the aboriginals, the Malays alone account for only 46.8 percent of the population of the Federation of Malaysia (Department of Statistics 1972, p. 3), to the Chinese 34.1 percent and Indian 9.0 percent, giving the latter two together a challenging 43.1 percent. The rest are aboriginals and "others." With the Bumiputera/*kaum pendatang* opposition, however, the proportions become 55.5 percent and 43.1 percent respectively, the balance being made up of a smaller number of "others." It is important to note that, although the government has attempted to invest the Bumiputera status with the quality of indigeneousness, the status has never quite succeeded in acquiring the emotional and motivating capacity of a true primordial identity. Aside from official documents, the term is rarely used, and in popular usage Malays still cling stubbornly to the old Malay/non-Malay and other distinctions described above. Clearly, primordiality cannot be legislated. Significantly, in the latest (third) government Five-year Plan (1976-80), the term Bumiputera is nowhere to be seen, having failed, so it seems, to gain fully ethnic currency. It may be worth noting that, while the term was in official use, the Jawi Peranakan and Indian Muslims were occasionally referred to by the epithet Brahmaputera, to stress the Indian component, hence separation from *Melayu jati*.

Another recent phenomenon in Malaysia society is a remarkable religious revival within the Islamic community. Comparable to the religious fervor of the 1920s and 1930s, during which the "marginal" Arabs, Jawi Peranakan, and Indian Muslims mustered and asserted a new ethnic unity, the modern movement, known as *dakwah*, seems to be part of an affirmation of ethnic identity. At its broadest, the purpose of the *dakwah* is to eliminate the most damaging influences of secular western culture, especially the emphasis on things material, and concomitantly to elevate the spiritual life of Muslims. More narrowly, however, and particularly important in the local community context, is its symbolic role in differentiating Malays (including "marginal" Malays) from others, predictably of course the Chinese. Thus, it is popularly said (if not theologically accurate), that other communities can have their own *dakwah,* for example, *dakwah Cina,* by which logic the equation between religion and ethnic identity is implicitly introduced. When generalized thus, the *dakwah* acquires a primordial quality, something exclusive to, and bred in, certain peoples only. Organizationally, this is reinforced by the adoption and propagation of the *dakwah* cause by a militant Muslim missionary association that has branches in most Malaysian towns. Once again, as in the case cited above, this association does not incorporate Chinese converts directly as full-status members, but maintains for them instead the separate Chinese Muslim Association. Similar religious phenomena have been observed on a smaller scale in some of the more traditional Malay states, such as the *Sabilullah* movement of Kedah. This was largely a Malay movement against Chinese financial interests, cloaked in terms of a religious war, *Angkatan Jihad.* Thus, religion in some contexts is primordialized, and at its widest generously embraces a large section of the Malaysian Muslim population, whether of Arab, Indian, or Indonesian origin. Its stopping short of the Chinese highlights the intervention of other (circumstantial) factors, and that other conditions and relations of the local community become generalized and reflected in another idiom and expression of opposition. Hence the need for flexible, alternative, and situationally apposite primordial devices to use as charters of ethnic identity.

Finally, in the context of post-Independence Malaysia, the politically central position of the Malays confers upon them, among other things, the ability to legislate and control ethnic charters and hence ethnic boundaries, and this gives them a unique position within the federation. The Malays are becoming, as Geertz would phrase it, "candidates for nationhood." This means the Malays have a political legitimacy and level of organization and mobilization transcending the merely "ethnic," or one among many, which enhances the value of Malay status. It is to be expected that in these circumstances more eligible Muslims will attempt to claim Malay identity, although if demand becomes too heavy, official charters of admission may be revised. It should be apparent from the foregoing, however, that administrative definitions, from colonial times on, have always been subject to rearrangement and reshaping at the local level. What is an important consideration and boundary for government purposes may not necessarily correspond to those meaningful in the neighborhood.[7] The issues that determine which ethnic boundaries will be erected, and in turn, which primordial qualities will be invoked by way of support, are ultimately dependent upon the social scale or level of action. Thus, a Jawi Peranakan at the local level may be officially classified, on the basis of religion, as a Malay for purposes of, say, a loan application by a government agency.

CONCLUSION

To return to the questions raised at the beginning, we may now hazard a few statements, based on the Malay material, on the general nature of ethnicity, and how boundaries are erected and defined.

At the risk of taking a position on the fence, it would seem that both the circumstantialist and the primordial approaches to ethnicity can be accommodated. It is not difficult to provide convincing illustrations of the first position, for examples of the stimulation by external factors of collective awareness and even action are not hard to come by. The changing definitions of Malay identity and the various charters adopted over the centuries have clearly been affected by political, economic, and demographic considerations, and by the nature of the significant others. The expansion of the frontier and the effects of massive immigration by large alien populations have also played an important role in crystallizing new identities. Here, a combination of administrative policies and local interests, particularly those pertaining to trade and the creation of a new political society, were strongly reflected in ethnic idioms, although not always mutually congruent ones.

The role of the primordial element, on the other hand, has until recently proved more difficult to demonstrate and justify, especially in view of the implicit positivistic tenor of the social sciences. On consideration of the evidence, however, the sole unique feature about the "ethnic" as a concept, category, or group, by which it can be distinguished from all other concepts (e.g., class) involves the nature of the charter membership, and in the ethnic case, this is primordial. Charters of identity that draw on a (putative) notion of common blood, origin, descent, or kinship connection as a reason for being or acting may be labeled ethnic. It matters little that such charters may be fabricated or manipulated, for as in the case of genealogies,

7. This is also a point to consider in studying stratification in Malaysian society, when the administrative stress on ethnic inequality constantly mutes attention to inequality by class.

it is the message they carry that counts. Further, different cultural attributes may variously play a primordial role. Sometimes race is used primordially, sometimes not. Religion may acquire in the folk view an association with blood and primary group ties that confers on it a primordial power, the power to define the ethnic boundary. Otherwise, religion is just another, incidental, cultural attribute, and not a crucial underpinning of ethnic identity.

Finally, to distinguish ethnicity from kinship alone, we must add to the definition of the former its potential as a self-sufficient, self-reproducing community, as opposed to those dependent on other, like units, for social survival.

Nonprimordial cultural traits, which by the above definition, are not essential in marking ethnic identity, are subject to rise and fall, maintenance or rejection, without absolutely jeopardizing ethnic status, for as in the case of the Arabs or Indian Muslims, claims to Malayness can be made in defiance of a wide variation of cultural practice.

Ethnic identity then is a unique blend of affective, expressive and basic ties, sentiments and loyalties with (sometimes blatantly) instrumental, calculated, political interests, and the latter are explained and given meaning by the former. The two ends of the *Gemeinschaft-Gesellschaft* continuum here come full circle.

REFERENCES ──────────────────────────────────

Anonymous
    1976 "Dakwah: Kembalikan Masyarakat Kepada Islam." *Dewan Masyarakat,* September 15, 1976, pp. 2-4.
Barth, Fredrik
    1970 *Ethnic Groups and Boundaries: The Social Organisation of Cultural Difference.* London: Allen and Unwin.

Brass, Paul
  1976 "Ethnicity and Nationality Formation." *Ethnicity* 3, no. 3: 255-41.
Census Department, Malaysia
  1911 *Census of the Federated States: Reports of the Census of Kedah and Perlis.* Penang: Criterion Press.
Clodd, H. P.
  1948 *Malaya's First British Pioneer.* London: Luzac.
Cohen, Abner
  1969 *Custom and Politics in Urban Africa.* London: Routledge and Kegan Paul.
  1974 *Urban Ethnicity.* ASA Monographs, no. 12. London: Tavistock Publications.
Department of Statistics, Malaysia
  1972 *Population and Housing Census of Malaysia: Community Groups.* Kuala Lumpur: Government Printer.
DeVos, George
  1975 "Ethnic Pluralism: Conflict and Accommodation." In *Ethnic Identity: Cultural Continuities and Change,* ed. G. DeVos and L. Romanucci-Ross, pp. 5-41. Palo Alto, Calif.: Mayfield Publishing.
Eisenstadt, S. N.
  1970 "Breakdowns of Modernization." In *Readings in Social Evolution and Development,* ed. S. N. Eisenstadt, pp. 421-52. Oxford: Pergamon Press.
Epstein, A. L.
  1958 *Politics in an Urban African Community.* Manchester: Manchester University Press.
Foster, Brian
  1974 "Ethnicity and Commerce." *American Ethnologist* 1, no. 3: 437-48.
Geertz, Clifford
  1963 "The Integrative Revolution." In *Old Societies and New States,* pp. 105-57. New York: Free Press.
Glazer, N. and Moynihan, D., eds.
  1975 *Ethnicity: Theory and Experience.* Cambridge, Mass.: Massachusetts Institute of Technology Press.
Gordon, Milton
  1964 *Assimilation in American Life: The Role of Race, Religion and National Origins.* New York: Oxford University Press.
Haaland, Gunnar
  1970 "Economic Determinants in Ethnic Processes." In *Ethnic Groups and Boundaries,* ed. F. Barth, pp. 58-73. London:

Allen and Unwin.

Hechter, Michael
    1976 "Ethnicity and Industrialization: The Proliferation of the Cultural Division of Labor." *Ethnicity* 3, no. 3: 214-24.

Inkeles, Alex
    1969 "Participant Citizenship in Six Developing Countries." *American Political Science Review* 64, no. 4: 1120-41.

Isaacs, Harold
    1974 "Basic Group Identity: The Idols of the Tribe." *Ethnicity* 1: 15-42.

Keyes, Charles
    1976 "Towards a New Formulation of the Concept of Ethnic Group." *Ethnicity* 3, no. 3: 202-13.

Kuper, Leo
    1969 "Plural Societies: Perspectives and Problems." In *Pluralism In Africa,* ed. L. Kuper and M. G. Smith, pp. 7-26. Berkeley: University of California Press.

Low, James
    1972 *The British Settlement of Penang.* Kuala Lumpur: Oxford University Press.

Leach, Edmund
    1954 *Political Systems of Highland Burma.* London: London School of Economics.

Macalister, Norman
    1803 *An Historical Memoir Relative to Prince of Wales Island.* London.

Mitchell, J. Clyde
    1956 *The Kalela Dance: Aspects of Social Relationships among Urban Africans of Northern Rhodesia.* Manchester: Manchester University Press.

Nagata, Judith
    1974 "What is a Malay? Situational Selection of Ethnic Identity in a Plural Society." *American Ethnologist* 1, no. 2: 331-50.

    1975 "Perceptions of Social Inequality in Malaysia." In *Pluralism in Malaysia: Myth and Reality,* ed. J. Nagata, pp. 113-36. Leiden: E. J. Brill.

    1976 "The Status of Ethnicity and the Ethnicity of Status," *International Journal of Comparative Sociology* 17, nos. 3-4: 242-60.

Naroll, Raoul
    1964 "On Ethnic Unit Classification." *Current Anthropology* 5, no. 4: 283-312.

Obeyesekere, G.

    1975 "Sinhalese-Buddhist Identity in Ceylon." In *Ethnic Identity: Cultural Continuities and Change,* ed. G. DeVos and L. Romanucci-Ross, pp. 231-58. Palo Alto, Calif.: Mayfield Publishing.

Patterson, Orlando

    1975 "Context and Choice in Ethnic Allegiance." In *Ethnicity: Theory and Experience,* ed. N. Glazer and D. Moynihan, pp. 305-49. Cambridge, Mass.: Massachusetts Institute of Technology Press.

Pillsbury, Barbara

    1976 "Blood Ethnicity: Maintenance of Muslim Identity in Taiwan." Paper presented at Conference on Taiwan, Portsmouth, England.

Porter, John

    1975 "Ethnic Pluralism in Canadian Perspective." In *Ethnicity: Theory and Experience,* ed. N. Glazer and D. Moynihan, pp. 267-304. Cambridge, Mass: Massachusetts Institute of Technology Press.

Roff, William

    1967 *The Origins of Malay Nationalism.* Kuala Lumpur: University of Malaya Press.

Rousseau, Jerome

    1975 "Ethnic Identity and Social Relations in Central Borneo." In *Pluralism in Malaysia: Myth and Reality,* ed. J. Nagata, pp. 32-49. Leiden: E. J. Brill.

Schrieke, B.

    1966 *Indonesian Sociological Studies.* The Hague: Van Hoeve.

Shils, Edward

    1957 "Primordial, Personal, Sacred and Civil Ties." *British Journal of Sociology* 8, no. 2: 130-45.

Smith, M. G.

    1965 *The Plural Society in the British West Indies.* Berkeley and Los Angeles: University of California Press.

Stavenhagen, Rodolfo

    1975 *Social Classes in Agrarian Societies.* New York: Anchor Books.

Van Leur, J. C.

    1967 *Indonesian Trade and Society: Essays in Asian Social and Economic History.* The Hague: Van Hoeve.

Vaughan, J. D.

    1857 "Notes on the Malays of Penang and Province Wellesley." *Journal of the Indian Archipelago and Eastern Asia,* n. s. 2, no. 2: 115-68.

Wallerstein, Immanuel
1972 "Social Conflict in Post-Independence Black Africa: The Concepts of Race and Status Group Reconsidered." In *Racial Tensions and National Integration,* ed. Ernest Q. Campbell, pp. 207-23. Nashville: Vanderbilt University Press.

In this paper, Bentley discusses the ethnic segmentation of the economy and political stratification that traditionally have been strongly related in social relations among the Tausug, Samal, and Bajau peoples living in the Sulu Archipelago of the Philippines. The Tausug dominate the area politically through the Sulu sultanate, economically through control over markets and a monopoly on favored productive lands, and ideologically through control of key Islamic symbols. Samal produce for subsistence and for the market, are clients of Tausug nobility for the most part, and often aspire to Tausug identity. The Bajau are a boat-dwelling pariah group with restricted participation in most areas of social life. Bentley shows how current origin myths, which give content to primordial identities, express the status relationships between the groups by portraying the Tausug as "good Muslims" and by deprecating the Samal and Bajau by recalling un-Islamic episodes associated with their putative entry into the archipelago. Political-economic dominance has given the Tausug the means to maintain the system of ethnic differences in the archipelago and this system has, in turn, generated the resources supporting the Sulu sultanate and other instruments of Tausug dominance. Sulu history thus shows how culturally marked status differences have been translated into profound ethnic cleavages.

G. CARTER BENTLEY

Migration, Ethnic Identity, and State Building in the Philippines: The Sulu Case

INTRODUCTION

In the southern Philippine Sulu Archipelago, migration, frontier expansion, and revolutionary restructuring of social relations were all involved in the development of a structured system of interrelated but hierarchically stratified ethnic groups. In the following discussion the structure of status differentiation and ethnic group boundaries in the archipelago will be discussed, the political and economic structures underlying the system of ethnic stratification will be described, mythic charters for Sulu ethnic stratification will be analyzed, and a probable historical model of processes leading to the present structure of interethnic relations will be delineated. The discussion is intended to illustrate four issues: 1. the relation between political centralization

Dependent as this paper is on extant literature, I owe a considerable debt to those who helped me obtain needed sources. Particular thanks are due Kemp Pallesen and William Geohegan who arranged access to Mr. Pallesen's dissertation draft,

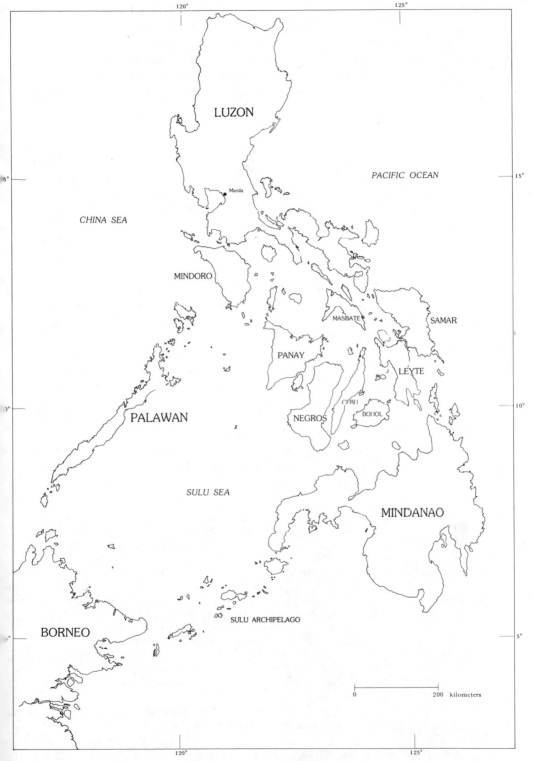

Figure 1. The Philippines

and clarity of ethnic self-identification; 2. symbolic and functional relations between politico-economic and ethnic segmentation; 3. the origin point for historical reckoning in stratified ethnic systems; and 4. the historical processes by which ethnic cleavages may develop.

THE REGION

The Sulu Archipelago is composed of more than five hundred islands ranging from high volcanic to low coral types lying between the large southern Philippine island Mindanao and North Borneo (see fig. 1). It separates the South China and Celebes seas. The archipelago lies on the traditional trade route that linked the Philippines with Borneo and the rest of insular Southeast Asia. The archipelago has long been considered by outsiders to be part of "Moroland," that portion of the southern Philippines primarily inhabited by Muslim indigenes, a religio-ethnic minority comprising about 5 percent of the total Philippine population.

Of the seven major "Moro" ethnic groups found in the Philippines, three inhabit portions of the Sulu Archipelago: Tausug, Yakan, and Samal.[1] Tausug are the dominant ethnic group, both politically and numerically. Their major population center is Jolo, northernmost major island next to Basilan. While Jolo holds the largest concentration of Tausug, other high volcanic islands (e.g., Basilan, Tupul, Lugas, and Siasi) also have significant Tausug populations. In general those islands suited to upland dry rice cultivation are inhabited by Tausug. The exception is the northernmost island, Basilan, inhabited almost entirely by Yakan. Marginal niches on the high islands and the lower atolls are left to Samalan groups. Small aggregations of boat-dwelling

and to Tom Kiefer who graciously gave permission to cite and quote his unpublished paper. I also owe a great deal to Charles Keyes and to the other participants in the CSEN seminar series for their incisive and insightful comments, which aided in revising the original draft of this paper. I am, however, solely responsible for the interpretations contained herein.

At the time I wrote the paper I did not have access to James Warren's excellent dissertation, "Trade, Raid, Slave: The Socio-Economic Patterns of the Sulu Zone, 1770-1898" (Ph.D. diss., Australian National University, 1975). Warren's data and analysis add immeasurably to the understanding of politics, economics, and the assimilation of foreign peoples as factors in the growth of Sulu power. He also discusses the activities of Iranun and Samal slave raiders as adjuncts to the marketing centers of Sulu, and the effects of demographic changes (native vs. foreign population) on the rigidity of ethnic stratification in the Sulu sultanate. For the period it covers, this work is authoritative.

1. Others are the Maranao, Magindanao, and Sangir of Mindanao, and the Jama Mapun of Cagayan de Sulu (Kiefer 1969, p. 30n).

Bajau, a Samalan-speaking group, are scattered in sheltered moorages throughout the archipelago.

The archipelago, except for Basilan (the home of the Yakan), makes up Sulu and Tawi-Tawi provinces. According to the 1960 provincial census approximately 60 percent of the population speak Tausug as their primary language, about 30 percent speak Samal, and about 2 percent are listed as Bajau (Stone 1962, p. 110). The remainder of the population is made up of nonindigenes, primarily Chinese and Christian Filipinos from the central (Visayas) and northern islands.[2] As of 1960 the estimated Tausug population of the islands was 325,000 of whom 175,000 lived on Jolo. Samalan speakers (excluding Bajau) numbered about 160,000, and Bajau were estimated to number between 4,500 and 6,0000 (Kiefer 1972a, p. 2; Arong 1962, pp. 140-41).[3]

ETHNIC BOUNDARIES AND STRATIFICATION

The following characterization of Sulu society refers to conditions as they existed in the mid-1960s and as they presumably existed for several decades prior to that time. Since then open conflict between government forces and those of the Moro National Liberation Front and other rebel groups has caused major social, political, economic, and cultural dislocations in Sulu, as well as in other Muslim Philippine

2. For clarity in argument, the nonindigenous people will be considered in the following discussion only when they significantly influence relations between indigenous groups.

3. In Philippine censuses prior to 1970, initial ethnic breakdowns were religious in nature, defining Christian-Muslim-Pagan as the relevant classes. Ethnic divisions within these gross classes were based primarily on linguistic affinity. In the 1970 and 1975 censuses, "mother tongue" was used as a proxy for ethnic origin and religious designations were deleted. The population estimates used here are considerably higher than the figures given in the 1960 census, which is considered unreliable. The 1970 and 1975 censuses indicate a substantial drop in total population (nearly 10 percent in five years) and a major shift in "mother tongue" with those listed as Tausug dropping from 65 percent (1970) to 58 percent (1976) and those listed as Samal rising from 29 percent (1970) to 40 percent (1975). Chinese are no longer listed in the censuses and categorizations of Filipinos nonindigenous to Sulu have changed considerably. To what degree these changes reflect actual population changes, alterations in the ethnic hierarchy, and census error cannot be assessed. While the political disorder in the region since 1970 has caused some population movement (especially exit by Chinese and other nonindigenes), its major effect has doubtless been to exacerbate the already egregious inaccuracy of Philippine censuses (National Census and Statistics Office 1970, p. 324; National Census and Statistics Office 1975, p. 104; O'Shaugnessy 1975; Pallesen 1977, p. 11).

areas. Refugee movements have generated large population shifts, trade and production have been seriously dislocated, and ethnic boundaries have been redefined and have shifted in relative importance. Sulu society is now in rapid flux and specific changes cannot be assessed because of the impossibility of conducting field research in the region. In using the present tense to describe past conditions I am following the anthropological convention of writing in the ethnographic present, that is, taking as the present the time when observations underlying the analysis were made.

The ethnic universe of the Sulu Archipelago is highly stratified. Tausug are ranked highest, followed by Samals (of various sorts), with Bajau comprising a pariah group. The Yakan stand somewhat apart from this ranking system and will not be considered in the following discussion. Before characterizing the stratification system itself some preliminary description of the constituent groups is required.

Although the name *Tausug* (glossed as "people of the current") implies a maritime orientation, the Tausug, both in residence and subsistence, are essentially land based.[4] The primary Tausug subsistence staple is rice, supplemented by starchy root crops (e.g., taro and cassava). Tausug settlements are located in areas suitable for rice cultivation and also for access to the sea since sea-borne trade has long provided important income and Tausug military power was traditionally naval in orientation. The only urban center in the archipelago is the town of Jolo (on Jolo Island), former seat of the Sulu sultanate and the most important port between Zamboanga and North Borneo (see fig. 2). Jolo city is inhabited primarily by Tausug with some Chinese and other nonindigenes involved in overseas and interisland trading (Kiefer 1969, p. 4).

Most Tausug use the name Samal to designate all non-Tausug indigenes in the archipelago, with the exception sometimes of the Bajau. There is a linguistic basis for this grouping since all non-Tausug indigenes speak related Samalan languages. Aside from linguistic affinities, Samalan groups also contrast with Tausug in that no Samalan group engages in the upland rice cultivation characteristic of the Tausug.

Tausug break down the general Samal category into subcategories

4. Spanish corruptions of the Tausug words meaning "ocean current," *sulug* or *sug*, also are supposed to have provided the names Jolo (pronounced with the silent Spanish *j*) and Sulu (Kiefer 1969, p. 1). Some informants say the name *Tausug* derives from the words *tau* and *suk*, giving a literal meaning of "people of the market." As will be shown below, this possible etymology points to an important feature of Tausug society. Pallesen (1978) suggests that *suluk* is a proto Sama-Bajau term designating both the island of Jolo and its people. This etymological puzzle remains to be unraveled.

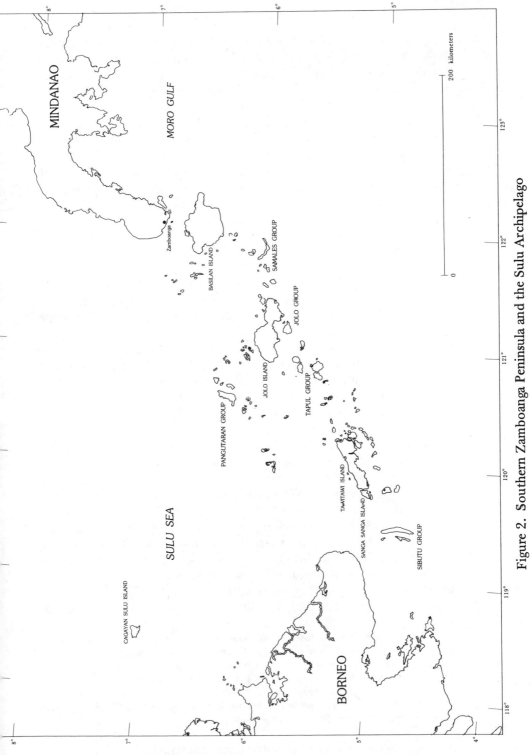

Figure 2. Southern Zamboanga Peninsula and the Sulu Archipelago

according to the ecological niches inhabited by various Samalan groups. *Samal Talon* ("wild Samal") live in the mountainous interiors of volcanic islands in areas unsuitable for rice cultivation. They practice shifting swidden agriculture and seldom associate with lowland groups. *Samal Gimba* ("forest" or "field Samal") engage in fishing for home consumption but depend on farming for primary subsistence. Members of this group typically reside on farm lots near beach or strand areas. *Samal Laut* ("sea Samal") build their homes over water in strand areas (Arong 1962, p. 136) and depend heavily on fishing for subsistence, generating income and obtaining starch staples through marketing of fish and trade with Tausug or Chinese. Each of these categories implies some contrast with Tausug life styles.[5]

The Sulu Bajau are a Samalan-speaking group of sea nomads who live in moorage clusters scattered throughout the archipelago. They share elements of life style with other "sea gypsies" in coastal areas throughout Southeast Asia (Sopher 1965). Local use of the name *Samal Pala'u* in some parts of the archipelago distinguishes Bajau from all other Sulu groups since it refers to their signal characteristic, the *pala'u* or boat home (Arong 1962, p. 136). The Sulu Bajau are usually characterized as nomadic, their movements tied to fishing opportunities, chances to visit relatives, and special social events such as marriages, burials, and circumcisions (ibid., p. 140; Sopher 1965, p. 135). Despite their propensity to travel, however, most Bajau identify one village (moorage) as a home port and spend most of their time there (Nimmo 1965, p. 423).

Aggregation of all non-Tausug indigenes into a single category usually labeled Samal by Tausug (note that Bajau are sometimes called *Samal Pala'u*) expresses both their linguistic commonalities and also their common distinctness from the Tausug. The latter point is important in that the category subsumes considerable cultural variation. As Nimmo (1972, p. 11) writes "Dialectical differences, occupational specializations, value systems, material culture, religious beliefs, and, in some cases, physical differences, tend to set off the various groups. As a result, the Samal-speakers normally identify themselves by their islands, sometimes even by villages, rather than by *Samal,* which because of its generic nature, has little value as identification among

5. For a different breakdown of the Samal category, this one based on regional and cultural factors rather than ecological differences, see LeBar (1975, pp. 5-13). Kashim (1978) argues that Samal is a misnomer, a pejorative label imposed by Tausugs. According to this view, the proper name of the people is *Sama,* meaning "together." Notably, Geohegan (1975) and Pallesen (1977; 1978), both of whom have done recent research among Sama peoples, prefer the Sama label. In this paper, however, I follow the traditional usage.

them." Elsewhere Nimmo (1972a) reported considerable difficulty in getting Samalan-speaking informants to generalize about all Samal or all Bajau. In contrast Kiefer (1972a) reported no difficulty in getting Tausug to generalize about all Tausug, or about all Samal, or all Bajau.

In the Sulu Archipelago Tausug identity serves as the touchstone from which all other ethnic identities are reckoned. For this reason, Tausug identity contrasts with other ethnic identities at varying levels of inclusiveness. As Kiefer (ibid., p. 2) notes,

When a man says "I am a Tausug," he may be referring to any of three things. First, he may be saying that he is a member of an ethnic group which speaks the Tausug language and has a particular form of adat, of custom, which sets him apart from the other Moslem ethnic groups in Sulu. Second, he may be saying that he is a person who has some primary loyalty to the Tausug sultanate at Jolo with its legal and political institutions; this sets him apart from other Filipinos. Third, he may be saying that he is a Moslem; this sets him apart from nonbelievers, especially Christians. In most cases a person will refer to himself as a Tausug on all of these levels of meaning.

The conceptual location of Tausug identity, in contrast to other non-Sulu identities, describes the universe within which other Sulu ethnic groups define themselves. As noted above, Samalan groups do not usually perceive Samal to be a real category of people, even though they are so conceived by outsiders. For them the most important elements of identity are those that relate them to the Tausug world and to each other. Hence the frequency with which they identify themselves by village or island. It is largely through their relationships to Tausug that their relationship to the rest of the world is defined.

The focus of Tausug identity corresponds to their elite social standing in Sulu. The Tausug language is the lingua franca of the islands. All Samalan-speaking men are also able to speak at least some Tausug but few, if any, Tausug deign to learn Samalan dialects, considering the language beneath them (Stone 1962, p. 112; Kiefer 1972a, p. 49; Nimmo 1972a, pp. 60, 65, 69, 71). Tausug cultivate and eat rice, the staple of prestige throughout the Philippines, while Samal and Bajau subsist on root crops.

The ethnic stratification of Sulu is amply demonstrated in the contrasting images that are held of Tausug, Samal, and Bajau in Sulu. Nearly all characteristics of Tausug behavior are highly valued; Bajau, as a pariah group, are held to exhibit all the corresponding negative characteristics. Normally non-Bajau Samalan groups are ranked somewhere between the other two.

Perhaps the most critical value standard is that of ranking itself.

In Philippine Muslim societies the concept of rank honor is pervasive and important. Among the Tausug the frequently used terms *maltabat* ("rank honor") and *sipug* ("shame") refer to this value (Kiefer 1969, p. 118). "Rank honor" is that personal attribute that defines how each person in Tausug society should act toward other people. "Shame" may refer both to actual dishonor or to the capacity of the virtuous person to feel shame or embarrassment. As Kiefer (ibid., p. 120) notes, "The basic element in shame is the discrediting of the self in front of others. In Tausug culture, the idea of bravery and masculinity is a major facet of a typical adult male's image of himself. Cowardice is a cause for ridicule and embarrassment for the individual. It deflates the image a person has of himself and the image others have of him." To be ashamed is intolerable, a cause for blood revenge or suicide, a point made succinctly in a Tausug proverb quoted by Kiefer (ibid., p. ii), "The thing that kills a man is embarrassment." At all costs a Tausug man must appear unafraid, and Tausug ridicule Samal and especially Bajau as cowardly, humble, and ashamed (Nimmo 1972a, pp. 44, 47, 52, 57). To illustrate the contrast between themselves and the Bajau, Tausug point out (often to exaggeration) that Bajau are afraid of dogs and that they even fear the very sea they live on (Kiefer 1969, p. 26; Sopher 1965, p. 140). Attribution of humility, shame, and cowardice to the Bajau severely stigmatizes them according to prevailing value standards. To a lesser degree Samalan groups are similarly devalued.

These contrasts in attitudes are reflected in the behaviors adopted in interpersonal encouters. Stone (1962, p. 112) observes that "The Tausug is, generally speaking, a fiercely proud, uncompromising, even arrogant, individual, and these particular qualities show in his face; the Samal quite simply does not possess this arrogance of manner but is, indeed, deferential in face to face relationships with the other groups (Bajau excepted)." From the Tausug perspective this behavior is appropriate and highly valued. In contrast Bajau are usually deferential, even servile, in face-to-face relationships. From the Bajau perspective, Tausug are frequently unpleasantly arrogant and aggressive and land Samal share these attributes, although to a lesser degree (Nimmo 1972a, pp. 44, 49, 52, 57).

As a pariah group, Bajau contrast with Tausug on nearly all other scales of value as well (Kiefer 1972a, p. 25). Tausug regard them as unclean, incestuous, and dishonest, among other negative attributes. While Bajau insist that they are Muslim, and say that they follow Muslim practices of washing after urination and defecation, that they practice Muslim rites of marriage, burial, and circumcision, observe the pork and alcohol taboos and use Islamic prayers, Tausug refuse to accept their professions of faith and claim that Bajau practices are not Muslim but pagan. Ethnographers point out that because they live on boats Bajau are uable to observe the strict hygienic practices and sexual segregation prescribed in Tausug society (ibid., p. 26). Many Bajau practices do differ from their Tausug analogs but the differences between the two groups are exaggerated by most Tausug (ibid.; Nimmo 1972a; Sopher 1965, p. 140).

As polar opposites on most value scales, conceptual and social distance between Tausug and Bajau is maintained at the extreme. Boundaries between Bajau and Tausug identities are considered impermeable. Tausug vehemently deny that a person can simultaneously be both a Bajau and a Tausug (Kiefer 1972a, p. 50). A Tausug man can marry a Bajau woman (if she "converted to Islam"), but this is reportedly very rare.[6] Under no circumstances can a Bajau man marry a Tausug woman. Tausug hold this prohibition to be an absolute rule. While Bajau report knowledge of no such rule, they acknowledge that such marriages never occur (ibid.; Nimmo 1972a, p. 65). Friendship between Tausug and Bajau is inconceivable to members of both groups (Stone 1962, p. 120).

Non-Bajau Samal[7] occupy intermediate levels in the Sulu ethnic hierarchy. They are generally admitted to be Muslims by Tausug, but Muslims of an inferior degree (Kiefer 1972b, p. 22; 1972a, p. 36). As recognized Muslims they share at least one element of Tausug identity unlike the Bajau who contrast with Tausug on all counts.[8] Just as the differences in valuation between Samal and Tausug are not so great as those between Bajau and Tausug, so also are the boundaries between them more permeable. While marriage between Samal and Tausug is not encouraged, it is tolerated and occurs fairly frequently (Stone 1962, p. 121; Kiefer 1972a, p. 59). In most such marriages a Tausug man takes a Samal wife, but the reverse also happens on occasion (Stone 1962, p. 121; Kiefer 1972a, p. 59). Residence is open to the choice of the couple.

Unlike the Bajau who have been prevented from assimilating to Tausug society and culture, at least in those areas where Tausug control is strong enough to enforce such restrictions, assimilation of agricultural

6. In his travels throughout the islands, Stone (1962, p. 112) found only one such marriage.

7. Hereafter simply called "Samal."

8. Kiefer (1972b, p. 22) notes that Tausug often distinguish between Samal Islam and Samal Luwaan. The former correspond to the members of the category "Samal" used here. *Samal Luwaan* are the Bajau and the name glosses as "Samal vomited out by God." The contrast between the two types of Samal will be explained in greater detail later.

Samal to Tausug society has occurred and still does occur (Stone 1962, p. 115; Kiefer 1969, p. 8). While old reports refer to Samal communities living on Jolo, none exists today. All Samalan peoples on Jolo except the Bajau appear to have been fully assimilated to Tausug society and culture. On the outskirts of Tausug influence (in the southern islands of the archipelago) linguistic assimilation is taking place at a rapid rate (Kiefer 1969, p. 9). The permeability of Tausug-Samal boundaries is further indicated in agreement by members of both groups that a person can simultaneously be both Samal and Tausug, although it is assumed that given a choice one will espouse Tausag identity (Kiefer 1972a, p. 50; Nimmo 1972a, pp. 78, 83, 86-90). Similarly, Samal-Tausug friendships are possible, although these are probably based primarily on economic reciprocity (Stone 1962, p. 120).

Samal-Bajau borders are at least partially permeable. Economically based friendship relations can exist between members of the two groups and marriages across the ethnic boundary occasionally take place, invariably between a Samal man and a Bajau woman, with the couple residing in the Samal community (Nimmo 1972a, pp. 78, 83, 86, 90).

Tausug-Samal-Bajau interethnic relations indicate that social mobility is possible incrementally within the status hierarchy but that movements or even contacts between the extremes are resisted.

The value differentials described above are not merely analytical inferences. There is consensus among Tausug, Samal, and Bajau about the stereotypic characteristics of all three groups (Kiefer n.d., p. 4).[9] Members of all three groups agree that Tausug are the proudest and the greatest troublemakers. On each of these dimensions they are followed by Samal and Bajau. Bajau are considered by all to be the dirtiest. The only real disagreement in characterization is between the Samal and the Tausug, each of which claims to be the most religious of the three; Bajau responses on this dimension are equivocal. Tausug make a strong claim to being the most "civilized" of the three groups. Bajau pariah status is reflected in their claim to being the most honest of the three; they see the Tausug as the most dishonest. Both Tausug and Samal respondents see it the other way (Stone 1962, p. 132).

POLITICAL-ECONOMIC STRUCTURES AND ETHNIC SEGMENTATION

Conceptual boundaries between ethnic groups in Sulu reflect and

9. These conclusions summarize results of a survey of intergroup attitudes and stereotypes conducted by Stone (1962) in a variety of Sulu locales. The numerical results, in tabular form, are found in Stone (1962, p. 120).

reinforce political and economic boundaries between them. Prior to its decline under Spanish and American colonial pressure, the Sulu sultanate, an ethnically Tausug polity, united all Sulu ethnic groups (theoretically at least) under the suzerainty of a single Tausug leader (Kiefer 1972c, p. 3). Although the sultanate lost power under colonial rule, ceding sovereignty to the United States under the Bates Agreement (1899) and the Carpenter Agreement (1915) (see Gowing 1977) and formally ceasing to exist in 1936 when the Commonwealth government refused to recognize any of the contending heirs to the throne of the late Sultan Jamalul Kiram II (Noble 1977, pp. 36-37), the clarity and focus of Tausug ethnic identity still derive from its former embodiment in the Islamic polity.[10] Many of the privileges and functions of the elite under the traditional system have been maintained, albeit unofficially since the prerogatives of their former titled offices in the sultanate are now attached to offices of the Philippine government. Although the government has tried to suppress traditional Sulu political forms in the interest of "modernization," members of the Tausug elite have often succeeded in using their traditional status and followings to gain elective or appointive office (see Arce 1968). External influences have produced changes, of course, but the following description of precolonial Tausug society still accurately characterizes Tausug social structure and the ethnic hierarchy in the Sulu region.

Tausug calculations of social position were based on a number of principles of affiliation, each of which described one facet of an individual's relationship to the conceptual center of Tausug society, a position occupied by the sultan. In general these principles involved kinship, residence, military alliance, religiosity, and accession to titled positions in the political structure.[11] None of these principles generated permanently corporate groups. Each provided an associational medium through which networks of interpersonal alliance could be constructed.

Rights to positions of legitimate authority, embodied in political and religious titles, were inheritable, but since kinship, inheritance, and succession were all reckoned cognatively, far more people could claim rights to titles than could wield the authority associated with them.[12] Estate (hereditary class) ranking ideally provided for dif-

10. To substantiate its territorial claims to Sabah, the Philippine government (in 1962-63) took up the cause of Sultan Kiram's heirs in their demand for compensation from the British government. For an analysis of this convoluted diplomatic episode, which affected Philippine-Malaysian relations and relations between the government and the Sulu elite, see Noble 1977.

11. Kiefer (1969, pp. 22-46) analyzes these principles in considerable detail.

12. This situation is common to all Philippine Muslim sultanates. Baradas

ferentiation between social ranks in great detail, but the only status boundaries that in practice restricted social mobility significantly were those between *bangsa mataqas* (*datuq* or "noble lineages"), *bangsa tay way* ("commoner lineages"), and *banyana* or *iqipun* ("slaves") (Kiefer 1969, p. 26).[13] Movement between these gross social segments was possible but difficult, while movement within them was rapid. Anyone with a hereditary claim to *datuq* ("noble") status could aspire to positions of high authority, if he could accumulate sufficiently powerful supporters. Actualization of any individual's claim to position depended on his ability to construct and maintain networks of supporters. These networks were based on dyadic alliances between a leader and each of his followers. An essential feature of clientage relations (hierarchical dyadic alliance) was a commitment of leader and follower to aid each other (often militarily) when called upon to do so. In return for a pledge of support and payment of some tribute and labor services, a man could secure protection for himself, his family, and his possessions. Anyone remaining unallied stood essentially defenseless in a society with a propensity for armed violence (Mednick 1957, p. 47; Kiefer 1969).

The resulting system was that termed by Nicholas (1966) "segmentary factionalism," in which leaders of nested factions were themselves factional supporters of people at succeedingly higher levels in the political structure. In this way power accrued to the sultan, the apex of the factional pyramid and at the same time the source of all symbolic and moral authority. As Kiefer (1972c, p. 39) describes the system, "In the Tausug polity the realities of power moved upward in an ever more precarious system of alliances, while the symbols of power—the titles which legitimated authority—moved downward to bring even the remote local headman at least within the ritual sovereignty of the state." A prime characteristic of the segmentary factional system was that it could "join almost any number of villages or settlements into a single political unit" (Mednick 1957, p. 43).

Titles in the sultanate did not indicate functional distinctions among their holders. They did not confer any power on a holder that he did not possess prior to his accession.[14] Because power rested

---

(1973) examines the ambiguities introduced into rank differentiation because of cognatic kinship.

13. This three-way stratification system was common in lowland Philippine societies. It was more elaborately articulated in the Muslim sultanates than elsewhere.

14. Kiefer (1972c, pp. 42-43) describes this character of the Sulu sultanate as follows "There was no authority available to the sultan as head of the state which was not simultaneously available to each of the regional and community head-

on dyadic alliances loyalty was granted only to the leader immediately above a given follower, and a leader could only expect obedience from his immediate following (Kiefer 1972, p. 41).[15] Titles served to validate the power an individual demonstrably already had by locating it within an Islamic political model of society and an Islamic conceptual/moral model of the universe (Kiefer 1969, p. 40).[16] According to Majul (1974, p. 5): "Islamization introduced new laws, novel ethical standards, and a new outlook on the meaning and direction of life. The Arabic script was adopted for writing local languages, and the Arabic language itself was used for ritual and theological matters. Moreover, Malay became the commercial and court language. All this helped to make the Philippine Muslims more and more an integral part of an expanding Islamic Malay world."

Although the state structure based on the Islamic model did not produce functional specialization of titleholders, it did legitimate

---

men. . . . The differences between them was a matter of quantity of power and its extent rather than differences in quality. . . . The sultan did possess ritual and religious functions by virtue of his office as head of a self-consciously defined Islamic state, and many of these ritual functions were unique to the sultan. Yet his ritual role did not give him any specific political functions which were simultaneously denied to any of the subsidiary officials. His ritual role was a source of prestige, which was of enormous value in the practical problems of everyday politics."

15. Expectation of obedience was not based on an ability to compel cooperation. Each individual calculated his stake in a given venture, advantages to be gained, and risks. Alliances were always contingent on continuing mutual advantage. As a result, alliances were necessarily fluid. Lacking absolute authority, a leader could not unilaterally dictate actions to be taken by his followers, nor could he compel settlement of disputes between two of his followers, although a titled leader was the proper medium for arriving at settlements and could claim a fee for assisting. Thus in 1821 the trading vessel *Sunflower* was given safe passage by the sultan of Sulu at Jolo but was later attacked by a lesser Sulu *datu* near Tawi-Tawi. The sultan apologized but left the ship's captain with the distinct impression that there was nothing he (the sultan) could do about the attack. The captain concluded that the Sulu political structure was an aristocracy rather than a monarchy because, "though there is a Sultan he has very little power, every measure being carried by the will of the *datus* who sometimes attack each other without consulting the Sultan upon the subject" (quoted in Tarling 1963, p. 147). The balance between centripetal forces of power centers and the *datus'* assertion of independence, and the role of Islam in this balance is discussed by Majul (1973). For a good account of Sulu piracy during the nineteenth century, see Tarling's chapter on the Iluanans and the Balingingi (1963, pp. 146-85).

16. The balance of centripetal and centrifugal forces in Sulu society is similar to that described by Geertz (1967) in his study of Balinese politics. Ideas of power that accompany such structures are described in Anderson's (1972) excellent essay on power in Javanese society.

a number of rights attached to all offices (again in differing degree). According to Kiefer (1972c, p. 43) these were "1) rights to act as the Law, 2) rights to control territories and subject peoples, 4) rights to control markets, 5) rights to control land ownership and use, 6) rights to control religious officials, and 7) rights to wage external war." All of these rights contributed to maintenance of the state, and to titleholders' power. In particular, rights to collect tribute, to control markets, to control subject territories and people, to control land use, and to wage war provided in various ways the income necessary for a leader to maintain his position. They also provided for the incorporation of subordinate ethnic groups into the political realm of the sultanate. Villages of Samal were usually treated as local factions, with their local headmen forming clientage relations with Tausug leaders at appropriate levels in the segmentary hierarchy (rights to control subject Samal villages were often appended to titles rendered by the sultan). Samal leaders who gave excellent service to the sultan could even aspire to titled positions in the sultanate themselves. The eastern Sulu Balingingi Samals were widely known as pirates and slave traders, ranging from the Visayas (central Philippine Islands) to Malaysia and Western Indonesia (see Geoghegan 1975, p. 6; Tarling 1963). Balingingi Samal leaders on occasion became titled advisors to the sultan, particularly on matters concerning piracy and naval warfare (see Sather 1971, p. 60).[17]

A similar means of incorporation was employed for the Bajau but its idiom was more invidious. Tausug *datus* were frequently said to own Bajau communities. The degree to which "ownership" actually linked Bajau communities to the larger Tausug polity depended largely on the communities' relative proximity to the center of power. Those communities near Jolo enjoyed special clientage relations with Tausug royal *datus* (and in some cases still do), but at the extreme reaches of Sulu influence, political patrons of boat-dwelling Bajau were often headmen of Bajau groups who had recently settled on land (ibid., p. 59). The clientage relations themselves were not always as exploitive as the term "ownership" implies, even though Bajau typically viewed them that way (Sather 1975, p. 10).[18] Like clientage relations among Tausug, those between Tausug and Bajau were contingent on continuing calculation of mutual advantage. Bajau were able to sever the

17. According to Tarling (1963, pp. 152-53) the British were convinced that the sultan, at least during the 19th century, acknowledged or even sponsored Balingingi raids and that he received a portion of the loot.

18. Sather (1971) points out that while threat of violence ultimately underlay ethnic stratification, interethnic relations did not usually involve violence.

relation simply by moving to a different moorage and patron, if their original patron became too demanding or was unable to adequately protect them (Sather 1971, pp. 59-60). Cases of Bajau villages disappearing overnight were well known (see Nimmo 1968; 1972a, p. 14).

The advantages to be gained in these clientage relations by subordinate Samal and Bajau were readily apparent. They gained protection, without which they would be subject to predation from all quarters.[19] Sather (1971, pp. 59-60) writes, "a majority responsibility of the patron was to protect his clients from raids and depredation directed against them by other outsiders. While the Baujau Laut were sometimes harassed, and occasionally looted or taken captive in the past, the clientage system seems to have been fairly effective in this regard and resulted generally in a precarious stand-off."

The same generally applied to Samal. Although some Samal (especially such militaristic groups as the Balingingi) were better able to defend themselves than Bajau, who were tactically vulnerable because of their boat-dwelling life style, greater security was to be gained through alliance with Tausug patrons.[20] Kiefer (1969, p. 153) records that in some wars the sultan was able to mobilize several thousand armed men in a short time. No Samal community, no matter how well organized, could field a comparable force.

The more pertinent question for purposes here is what the Tausug gained by incorporating subordinate groups into the sultanate. Prestige gained would seem insufficient by itself to justify maintaining obligations to protect groups particularly open to attack. The explanation lies in occupational specialization of the different ethnic groups, resultant trade, and Tausug abilities to exploit that trade to their advantage.

Because Sulu ethnic groups occupied different sets of ecological niches, each produced products valuable to the other groups. Underlying all other trade relations was the exchange of subsistence products: protein (mostly fish) for starch (rice, cassava, etc.). Bajau and Samal possessed the knowledge necessary to become successful fishermen,

19. The importance of protection for Bajau is starkly illustrated in Kiefer's (1969, p. 179) statement that, with regard to Tausug piracy, "Boat-dwelling Samal (Bajau) are always fair game, although piracy committed against them is more likely to involve a strictly pecuniary motive, as they are such easy targets and seldom resist."

20. The Balingingi were able to enjoy a relatively independent political existence because of their military prowess and aggressiveness. The Balingingi Samal and Tausug seemed to have mutually chosen accommodation over confrontation (Sather 1971, p. 60).

and they were also adept at producing the materials needed to exploit the sea. Because of their mobility, Bajau were well situated to take advantage of fishing cycles, and many of their movements were coordinated with changing fishing opportunities in different parts of the archipelago (Nimmo 1972b, p. 15; LeBar 1975, p. 10). Bajau and Samal fisherman had to obtain starch staples from outsiders, just as Tausug depended on other groups for protein. Although some Samal, in areas outside of direct Tausug control, were able to plant gardens and to become relatively self-sufficient, those living near Jolo or in other areas of major Tausug settlements were prevented from owing farm land, or from producing fixed field crops (LeBar 1975, p. 8).[21]

Tausug dominated the local trade in subsistence products. Markets in Sulu operated under the aegis of individuals who could guarantee the safety of people who traded there. Given the opportunities for confrontation and violence in exchange situations, only those who could call upon a large number of armed supporters could sufficiently guarantee law and order. With very few exceptions such persons would be Tausug. In return for these services market patrons extracted a small tax from all vendors.[22]

In addition to controlling the market setting itself, Tausug (along with Chinese) dominated the entrepreneurial positions in the market. Samal and Bajau were unable to penetrate the realm of Tausug consumption directly because their patrons normally held exclusive rights to market their clients' produce as a condition of the clientage relation between them. Samal importance to the market process is indicated in a Tausug comment that, "Without the Samal there would not be a market place. The Samal are the fisherment of Sulu. Tausug are not food fishermen, and it is necessary for the Samal to supply the market place with fish if the people are to live normally there" (Stone 1962, p. 117).

Because of their subordinate position, Samal and Bajau were unable to fully exploit the produce of their labors. While they obtained the starch staples they needed for survival, surpluses of production were alienated by Tausug patrons and traders, providing part of the income Tausug needed to maintain their superordinate status and military power.

Nonsubsistence goods produced by Samal and Bajau were handled similarly. Bajau collected shells and pearls highly valued by the Tausug

21. Tausug titular rights to control landownership and use were used to prevent Samal, and especially Bajau, from farming and adopting sedentary lives.

22. This system has been recorded as early as the 17th century on Jolo (see Spoehr 1973, p. 268). It seems highly probably that it is of even greater antiquity.

elite. Some Samal villages specialized in building boats and pottery manufacture. As Spoehr (1973, pp. 266-67) notes, "There is no Tausug tradition of making pottery. Within the memory of residents of Parang, local earthenware was obtained from Samal. The earthenware sherds recovered from the cottas are evidence of a continuing internal trade between Tausug and Samal communities probably located in outlying islands." Their facility at building ocean-going *praos* gave some eastern Sulu Samal, notably the Balingingi, a privileged place within the patronage system. They operated as naval retainers of Tausug nobles, engaging in both trade and piracy at their behest (see Geohegan 1975; Warren 1975). These relations also fell within the purview of interethnic clientage, as did trade in goods used by Tausug for overseas trade, probably the most important of the trade sectors for maintaining ethnic stratification.[23]

Jolo was the entrepôt for trade throughout the archipelago, a centralization dictated partially in the interest of maximizing potential profits, but more specifically to minimize losses due to piracy. Being involved in both piracy and protection, the sultan and royal *datus* could bring nearly all trade, even that by Chinese and later by Europeans, within their control. Their control of local markets and dominance in entrepreneurial positions generated the maximum possible income.[24] At the same time, as military power generated profits, it also was used to exclude potential competitors for those profits. Bajau, Samal, Chinese, and Europeans were for centuries prevented from developing trade centers independent of Tausug control. Spoehr (1973, pp. 274-75) notes the interaction of trade, military power, and stratification: ". . . in the past, the status of one ethnic group vis-à-vis another seems to have been based on relative access to external trade. Tausug political superiority was certainly linked to their control through the sultanate of foreign trade with other parts of Southeast Asia, China, and later, Europe." Forrest (1779, p. 335) noted the importance of trade in maintaining political power when he observed that, "The datoos are all traders. Even the sultan is a merchant."

23. While local subsistence trade was traditionally carried on through barter, Forrest (1779, p. 330) reported that in the 18th century Sulu used a copper currency in overseas trade, a feature lacking in most of the other Philippine sultanates.

24. Foreign traders apparently paid a commission directly to the sultanate for rights to establish outlets in Sulu. A Chinese trader told Forrest (1779) that he paid a 5 percent commission on every shipload of goods brought into Sulu. State-building based on trade centralization was a common feature of southeast Asian history. See Shriecke 1957 and Van Leur 1955, for descriptions of this pattern in Java and elsewhere in insular southeast Asia.

The range of goods excavated from a Tausug *cotta* indicates early foreign trade. These included "glass fragments, Chinese and British coins with a few doubtful specimens of possible Sulu coinage, fragments of iron vessels, and musket balls, musket flints, and cartridges demonstrating the possession of firearms. The brass betel nut boxes, lime containers, ornaments, and chest fittings could have been imported from Borneo, Mindanao, or even in some cases from China" (Spoehr 1973, p. 267). Nearly all these items were apparently imported through overseas trade. Exports from Sulu may be inferred from a fifteenth-century Chinese account of important articles of trade (see Majul 1966, p. 145). Sulu exports listed in this manifest included pearls, beeswax, tortoise shell, and rare woods. These were exchanged for ceramics, beads, iron, and cloth. Eighteenth-century English accounts indicated that the goods available at Jolo (many of which came originally from Borneo and the Moluccas) included spices, trepang, birds' nests, beeswax, resins, rare woods and rattan, pearls, pearl shells, cowries, tortoise shell, and abaca (Spoehr 1973, pp. 267-68).

Those items listed as exports from Sulu were not the sort of items to which Tausug had direct access. Woods, resins, beeswax, and rattan were the products of forest dwellers, primarily Samal. Marine products came from Samal and Bajau. Of particular importance in the overseas trade were pearls. Forrest (1779, pp. 327-28) writes, "At Sooloo, and the many islands around, which form a great Archipelago, the pearl fishery has been famous many ages. This is the source of their wealth, and sets them more at ease than any Malays I ever knew, though their island does not generally produce so much rice as they consume. They trade therefore to Magindanao with Chinese articles for that grain, and make great profits, as no Chinese junks have for a long time gone thither." Tausug did not find their own pearls. These were found by Samal and Bajau fishermen and some Bajau who specialized in diving for shellfish. Forrest (ibid.) also described how Tausug *datus* came into possession of pearls for trade: "The large pearls are the property of the Datoos, on whose estates they are found, for whose paramounts claim the property of the banks as well as of the dry land."

This element of *adat* ("customary law") was still in force when Americans occupied the Philippines in 1899. Under an agreement in that year, the United States government recognized the right of the sultan of Sulu (or his designated subordinate) to any pearl found by one of his subjects (Tan 1967, p. 126).

Even today the blatantly commercial character of clientage relations with Bajau, at least from the Tausug point of view, is indicated in the response of a Tausug informant who, when asked what virtues the Bajau had, responded, "They sell us fish and buy things from our stores. The only good thing about them is that they have economic reciprocity with us; otherwise all their customs are bad" (Kiefer 1972a, p. 25).

While Samal and Bajau contributions are still essential to the trade on which Tausug welfare depends, they are not allowed participation in foreign trade. As Stone (1962, p. 117) puts it, "The path of quickest economic mobility and heaviest profit are closed to the Samal—that of trading, on the North Borneo run. Tausug realize that this is the easiest way to high economic and consequently high social status, and as such, it is closed to all except Tausug and their Chinese financiers." Since the sultanate is no longer a real political structure the mechanisms of stratification and control are today somewhat different. However military power and protection are still needed since this "trade" consists of smuggling goods past Philippine government controls specifically intended to stop them and piracy is by no means rare in the region (see Tan 1967, pp. 141-44).[25]

Economic stratification is maintained in the other elements of economy where opportunities for capital accumulation and profits are greatest. Production of *daing* ("dried salt fish") for export is largely controlled by Chinese (Stone 1962, p. 117). Arong (1962, p. 142) reports that recently Chinese financial backers have become dissatisfied with the inability of Samal to meet increasing market demand with their traditional fishing methods. As a result the financiers have begun liquidating the fishing equipment used by Samal and reinvesting in modern fishing boats crewed by Visayan (central Philippine) immigrants. As their traditional skills are outstripped by technological innovations, even those niches traditionally reserved to them are denied Samal and Bajau.

Samal participation in wage labor and small-scale enterprise is fitful and sporadic. Managers report that they are target workers and are unreliable (Stone 1962, p. 113). Capital concentration in Tausug and Chinese hands tends to be self-reinforcing as Stone (ibid.) found that Samal and Bajau are much more likely to be dependent on extra-ethnic credit sources than were either Tausug or Chinese. Where the latter usually obtained credit from family or friends, Samal and Bajau usually had to get it from their political patrons (Tausug) or from Chinese financiers.

Ethnic stratification in the archipelago developed as a combined function of economic sectioning and political incorporation. The two

---

25. Recently the government has established a "Barter Trade Zone" in Zamboanga where goods imported from Borneo may be sold tax free. In effect, Sulu smuggling has been partially legalized, but piracy and the need for armed power to participate in the trade continue unabated.

were mutually reinforcing, since the former generated trade, and the latter the means to exploit it. The Sulu state operated not only to take advantage of local and overseas trade but also to reinforce the conditions under which that trade continued to be profitable to Tausug. The growth of the Sulu state may be loosely compared to a market monopoly based on an elaborate protection racket. Social standing and opportunities for advancement derive from proximity to the "king-pin," in this case the sultan of Sulu.[26]

CHARTERS FOR SULU ETHNIC IDENTITIES

Just as all elements of Sulu social organization are identified by their distance from the center of power, all ethnic identities are identified by their distance from the symbolic focus of Tausug identity (see Kiefer 1972b, p. 2). The symbolic primordiality of Tausug identity in the Sulu ethnic universe is indicated in responses given by members of different groups to the question, "According to the beliefs of your ancestors before the Europeans came, who were the first human beings in the world?" Tausug answers varied in specifics, but all the named "first humans" shared a common characteristic: they were all Tausug. Two responses are typical: "The first human was Salip Muda, cousin of the prophet Mohammed. He was the first person and was a Tausug. Some people say that Adam and Eve were the first people; anyway they were Tausug" (Kiefer 1972a, p. 13). "The ancestors believed that the first humans were the Tausug, that Adam and Eve were Tausug. Even today most people believe that" (ibid., p. 11). On the other hand, Bajau, when asked the same question, responded that they had

26. Change in the Sulu Archipelago has opened new avenues for social mobility for Samal and Bajau. While Tausug dominance continues, the institutional means of maintaining it have lost much of their potency; Bajau have come ashore in numbers in Sitangkai (see Fig. 2; Nimmo 1972b). Samal are beginning to make inroads into teaching and other new high-status occupations. Two Tausug teachers respond to these changes very differently: (1) "Tausugs do not try to improve themselves. They think they are the nobility, the privileged people, so they do not try to gain betterment. The Samals are different. Now you find many of them who are teachers, who want to get an education and help their people. They try very hard. When they get an education, then they are better then Tausug." (2) "The Tausug must regain their former place. It is true that the nobility had degenerated but if a true renaissance can be started, true Islam will be enforced and the Tausug will regain their rightful place" (Stone 1962, p. 119). Kiefer (n. d., p. 30) has noted that as social mobility for Samal and Bajau has increased, they have increasingly come into direct competition and even open conflict with Tausug.

no knowledge of the first people in the world (Nimmo 1972a, pp. 14, 17, 20, 22).

Similarly, beliefs about group origins indicate that Tausug are the cardinal, the "unmarked" category, in the Sulu ethnic structure. Tausug generally believe that they have always lived on Jolo (the cultural center) and that Jolo Island was among the first lands created by God (Kiefer 1972a, p. 16).[27] In contrast both Tausug and Samalan groups have numerous myths that explain the origins, life style, and pariah status of the Bajau. Tausug myths of Bajau origins emphasize their association with water and their fall from favor with God. Kiefer recorded on Jolo a myth that he regards as typical of Tausug explanations:[28]

One of the descendants of the prophet called Fatima had a small store near the beach. Her husband Ali wanted to eat fish, so he asked a Samal who was drinking coffee to bring some the next day. When he gave the fish to Fatima the next day he (the Samal) said, "I do not want any money for this fish, I only want to sleep with you." Fatima told him she would bring the fish home first. When she returned to him she brought some coconuts with her. She threw the coconuts at the Samal which became cats, chasing after him and biting his penis. He died and the rest of the Samal went back to their island home in the sea.

Later, Ali went to their home and asked them why they do not pray like other Moslems. They answered that it was because they were naked and ashamed. Ali gave them clothes, and he was happy because they were going to begin to pray. But they only prayed once, and then they traded all their clothes for cassava. He went back, and they again promised to begin praying. To show their good faith, they cooked a splendid meal for him, but unthinkingly served him slices of dog meat. Fortunately Ali said a prayer before eating and all the slices of meat turned into dogs. He was very angry and left.

When Ali was a safe distance from the island it began to sink to the bottom of the ocean. All the Samal were killed except for one pregnant woman. But she was not forgiven by God, and she and her children were cursed forever by Him; they were permanently vomited out. The only other animals which survived the flood were the monkeys that climbed to the top of the trees; thus these people and the monkeys come from the same race. [Kiefer 1972b, pp. 22-23]

Prominent themes in this myth include the conceptual separation of sky, earth, and sea, with earth being the only proper habitation for human beings.[29] Bajau (Luwaan) here are compared to monkeys, for both inhabit nonhuman places. Samal are shown in this myth to be

27. Tausug myths vary enough to make generalization hazardous. There is a high value placed on originality and virtuosity in Tausug storytelling. An alternate origin myth may be found in a translation of Mullug's story, "In Atu Nakauna," in Damsani et al. (1972).

28. Personal communication from Kiefer.

29. The earth-sea-sky trichotomy appears frequently in a variety of Tausug myths.

lustful, dishonest, lazy, and not devout. All the actions attributed to them in the story show their deviation from the Tausug standards of behavior. The myth thus validates Tausug ascendancy in Sulu and explains Bajau (and more generally, Samal) servility (Kiefer 1969, p. 7).

Similar myth fragments, which pursue the same themes, are found among Tausug living on southern islands of the archipelago:

> [L]ong ago all the people in Sulu lived as a single group. One day a great tidal wave was seen approaching the islands; to save themselves from the wave, half the people built boats while the other half ran to the mountains. The people who built boats were washed to sea and became the boat-dwelling people of Sulu, whereas those who had run to the mountains became farmers and are the present Tausug population. . . . Another Tausug story tells of an ancient time when the Bajau were very devout Muslims. One Friday when they were praying in their mosque, built on piles over the sea, they saw a school of fish pass below. Forgetting their prayers, they jumped into the sea after the fish. God became angry and would not let them return to the mosque; ever since they have been wandering the seas as pagans. [Nimmo 1968, p. 41]

Note the separation of land and sea in the first fragment and the Bajau lack of piety, with consequent rejection by God, in the second fragment.

On the Bajau side, mythical explanations of their origins and present conditions emphasize their dispersion from a common origin point, their migration across great expanses of sea, and in some cases their fall from favor. The first two themes are central to the following version:

> The Bajau of Tawi-Tawi and Sibutu tell of a time long ago when their ancestors lived at Johore, a place to the west near Mecca, in villages of boats much as some of them still live today in Tawi-Tawi. One day a strong wind began to blow, and so the leader of the village stuck a pole into what he thought was the ocean floor and tied his boat to it. The other villagers, also fearing the wind, tied their boats to that of the leader. It turned out, however, that instead of going into the sea floor, the pole had dug into the nose of a giant sting ray which lay sleeping under the flotilla. That night when the villagers were sleeping, the ray awakened and swam out to sea, pulling the boats with it. When the people awoke the next morning, they were far in the open sea and did not know the way back to Johore. For one week they drifted helplessly on the sea, until finally the leader pleaded to God for help. Within minutes, God sent down a spirit which entered the man's body and instructed him to sail for two days toward the east. Upon reaching shore the Bajau stuck a large pole (called *samboangan* in Samal) into the sea floor and all the boats were tied to it. This was the first mooring place in the Philippines for the Bajau and thus was called "Samboangan." Today it is still called this by the Bajau while the rest of the world knows it as Zamboanga. Shortly after their arrival in Samboangan, the boat-dwellers became subjects of the powerful Sultan of Sulu. During the course of his many marriages throughout Sulu, the Sultan gave groups of Bajau as portions of his brideprice; consequently the Bajau became

scattered throughout the Sulu Archipelago, as they are presently found. [Ibid., pp. 39-40]

Both Bajau dispersion from Johore and their fall from favor with God are accounted for in the following myth:

Many years ago the sultan of Johore decided to marry, but he desired the most beautiful woman in his kingdom. He sent trusted aides to search out the beautiful women, and they brought him women from throughout the country but none would suit him. Finally, he himself saw a beautiful woman walking in his garden, and it was his sister. It is forbidden to marry one's sister, but the sultan was so filled with desire that he determined that he would marry her. He sent for the imam, who refused, and fled the country. Then he sent for another imam and the same thing happened. Finally, he told the third imam that he would behead him if the marriage was not performed. The imam hesitated but finally agreed on condition that it would be performed in the middle of the ocean, for to marry one's sister on land was against Allah's will. The sultan agreed, and called together all his people and told them they must build a bridge of boats far into the sea, for he was to be married in the middle of the ocean. This they did, and the sultan arrived with the imam and his sister. Just as the imam began to chant the marriage rites, a great wind arose, and scattered the boats far and wide. The sultan and his sister, and the imam were swept into the sea and drowned. The boats were carried far to the east, and finally they arrived in the Sulu islands. [Stone 1962, p. 122]

On the basis of the myth immediately above, it appears that Bajau accept the Tausug definition of them as fallen Muslims (see Kiefer 1972a, p. 15). In this version the Bajau fall is caused by a sultan's abrogation of cardinal rules of moral conduct. Because of their association with him, his people were cast down. If the Bajau were not blamed for their downfall, it still tainted them.

Tausug have used coercion to reinforce these traditions to prevent Bajau from adopting practices that would disconfirm their identity as pariah pagans.

Traditionally the Bajau Laut were physically debarred from coming ashore, except temporarily, and were not allowed to enter mosques or other religious structures or to build mosques of their own. While ostensibly "religious," this prohibition had important political implications. The construction of a mosque signalled the emergence of a leader within a community capable of mobilizing its wealth and power and meant, as a consequence, an end to its clientage status. . . . the final loss in their (Bajau) loss of social stigma appears to have been the construction of a mosque and their acceptance by others as Muslims. [Sather 1971, pp. 61-62]

MIGRATIONS, CHARTERS, AND STATE BUILDING IN SULU HISTORY

While mythic charters justify and help maintain Bajau pariah status, the question of the origins of Bajau, Samal, and Tausug, the conditions of their contact, and the processes leading to intergroup relations in the historic period remain. Mythic traditions are frequently assumed to be at least partially true to historical fact, especially with reference to group migrations and origins (Vansina 1965). Given Tausug insistence on their local origin we might accept as fact the later intrusion of Samal and Bajau into Sulu. Bajau stories of their migration from Johore support this origin. Further mythic confirmation for Johore origins is found in prevalent origin stories collected in Sulu by nineteenth- and early twentieth-century observers (see Sopher 1965, pp. 141–42). In general, these tell of a beautiful princess of Johore who was desired by competing sultans. To avoid the resulting conflict, the Bajau boat people left Johore to wander the seas.[30] Based primarily on this mythic tradition Sopher (ibid., p. 352) locates the ultimate Bajau origins point in the Rious-Lingga Archipelago, a dependent territory of Johore off the southern tip of the Malay Peninsula at the eastern end of the Malacca Strait. He argues that the dispersion of Bajau from Johore took place alongside increases in Arab and Chinese Muslim trade during the twelfth–fifteenth centuries (ibid., p. 353). According to this theory Bajau occupied those marginal niches not already occupied by indigenous Tausug.

The mythic themes of late arrival of Bajau in Sulu, and the circumstances of their migration, validate current interethnic relations in Sulu. They support ethnic stereotypes of Bajau as cowardly vassals of lordly Tausug by whose leave they are suffered to remain. However the mythic history is contradicted by linguistic evidence. Recent studies have shown that Tausug is intrusive in Sulu (Chretien 1963). Its relatedness to Visayan languages, spoken to the north, is clear (see Vogelin and Vogelin 1965, pp. 62, 69; Thomas and Healey 1962, p. 22), and Tausug does not show significant dialectal variation, especially in comparison with Samalan languages (Kiefer 1969, pp. 7–8). Tausug occupation of a single ecological niche and subsistence base is also significant when compared to Samal speakers' occupation of a variety of niches. It seems unlikely that Samal immigrants would have adapted to a much wider variety of ecological settings than indigenous Tausug.

Recently, Pallesen (1977) has undertaken detailed linguistic re-

30. Similar tales of Johore origins are found among boat dwellers on Celebes (Sulawesi), west and south Borneo, and among land dwellers on southern Mindanao (Sopher 1965, pp. 151, 355). The 18th-century English captain Thomas Forrest described "Badjoos" in Borneo who were said to have come from Johore, at the east end of the Malacca Strait (see ibid., p. 297). Based on this ubiquitous mythic theme, the early ethnographer Saleeby (1908) was lead to conclude that the origin stories were accurate accounts of historical incidents.

constructions of southern Philippine language interrelationships. Despite the difficulties in lexicostatistical and glottochronological inference of absolute dates of linguistic divergence, these techniques can be effectively used to establish genetic relationships between languages and to infer *relative* dates of origins and divergence. From Pallesen's data a probable model of origins, contact, and historical development of ethnic boundaries in Sulu may be inferred. Pallesen has established with reasonable certainty that a proto-Samal Bajau language was spoken in the Basilan-Zamboanga area well over one thousand years ago (Pallesen's suggested date is ca. 1,200 years before the present). Since local dialect variation is far greater in this area than in any other where Samalan languages are spoken, Pallesen has posited Zamboanga as the origin point for the Samal migrations (ibid., pp. 165-76).[31] This date far precedes estimates of the Bajau dispersion from Johore. Pallesen's conclusions of course do not preclude a reverse migration at a later date, for which Sopher (1965) has argued.

If Samalan speakers were Sulu indigenes and Tausug intrusive, three questions arise. First, where did Tausug originate? Second, how was Tausug introduced into the Sulu Archipelago? Third, what factors led to Tausug ascendancy throughout the archipelago?

In answer to the first question one can first consider linguistic evidence. The extant Philippine language most closely related to Tausug is Butuanun, spoken in the province of Agusan del Norte in Mindanao (Pallesen 1977, pp. 338-39). Pallesen estimates that these two languages diverged perhaps 800 to 900 years ago. Contact between Tausug and Sulu Samalans probably took place at about the same time (ibid., p. 340). The timing of contact accords with the probable date of divergence of several Samalan languages.

The introduction of Tausug into Sulu was probably associated with dynamic changes in trade patterns in the Malay and Indonesian islands. Huang Ch'ao's massacre of foreign traders in South China A.D. 878 caused a major migration of traders, mainly Muslims, into the Malay Peninsula (Majul 1973, p. 38). Intensification of local trade in a variety of areas resulted from this diaspora. The Philippines probably were incorporated into the trading network during the following century, judging from Sung dynasty coins excavated from Philippine graves (Fox 1967, p. 43).

Archaeological discoveries in Sarawak show abundant evidence for T'ang dynasty trade with Borneo at least by A.D. 732 (ibid, p. 52).

---

31. Based on further reconstructions Pallesen (1977, p. 338) estimates that the parent languages of Tausug and Samal diverged some 3,000 to 5,000 years ago. Their ultimate origins are unknown.

Chinese contacts with the Philippines during this period were sporadic at best (ibid. pp. 43, 51). During the Sung dynasty (tenth to twelfth centuries), Arab trade linking China to the islands increased, while during the twelfth century, Chinese merchants began to compete in the trade. Prior to the Arab diaspora trade seems to have followed the expansion of the kingdoms of Srivijaya and Madjapahit centered in northern Indonesia (Rausa-Gomez 1967, pp. 92-93). Once the Arabs and Chinese became involved, the boundaries of the trade networks steadily expanded. It is during this period that Samalan languages apparently began to disperse from the Basilan-Zamboanga region, and that Samal and Tausug speakers first came into contact.

The Agusan River is one of two readily navigable rivers in Mindanao (see fig. 1). Access for trade into the interior of Mindanao was nearly impossible except by using these two rivers. Trade contacts between Samal traders and indigenes in the Agusan basin is likely. The presence of some Samal loan words in languages in this area, and the presence of Samal settlements to the north provide evidence for such contacts, probably continuing over a long period of time (Pallesen 1977, pp. 343-46). The ubiquity of the word *daing* (salted dried fish) and its derivatives among both inland and coastal peoples in the Agusan basin also argues for such contacts especially since *daing* is known, from Chinese records, to have been a major Samal trade product. Pallesen's analysis (ibid., pp. 346-47) suggests that north Sulu Samals, known to have been wide-ranging traders and pirates, were probably the group that made contact. While the needs of seagoing travelers for terrestrial starch products would have been sufficient reason to land in the Agusan region, the chance to procure inland forest products highly valued elsewhere would have added inducement to such ventures. The apparent long-term presence of Samalan speakers in the vicinity of the Agusan River suggests very frequent if not continuous trade relations between Sulu and northeastern Mindanao.

Since trading often kept men away from home for long periods of time, the taking of local wives would not have been unlikely, and marriage between traders and local women was common throughout southeast Asia for cementing valuable relations of reciprocity for successful trading. Since most Tausug terms intrusive into Samalan languages are female in association (e.g., household items, prepared foods, body-parts, names), semantic data supports the supposition that the carriers of Tausug from the Agusan area to Sulu were predominantly women (Pallesen 1977, pp. 365-70). Thus, while the impetus for initial contact was probably mercantile, Tausug was probably introduced into Sulu through intermarriage.

"There is the likelihood that there was a network of intermarriage uniting the Tausug immigrant to mercantile Sama families, mainly by the marriage of Sama men to Tausug women. It seems probable that the number of Tausug speakers who made the journey to settle in Sulu was considerable, but rather than posit large numbers of Tausug wives it seems more reasonable to suppose that these Tausug speakers included Tausug women and their children by Sama men" (ibid., p. 370). It is possible that slave-taking for ransom, a common adjunct to trading activities, may also have contributed to the presence of Tausug speakers in Sulu (ibid., p. 363).

Tausug failed to converge completely toward the surrounding Samalan languages because of its function as a class/status marker. "Considerable prestige, and inevitably, political power, must have been enjoyed by the mercantile class, and it is apparent, from the foregoing discussion, that one section at least of this class was distinguished by Tausug-Samalan bilingualism" (ibid., p. 372).

Mercantile elite prestige was maintained by control over specialized economic activities that, because of the capital, manpower, skills, and military risks they entailed, were not easily undertaken, and by control over the symbols by which elite status was marked. The high status associations of Tausug would have encouraged its spread, and some Tausug words did find their way into Samalan languages. However, the linguistic environment of Sulu was, at the time, overwhelmingly Samalan, conditions favoring convergence toward Samalan. Concentration of the small community of Tausug speakers in parts of Jolo Island may have contributed to Tausug's persistence (Majul 1973, p. 52; Kiefer 1969; Pallesen 1977, pp. 367-69). In addition to spatial concentration, the intimate connections between trading and military power would have set Tausug-Samal bilinguals apart as a specialized elite. While some convergence took place, evidence points to the existence of a distinctly bilingual elite with regional commercial and political power by the fourteenth or fifteenth century.

At this point the introduction of Islam and the construction of the Sulu state provided a symbolic and institutional focus for Tausug identity, and the means by which Tausug became dominant throughout Sulu. The Tausug language was, as noted above, associated with trading, and Islam was introduced into Sulu through that medium. The earliest records indicate contact between Muslim traders and the west Jolo Tausug-Samal trading centers. Marriage of a Muslim trader with a Jolo woman is documented in Sulu *tarsilas* ("genealogies") in the early fourteenth century (Majul 1973, pp. 52-53, 60). A number of other events in this area, such as the building of a mosque at Jolo town by Karim al Mukdam, the arrival of Rajah Buginda from Minangkabau and his founding of a dynastic line, and the deaths of several Muslim

Sulu chiefs indicate that Islam took root early in Jolo. The title of "founder" and first sultan of Sulu is given to Abu Bakr (renamed Salip al-Hashim) because of his introduction of Islamic political institutions (ca. 1450) and his conversion of the hill peoples in the interior of Jolo (ibid., pp. 57-58). After Salip al-Hashim, the line of Sulu sultans was unbroken and the spread of Tausug hegemony was steady. Even so, the primary sphere of influence for all the sultans, their seat of power, remained in west Jolo.

Sather (1971, p. 62) suggests that Tausug may not have encouraged Islamization in Sulu, that, "Rather than being fostered by those in power, Islam may have been adopted by subordinate groups . . . as a way of assisting themselves actively into the political system." By the time of Spanish colonization (begun by Legaspi in 1565) the Sulu sultanate was firmly established as a military power. Sultanates had been established as far north as Manila, which was burned by the Spanish in 1571 (Majul 1973, pp. 74-75). Spanish attacks on the Brunei sultanate (1578-91) and Magindanao (after 1591) inevitably brought the Sulu Tausug and the Spanish into conflict (ibid., pp. 108-16). The Spanish attack on Jolo in 1602 heralded 300 years of Spanish-Tausug fighting.[32] Despite Spanish military pressure the sultanate continued to expand its territorial control, until by 1850 the sultan of Sulu reigned over the entire Sulu Archipelago and also regions of Mindanao and Sabah, regions with a total subject population of over 400,000 (Kiefer 1972c, p. 23). In fact, it appears that Spanish military adventures may have assisted the sultanate's spread since they forced opposing groups to seek aid and protection from the sultan of Sulu. Not until 1851 were the Spanish able to occupy Jolo. Their success was based on Spanish possession of steam warships that, as Kiefer (ibid., p. 12) notes, "for the first time in 300 years gave them a clear naval advantage over the Tausug." Sulu power then began to wane although the Tausug were not effectively brought under colonial control until the American "Moro Wars" of 1902-13.

With the institutionalization of Islam in the ethnically Sulu sultanate, linguistic convergence of Tausug to Samalan languages ceased. Where convergence still took place it was in the reverse direction, with Samalan languages taking on lexemes from Tausug (Pallesen 1977, pp. 373-75). Tausug identity became congruent with a hegemonic political structure symbolically and ideologically undergirded by Islam. The combination served to institutionally demarcate the

---

32. During this period the Spanish were fighting almost constantly with one or more "Moro" groups. The Sulu wars are only one aspect of that extremely complex history.

boundary between Samal and Tausug, and it provided an institutional means of preserving Tausug elite status.

The establishment of a Sulu sultanate and an elaborate court structure based on the Malay pattern may have favored the political ascendancy of a Tausug-speaking elite, and probably accentuated the social distinction between Tausug and northern Sulu Samal. North Samal speakers, however, evidently continued to play an important function in the structure of the sultanate; the tradition of a navy manned by Balingingiq is probably a local (Tausug) historian's "rewrite" of what was originally a balanced division between land-oriented and sea-oriented power. However, it is evident that [the early history of the Muslim sultanate] became increasingly dominated by Tausug speakers. [Pallesen 1977, p. 373]

The introduction of Tausug into Sulu and its subsequent social consolidation and spread represent a transformation of an internal class/status distinction into an ethnic distinction. While specialization in trade accounted for the initial differentiation of the Tausug-Samal community in Sulu from its Samalan surroundings, the association of Islam and the Sulu sultanate with Tausug identity allowed a linguistically marked status gradient to become a disjunction between two entirely separate ethnic groups. It is interesting to note, however, that the origin myths of the different groups do not reflect this process of ethnogenesis but instead mirror current relations between the groups.

Tausug were almost certainly not the first people in the Sulu Archipelago, or even on Jolo. By assigning themselves priority their origin myths serve to validate, ex post facto, the extant social ordering of Sulu ethnic groups. Tausug origin myths have been adapted to include elements of Islam identifying Adam and Eve as Tausug.[33] Combining Islamic elements with prestige social status, the myths center on the symbolic origin point of their current society and culture, the entry of Islam.

Bajau myths share a similar orientation. The Johore origin story probably does have an historical referent. Saleeby (1976) states that Sharif Kubungsuwan, founder of the Magindanao sultanate, was accompanied in his travels from Johore by Bajau. Kubungsuwan was a Malay-Arab who traveled to Mindanao via a roundabout route, including stops in Java, arriving in about 1515 (Majul 1973, p. 65). The Bajau who accompanied him may well have come from the Riouw-Lingga Archipelago as Sopher argues. Their movement may have been part of a

33. Some Philippine Muslim documents exhibit much more sophisticated knowledge of origins than do these myths. Since these would have been accessible only to scholars and religious functionaries they cannot be considered representative of popular understanding of Tausug origins (see Majul 1973, pp. 4-5).

more extensive migration associated with the founding of Malacca in 1400 and conversion of its leader to Islam in 1414. This event and subsequent growth of Malacca influence would have had enormous impact on the maritime communities under its suzerainty. Increases in trade, the establishment of networks of economic and political alliance throughout insular southeast Asia, and the spread of Islam all would have encouraged Bajau migration, as would their apparent aversion to residence near major power centers (Sopher 1965, pp. 367-68). Assertion of Johore as their ancestral home thus identifies Bajau relatedness to the cardinal historical focus in island history, the spread of Muslim influence throughout Indonesia.

This history does not explain Bajau pariah status. Factors include the inability of Bajau to behave according to Tausug values because of their ecological specialization, economic segmentation, their lack of "honor" as a result of military vulnerability and lack of assertiveness, and their transgression of important Tausug conceptual boundaries (see Douglas 1966; Sather 1971; Kiefer 1972a). Those myths that do offer explanation for pariah status combine the fall from favor with God (the Islamic theme) with the migration from Johore. Both migration and status are explained with reference to Islam.

CONCLUSIONS

Through the examination of ethnicity in the Sulu Archipelago, the interrelations of migration, ethnic identity, and state-building have been illustrated. While this has been primarily an empirical examination, it reflects on several theoretical issues in studies of ethnicity.

First, the degree to which a group is characterized by political centralization does seem to correlate positively with the degree to which that group possesses a clear ethnic self-identity (Kiefer n.d., p. 2; Levine and Campbell 1972, pp. 81-113). Tausug clarity of identity and political centralization both devolve from the Islamic state. The identity symbols and political practice are self-reinforcing. Neither would be possible without the other.

Second, ethnic segmentation of the market economy not only reinforces ethnic distinctions conceptually, but it also generates the surpluses by which ethnic segmentation may be coercively maintained. Tausug control of marketing systems produced and continues to produce the profits necessary to maintain Tausug military power and state institutions, the organizational means by which the Tausug assert control.

Third, in an ethnic universe characterized by marked status differentiation, the origin point from which groups reckon shared descent (see Keyes 1976, pp. 205-6; Shibutani and Kwan 1965, p. 47) depends on the symbolic focus of the dominant cultural tradition. Tausug origins are assumed to be continuous with Islam. The Tausug myth is an adaptation of the Quranic origin story. Bajau origin myths do not refer to ultimate Bajau origins, but the historical instance most significant to their relationship to the dominant Sulu groups. That event was the introduction of Islam and their migration from Johore.

Fourth, culturally marked class-status distinctions in relatively undifferentiated economies can develop into profound ethnic cleavages. The intrusion of Tausug culture as a prestige mark started a process that eventually resulted in the existence of separate and bounded groups. Tausug used ethnic criteria to defend their superordinate status position. The consolidation of identity and institutionalization of status differences was a product of political revolution, of a sort, the formation of the state. Whether a process of ethnicizing class differences can proceed this far in more highly differentiated economic systems is unclear. Hechter's studies (1971, 1974a, 1974b) suggest that cultural distinctions are crucial in maintaining class distinctions in industrial societies. However it is not clear whether class distinctions themselves generate sufficiently profound cultural differences that these identities may become primordial (see Keyes 1976, pp. 204-5). How the complementarity of exchange relations is involved in the generation and structuring of ethnic differences remains a question needing theoretical and empirical examination.

REFERENCES

Anderson, B. R. O'G.
1972. "The Idea of Power in Javanese Culture." In *Culture and Politics in Indonesia,* ed. Claire Holt, pp. 1-71. Ithaca, N.Y.: Cornell University Press.

Arce, W.

    1968. "Leadership in a Muslim-Christian Community in the Philippines." Ph. D. dissertation, Cornell University.

Arong, J. R.

    1962. "The Badjaw of Sulu." *Philippine Sociological Review* 10: 134-47.

Baradas, D.

    1973. "Ambiguities in Maranao Rank Differentiation." *Philippine Sociological Review* 21: 273-78.

Chretien, D.

    1963. "A Classification of Twenty-One Philippine Languages." *Philippine Journal of Science* 91: 485-506.

Damsani, M., E. Alawi, and Rixhon, G.

    1972. "The First People of Sulu." In *Sulu Studies,* ed. G. Rixhon 1: 245-54. Jolo, Sulu: Notre Dame of Jolo College.

Douglas, M.

    1966. *Purity and Danger.* Baltimore: Penguin.

Forrest, T.

    1779. *A Voyage to New Guinea and the Moluccas from Balambangan Including an Account of Magindanao, Sooloo, and Other Islands.* London.

Fox, R. B.

    1967. "The Archaeological Record of Chinese Influences in the Philippines." *Philippine Studies* 15: 41-62.

Geertz, C.

    1967. "Politics Past, Politics Present." *Archives of European Sociology* 8: 1-14.

Geohegan, W.

    1975. "Balingingi." In *Ethnic Groups of Insular Southeast Asia,* ed. F. LeBar 2: 6-9. New Haven, Conn.: Human Relations Area Files Press.

Gowing, Peter G.

    1977. *Mandate in Moroland: The American Government of Muslim Filipinos 1899-1920.* Diliman, Quezon City: Philippine Center for Advanced Studies, University of the Philippines System.

Hechter, M.

    1971. "Towards a Theory of Ethnic Change." *Politics and Society* 2: 21-55.

    1974a. "The Political Economy of Ethnic Change." *American Journal of Sociology* 79: 1151-78.

    1974b. *Internal Colonialism: The Celtic Fringe in British National Development, 1536-1966.* Berkeley and Los Angeles: University of California Press.

Kashim, A.
1978. "Samal is Not the Ethnic Sama." *Dansalan Research Center Research Bulletin* 4, nos. 3-4: 9-11.

Keyes, C. F.
1976. "Towards a New Formulation of the Concept Ethnic Group." *Ethnicity* 3: 202-13.

Kiefer, T.
1969. "Tausug Armed Conflict: The Social Organization of a Philippine Moslem Society." *Philippine Studies Program Monograph,* no. 7. Dept. of Anthropology, University of Chicago.

1970. "Affect, Tradition, and Reason in Tausug Private Warfare." *Man* 5: 586-96.

1972a. *The Tausug.* New York: Holt, Rinehart, & Winston.

1972b. *Tausug of the Philippines.* New Haven, Conn.: Human Relations Area Files.

1972c. "The Tausug Polity and the Sultanate of Sulu: A Segmentary State in the Southern Philippines." In *Sulu Studies* ed. Rixhon 1: 19-64. Jolo, Sulu: Notre Dame of Jolo College.

n. d. "The Tausug of the Philippines." In *Ethnic Boundaries and Intergroup Relations,* ed. R. Levine. Forthcoming.

LeBar, F. M., ed.
1975. *Ethnic Groups of Insular Southeast Asia.* Vol. 2, *Philippines and Formosa.* New Haven, Conn.: Human Relations Area Files Press.

Levine, R. and Campbell, D. R.
1972. *Ethnocentrism: Theories of Conflict, Ethnic Attitudes, and Intergroup Behavior.* New York: John Wiley and Sons.

Majul, C. A.
1966. "Chinese Relationships with the Sultanate of Sulu." In *The Chinese in the Philippines,* ed. A. Felix, pp. 143-59. Manila.

1973. *Muslims in the Philippines.* Quezon City: University of the Philippines Press.

1974. "The Muslims in the Philippines: An Historical Perspective." In *The Muslim Filipinos,* ed. P. Gowing and R. McAmis, pp. 1-12. Manila: Solidaridad.

Mednick, M.
1957. "Some Problems of Moro History and Political Organization." *Philippine Sociological Review* 5: 39-52.

National Census and Statistics Office
1970. *1970 Census of Population and Housing.* Manila, National Economic and Development Authority.

1975. *1975 Integrated Census of the Population and Its Economic Activities*. Manila: National Economic and Development Authority.

Nicholas, R.
1966. "Segmentary Factional Political Systems." In *Political Anthropology*, ed. M. Swartz, V. Turner, and A. Tuden, pp. 49-59. Chicago: Aldine.

Nimmo, H. A.
1965. "Social Organization of the Tawi-Tawi Badjaw." *Ethnology* 4: 421-39.
1968. "Reflections on Bajau History." *Philippine Studies* 16: 32-59.
1972a.*Bajau of the Philippines*. New Haven, Conn.: Human Relations Area Files.
1972b.*The Sea People of Sulu*. San Francisco: Chandler.

Noble, L. G.
1977. *Philippine Policy toward Sabah: A Claim to Independence*. Tucson: University of Arizona Press.

O'Shaughnessy, T. J.
1975. "How Many Muslims Has the Philippines?" *Philippine Studies* 23: 375-82.

Pallesen, A. K.
1977. "Culture Contact and Language Convergence." Ph. D. dissertation, University of California.
1978. "What is the Meaning of Sulu?" *Dansalan Research Center Research Bulletin* 4, nos. 3-4: 11-12.

Rausa-Gomez, L.
1967. "Sri Vijaya and Madjapahit." *Philippine Studies* 15: 63-107.

Saleeby, N.
1963. *The History of Sulu*. 1908. Manila: Filipiana Book Guild.
1976. *Studies in Moro History, Law and Religion*. 1905. Manila: Filipiana Book Guild.

Sather, C.
1971. "Sulu's Political Jurisdiction over the Bajau Laut." *Borneo Research Bulletin* 3, no. 2: 58-62.
1975. "Bajau Laut." In *Ethnic Groups of Insular Southeast Asia*, ed. F. LeBar, pp. 9-12. New Haven, Conn.: Human Relations Area Files Press.

Schriecke, B.
1957. *Ruler and Realm in Early Java*. The Hague and Bandung: W. van Hoeve.

Shibutani, R. and K. M. Kwan
1965. *Ethnic Stratification.* New York: Macmillan.
Sopher, D. E.
1965. *The Sea Nomads.* Vol. 5, *Memoirs of the National Museum.* Singapore: National Museum.
Spoehr, A.
1973. "Zamboanga and Sulu: An Archaeological Approach to Ethnic Diversity." *Ethnology Monographs,* no. 1. Pittsburgh: University of Pittsburgh.
Stone, R. L.
1962. "Intergroup Relations among the Taosug, Samal, and Badjaw of Sulu." *Philippine Sociological Review* 10: 107-33.
Tan, S. K.
1967. "Sulu under American Military Rule, 1899-1913." *Philippine Social Science and Humanities Review* 32: 1-187.
Tarling, N.
1963. *Piracy and Politics in the Malay World.* Melbourne: F. W. Cheshire.
Thomas, D. and Healey, A.
1962. "Some Philippine Language Subgroupings: A Lexicostatistical Study." *Anthropological Linguistics* 4, no. 9: 21-33.
Van Leur, J. C.
1955. *Indonesian Trade and Society.* The Hague and Bandung: W. van Hoeve.
Vansina, J.
1965. *Oral Tradition.* Chicago: Aldine.
Vogelin, C. F. and F. M. Voeglin
1965. "Languages of the World: Indo-Pacific Fascile Four." *Anthropological Linguistics,* vol. 7, no. 2.
Warren, James
1975. "Trade, Raid, Slave: The Socio-Economic Patterns of the Sulu Zone, 1770-1898." Ph.D. dissertation. Australian National University, 1975.

Tessler is here concerned with the process of change that applies to ethnic groups that have in common an inferior political status in societies where the political identity of the state is formally tied to the ethnicity of the majority. In specific, he considers the Jews in Tunisia and Morocco and the Arabs in Israel as examples of an ethnic group that he calls "nonassimilating minority." He argues on the basis of historical information and the analysis of survey data that four different types of change can be identified, differentiating between increasing or decreasing communal solidarity and between identification of groups with external or internal social systems. The first type, "diasporization," is exemplified by urban Jews in Tunisia and Morocco who have undergone a decrease in communal solidarity and an increase in identification with European civilization. Nonurban Jews in Tunisia provide an example of the second type, "assimilation," in that while they have also experienced diminishing communal solidarity, they have increasingly identified with the civilization of the country's Arab Muslim majority. Urban Arabs in Israel provide an example of the third type, "irrendentism." They have experienced increased communal solidarity while also coming to view themselves as a part of a broader Palestinian nation. Finally, the fourth type, "communalism," is exemplified by nonurban Arabs in Israel who have also experienced increased communal solidarity, yet have increasingly identified with Israeli society rather than with the larger Arab world. Tessler concludes his paper by focusing on the demographic and social structural attributes of the communities of nonassimilating minorities considered to derive general hypotheses about the conditions that lead to one or the other type of ethnic change he has identified.

MARK A. TESSLER

Ethnic Change and

Nonassimilating Minority Status:

Jews in Tunisia and Morocco

and Arabs in Israel

THIS paper seeks to describe and explain ethnic change among Jews in Tunisia and Morocco and Arabs in Israel. The groups have been selected for study because they reside in particular political circumstances, being religious and cultural minorities in states where there are strong and official linkages between the political system and the ethnic identity of the dominant majority. The Jews in Tunisia and Morocco and the Arabs in Israel are examples of what we shall call nonassimilating minorities and they are considered here to develop generalizable insights about the effect on ethnic change of this kind of minority group situation.

This research was supported by grants from the Social Science Research Council, the American Philosophical Society, and the University of Wisconsin, Milwaukee. While in Tunisia, the author received administrative assistance from the Centre d'Etudes et de Recherches Economiques et Sociales. The support of each of these institutions is gratefully acknowledged. The author also acknowledges with appreciation the useful comments on an earlier draft of this paper provided by Joel Migdal, Larry Rosen, and Crawford Young.

MARK A. TESSLER   155

The purpose of this section is to characterize the particular minority group situation whose effect on ethnicity we seek to assess. Since the cases to be examined are from the Middle East, we shall describe this situation in relation to that area. But we shall characterize it in conceptual rather than descriptive terms, thereby making questions about Jews in Tunisia and Morocco and Arabs in Israel part of a general theoretical inquiry. The circumstances of these minorities constitute the independent variable in our analysis.

An introductory definition of ethnicity and ethnic identity is provided by Bell and Freeman (1974, p. 10). They suggest that these terms imply cultural and subcultural traits that set one group apart from another, values and patterns of behavior being involved as well as self and other identifications. We agree with Rosen that in heterogeneous societies ethnicity is only one of many lines of social cohesion and its importance is not the same in all situations (1972, pp. 155-57). We also agree with those who argue that an adequate conceptual formulation of ethnicity must consider not only cultural elements but also factors like descent (Keyes 1976) and economic specialization (Hechter 1975). For purposes of the present analysis, however, the formulation of Freeman and Bell seems adequate. Membership in the groups with which we are concerned is readily ascertained by religion; available data permit us to examine only selected dimensions of ethnicity; and we are concerned principally with describing and explaining change on these dimensions rather than with defining ethnicity as completely as possible.

There is growing agreement among social scientists that ethnicity is not immutable, that forces of social and political change modify both the objective and subjective elements of group identities. In the introductory chapter of this volume, Keyes identifies three changes in political economy that affect ethnic identity. One is migration, which primarily involves movement from tribal or peasant communities to more complex urban milieux. Another is frontier expansion, which today usually means incorporation into a modern nation-state. A third is revolution, the central element of which is a restructuring of power relationships and attendant cultural and ideological patterns. All three of these dynamic processes have been operating for some time in the Middle East, fostering ethnic change among the majority of the population and, by extension, affecting the environment within which reside the area's minorities.

For most of the Middle East's peoples, changes in political economy have transformed religion, culture, and ethnicity into bases of nationalism and political action. Long before most countries in the Middle East were independent, urbanization and related social change processes raised questions about the relevance to modern life of ancient religious and cultural traditions. Frontier expansion was also occurring: European colonialism entered the Middle East, pogroms invaded Jewish communities in Eastern Europe, and intellectual responses to these challenges spread to the hinterland. A result of these developments was the emergence of modern Arabo-Islamic nationalism and modern Zionism. Of course Jews and Muslim Arabs had existed as political communities in the past. But, during the last 100 years or so, each has experienced a reemergence of political consciousness and defined the ideological content of its nationalism in terms of traditional religious, cultural, and ethnic attachments (Haim 1962; Hourani 1966; Hertzburg 1970).

Since independence, urbanization and other aspects of modernization have accelerated these developments in the Middle East. Frontier expansion has also assumed increased importance as leaders work to inculcate common political values among the masses. For example, the content of school curricula is controlled by the state to assure that future generations will appreciate and identify with the national patrimony, as it is understood and defined by the political elite. Finally, and most important, many governments have effected a political as well as a cultural revolution by formally tying the identity of the state to the ethnic attributes of the majority. Most Arab states are officially Muslim and Arab, for example. Constitutions make Islam the religion of state and Arabic is the national language by official decree. Similarly, Israel's first commitment is to Jews and Judaism. This pattern, which is not unique to the Middle East, involves an explicit rejection of Western-style secularism (Tessler 1975; Smith 1971). It means that the heritage of some but not all groups in a culturally heterogeneous society is incorporated into the political identity of the state. As mentioned, the rejection of secularism has its origins in both historical and contemporary patterns of political economy in the Middle East. At the present time, however, it is institutionalized and made official by formal government action.

Secularism does not refer only to the separation of religion and politics, although religion is a particularly significant focus for the discussion of secularism in the Middle East. More precisely, secularism refers to a disassociation of politics and the defining attributes of any particular group—religious, racial, cultural, or other. Alternatively, if an avowed purpose of political association is the defense and service on a priority basis of a particular community of individuals, rather than all individuals living within a state, then secularism is absent.

In Tunisia and Morocco, for example, values having to do with Arabism, as well as Islam, are part of the official identity of the state. It should also be noted that where religion is salient, a rejection of secularism does not necessarily imply the acceptance of theocratic models of statehood. In Tunisia, Morocco, Israel, and elsewhere, conceptions of religion are changing and there are intense debates about what is appropriate for a state seeking to make religion a part of its raison d'être. Nevertheless, the official and continuing tie between religion and politics in all three countries, as well as between Arabism and politics in the North African cases, constitutes a clear rejection of secularism. The result is that groups not possessing these attributes can share only marginally in the state's political identity and mission.

The rejection of secularism is viewed by most people in the Middle East as an appropriate expression of the will of the majority and a natural culmination of the efforts of nationalist movements striving for ethnic pride and cultural self-determination, as well as political independence. Yet this situation gives religious and cultural minorities, through no fault of their own, a political status inferior to that of the dominant majority. Even where discrimination is prohibited and the minority is relatively prosperous, as is the case for Jews in Tunisia and Morocco and Arabs in Israel, the tying of the country's political mission to the identity of a particular group makes those with different communal identities incapable of embracing or being embraced by the national ethic that is the basis of statehood and political legitimacy. As an observer notes about Israel, for example, "Both Jews and Arabs are aware that the Arabs are not truly welcome. Few Jewish tears would be shed were all of Israel's Arabs voluntarily to leave the country. Israel's ideology, however much it has come to be an ideology of nationalism, is still a Jewish ideology, in which Arabs have no role to play" (Fein 1966, p. 61). In sum, the rejection of secularism constitutes a political situation wherein some groups of citizens have a privileged claim on the power and resources of the polity while others have a distinctly inferior political status.

The rejection of secularism in the Middle East has been described in detail and evaluated elsewhere (Tessler 1975). It concerns us at present as a contextual stimulus, calling attention to a particular minority group situation whose impact on ethnic change we seek to assess. It may be noted in passing that groups whose political status is made marginal by a rejection of secularism may in fact be the numerical majority, as in South Africa, for example. Thus, while only minorities are examined in the present analysis, it is possible that findings about Jews in Tunisia and Morocco and Arabs in Israel will have relevance for ethnic enclaves that are numerically dominant but nonetheless reside in comparable political circumstances. In any event, since our objectives in the present paper are theoretical, it is important to characterize this situation in conceptual rather than descriptive terms; and toward this end the literature on pluralism is relevant. Kuper (1969 and 1974), van den Berghe (1969) and others wisely suggest considering the social, political, and demographic attributes of plural society as dimensions that may be treated, separately or in combination, as independent or specification variables. Among the dimensions they discuss are segregation-assimilation and equality-inequality, both of which are relevant to the present study. Armstrong (1976) also writes of the need for conceptual categories in the analysis of pluralism and ethnic group relations and shows the utility of combining dimensions to form broader analytical constructs, some of which approach ideal types.

Following these scholars, we shall characterize the situation of religious, cultural, and ethnic minorities in nonsecular states as involving "nonassimilating minority status" and we shall conceptually define that status in terms of a concatenation of tendencies along several selected dimensions. First, these groups are indigenous. Based on historical considerations, they would normally expect to have full claim on the resources of the state, equal to that of other citizens. Second, they reside in societies where the dominant group views as legitimate an association of its own ethnicity and the nationalism of the overall community. In situations where the dominant group is also numerically preponderant, this means that nonassimilating minority status results from a realization of the will of the majority. Its abolition would increase minority rights but at the price of denying powerful and historically legitimated aspirations of the majority. Third, these groups reside in societies where the government has institutionalized this view by formally tying the identity of the state to a single group; and, as stressed, this means that all other groups are relegated to a separate and unavoidably inferior political position. In sum, nonassimilating minority status involves residence in a particular sociopolitical context and constitutes a stimulus that may be presumed to influence many of the orientations and behavior patterns of groups that possess it.

Having defined the sociopolitical situation whose impact upon ethnic change we seek to determine, we turn to Jews in Tunisia and Morocco and Arabs in Israel. A research design comparing each group to a reasonably comparable "assimilating" minority would be desirable, but this is beyond the scope of the present study. Nevertheless, generalizable insights may be derived from a series of interrelated case studies through a comparative analysis that focuses on both similarities and differences with respect to the dependent variable, ethnic change in this instance. Similarities constitute potential generalizations about the relationship between nonassimilating minority status and ethnic change. Differences give information about the range of ways that ethnicity varies among nonassimilating minorities and about the conditions under which these minorities experience particular kinds of ethnic change.

THE GROUPS

More complete accounts of the historical and contemporary situation of Jews in Tunisia and Morocco and Arabs in Israel are available (see, for example, Chouraqui 1968; Hirschberg 1974; Stock 1968; Landau 1969; Tessler 1977, 1978, 1979, 1980a, 1980b, 1981), but a substantive introduction is presented here for three reasons. First, since our analysis involves a case study methodology, at least some background information about groups under study should be provided. Second, this information contributes to fuller understanding of nonassimilating minority status. Finally, the information provides a basis for differentiating among the groups and identifying relevant specification variables should it be necessary to account for intergroup variations with respect to ethnic change.

Some believe Jews entered North Africa as early as the destruction of the first Temple in Jerusalem in 586 B.C.E. Much larger Jewish migrations to the area took place after the Romans destroyed the second Temple, in 71 C.E. Thus, almost six hundred years before the Arabs entered the Maghreb, thriving Jewish communities existed there. In addition, it is believed that many of the indigenous Berbers converted to Judaism, although most later embraced Christianity and, subsequently, Islam.

In medieval times, the position of Jews in the Middle East and North Africa was defined by Islamic law. Like Christians, Jews were People of the Book, having specific rights and obligations but never full membership in the Muslim community. Jews fared reasonably well in this situation, although harassment and violence were by no means unknown. They were economically integrated into Muslim society yet generally free to follow their own law and to maintain their own communal institutions. In the western Maghreb, Jews lived as did their Berber neighbors, who were almost completely Islamicized by the eighth century. In the eastern Maghreb, and elsewhere in urban areas, Arabism as well as Islam took root after the eleventh century and Jews adopted attributes of Arab culture. Yet urban Jews were increasingly required to reside in special quarters, adding physical separation to the legal, religious, and institutional distance between them and the Muslim majority.

With the Spanish Inquisition, many Jews fled to North Africa from the Iberian Peninsula and Balearic Islands. Muslims arrived too, introducing an Andalusian component into North African civilization. Spanish Jews rarely settled in the countryside. In the cities, however, immigrant and indigenous Jews came into direct contact, the result being conflict in some instances but, over-all, a reorganization and enrichment of communal life. Literacy and religious education increased, for example. In addition, the expansion of commercial relations with Europe after the sixteenth century created a class of prosperous and well-connected Jews, of which there was no counterpart in Muslim society. Nevertheless, Jews remained politically subject and many continued to live in impoverished conditions.

French colonial rule was established in Algeria in 1830, in Tunisia in 1881, and in Morocco in 1912. The French conferred many privileges on North African Jewry, partly to justify their claim to be liberators and partly to divide the indigenous population. In 1870, most Algerian Jews were given French citizenship, for example. Also, the Alliance Israelite Universelle began its work in North Africa about this time, establishing modern schools in cities and towns throughout the Maghreb. As a result, large numbers of Jews were drawn into the French cultural and political orbit, learning the French language and frequently coming to regard themselves as Frenchmen. Among Muslims, on the other hand, the dominant response to colonialism was nationalism. This occurred at different rates in Algeria, Tunisia, and Morocco, but after World War I intellectuals in all three countries called for independence. Further, to provide an ideological foundation for opposition to the French and to rally the masses, the nationalists usually stressed Islamic themes, which excluded Jews from the mainstream of nationalism and increased Jewish identification with France.

Jewish communities prospered greatly during the colonial period. Lingering tensions between Jews of different origins diminished substantially and new communal organizations came into existence. Also, though rural communities in Morocco and southern Tunisia remained relatively untouched by the new currents, a measure of unity emerged among the Jewish population of each Maghreb country. There were national networks of Jewish schools, clinics, and religious courts and in the cities there were newspapers and radio programs designed for Jews; even many smaller towns had Jewish clubs and youth groups.

By the end of World War II, there were approximately 100,000 Jews in Tunisia, 175,000 in Algeria, and 275,000 in Morocco. In all three countries, Jews were a significant national minority and constituted a particularly important component of the educated and professionally skilled urban population. Within a few years, however, large-scale Jewish migrations from North Africa were underway. Motivated by traditional religious convictions, Jews from the Moroccan interior and the Tunisian south began to leave when Israel became independent in 1948. A more important stimulus to migration was the cultural and political distance between urban Jews and the Muslim majority. Few Jews identified with North African nationalism and, after independence, policies promoting Arabism and Islam reinforced this alienation. For example, since Jews were rarely literate in Arabic, they naturally felt threatened by Arabization. All but a handful of Algerian Jews left after the revolution. More Jews remained in Tunisia and Morocco, but large and continuing migrations have been going on in both countries since independence.

Other factors have also contributed to Jewish emigration in independent Tunisia and Morocco. Educational advances in both countries have reduced dependence on Jews and foreigners and created pressures for economic discrimination in favor of Muslims. Also, especially in Tunisia, government policies have disadvantaged the middle class and disallowed independent political institutions, religious or otherwise. Although these policies have been applied equally to Muslims, this does not reduce their effect on Jews. Further, acts of harassment, though officially discouraged, frequently occur on popular levels. Rapid urbanization has brought to North Africa's cities many illiterate individuals without prior contact with Jews. Bitter about social injustice, these persons are often receptive to ideologies attributing problems to Zionism or colonialism and this generates hostility toward Jews. Finally, since the existence of the critical mass necessary to maintain communal institutions and carry out normal social and religious activities is increasingly in doubt, the diminishing size of Jewish communities has itself fostered emigration.

Despite this exodus, Jews for a time retained some of their social and economic advantages. Individual Jews assumed positions of importance and for a few years both Tunisia and Morocco even had a Jewish cabinet minister. Nevertheless, the marginality and weakness of North African Jewry increases every year. As of 1973, there were fewer than 9,000 Jews in Tunisia and only about 25,000 in Morocco. Today the numbers are approximately 6,000 and 18,000, respectively. In each country, a parallel internal migration has also been occurring. Most Jews from small towns and rural areas have abandoned their homes and regrouped in a few cities. In addition, there is a high proportion of children and older persons, creating a disproportionately inactive and indigent population. Finally, schools and other communal institutions are steadily closing and most that continue to operate depend on subsidies from abroad. Thus the viability of North Africa's remaining Jewish communities is rapidly declining.

Though generally comparable, there are also important differences in the situation of Tunisian and Moroccan Jewry. The number of Jews in Tunisia is far smaller and, with the exception of Jews in Djerba, the community is concentrated almost exclusively in Tunis and its suburbs. Moroccan Jewry includes sizable concentrations in six cities and numbers of moderate size in at least half a dozen other towns. The proportion of young, middle-class, and professionally active Jews, though shrinking, is also higher in Morocco, giving that community a more nearly normal demographic and economic structure. Perhaps most significant, communal institutions are more numerous and effective in Morocco than in Tunisia. Jewish courts and several Jewish school systems continue to operate. National and local political councils, clinics, and youth groups are also active. Thus, while the vitality of Morocco's Jewish community should not be overstated it does contrast noticeably with that of Tunisia. Among the reasons for these differences are the substantially greater size of Morocco's Jewish community prior to independence and the greater tolerance of Morocco's government toward independent Jewish activity.

Another particular concerns Jews in two small villages on the island of Djerba in southern Tunisia. The island's approximately 1,100 Jews constitute the only Jewish community in North Africa to which the trends noted above do not readily apply. First, this community proudly traces its origins to the destruction of the second Temple and it deliberately remained outside the French colonial experience, maintaining its traditions of religious orthodoxy and an attachment to Arab cultural patterns. Second, it today possesses more than 20 percent of its original number and its population has remained stable in recent years. Some estimates even suggest a population increase. Third, while the community is under the control of a head rabbi and maintains some ties to national Jewish institutions in Tunis, contact with Muslim society is increasing and the community is modernizing within its Tunisian context. Its children attend Tunisian public schools, for example—something virtually unknown among Jews in Tunis—and, ironically, are among the first Djerban Jews to learn French. They are also among the first Djerban Jews to become literate in Arabic. In addition, Jews participate in and benefit from government efforts to promote tourism on Djerba and indeed social change generally has eroded the isolation of the island and fostered Jewish interaction with a broader spectrum of Tunisian society. Finally, in the last few years Muslims have begun to settle in the Jewish villages on Djerba. Thus the situation of Djerban Jewry is different from that of other Jews in the Maghreb and they are today the only potentially viable nonurban Jewish community in North Africa.

In summary, North African Jews have long lived in relative harmony with the majority, yet the structure of both Islam and Judaism has permitted and indeed required a high degree of communal autonomy. Under colonialism, and with the rise of Arabo-Islamic nationalism, distance between Jews and the majority grew. At the same time, Jewish communities prospered and, in the aggregate, became advantaged relative to the majority. Since independence, this situation has changed. Many Jews have migrated from North Africa, and diminishing size reduces the viability of the remaining Jewish communities of the Maghreb. Further, pressures on Jews have been intensified by governmental policies and social change among the majority. But while continuing departures, demographic dislocation, and institutional decay are everywhere visible, there is less of this in Morocco than Tunisia, although in one locality in Tunisia, Djerba, the community is relatively stable and Jewish alienation from Muslim society is not increasing.

We now turn to Arabs in Palestine and Israel. With the end of the second Jewish commonwealth in Roman times, Christianity soon became the dominant religion in Palestine. But Jews continued to live there and, a few centuries later, a Muslim component was added. Arab raiders entered Palestine during Mohammed's lifetime and by the middle of the seventh century the country was part of an Arab empire ruled from Damascus. Jews, for their part, welcomed the Arabs, believing they would fare better under Islam than under Christianity. Yet, despite affinity between the Arabs and Palestine's Semitic population, the spread of Islam and Arabic was not rapid. Christianity remained the religion of the majority until the ninth century and Christians continued to dominate many professions. Aramaic also did not give way to Arabic until the ninth century.

Arabo-Islamic civilization flowered in the years that followed. Palestine was part of empires ruled successively from Iraq, Tunisia, and Egypt; but it was a peripheral province in all of them, contributing little to the arts and sciences of the day and never occupying center stage in the drama of contemporary Middle East history. In Palestine itself, conversion to Islam was growing and the millet system came into existence, with Christians and Jews functioning as semiautonomous communities in the wider Muslim society. The situation of Jews and Christians appears to have been characterized by official toleration and by opportunity at the elite level but by growing pressure from Muslims in the street, especially where minorities appeared to be in a privileged position.

Following the eleventh century, the Arab world entered a period of decline and stagnation from which it did not begin to emerge until the nineteenth century. During these years, Palestine endured the Crusades and then was ruled first by Mamluks from Cairo and thereafter by the Ottoman Turks from Constantinople. The country suffered as much as or more than most other parts of the Arab world. Commercial activity declined. Cultivators were oppressed by Mamluk rulers and by local feudal lords who succeeded them under the Ottomans. Christians, Jews, and Muslims were all affected, although Jews did benefit from a brief renaissance in the early years of Ottoman rule. By the eighteenth century, much land was out of cultivation and the population had declined to as few as 200,000 residents, among them less than 20,000 Jews. There was almost no professional or middle class in Palestine at this time: beyond a small land-owning elite and some ruling officials, the settled population was composed overwhelmingly of agriculturists, artisans, and petty merchants. Finally, Turkish indifference to local feuds fostered a climate of insecurity by permitting Bedouin, Druzes, and others to sack towns and destroy valuable agricultural land.

The present-day character of Palestine began to take shape in the nineteenth and early twentieth centuries with the rise of modern Arabo-Islamic nationalism and Zionism. Arab nationalism emerged first in Egypt, where it had Islamic overtones and was directed against Ottoman rule. Egypt broke away from Ottoman domination early in the nineteenth century and in the 1830s took control of Palestine. But it failed to arouse nationalist feelings in Palestine, probably because of the small middle class and intelligentsia. Another early center of nationalism was Lebanon, and here the contribution of Christian intellectuals made Arabism an ideological pillar in the quest for solidarity. This nationalism also had little significance for Palestine, however. Nationalist activity intensified with the Young Turk revolution and the approach of World War I and for the first time Palestinians did participate in various movements, led in many instances by Lebanese and Syrians based in Egypt or Europe. These Palestinians were not numerous and their presence did not represent any explicitly territorial preoccupation, but most were from leading families and had influence in Palestine beyond their numbers. Their goal was the inclusion of their country in an independent Arab political unit.

Modern Zionism also emerged during this period and organized Jewish migrations from Europe to Palestine began in 1882. By the end of World War I, the number of Jews had risen to 80,000 and almost 100,000 more arrived in the next decade. In addition, international Zionist organizations were established to buy land and promote Jewish settlement in Palestine. Like Arab nationalists, Zionists were often divided about the kind of society they wished to found. But there was wide agreement on the basic objective of creating a homeland oriented toward Judaism and world Jewry.

Following the First World War, the British became the third political force in Palestine, having made conflicting promises to their Arab, Zionist, and French allies during the fighting. To the Arabs they promised independence if the Turks were defeated. To the Zionists they gave assurances of support for a Jewish homeland. To the French they promised cooperation in establishing European spheres of influence. The result was an unhappy compromise: the Arabs obtained nominal independence in Iraq and Transjordan and autonomy in Arabia; France, with British acquiescence, seized Syria and Lebanon; Britain took Egypt and other areas, including Palestine, over which it established a mandate in 1922; the Zionists received temporary British support for continued immigration and assurance that Britain continued to favor the eventual creation of their desired homeland.

During the mandate period, Arab nationalism came of age in Palestine, motivated by resentment against the British and rising fears of Zionism. Local political clubs sprang up and sent representatives to an All-Palestine Congress, which met annually for a number of years. The congress in turn sent representatives to meetings of Arab nationalist organizations outside Palestine. Though Muslims and Christians were both involved in these activities, the Palestinian political elite remained fragmented on the basis of religion, family, and social status. Moreover, the dominant nationalist orientation was pan-Arabist, rather than purely Palestinian in focus. Nevertheless, political agitation became increasingly militant and popular in scope, culminating with a general strike and communal violence in the late 1930s. The Zionists, for their part, were growing in numbers and, like the Arabs, they did everything possible to force concessions from the British. Under these conditions Britain soon lost control and after World War II the newly formed United Nations was asked to deal with the problem. The situation was extremely difficult. Nazi atrocities produced worldwide sympathy for Jews and increased the latter's determination to establish a state of their own. At the same time, Arab nationalism was maturing and independence was coming to most other parts of the Arab world.

In 1947, the United Nations voted to partition Palestine into an Arab state and a Zionist state. The Jews accepted this as giving them "an indispensable minimum." Arabs, on the other hand, argued that the world was paying its debt to the Jews with Arab land and went to war to liberate Palestine. They lost this war, however, and at its conclusion the State of Israel was not only firmly established but in control of some of the land originally proposed for the Arab state. The demographic character of Palestine was also radically altered by the war as thousands of Muslim and Christian Arabs fled their homes. Roughly 800,000 Arabs lived in the territory occupied by Israel prior to its independence; about 160,000 remained after the war. Further, the Arabs who left included almost all of the country's elite and most of its educated middle class. Finally, some Arabs who remained in Israel lost their homes when they fled from one part of the country to another. Thus, within the borders of the new Jewish state was a large number of non-Jews, disorganized, leaderless, cut off from the rest of the Arab world, and poorly prepared for life in a predominantly European-oriented society.

Arabs in Israel have been politically and socially divided on the basis of religion, village, and kinship. About 17 percent of the Arab population is Christian, about 8 percent is Druze, and the rest is Muslim. There are no national organizations serving or representing the whole of the Arab community. The majority of Israel's Arabs live in villages and most villages are dominated by one or more *hamula*, or extended family association. Some believe that Israeli institutions have helped to maintain the *hamula* system. Others believe it is the traditionalism of Arabs themselves that has kept the system intact. In any event, these associations reinforce other divisions in Arab society and have tended to perpetuate conservatism and fragmentation among much of Israel's Arab population.

Although Arabs are, in theory, full citizens of Israel, they are outside the political mainstream. Separation from Jews and domination by them is deeply rooted in most of the country's political and institutional machinery. Unitl 1966, for example, areas inhabited primarily by Arabs were governed by a military administration, which Israel claimed was necessary for security reasons. Arabs and some Jews questioned this and complained that it violated Arab rights. More generally, most Arabs are excluded from military service in Israel and there are also strong taboos against employing Arabs in many of the industries associated with defense. The economic as well as the psychological impact of this is significant. Since these considerations derive at least partly from security concerns, it is important to note that many national organizations are explicitly Jewish and their resources reserved primarily for Jews. This is particularly true of international Zionist agencies. Many have quasi-official status in Israel and perform functions that elsewhere would be carried out by the government. Similarly, almost all political parties have ideologies associated with Judaism and Zionism, and this inevitably discourages Arab identification with them. Finally, some government ministries and other national organizations have separate departments for Arab affairs, which are charged with supervising Arab activities and are almost always run by Jews. Perhaps the best example of this institutional separation is in the field of education. Most Arabs go to all-Arab schools, even in cities where Arabs and Jews both reside. They also study according to a curriculum different from that of Jews, yet carefully regulated by the Arab Department of the Ministry of Education. Although Arabs are permitted to use their own language and study their own history, they claim their schools receive too little money and are far inferior to those of Jews. In any event, the educational system reflects Arab exclusion from the Israeli mainstream and Jewish domination of institutions regulating Arab life.

The Arab community in Israel has been undergoing significant change in recent years and, despite their disadvantaged position relative to Jews, Arabs benefit in many ways from incorporation into Israeli society. Their population has tripled in the last twenty-five years and the Arab birth rate is far higher than that of Jews, causing some Zionists to fear that the greatest threat to Israel's existence as a Jewish state is internal rather than external. Israel's Arabs are also increasingly well educated. Almost all Arab children are today in school, in contrast to less than half in 1947, and Arab illiteracy is lower in Israel than in any Arab country. Other changes are the rapid urbanization and increasing prosperity of the Arab population. In both villages and urban areas, unemployment among Arabs is low, for example, although many jobs involve unskilled labor and are of fixed duration. Also, investment in the Arab sector is limited and villagers must often commute to cities or Jewish towns for work. Nevertheless, wages are high, work is plentiful, and living standards are reasonably high and gradually improving. Finally, Israeli Arabs have considerable political liberty. Freedom of speech and the press are as complete as anywhere. Freedom to organize is more limited and some attempts to build independent political institutions have been suppressed. On the other hand, the Arab-oriented Communist party carries on activities with relatively little interference.

Since 1967, and especially since 1973, changes in Arab society have intensified and assumed greater political significance. After the 1967 Six-Day War, Israel occupied the West Bank and other territories, enabling its own Arab population to interact directly with citizens of Jordan and other Arab countries. The 1973 war was another military victory for Israel. But the Arab countries also had military successes and were the major political beneficiaries of the conflict, producing a surge of confidence in the Arab world. For Israel's Arab population, these experiences have contributed to increasing militancy in the expression of grievances and to institutional development at both the national and local level. An illustration of these tendencies is the growing electoral success of the Israeli Communist party, an anti-Zionist party emerging as a de facto national Arab organization, whose success suggests increasing unity among Israel's traditionally divided Arab population. Local associations with political overtones are also increasing in number and becoming more active. So far as Jews are concerned, these developments have prompted both attempts to suppress and attempts to accommodate Arab demands. The former tendency is illustrated by a recently published secret plan to reduce Arab demographic pressure and political activity in the Galilee. The latter tendency is illustrated by the creation of three major Arab-Jewish study panels in the last two years.

In summary, like Jews, Christians and Muslims are indigenous to Palestine. Indeed, prior to the advent of large-scale Jewish immigration, Muslim and Christian Arabs were the overwhelming majority in Palestine. The Arabs were divided into largely autonomous subcommunities; and because Palestine was one of the less developed parts of the Arab world, its inhabitants had little social mobilization and, until the mandate period, were affected only marginally by Arab nationalism. Arab society did change significantly under the British, but Jews were by then the most modern and well-organized segment of the population and their dominance was assured by the exodus of the Arab majority in 1947-48. In independent Israel, the Arab remnant is fragmented, weak, and disadvantaged in comparison to Jews. Yet Israel's Arabs enjoy many benefits and their situation is changing in many ways. Increasing size and social mobilization, coupled with growing militancy, unity, and institutional strength, have greatly enhanced the influence and political significance of the Arabs in Israel in recent years.

PATTERNS OF ETHNIC CHANGE

Ethnicity is the dependent variable in this analysis. Our general concern is to contribute to an understanding of how and why ethnicity changes. Our specific objective is to suggest whether and how ethnicity is affected by nonassimilating minority status.

To assess ethnic change among Jews in Tunisia and Morocco and Arabs in Israel, we shall examine the attitudes of individual members of these groups. The previously discussed demographic and institutional attributes are also relevant, but these will be treated as specification variables and considered again later when attempting to explain ethnic change. The present section seeks only to describe ethnic change and it focuses on individual orientations toward this end. In Tunisia and Israel the views of urban and nonurban minority group members will be considered separately, since dissimilar patterns of ethnic change are occurring among each subcommunity. In Morocco, all minority group members reside in urban areas.

The attitudinal data for this study were collected through survey research in Tunisia, Morocco, and Israel. Interviews were conducted by the author and several trained assistants between 1973 and 1975. The survey instruments were prepared in collaboration with knowledgeable members of the communities under study and with qualified local social scientists. Standard procedures for assuring the accuracy and comparability of the translations were carried out and the instruments were carefully pretested prior to actual use. Practical and political difficulties prevented the use of random sampling procedures. Thus, in all three countries, stratified quota samples were selected on the basis of age, sex, socioeconomic status, and place of residence. Religion was also a variable of sample stratification in Israel. The sample sizes were small in North Africa: 89 Tunisian Jews and 161 Moroccan Jews were surveyed. In Tunisia, however, Jews were surveyed in Djerba as well as Tunis and, given the small size of the Jewish population, the sample actually represents about 5 percent of the total active adult population. Moreover, a matched sample of Tunisian Muslims was interviewed, providing data with which to determine rigorously whether Jewish attitudes are different from those of other Tunisians. Muslims were matched to Jewish respondents with respect to age, sex, education, income, and place of residence. In Morocco, persons were interviewed in Casablanca, Rabat, Fès, and Meknes and the sample size is about 2 percent of the total active adult population, also a very large proportion for a national survey. In Israel, 348 Israeli Arabs were interviewed. The survey was conducted primarily in the northern part of the country, with interviewing done in Haifa, Acre, Nazareth, Jaffa, Majdel Krum, Miilya, and Shefa Amr. Over-all, the Israeli data base is large and reasonably representative and compares well to the few other national surveys of Israeli Arabs that have been conducted (see Peres 1970; Smooha and Hofman 1976-77.)

One limitation of the data base concerns the obvious difficulty of attempting to assess change with evidence from a single point in time. The solution attempted in this paper is to infer longitudinal variation from cross-sectional variation, asking specifically how the generation of young and well-educated individuals presently coming into the mainstream of society differs from other, more traditional elements within each community. This kind of generational analysis has proved useful in other studies of the Middle East (Tessler 1976a) and appears to be a reasonable, though of course imperfect, basis for drawing conclusions about the ways that values and identities are changing. The tables presenting survey data will thus show the attitudes of younger and better educated respondents and of those who are older and/or less well educated, younger persons being defined as those aged thirty-five or less and better educated respondents being those with at least a high-school education. A second problem results from the political sensitivity of the research and a resultant inability to include on interview schedules all of the questions one might ideally wish to ask. This was not significant in Israel, but it was to some degree in Morocco and was particularly so in Tunisia. In Morocco and Tunisia measures of attitudes toward ethnicity are thus somewhat indirect. Looked at differently, however, it has been possible to collect considerable information under difficult circumstances and these data, despite their limitations, reveal a great deal about the groups under study. Further, the relatively large size of the North African samples and the availability of comparative data on Tunisian Muslims are at least partially compensating factors so far as the validity of conclusions to be drawn from the data are concerned.

We begin with Jews from Tunis, presenting in table 1 their responses and those of matched Muslims to a selection of items from the Tunisian interview schedule. All respondents are divided into two subsets, those under thirty-five who have completed high school and those who are older and/or less well educated. Items in the table are organized into three subject categories: Arab and European culture, Tunisian national identity, and political culture. Since differences between the subsets into which Jewish respondents have been divided are substantial, we may infer that significant ethnic change is occurring. Further, responses to individual items suggest that this change involves a waning of the group's traditional ethnicity and its members' consequent identification with a larger and more diffuse cultural community, one whose population and political center is outside Tunisia. We shall call this pattern of ethnic change "diasporization."

Although interested readers may consult the table for details, we shall outline the major response patterns on which our general conclusion about Jews from Tunis is based. The first set of items, despite a few variations, shows that young and well-educated Jews are more completely oriented toward European culture than other Jews, that similar but smaller differences between respondent categories exist among Muslims, and that differences between Jews and Muslims are greater among young and better educated persons. Jews in Tunis are thus becoming less positively oriented toward the culture of the dominant majority and as a result, despite currents of change in Muslim society, the cultural and psychological distance between these Jews and Tunisia's Arab population is growing. Similarly, cultural differences between Tunisia's urban Jews and Jews in France and elsewhere are diminishing. These conclusions are not surprising, since the Europeanization of Tunisian Jewry has been underway since the colonial period.

Despite a few ambiguities, the second set of items, on national identity, shows that young and better educated Jews are more likely than other Jews to believe that aspects of Arabo-Islamic civilization should be tied to Tunisia's political identity, that among Muslims, young and well-educated respondents are more likely than others to believe that Tunisia's identity should incorporate nonindigenous as well as Arabo-Islamic cultural traditions, and that attitudinal differences between Jews and Muslims are much smaller among young and well-educated individuals than among other persons.

Increasingly assimilated into European culture and believing that Tunisia is and ought to be a country primarily for Arabs and Muslims, Jews in Tunis must inevitably conclude that there is no place for them in the mainstream of Tunisian society. Perhaps a few permit themselves to wonder whether currents operating among the majority will transform Tunisia sufficiently to enable those who are not Arabs and Muslims to share equally in the mission of the state. More probably, however, Jews increasingly are not even concerned about this possibility. They no longer consider themselves as having a permanent stake in Tunisia. Their growing support for a national identity cast in terms of Arabism and Islam reflects an abdication of the Tunisian component of their own ethnicity.

The last group of items, dealing with more explicitly political orientations, shows that, among Jews, the younger and better educated are less able than others to identify political leaders, less likely to feel politically efficacious, and less likely to express attitudes reflecting deference toward political authority. Comparable Muslims are better informed politically, higher in political efficacy, and generally, though not consistently, more negative in their attitudes toward political authority. The trend among Muslims does not auger well for political stability in Tunisia. A modern political culture is forming, but people have growing doubts about their political system (Tessler 1976b). Jews, however, are our principal concern and they are increasingly disinterested in Tunisian politics but not increasingly politically alienated. Jews in Tunis do not appear to be politically insecure, but their identification with the Tunisian political system is low and diminishing and this includes identification with the Tunisian Jewish community.

TABLE 1

RESPONSES TO SELECTED ITEMS OF JEWS AND MATCHED MUSLIMS FROM TUNIS CATEGORIZED BY AGE AND EDUCATION

Item	Jewish Responses		Muslim Responses	
	Young/well educated (N=26)	Others (N=30)	Young/well educated (N=26)	Others (N=30)
	(In percentages)			
Cultural Orientations				
Knows Arabic well	42	70	100	100
Knows English well	73	30	69	33
Does not prefer Western music	29	41	68	81
Does not prefer Western films	4	23	20	30
Does not prefer European cooking	54	70	77	80
More important for a child to respect than love his father	31	65	58	57
A married woman should not go out socially without her husband	30	54	54	86
National Identity				
Public official knowing French but not Arabic is not qualified	80	43	65	52
Unacceptable for French to be more important than Arabic	74	59	92	87
Unimportant for Tunisian pupils to study French history	38	8	37	54
Important for Tunisian pupils to study classical Arab history	65	32	75	75
Mufti plays an important social role	30	17	26	43
Tunisia more like rich Arab country than rich bicultural country	54	19	54	84
Europe has nothing important to learn from the Arabs	45	56	29	26
Political Orientations				
Can identify				
Tunisian cabinet minister	24	32	46	39
Jewish community leader	31	44	12	14
Politics too complicated to understand	32	54	48	59
Has little political influence	70	69	75	63
Must help country at all costs	55	83	88	78
Much respect for profession of government minister	35	46	37	46
Should share wealth with one's community	40	50	46	63
Government does not care about people like respondent	59	57	52	57

Findings are consistent and point to a significant transformation of the ethnic identity of Jews in Tunis. They increasingly identify with European culture, accept and deem appropriate the predominance of Arab and Islamic cultural orientations in Tunisia, and are ignorant about and uninterested in things Tunisian. It is possible that as Tunisian Jewry reconstitutes itself in France and elsewhere, a North African component of its identity will survive and assume greater relative importance. Indeed, we have argued elsewhere that the advent of greater solidarity among Afro-Asian Jews in Israel could be a stimulus for the development of an identifiable "oriental" Jewish ethnicity, which would be based in part on the traditional values of immigrants from the Maghreb (Tessler 1978). But the vast majority of Tunisia's departing Jews have emigrated to France rather than to Israel, and it is more probable that the specificity of European Jews of North African origin will disappear completely in a generation or two. In any event, cultural distinctiveness and communal consciousness are waning among Jews who remain in Tunis. At the same time, these Jews are not assimilating into the mainstream of their host society; they are increasingly identifying with an alien civilization. We believe it is appropriate to characterize this process as diasporization, the replacement of a group's traditional ethnicity by its members' identification with a cultural community outside their homeland.

Table 2 presents responses of Djerban Jews and matched Muslims to the items given in table 1, and a few additional statements pertaining primarily to Jewish-Muslim relations. Our general conclusion about Jews in Djerba is that they are changing less radically than Jews in Tunis but that change is occurring nonetheless, and it is in the direction of greater assimilation into Tunisian society. On the first group of items, Jews are in some cases becoming more strongly oriented toward Arab culture. In other instances, their interest in things European is increasing but no more than among Muslims and/or they remain less positively oriented toward European culture in absolute terms than Muslims.

In the battery on national identity, some statements show that change among Jews involves greater acceptance of the relevance of European culture for Tunisia. But, in most of these instances, Jewish attitudes are changing no more than those of the Muslims, and in absolute terms Jews are more likely than Muslims to accept the primacy of Arabism and Islam. Further, on other items, Jews increasingly attach importance to Arab and Islamic components of Tunisian identity and to Arabo-Islamic traditions generally. Moreover, Muslims are becoming more critical of Arabs and Islamic orientations, making the attitude shifts occurring among Jews that much more striking.

TABLE 2

RESPONSES TO SELECTED ITEMS
OF JEWS AND MATCHED MUSLIMS FROM DJERBA
CATEGORIZED BY AGE AND EDUCATION

	Jewish Responses		Muslim Responses	
	Young/well educated* (N=22)	Others (N=8)	Young/well educated* (N=22)	Others (N=8)
Item	(In percentages)			
Cultural Orientations				
Knows Arabic well	100	100	100	100
Knows English well	5	0	14	0
Does not prefer Western music	95	88	95	100
Does not prefer Western films	55	25	65	50
Does not prefer European cooking	50	75	57	75
More important for a child to respect than love his father	91	100	90	84
A married woman should not go out socially without her husband	91	100	100	100
National Identity				
Public official knowing French but not Arabic is not qualified	77	95	52	57
Unacceptable for French to be more important than Arabic	95	100	73	71
Unimportant for Tunisian pupils to study French history	5	0	61	71
Important for Tunisian pupils to study classical Arab history	53	0	84	100
Mufti plays an important social role	89	83	76	57
Tunisia more like rich Arab country than rich bicultural country	43	29	23	57
Europe has nothing important to learn from the Arabs	71	100	40	0
Political Orientations				
Can identify				
Tunisian cabinet minister	18	0	50	43
Jewish community leader	5	0	10	0
Politics too complicated to understand	73	100	65	86
Has little political influence	64	83	65	57
Must help country at all costs	100	100	95	100
Much respect for profession of government minister	71	88	29	43
Should share wealth with one's community	59	38	71	88
Government does not care about people like respondent	85	100	67	100
Others				
Life is getting better	86	62	82	100
Relations with persons of different religion are good or excellent	62	43	47	40
Muslims should not marry non-Muslims	16	28	20	61

*Given the low levels of education in Djerba, the cutting point for education is primary rather than high school.

The third group of responses shows Jews to be increasingly positively oriented toward political life, both on dimensions of efficacy and knowledge and with respect to attitudes toward system performance. The political orientations of Muslims, on the other hand, are not becoming more positive as consistently or to the same degree, and some responses suggest growing alienation. Thus, while Djerban Jews do not have highly positive political orientations in absolute terms, their attitudes are becoming more civic and supportive and they are generally more politically content than comparable Muslims.

The three additional statements presented to Djerbans show that Djerban Jews have increasingly satisfactory interactions with Muslims and, added to the trends noted above, these response patterns suggest that Jews in Djerba consider themselves to be Tunisian in important respects and are becoming more rather than less well integrated into Tunisian society. Overall, they are more oriented toward the Arab civilization of the dominant majority than toward European civilization, and their personal immersion in Arab culture is increasing, as is their disposition to view Tunisia as a society with an Arab and Islamic identity. They also show increasingly positive and supportive political orientations and have improving relations with non-Jews.

These trends indicate increasing Jewish assimilation into Muslim society. There may be limits to this assimilation, since Judaism is associated with life-style attributes that tend to perpetuate cultural distinctiveness. But Jews are increasingly served by state schools, courts, and the like, and our survey data suggest that the ethnic identity of Djerban Jews is changing and the Tunisian component of that identity is growing rather than diminishing in importance.

Table 3 presents the responses of Moroccan Jews, all from major cities and the majority from Casablanca, where most of Morocco's Jewish population currently resides. Items from the Moroccan interview schedule are divided into five categories and responses show, in general, that Moroccan Jews are experiencing the same kind of ethnic change as Jews in Tunis. The North African component of their ethnicity is diminishing and communal consciousness is given way to a more general self-image based on identification with the European culture.

Responses to the first statements show that age and education are strongly associated with cultural orientations. As among urban Jews in Tunisia, identification with Arab culture is diminishing and assimilation of European cultural patterns is on the rise. Responses to the second battery of items also parallel those of Jews in Tunis: increasing support for Arabization, increasing importance attached to the study of Arab history, and a declining belief that European civilization is superior to Arab civilization.

TABLE 3

RESPONSES TO SELECTED ITEMS
OF MOROCCAN JEWS
CLASSIFIED BY AGE AND EDUCATION

Item	Young/well educated (N=63)	Others (N=98)
	(In percentages)	
Cultural Orientations		
Knows Arabic well	35	49
Does not prefer French language radio and TV programs	5	11
Does not prefer Western music	13	33
Regularly reads newspapers from France	54	39
Muslims should practice their religion as did their fathers and grandfathers	40	67
A married woman should not go out socially without her husband	57	84
Children should be encouraged to think for themselves, even if they occasionally disobey their parents	95	73
National Identity		
Favors Arabization policies	38	26
Unimportant for Moroccan pupils to study French history	45	28
Important for Moroccan pupils to study classical Arab history	49	39
Arabs should learn moral principles from Europe	21	31
Europe has nothing important to learn from the Arabs	46	73
Relations with Non-Jews		
Has few Muslim friends	82	74
Relations with non-Jews are good or excellent	34	40
The principal mission of Moroccan Jewish institutions is to facilitate emigration	39	28
Political Orientations		
Can identify Moroccan cabinet minister	21	36
Frequently asked to explain political events	67	54
Has little political influence	36	57
Punishments of Moroccan courts are too severe	70	55
Reads opposition newspaper regularly	52	31
Government does not care about people like respondent	62	50
Sense of Community		
Does not eat nonkosher food	67	76
Strictly observes the Sabbath	17	30
Moroccan Jews are not sufficiently religious	50	66
Prefers European to Moroccan Jewish cooking	23	11
There are important cultural differences between Moroccan Jews and French Jews	34	43
Participates in Jewish community affairs	33	47
Can identify Jewish community leader	33	41
Strongly opposes Jews marrying non-Jews	27	46
Religious affiliation will not influence respondent's future	51	40

As in Tunis, Jews are becoming more European in thought and behavior and more likely to believe that non-Jewish Moroccans should assert their Arabo-Islamic identity. The third section reinforces this interpretation, showing that Jewish involvement with Muslims and Muslim society is diminishing.

The change in political orientations involves declining political information and interest, increasing political efficacy, and a rise in dissatisfaction with the government. The latter trend, which was not noted among Jews in Tunis, suggests that Jews still care about politics in Morocco. But, in general, they are clearly moving toward the kind of political marginality observed in Tunis, and growing discontent can only further weaken their ties to Moroccan society.

A final category of items deals with religious and communal orientations and reveals similar patterns of change. Responses show a decline in the observance of Jewish ritual and law as well as a decline in interest, participation, and support for the Jewish community and its institutions.

Table 3 suggests that the future of Morocco's Jewish community as a distinctive and viable ethnic group is in serious doubt. Ethnic change involves movement away from communal consciousness and toward identification on an individual basis with European society, a pattern we have characterized as diasporization. Its members increasingly think of themselves as belonging to a more diffuse cultural tradition, whose population and political centers are outside their homeland.

We turn now to urban Arabs in Israel and their responses in table 4 to selected items from the Israeli interview schedule. Today, 35 to 40 percent of Israel's Arabs live in cities and, in the present study, respondents are drawn in approximately equal proportions from the mixed Arab-Jewish cities of Haifa, Jaffa, and Acre and the all-Arab city of Nazareth. Differences asssociated with the two types of urban setting are rarely significant, though a few exceptions are noted in the table. Items in the table are divided into five categories: cultural orientation, communal solidarity, relations with Jews, political orientation, and communal identity. The last category, which has not been employed previously, contains items that ask about the content of a respondent's ethnicity—about his identification as either Israeli or Palestinian. The general conclusion about urban Arabs suggested by respondent attitudes is that substantial ethnic change is underway and that it involves increasing communal solidarity, political consciousness, and identification with the nationalism of a neighboring people. We characterize this as a kind of irredentism.

The obvious and uncontroversial conclusion to be drawn from

TABLE 4

RESPONSES TO SELECTED ITEMS
OF ISRAELI ARABS RESIDING IN CITIES
CLASSIFIED BY AGE AND EDUCATION

Item	Young/well educated (N=97)	Others (N=162)
	(In percentages)	
Cultural Orientations		
Not prefer Arab music	64	36
Important for Arab pupils to study European history	58	36
People of respondent's religion should observe their religion as did their fathers and grandfathers	6*	21
Children should be encouraged to think for themselves, even if they occasionally disobey their parents	80	54
A married woman should not go out socially without her husband	41	52
Sense of Community		
Religious affiliation defines respondent's identity very little	49	26
Muslims, Christians, and Druzes have few common concerns	21	34
Acceptable for Arabs of different religions to marry	65	49
Hamula plays negative political role	96	88
Is active in clubs and social groups	40	12
Can identify Arab political leader	55	41
Relations with Non-Arabs		
Relations with non-Arabs good or excellent	39**	48
Would oppose relative marrying a Jew	58*	73
Does not feel more comfortable in Arab country than in Israel	34	56
Political problems cause Arabs to leave Israel	56	33
A major reason for discrimination against Arabs in Israel is that Jews do not like Arabs	62	47
Political Orientations		
Can identify Jewish political leader	81	67
Reads Hebrew language paper regularly	70	18
Frequently asked to explain political events	77	54
Arab political leaders in Israel unqualified	88	68
Arabs poorly represented in Israeli politics	95	77
Arabs make more political progress in Israel than in Egypt or Jordan	24	39
Communal Identity		
Prefers radio and TV programs from Arab countries to those from Israel	50	31
Term "Israeli" does not characterize respondent well	56*	49
Meeting people from West Bank makes respondent feel more Arab rather than more Israeli	67	52
Considers self represented by Arabs outside Israel	50*	37
A major reason for discrimination against Arabs in Israel is that Israel is a state for Jews	80	60
Might move to Palestinian state if one established alongside Israel	69*	57
Might be active in political life of Palestinian state if one established alongside Israel	82	60

*Difference between respondent categories is large only in mixed Arab-Jewish cities
**Difference between respondent categories is large only in Nazareth

the first category of items is that social change is eroding long-standing cultural patterns and making people more receptive to nonindigenous values. The second set of responses indicates a growing sense of community among urban Arabs in Israel. Traditionally, Arabs in Palestine and Israel have been fragmented on the bases of family, village, and religion. Today, however, parochial loyalties are giving way to an expanding locus of social solidarity. Thus the modification of traditional cultural values is paralleled by an evolution of political identity.

The next two sections reveal that urban Arabs are increasingly dissatisfied with their relations with Jews and that they are becoming increasingly politically militant. Responses to the fifth group of statements suggests several additional trends: first, the state of Israel is declining as a focus for Arab identity; second, urban Arabs in Israel are increasingly aware of themselves as Arabs; third, there is increasing willingness to identify with and participate in the life of a Palestinian Arab state, should one eventually be established alongside Israel. Taken together, these trends suggest that urban Arabs see themselves more and more as belonging to the Arab world and not to Israel.

To sum up, ethnic change among urban Arabs in Israel involves an expansion of the traditional locus of communal identity and an increase in boundaries separating minority and majority. Like the urban Jews in North Africa, members of the minority are coming to regard themselves as foreigners in their country of residence, although to a considerable extent this has been the position of Israeli Arabs since 1948 and what is changing is concern for the situation rather than the situation itself. What particularly sets the experience of urban Arabs in Israel apart from that of urban Jews in North Africa, however, is the growing integration of the former, their identification with an external civilization on a communal rather than an individual basis—maintaining a subjectively important subcultural identity, probably as Palestinians—and their increasingly militant insistence that the dominant majority find a way to accommodate its own desires for nation-building with concern for the aspirations of the minority. As mentioned, these sentiments involve a kind of irredentism.

Using the same statements as in table 4, table 5 presents the responses of Arabs from three villages: one Muslim, one Christian, and one composed of both Muslims and Christians. These data show that among nonurban Arabs there is growing communal solidarity coupled with improving relations with the dominant majority and its political system. This pattern, characterized by increased identification with both Israel and a distinct Israeli Arab subcommunity, is familiar to students of cultural pluralism and is sometimes referred to as "communalism" or "communalization" (Deutsch 1953; Melson and Wolpe 1971; Cohen 1972; Young 1976).

TABLE 5

RESPONSES TO SELECTED ITEMS OF ISRAELI ARABS
RESIDING IN VILLAGES
CLASSIFIED BY AGE AND EDUCATION

Item	Young/well educated (N=36)	Others (N=53)
	(In percentages)	
Cultural Orientations		
Not prefer Arab music	39	33
Important for Arab pupils to study European history	68	40
People of respondent's religion should observe their religion as did their fathers and grandfathers	13	27
Children should be encouraged to think for themselves, even if they occasionally disobey their parents	83	47
A married woman should not go out socially without her husband	29	59
Sense of Community		
Religious affiliation defines respondent's identity very little	42	23
Muslims, Christians, and Druzes have few common conerns	10	27
Acceptable for Arabs of different religions to marry	40	39
Hamula plays negative political role	93	80
Is active in clubs and social groups	30	11
Can identify Arab political leader	52	39
Relations with Non-Arabs		
Relations with non-Arabs good or excellent	35	45
Would oppose relative marrying a Jew	61	84
Does not feel more comfortable in Arab country than in Israel	57	64
Political problems cause Arabs to leave Israel	65	54
A major reason for discrimination against Arabs in Israel is that Jews do not like Arabs	55	66
Political Orientations		
Can identify Jewish political leader	89	59
Reads Hebrew language paper regularly	74	44
Frequently asked to explain political events	84	53
Arab political leaders in Israel unqualified	70	59
Arabs poorly represented in Israeli politics	63	69
Arabs make more political progress in Israel than in Egypt or Jordan	50	39
Communal Identity		
Prefers radio and TV programs from Arab countries to those from Israel	42	45
Term "Israeli" does not characterize respondent well	26	26
Meeting people from West Bank makes respondent feel more Arab rather than more Israeli	58	56
Considers self represented by Arabs outside Israel	33	17
A major reason for discrimination against Arabs in Israel is that Israel is a state for Jews	70	77
Might move to Palestinian state if one established alongside Israel	71	73
Might be active in political life of Palestinian state if one established alongside Israel	79	83

Village residents respond to the first two batteries of items as do residents of urban areas. Cultural differences between respondent categories are greater than among city dwellers, suggesting that traditional values are changing even more rapidly among villagers. Changes are smaller and less consistent with respect to communal solidarity and the transcendence of traditional political affiliations, but parochial loyalties are also giving way and a more inclusive communal identity is forming.

Responses to the third and fourth item categories do not show the differences between respondents noted among urban Arabs. Relations between Arabs and Jews are not deteriorating and political dissatisfaction is not increasing. Indeed change is sometimes in the opposite direction. With respect to political information and competence the trend is similar to that of urban Arabs. Not being motivated by dissatisfaction, however, this does not indicate growing militancy but rather reflects only general cultural change and political modernization. Residents of Arab villages in Israel are thus expanding the locus of their social relations and communal loyalties, incorporating elements of Israeli society generally as well as of the sectors of Israel's Arab population with which they have traditionally had little association.

It is going too far to suggest that "Israeliness" is becoming a focus of identity for nonurban Arabs. Nevertheless, responses to the last group of items do reveal limited movement in this direction. The proportion of people unwilling to describe themselves as "Israeli" is relatively low and not increasing, and there is some movement toward rejection of the proposition that Arabs are discriminated against because Israel is a state for Jews. Further, identification with the Arab world and the Palestinian cause is not increasing. Thus, to the extent the transcendence of local identities continues and establishes the primacy of an ethnicity based on bonds among Israeli Arabs in general, the political and ideological arena of Israel rather than the larger Arab world will provide the context for these developments, assuring an Israeli component to the community's identity.

It is doubtful that a specifically "Israeli Arab" communal identity can endure in the long run. Increasing interaction between village Arabs and both Jews and urban Arabs with differing views will probably modify the orientations of the villagers. Also, the evolution of the Arab-Israeli dispute in its international context seems destined to increase the Palestinian consciousness of all Arabs of Palestinian origin (Tessler 1977). Nonetheless, for the present, ethnic change among village Arabs in Israel is characterized by improving social and political relations with the majority and a willingness to see Arab ethnicity evolve in an Israeli context. In sum, village Arabs are experiencing a modernization and expansion of their communal identity, increasingly regarding themselves as a distinct ethnic group and seeking to take their place in a society they are coming to regard as open and pluralistic. We have borrowed the term "communalism" to characterize this pattern of ethnic adaptation.

EXPLAINING ETHNIC CHANGE

The aspects of ethnic change on which our data enable us to comment are of course limited. We have focused principally on cultural preferences, communal solidarity, relations with the dominant majority, and attitudes toward the national political system. These considerations by no means exhaust the list of orientations relevant to ethnicity and ethnic change. Still, having to do with cultural traits, self identification, and group boundaries, they reside at or reasonably near the core of a group's ethnic identity. In the present section, we turn to a comparison of the cases, our objective being to develop generalizable insights about the relationship between nonassimilating minority status and ethnic change.

Since different patterns of ethnic change have been observed, the only proposition that may be advanced about nonassimilating minority status in general is that is produces instability so far as ethnicity is concerned. Movement related to ethnicity was noted in all cases examined, and thus we may hypothesize that circumstances common to the groups consistently lead to ethnic change of one kind or another. On the other hand, no single pattern of ethnic change seems particularly likely to occur in response to nonassimilating minority status. Even among the specific orientations examined—cultural affinity with the dominant majority, minority-majority relations, political satisfaction, and communal solidarity—there is no area in which the same kind of change was observed in every instance. Thus, to carry forward theoretical inquiry, it is necessary to determine the conditions under which nonassimilating minority status is associated with different kinds of ethnic variation, in effect to identify specification variables in the relationship between nonassimilating minority status and ethnic change.

Two underlying dimensions give conceptual unity to the observed patterns of ethnic change. The first dimension involves individual community identification: whether or not individual ties to a group are becoming stronger or weaker, of greater or lesser importance to the group's members. The second dimension involves internalism-externalism in systemic identification: whether a group's most salient sociopolitical attachment is to its host society or whether it views itself as an extension of a social system external to that society. Taken together, these dimensions permit observations about the significance of a group to its members and about the larger social and political system of which the group is seen as a part. In the present instance, our data reveal movement within each group on both dimensions. In addition, there is intergroup variation in the kind of movement taking place on each dimension. Finally, since intergroup variation in both cases pertains primarily to direction rather than rate of change, the two dimensions may be dichotomized with little loss of information. The result of juxtaposing the dichotomized dimensions is a typology of four varieties of ethnic change, each corresponding to a pattern noted among the groups studied. Figure 1 presents this graphically, showing possible combinations of the dichotomized dimensions and listing the pattern and group to which each combination corresponds.

Though inductively derived, this classification neatly organizes the variance observed. Even more significant, it provides a conceptual foundation for thinking about that variance. Instead of dealing with arbitrary designations attached to idiosyncratic patterns, the labels are given conceptual definitions in terms of dimensions relevant to all four patterns. Finally, the classification offers a partial response to inquiries about the

		Individual Community Identification	
		Increasing	Decreasing
Systemic Identification	Internal	Communalism: Village Arabs in Israel	Assimilation: Jews in Djerba
	External	Irredentism: Urban Arabs in Israel	Diasporization: Urban Jews in Tunisia and Morocco

Fig. 1. A Two-dimensional Classification of Ethnic Change

range of ways ethnicity can vary. It is not complete. The incorporation of other dimensions, as well as the refinement of ratings on those employed, will be necessary if other aspects of ethnicity are analyzed or if the study of additional groups reveals new forms of ethnic change. Nevertheless, it does suggest that ethnic change among nonassimilating minorities, and among other groups, too, in all probability, can be understood in terms of interrelated variation on a few important conceptual dimensions. In the present study, we have found that nonassimilating minority status leads to one of at least four possible kinds of ethnic change: diasporization, assimilation, irredentism, communalism. Each involves a different combination of changes in the growth or diminution of individual attachments to the group and in the location of the broader system of which the group is considered a part.

Individual community identification is increasing among Arabs in Israel. It is decreasing among Jews in Tunisia and Morocco, including Jews in Djerba. Characteristics of the Israeli examples that appear determinative are the relatively large size of the minority, the minority's traditionally low level of institutional complexity, its disadvantaged socioeconomic position relative to the majority, and the host society's high level of development. These factors set the Israeli cases apart from those of North Africa, where communal solidarity is declining rather than increasing, and define a context in which community identification tends to grow stronger. For this to occur, a group must be large enough to constitute a viable unit. The absence of well-developed traditional institutions, reflecting a weak and comparatively easily surpassed base for traditional identities, also appears to be a prerequisite. Finally, when individuals are aware of the privileges of others and in contact with technological and organizational modes more complex than their own, the result is apparently a kind of communal competition that increases ethnic solidarity and stimulates community development.

The decline of community identification among North African Jews appears to be encouraged by the small relative size of the minority, by its advantaged socioeconomic position, and by the fact that the majority is comparatively traditional but experiencing social mobilization. All of these attributes characterize the situation of North African Jewry and differentiate it from that of Arabs in Israel. Size is very important. Without meaningful numbers, a group cannot maintain the activities and institutions necessary to make it a significant focus for communal identification. The advantaged position of North African Jewry is particularly striking in urban areas, and this too is significant. The minority may move away from a strong and visible ethnic identity in order to minimize resentment by the majority. For the community as a whole, this involves carrying out a declining number of the activities necessary to promote solidarity. For the individual, it involves attempts to disassociate oneself from popular stereotypes about a privileged minority. In North Africa, resentment against Jews is based not only on cultural and economic disparities, but is compounded by Arab concern about possible Jewish sympathies for Israel and by past Jewish support for colonialism. Finally, social mobilization among a traditional majority also contributes to these tendencies. It raises popular expectations more rapidly than they can be satisfied, thereby inducing both negative feelings about those with privileges and a search for scapegoats on whom to vent frustration. A small group considered external to the mission of the state is particularly resented and vulnerable in this situation. Thus, in the final analysis, small size, minority privilege, and social mobilization among a traditional majority reinforce one another and define a context in which the members of a nonassimilating minority are encouraged to limit personal identification with their community.

Externalism in systemic identification is growing among urban Jews in Tunisia and Morocco and among urban Arabs in Israel. Each group, despite differences among them, is increasingly looking beyond the borders of the host society for its social and political identity, viewing itself and its members as part of a social system external to the society of the dominant majority. The present study suggests that this focus of systemic identification tends to occur in urban but not village settings or, in more conceptual terms, when minority exposure to members and institutions of the dominant majority is regular and intense and when levels of social mobilization are high, increasing political consciousness and providing information about potential reference groups beyond the national borders. In other words, nonassimilating minority status tends to externalize the systemic identification of a group when its members are keenly aware of their inferior political position and informed about their potential affinity with groups or cultural units in other countries.

Internalism in systemic identification, which ought to be the more normal situation, appears to occur among nonassimilating minorities only under certain conditions, when the minority is relatively isolated and traditional. Among both Jews in Djerba and village Arabs in Israel, contact with the dominant majority is far from absent and social mobilization is taking place. But, in both respects, levels are far lower than among minority group members in urban areas. Thus, though intensified social mobilization might in the future produce externalism in systemic identification among nonurban groups, our data suggest that a tendency to view a group and its members as part of the domestic system will prevail as long as contact with the majority remains somewhat limited and levels of social mobilization are below a critical threshhold.

To sum up, we may combine these observations and offer testable generalizations about the conditions under which nonassimilating minority status leads to each of the patterns of ethnic change that has been discerned.

1. Nonassimilating minority status tends to produce the diasporization of ethnic identity when a minority is small, high in social mobilization, and in a privileged position relative to the dominant majority, when the majority is comparatively traditional but experiencing rapid

social mobilization, and when interaction between the minority and majority is intense.

2. Nonassimilating minority status tends to produce ethnic assimilation when a minority is small, traditionally low in social mobilization, and comparable to the majority in socioeconomic position, and when there is moderate social mobilization among both majority and minority and regular but not intense contact between the two.

3. Nonassimilating minority status tends to produce irredentism with respect to ethnicity when a minority is large, without a well-developed institutional base, fairly high in social mobilization but nonetheless disadvantaged relative to the majority, in regular and intense contact with the majority, and aware of external groups with which its affinity may be significant.

4. Nonassimilating minority status tends to produce communalism as a form of ethnic adaptation when a minority is reasonably large, without a significant institutional base, and in a relatively disadvantaged socioeconomic position, and when it has a fairly low level of social mobilization and its contact with the dominant majority is limited rather than intense.

In concluding, the limitations of our categories and propositions should be acknowledged and directions for future research should be pointed out. First, as mentioned earlier, the patterns of ethnic change considered in this study do not exhaust the ways that ethnicity can vary. The literature on ethnicity suggests additional dimensions and patterns and some of these are undoubtedly relevant to nonassimilating minorities. Further, though not encountered in the present study, there may be conditions under which ethnicity remains stable for lengthy periods among nonassimilating minorities. Finally, it is important to determine not only the kinds of ethnic change that take place but the relative frequency with which each occurs. Our findings about determinants of certain patterns provide a base for predicting whether any is likely to occur in a particular instance, but we have not inquired about the the general distribution of cases across the categories of our classification. All of these concerns relating to our dependent variable are topics for future research. Our classification was inductively derived from the study of a small number of nonassimilating minorities. It should be refined and the empirical significance of each category assessed by examining additional groups.

Limitations concerning specification variables in our analysis must also be acknowledged. It is possible that the most significant conditions affecting the relationship between nonassimilating minority status and ethnic change have not been consistently identified. There are many attributes that differentiate among groups experiencing dissimilar kinds of ethnic change, a situation compounded by the small number of cases considered, and this forces us to make informed but ultimately subjective judgments about which are significant and which are not. In addition, we are required to infer causation when only associations are discernible. These limitations are inherent in the quest for social theory through comparative analysis at the societal level. But replication, involving the study of other groups by researchers with different values and preconceptions, will do much to increase confidence in the proposed relationships or, if appropriate, to stimulate their reformulation.

Finally, pertaining to nonassimilating minority status, our independent variable, the present study has employed a case-study methodology and examined only groups residing in a particular situation. It is not impossible that under appropriate conditions groups that are not nonassimilating minorities exhibit the same patterns of ethnic change that we have noted among groups that are, and thus we are again inferring causal relationships from observed associations with little control of extraneous variance. This concern confirms again the importance of future research. To the extent possible, comparative studies of nonassimilating and other minority groups should be carried out.

These limitations can rarely be resolved in a single study or by a single investigator. Thus, like this volume as a whole, our objective is not to provide definitive answers but to focus attention on important questions pertaining to ethnic change and to make a start in dealing with these questions by offering tentative answers and an approach to inquiry that may aid and encourage subsequent investigation. In the present study, we have sought in particular to explore the theoretical possibilities for an investigation of ethnic change among groups in a specific social and political position, and toward this end empirical data on a number of groups have been collected and analyzed and several testable propositions about the relationship between nonassimilating status and ethnic change have been derived. If confirmed, these insights will contribute significantly to our understanding of how and why ethnicity changes. In the meantime, as with the results from any single study, they should be considered tentative.

POSTSCRIPT 1979

The data on which the preceding analysis is based were collected between 1972 and 1975 and the analysis itself was prepared early in 1977. But Jews in Tunisia and Morocco and Arabs in Israel have experienced changes since the research for this paper was completed, and return visits to North Africa and Israel in 1979 make it possible to offer a summary of recent developments in each community by way of a postscript.

Among urban Jews in Tunisia and Morocco, the trend toward diasporization continues. In Tunisia, the urban Jewish community has dwindled to approximately four thousand individuals, with almost all Jews now living in Tunis and its suburbs, and many of those who remain are already preparing for eventual departure. Emigration in recent years has been particularly high among younger Jews, making the demographic distribution of the remaining community even more skewed than it was as little as five years ago. This is important because it bears out projections about declining communal solidarity that were offered earlier and because it suggests that, with an increasingly older and inactive population, the viability of Tunisian Jewish society will decline even more in the future. In addition, the atrophy of communal institutions adds to the weakness of Jewish society and encourages its members to seek an alternative focus for ethnic identity, contributing further to diasporization. Finally, Jews feel increasingly unwelcome in Tunisia, as the country intensifies its identification with inter-Arab politics. In this connection, the installation of the Arab League in Tunis in 1979 appeared particularly significant to Jews, and a related development is that not only are local Jews uneasy but far fewer departed Jews now living in France visit Tunisia than in the past. These trends suggest that within a generation, perhaps less, it will not be possible to think of the Jews of urban Tunisia as constituting a coherent community and that, barring radical and unlikely changes in Tunisian society generally, a Jewish presence dating back at least to Roman times will have virtually have come to an end, leaving as its remnant no more than a few unconnected individuals and families.

All of these trends are in evidence in Morocco as well as Tunisia. The Jewish population of Morocco was approximately twenty-five thousand in 1973 but it is now reliably estimated to be under seventeen thousand. Jewish schools and other community institutions are also gradually shutting down, suggesting that Moroccan Jewry is going the way of urban Jewry in Tunisia, and that earlier projections about declining communal viability and solidarity are again being borne out. A reasonable guess is that it will take about fifteen to twenty years for Moroccan Jewry to reach the demographic and institutional weakness of the urban Jewish community of Tunisia at the present time.

It is possible, of course, that forces operating in the broader Moroccan society could intervene, either to speed up or retard this evolution, and indeed Morocco has had fairly significant fluctuations of national policy in matters that bear on the status of its Jewish citizens. The country sent troops to fight Israel in the 1973 war, an event that created some local antipathy toward Jews; but the government began a policy of rapprochement toward Jews after 1975, issuing statements about Arab-Jewish cooperation and making overtures to foreign as well as local Jews. Prominent American Jews and even some Israeli officials visted Morocco in 1976, for example, and local Jews were visibly involved in arranging and hosting these visits. The Moroccan government also launched a campaign to encourage the return of departed Moroccan Jews, which had little success but which nonetheless made the Jews remaining in Morocco feel more secure. Nevertheless, Jewish emigration and institutional decay continued during this period, as they did at earlier historical junctures during which official policy was favorably disposed toward Jews. Moreover, the recent Moroccan overture toward Jews has been motivated more by a desire to win international and especially American support for the country's war in the Sahara than by a sincere interest in Arab-Jewish understanding; and in fact the relative psychological security about which Jews were talking in 1976 and 1977 had largely disappeared by 1979, in part because U.S. support for Morocco's Saharan initiative had not yet materialized but especially because of growing domestic opposition to many government policies, which were deemed responsible for the serious gap between rich and poor. In any event, Jews in 1979 tended to view their relations with Moroccan society as problematic; and even if Morocco's interest in improved Arab-Jewish relations were to continue, it is unlikely that the direction of ethnic change among Jews would be modified appreciably or that the rate of this change, this diasporization, would be slowed more than a little.

Jews of North African origin in both France and Israel have made some effort to establish organizations to give expression to their common heritage. Thus it is possible that the end result of diasporization among North African Jewry will not be identification on an individual basis with a society and civilization external to the countries in which they live, or from which they came, and that once they have left the diaspora, as it were, new forces will come into play to reinvigorate an ethnic identity that was in the process of disappearing while they were still in the Maghreb. Actually, this possibility seems somewhat remote. In Israel, solidarity among Jews of North African origin is limited and represents more of a class than an ethnic or cultural phenomenon. In France, although many older Jews, especially those of Tunisian origin, retain an active interest in their traditional culture, young Jews of Tunisian or Moroccan origin increasingly think of themselves as Frenchmen, in the same way as do the children of Jewish families that have been in France for several generations. Regardless of the ethnic response of North African Jews to their new social and political circumstances, however, urban Jews who are still in the Maghreb are continuing to experience diasporization. The solidarity of their communities is diminishing, identification with their host societies is low and decreasing, and the result is a focus for ethnic identity that is extenal to both. Moreover, it appears that in the social and political context within which urban Jews in Tunisia and Morocco reside, a context defined by nonassimilating minority status, a privileged socioeconomic position, and small numbers, diasporization is an unstable state that tends to produce emigration.

Ethnic change among urban Arabs in Israel was earlier characterized as involving irredentism, reflecting both growing communal solidarity and increasing ethnic and political identification with an emerging Palestinian nationalism. As with urban Jews in North Africa, this trend has intensified since field work for the present study was completed. In the last few years social and political movements uniting Muslim and Christian Arabs have grown substantially, and more recently Druzes have begun to affiliate with these movements as well. Moreover, there has been a marked increase in political militancy among Arabs in Israel, giving expression to discontent with their status as an involuntary and nonassimilating minority. Arabs strongly believe they receive far less than their fair share of national resources, principally because Israel regards itself, first and foremost, as a state for Jews. This militancy is evident in growing tension and hostility between Arabs and Jews in Israel and in significant attempts by Arabs to fashion national political institutions that will enable them to articulate their grievances and defend their interests more effectively. Finally, the identification of these Arabs with the politics and society of a broader Palestinian community is also increasing. Although historically Palestinian, this identification had little conscious ideological content during the early years of Israeli independence and thus remained more latent than manifest. Even as recently as five years ago, when the research for this study was being conducted, a sense of Palestinian identity was only beginning to crystallize among urban Arabs and public professions of this identity were unusual and controversial. Today, however, Israel's Arabs have a widespread sense of belonging to a greater Palestinian nation and many define their politics as well as their ethnicity in these terms, openly supporting the Palestinian Liberation Organization, for example. Growing communal solidarity, heightened political militancy, and an increasingly clear Palestinian identification among Israel's Arabs are leading some Jewish Israelis to conclude that there is a coming crisis in Arab-Jewish relations in Israel. There are also reasons to hope that this crisis can be avoided. One hopeful sign is the Egypt-Israel peace initiative, which began at the end of 1977 and has involved through 1979 increased normalization between Israel and its most important Arab neighbor. But, in any event, the projections offered earlier have clearly been borne out, suggesting that nonassimilating minority status and the other contextual factors structuring the social situation of Arabs in Israel do indeed lead to irredentism.

While the direction of ethnic change among urban Arabs remains the same, the rate of this change has been more rapid than might have been projected a few years ago. The reasons for this include decreased attention to Arab grievances by the Israeli government, especially with the election in 1977 of the first non-Labor government since independence; related government policies involving the appropriation of much Arab land, with the objective, moreover, of using it for the development of Jewish towns and Jewish agricultural settlements; and international considerations, including growing recognition of the P.L.O. and of the need to find a national solution to the Palestinian problem and increasing contact between Arabs in Israel and Palestinians residing in the territories Israel captured in the 1973 war and has administered since that time. The rather obvious general lesson to be learned from these events is that when the conditions for irredentism are present, the rate of ethnic change intensifies as the social and political distance between a nonassimilating minority and its host society grows and as contact between the minority and the society that is the object of its irredentist sentiments increases.

Earlier projections involving a pattern of ethnic change described as communalism for the village Arabs in Israel are in need of modification. The possibility that the irredentism characterister of unban Arabs would spread to Arabs in the villages was raised previously and this is in fact coming to pass. This is not to say that positive orientations toward Israeli society were not increasing earlier, interacting with growing communal solidarity to produce the communalization of ethnic identity, the view, in other words, that the Arabs constitute a coherent ethnic community within a broader and essentially multiethnic Israeli society. Indeed, despite the contradiction with Israel's self-proclaimed Jewish character, this is in principle the attitude of the Israeli government toward its Arab citizens. They are regarded as a separate community that is encouraged to develop its own culture and civilization, within the framework of a society that is dedicated to pluralism and democracy, as well as to the fulfillment of its special mission to Judaism and to the Jews. But while ethnic change within rural Arab society was for a time in conformity with this official view, as very possibly it was among urban Arabs as well at an even earlier period following Israeli independence, the contradictions of Arab life in the Jewish state have increasingly come to the fore. Like urban Arabs, village Arabs in Israel appear to be increasingly unfavorably oriented toward Israeli society, increasingly politically militant and mobilized, and increasingly likely to identify in their politics and their ethnicity with Palestinian nationalism. In short, village Arabs are increasingly experiencing the irredentist pattern of ethnic change that was observable among urban Arabs at an earlier period. These developments suggest as a generalization that nonassimilating minority status may be unlikely to produce communalism as a permanent and stable pattern of ethnic change and that, in most cases at least, the built-in political marginality of nonassimilating minorities will eventually lead away from increased communal solidarity coupled with a growing identification with the host society.

The factors that have modified the direction of ethnic change among village Arabs in Israel derive from those that have accelerated the rate of change among urban Arabs. Most notable is the increasing alienation of Arab land by the state, which naturally is felt with force among a village population that has traditionally been tied to agriculture. In this respect, March 1976 was a watershed for Arabs in Israel, that being a time of national demonstrations on what became known as "Land Day." These demonstrations were part of an Arab response to the government's announcement of new land seizures, to accelerate Jewish development in the country's northern Galilee region. The creation of new, national political institutions, which have won adherents in the villages to a much greater extent than existing Arab political organizations, was another part of the legacy of Land Day. Related to the issue of land has been the government's failure, or at least its inability, to create an economic infrastructure in most Arab villages. This means that villages tend to be economically underdeveloped and that, with the increasing loss of agricultural land, most residents must commute to the cities or to Jewish agricultural settlements to find work. The result has been an increase in both political discontent and contact with Jews and with urban Arabs, all of which has eroded the traditional autonomy and isolation of many villages and initiated currents of ethnic change comparable to those already existing among urban Arabs.

The situation of Jews in Djerba, North Africa's only remaining Jewish community that is not highly urbanized, is difficult to assess. Ethnic change appears to have proceeded more slowly than might have been expected six or seven years ago, yet the pressures for change remain very much present and the community seems to be moving toward an important social and political transition. Based on data from an earlier period, it was observed that communal solidarity was declining and that Djerban Jews were increasingly oriented toward their host society, which led to the proposition that ethnic change involved limited but nonetheless significant assimilation. With respect to communal solidarity, however, the community has exhibited considerable staying power. The size of the community, based on two neighboring villages with only limited interaction, has remained fairly constant since the research for this study was originally carried out. Equally important, community institutions, such as schools, synagogues, and a clinic, continue to operate, even though many appeared on the verge of closing when the community was first visited in 1972. In the principal Jewish village, there is also a small religious printing house that publishes work in Judeo-Arabic and in Hebrew, and a Yeshiva for the training of rabbis. Thus, with its religious and educational institutions still operating and its population not yet substantially diminshed, the community retains a considerable measure of autonomy and cohesion. On the other hand, Jewish emigration from Djerba is increasing, with the number of departures beginning to exceed the community's natural growth. Also, a fair number of Djerban Jews are relocating in Tunis, and many make intermittent return visits, which will probably stimulate others to follow their lead. This increased contact between Jews in Djerba and Tunis may also affect the psychology of Djerban Jews in other ways, suggesting an exposure to national currents parallel to that of village Arabs in Israel. In addition, Jewish children still rely on Tunisian public schools for much of their education, although many also complete their studies with several hours each day at one of their community's own schools. Finally, the villages that previously were inhabited only by Jews now contain a substantial Muslim population, intensifying interaction between Jews and Muslims, and reducing the Jewish community's traditional autonomy. Thus, it is not yet clear whether the community will experience the kind of diminishing solidarity and cohesion that was predicted earlier. This aspect of ethnic change has occurred to some extent since field work for the study was completed, and pressures for additional movement in this direction are clearly evident. Yet the continuing solidarity of the community appears to have been underestimated and projections about the future are therefore advanced with particular caution.

Change has been more dramatic in Jewish attitudes toward Muslim society and here, at least recently, movement has not been in the direction anticipated. There has been growing friction between Muslims and Jews on both individual and community levels. One turning point was the construction of a mosque in the major Jewish village two years ago, over Jewish objections, and the most significant developments involve fires set by Muslims at a synagogue and at the Jewish printing establishment in the spring of 1979. The fires, which appear to have evolved from a series of arguments that began with a fight between Jewish and Muslim children walking home from school, were probably set by vandals, by "boys of the street." Nevertheless, some Jews feel that local Muslim religious officials are encouraging anti-Jewish sentiment and, in any event, the fires go substantially beyond any of the petty incidents that occasionally complicated Arab-Jewish relations in the past, dramatically demonstrating to Jews their considerable vulnerability. These events found Djerban Jewry in a state of considerable tension in 1979; but it remains at least possible that earlier trends working for positive Muslim-Jewish relations will prevail in the long run. Jews remain well integrated in Djerban economy and are generally prosperous. Also, Jewish attendance at Tunisian schools has meant increased friendships between Muslims and Jews, as has living in closer proximity to each other. Thus intensified contact between minority and majority brings many positive associations, as well as the kinds of conflicts that came to the fore in 1979. It is difficult to say how this will turn out. If Arab-Jewish relations continue to deteriorate, emigration will accelerate and the ethnic orientation of Jews who remain will most probably come to resemble the pattern of diasporization characteristic of urban Jewry in North Africa. If the recent tension passes, however, with occasional and small-scale conflicts being the exception during a period of intensifying Arab-Jewish interaction, the present situation has the potential to endure for quite some time, with the strong possibility that communal solidarity will nonetheless gradually diminish and ethnic change will yet involve the partial assimilation projected earlier. It is clear, in conclusion, that the character of ethnic change among very small nonassimilating minorities, like the Jews of Djerba, is subject to considerable fluctuation, depending on their relations with the host society, and that as contact between the minority and majority intensifies, the direction as well as the rate of this change can easily be modified.

REFERENCES

Armstrong, John A.
    1976 "Mobilized and Proletarian Diasporas." *American Political Science Review* 70:393-408.
Bell, Wendell and Freeman, Walter
    1974 *Ethnicity and Nation-Building*. Beverly Hills, Calif.: Sage.
Chouraqui, Andre
    1968 *The Jews of North Africa: Between East and West*. Philadelphia: Jewish Publication Society of North America.
Cohen, Abner, ed.
    1972 *Urban Ethnicity*. London: Tavistock.

Deutsch, Karl
    1953 *Nationalism and Social Communication: An Inquiry into the Foundations of Nationality.* Cambridge: Massachusetts Institute of Technology Press.
Fein, Leonard
    1966 *Politics in Israel.* Boston: Little, Brown.
Haim, Sylvia
    1962 *Arab Nationalism.* Berkeley: University of California Press.
Hechter, Michael
    1975 *Internal Colonialism: The Celtic Fringe in British National Development, 1536-1966.* Berkeley: University of California Press.
Hertzburg, Arthur
    1970 *The Zionist Idea.* New York: Atheneum.
Hirschberg. H. Z.
    1974 *A History of the Jews in North Africa.* Leiden: Brill.
Hourani, Albert
    1966 *Arabic Thought in the Liberal Age.* London: Oxford University Press.
Keyes, Charles F.
    1976 "Towards a New Formulation of the Concept of Ethnic Group." *Ethnicity* 3: 202-13.
Kuper, Leo
    1969 "Plural Societies: Perspectives and Problems." In *Pluralism in Africa,* ed. L. Kuper and M. G. Smith, pp. 7-26. Berkeley: University of California Press.
    1974 "On Theories of Race Relations." In *Ethnicity and Nation-Building,* ed. Wendell Bell and Walter Freeman, pp. 19-28. Beverly Hills: Sage.
Landau, Jacob
    1969 *The Arabs in Israel: A Political Study.* London: Oxford University Press.
Melson, Robert and Wolpe, Howard
    1971 *Nigeria: Modernization and the Politics of Communalism.* East Lansing, Mich.: Michigan State University Press.
Peres, Yochanan
    1970 "Modernization and Nationalism in the Identity of the Israeli Arab." *Middle East Journal* (Autumn), pp. 479-92.
Rosen, Lawrence
    1972 "The Social and Conceptual Framework of Arab-Berber Relations in Central Morocco." In *Arabs and Berbers,* ed. E. Gellner and C. Micaud, pp. 155-73. Lexington, MA:

D.C. Heath.

Smith, Donald
1971 *Religion, Politics and Social Change in the Third World.* New York: Free Press.

Smooha, Sammy and Hofman, John E.
1976-77 "Some Problems of Arab-Jewish Coexistence in Israel." *Middle East Review* (Winter), pp. 5-14.

Stock, Ernest
1968 *From Conflict to Understanding.* New York: Institute of Human Relations Press.

Tessler, Mark
1975 "Secularism in the Middle East?" *Ethnicity* 2: 178-203.
1976a "Political Generations." In *Change in Tunisia,* ed. R. Stone and J. Simmons, pp. 73-106. Albany: State University of New York Press.
1976b "Single Party Rule in Tunisia." *Common Ground* 2: 55-64.
1977 "Israel's Arabs and the Palestinian Problem." *Middle East Journal* (Summer): 313-29.
1978 "The Identity of Religious Minorities in Nonsecular States." *Comparative Studies in Society and History* 20: 359-73.
1979 "Minorities in Retreat: The Jews of the Maghreb." In *The Political Role of Minorities in the Middle East,* ed. R. D. McLaurin, pp. 188-220. New York: Praeger.
1980a "Arabs in Israel." *American University Field Staff Reports,* no. 1.
1980b "The Political Culture of Jews in Tunisia and Morocco." *International Journal of Middle East Studies* 11 (January): 59-86.
1981 "The Protection of Minorities in the Middle East: Jews in Tunisia and Morocco and Arabs in Israel." In *The Protection of Minorities,* ed. Robert Wirsing. Elmsford, New York: Pergamon, forthcoming.

van den Berghe, Pierre
1969 "Pluralism and the Polity: A Theoretical Exploration." In *Pluralism in Africa,* ed. L. Kuper and M. G. Smith, pp. 67-81. Berkeley: University of California Press.

Wallerstein, Immanuel, ed.
1966 *Social Change: The Colonial Situation.* New York: Wiley.

Young, Crawford
1976 *The Politics of Cultural Pluralism.* Madison: University of Wisconsin Press.

This paper considers a form of ethnic change involving the emergence or intensification of what is called "ethnic nationalism." Ethnic nationalism is defined by the authors as the occurrence of political or quasipolitical groups whose organizing principle, mobilization of adherents, and appeals for redress of presumed inequities are based on ethnic identity. It is argued that ethnic nationalist movements develop in response to political changes entailing the increased intrusion of bureaucratic controls into the lives of some peoples. Typically, such increased bureaucratic controls are manifest in modern "welfare states." The authors also see a similar pattern as characteristic of certain bureaucratic colonial regimes. Ethnic nationalist movements gain saliency, the authors argue, because they are able to organize local populations differentiated by wealth, age, sex, education, residence, even religion and language, into political constituencies seeking redress from bureaucratic government. The authors examine three cases of ethnic nationalist movements—the French-speaking Acadian movement in New Brunswick, Canada, and Welsh nationalist movement in Great Britain, and a non-Brahman movement in South India—in light of their argument.

RICHARD G. FOX, CHARLOTTE H. AULL,

AND LOUIS F. CIMINO

Ethnic Nationalism

and the Welfare State

The European national revolutions of the last few centuries did not so much expand political rights as concentrate them in the state and reduce their investment in other sorts of governments. A large part of the process consisted of the state's abridging, destroying, or absorbing rights previously lodged in other political units: manors, communities, provinces, estates ... the right itself continued in more or less the same form, but under new management. In other cases, the right disappeared entirely. The right of a household to pasture its flock on the village common is a notorious example, the right of the household's head to punish its members is a less obvious one. [Tilly 1975, p. 37]

A South Asian proverb humorously relates that five Brahmans will require six separate cooking vessels, so great is each one's sense of

The initial research was funded by NSF grant SOC 75-16593. Aull's research on Wales was funded by the Social Science Research Council and Wenner-Gren Foundation. Cimino's research on the Acadians was funded in part by the Duke University Program in Canadian Studies.

pollution and "mutual repulsion." A similar scholarly fastidiousness unfortunately does not characterize the approach to ethnicity in a growing number of ethnic studies. Often in ostensibly disproving, for example, (American) "melting pot" ideology, many such studies reassert it in a new context; that is, in the potpourri of institutions, populations, allegiances, and identities all termed "ethnic." Used thus nondiscretely, the "concept" of ethnicity comes perilously close to being merely a label justifying or classifying a certain (but not well-defined) sort of scholarly inquiry, rather than being an analytic concept of some utility. Anthropologists have the precedent of such terms as *tribe* and *peasant* to warn us of how analytically empty and yet unfortunately long-lived such labels can be.

One way to avoid this dilemma is to presuppose that "something" called ethnicity exists and to investigate its characteristics and consequences. Whether ethnicity is situational or primordial, whether an ethnic division of labor exists and how its consequences are measured, why and in what circumstances ethnicity is or is not significant for the individual in interactions with others, how ethnic boundaries are crossed—all these valid questions lend analytic significance to the concept of ethnicity by specifying attributes like boundaries, situational employment, loss through assimilation, economic outcomes, and so forth. The danger is that since the "why" and the "wherefore" of the definition of ethnicity is not the object of investigation, that is, since ethnicity is treated as given or "real," it becomes increasingly difficult to deter other, perhaps less fastidious, scholars from adding their small bit of "ethnic" phenomena to an increasingly unsavory stew. WASPS, Appalachian highlanders, American southerners, triracial isolates like the Louisiana Freejacks, Koreans and Japanese or alternatively Asians, Scandinavian identities, Scottish highland gamesters, Frisians, Breton speakers, the Jewish Defense League, Latins—but also Cubans, Puerto Ricans, and Mexicans, the Syndicate, West Indians and Pakistanis in Britain—but also sometimes "Coloreds"; American Indian Movement—all are somehow equivalently ethnic, which makes ethnicity almost everything, and almost nothing.

Another way to avoid the labeling dilemma is to ignore ethnicity altogether, at least as a given, or starting point, for investigation. Our research proceeds from such an orientation, and the previous comments are a roundabout and somewhat querulous apology for addressing ethnicity and ethnic change backwards, that is, as an outcome of an analysis of state organization and the peculiar social movements that a specific form of the state (we believe) generates. Our argument is that by stipulating under what conditions in the wider society ethnicity occurs and how it varies with those conditions we can specify its salience for social behavior, the nature of ethnic boundaries, the role of acculturation, and so forth. The "outcome" we choose to label ethnic—politicized social movements called ethnic nationalisms— may cover only a very limited aspect of the phenomena others term ethnic. But like the Brahmans and their several cooking vessels, such discreteness, even though it denies analytic utility to the idea of ethnicity in the aggregate, promises less mix-up than the "melting pot" approach.

ETHNIC NATIONALISM

Ethnic nationalism can be defined as the occurrence of political or quasipolitical groups whose organizing principle, mobilization of adherents, and appeals for redress of presumed inequities are based on separate ethnic identity within a given culture. Such ethnic political movements are currently found in many of the most industrially advanced nations of the world: the Acadian revival and Quebec separatist movement in Canada; the Welsh and Scottish nationalist agitation in Great Britain; the Samish movement in Norway; the Breton, Corsican, Occitanic, and Alsatian autonomists in France; Basque terrorism in Spain; and the Cajun revival and Amerindian movement in the United States. These movements clearly differ in their organization and mass following, the ideology espoused, the protest activity undertaken, and the larger sociopolitical milieu in which they are set. Yet we believe there are certain underlying regularities to their occurrence and to the developmental phases through which they pass. These regularities have to do with the organization of political opposition by ethnic elites, rather than any upsurge of ethnic identity based on primordial loyalties not fully excised by the nation-state. Our thesis is that these ethnic nationalisms are novel means for (or attempts at) political mobilization under specific conditions of state organization, summed up in the term *welfare state*. Such ethnic movements are accommodations of or adaptations to the peculiar characteristics of such states, specifically their high levels of bureaucraticization and managerial capacity coupled with the weakening of class-based ideology and organization for political mobilization. Appeals to ethnicity, as one component in a larger set of political appeals based on so-called ascriptive criteria such as age, sex, and community, become a major means of mobilizing large populations for dissident political activities in such states.

The political nature of ethnic nationalist movements is best shown by the role of counterelites in their development, in the definition of ethnic ideology, in the employment of ethnic diacritica, and in the articulation of political protest. The developmental phases of these movements show their creation and manipulation by self-conscious counterelites, or ethnic elites, who use them to carve out, reinforce, or protect their access to power, wealth, and other perquisites at first as local influentials and then later as brokers between an increasingly bureaucratized state government and the ethnic collectivity. As the government bureaucratizes further and intrudes even more strategically in the social life of communities and regions, the ethnic elite must increasingly mobilize their self-defined ethnic brethren to maintain credibility as mediators between government and the (actually or potentially) dissident demands of the latter population.

Since increasing bureaucratization and state intrusion on community institutions is the major impetus behind ethnic nationalism, similar movements and their elites should develop wherever equivalent forms of the state exist, even if these are not conventionally called welfare states. Our research suggests that under certain bureaucratic colonial regimes, where the state was the major source of power and employment, ethnic nationalist movements arose that in form and development were similar to those of contemporary America and western Europe. In such cases, class-based forms of political mobilization had not been superseded; rather, ethnicity represented an original means of organizing political opposition in such heterogeneous and recently preindustrial states.

The following sections develop this thesis in greater detail and illustrate it with case materials from the Acadian, Welsh, and South Indian non-Brahman ethnic nationalist movements.

THE WELFARE STATE AND THE "END OF IDEOLOGY"

The history of industrial nations over the last century but especially since World War II shows a reduction in economic class conflicts and an increase in managerial (rather than political) approaches to social problems, as the ever more powerful welfare state expands regulation into all aspects of economic, political, and social life (see Janowitz 1976; Gouldner 1970, pp. 349-50). An outgrowth partly of the need for wide-scale governmental regulation and control during the Great Depression and World War II and partly a simple response to the possibilities introduced by the new technology of communication and transportation, the concentration of control by the welfare state over education, social welfare, economic planning, transportation networks, communication facilities, agricultural production, exports and imports, currency, and even public morality has increasingly abrogated most community and locality autonomy or independence (compare Reiter 1972; Bensman and Vidich 1958).

The enlargement of the welfare state's capacity for control has developed coterminously with its increasing capability of producing wealth and its growing commitment to supplying at least minimal social services on an equalitarian basis. The strange but popularly accepted conjunction of state intervention in the economy with private capitalism and individual profit-making means that the former class-based ideological battles between right and left are replaced with a less contentious dispute over relative economic and political priorities, a dispute that takes on a basically managerial rather than ideological cast. As Lipset, summarizing a 1955 conference, writes:

. . . the general agreement among the delegates, regardless of political belief, [was] that the traditional issues separating the left and the right had declined to comparative insignificance. . . . The socialists no longer advocated socialism; they were as concerned as the conservatives with the danger of an all-powerful state. The ideological issues dividing left and right had been reduced to a little more or a little less government ownership and economic planning. No one seemed to believe that it really made much difference which political party controlled the domestic policies of individual nations. [Lipset 1960, p. 401]

Similar statements are to be found in many sources (Waxman 1968 contains excerpts of the arguments, both pro and contra) of this trend towards the "politics of consensus" (Lane 1965, p. 877) "depoliticization" (Torgerson 1962, p. 160), or "the waning of opposition" (Kirchheimer 1957, p. 150), although Bell's notion of an "end of ideology" is probably most widely known (Bell 1962).

The scholarly controversy that has swirled around Bell's statement has been clouded by many tangential issues—what ideology is, what must happen to declare it at an end, who has it—and the political affirmation of an "end of ideology" by Bell and others has not cleared the air. We do not wish to become embroiled in either the scholarly or political tangents involved in this notion, nor do we make any value judgments on the benefits of this process for Western society. We especially disavow any idea that participatory democracy and effective economic redistribution are inherent and present qualities of welfare states (see Thoenes 1966, pp. 136-37). However, two propositions contained in the "end of ideology" concept are worth conserving because they are generally echoed in the political science literature on the Western welfare state. These are that decision making and ideology in the welfare state are basically managerial rather than (class) ideological and consequently that there is a decline in or demise of political conflict and mobilization by movements and ideologies grounded in class opposition.[1] (Compare Lipset 1977 for the most recent statement of this position, in which he sums up opinions on both the right and left that confirm this notion).[2]

At this point our discussion must appear far removed from the Welsh National Eisteddfod or even the acts of violent sabotage by A. I. M. To link the welfare state with ethnic nationalisms we must understand the mechanism by which the (class) "depoliticization" is spread to the population in these welfare states and the manner in which alternative political ideologies, such as ethnic nationalism, are generated.

Field and Highley, in a pioneering study of political elites in the most advanced industrial nations, have identified the mechanism; they suggest that the widespread dissemination of an elite managerial orientation leads to general political stability. The first requirement is a unified elite, that is, one whose "members prefer system continuity over factional or personal advancement in cases where these two elite interests conflict. This implies that there exists among elite persons an implicit, and sometimes explicit, consensus about the nature and desirability of the society they manage and direct" (Field and Highley 1972; p. 15). This consensus is based on the elite's expectation that continuance of the system will provide sufficient rewards, participation, and power to satisfy all competing elite interest groups or conversely, that opposition would bring punishment, poverty, and powerlessness.[3] Field and Highley evidently believe that such unified elites and their managerial orientations can develop in advance of industrialization and the welfare state (Field and Highley 1972). However, the evolving welfare state acts to unify elites by reaching high levels of productivity coupled with a ramified bureaucratic organization; it therefore provides greater rewards for proper management than for divisive political challenge.

This managerial consensus is spread widely as an increasing pro-

1. This statement does not necessarily mean that party identification lessens, but rather that party identification, like the parties themselves, become less grounded in class ideology, just as the election of one party or another has fewer national and individual consequences in terms of class or a class-based political program (compare Lane 1965, p. 884).

2. Bell (1975) also addresses the "end of ideology" argument again and suggests that ethnicity may be a response to the welfare state similar to those expressed in this paper.

3. Field and Highley seemingly conceive of unified elites brought about by voluntary consensus in an atmosphere of free political choice. The history of nation-state formation in Europe appears to show that such voluntary distributions of power, representation, and rewards among elites or to the masses are not typical (see Tilly 1975, pp. 37-38).

portion of the state population is brought into enduring involvement with bureaucratic institutions and becomes dependent on them for direction and rewards (Field and Highley 1972, pp. 14-15). Consequently "class-centered" attitudes toward political ideology and institutions decline markedly. However, Field and Highley believe that the elite complacency attributed by Bell and others to the welfare state is short lived. As the welfare state proves incapable of final solutions to poverty and disaffection, there emerge conditions that could lead to new political mobilization by dissatisfied members of the political elite. Yet Field and Highley do not foresee a return to political ideologies and oppositions linked to class because the classes to which the latter were historically linked have largely been diluted by involvement in and rewards from the bureaucratic welfare state. Nor do they envision a new set of ideologies developing because there will be no "crystallization of social classes" to which such ideologies could adhere—*except*, they suggest, for certain groups like the residual poor or youth, who are sufficiently disaffected from or unrewarded by the major institutions of production and management in the society. But since these groups provide services of such minimal societal value, they have little power; therefore they will be unable to invade the political process, as did the middle class and working class before them (Field and Highley 1972, pp. 40-41).

The conclusion that no new ideologies of (effective) political mobilization and no new elites to wield them will surface in welfare states appears premature. Even in the early 1970s Field and Highley could have seen them and their institutional embodiment in parties or other protest activities aimed at gaining influence in the political process. Perhaps they ignored them because their ostensibly ascriptive ideologies appeared only as recrudescences of primordial sentiments and therefore hardly novel. Yet our thesis is that ethnic nationalisms represent such new ideologies and forms of political protest, part of a larger set of novel political movements based on presumed ascriptive characteristics such as age, sex, community, and ethnicity. However, ideologies and institutionalized protest based on sex and ethnicity are potentially the most successful for dissident elites to mobilize because they involve populations that perform important productive and managerial functions (by virtue of numbers and skills) in welfare states.

Ethnic nationalism can best be explained, therefore, as a new organization and ideological form for political protest that occurs in welfare states as an alternative to and replacement for class-based forms of political opposition (their appearance in colonial societies will be discussed later). The salient characteristic of ethnic nationalism is its ability (or attempt) to bind local populations differentiated by wealth, age, sex, education, residence, even religion and language, into a new political constituency seeking redress from the bureaucratic government. The appeal to ethnicity, and the cultural diacritica like language, religion, homeland, common economic status, or history that symbolize it, may provide an effective base for elite political mobilization that overcomes the separate and sometimes antagonistic loyalties, statuses, and roles in a complex welfare state. At least ethnicity is a logical choice, to the extent that it can be ideologically created or reinvigorated, but in any case redefined in a new (political) context and for novel ends (directed against the welfare state). This thesis explains why ethnic nationalisms have only recently burgeoned into large-scale or even mass political protest, even though elite activity and ethnic ideology were often set in motion over a century ago. The full onset of the welfare state and the wealth and technology upon which it depends is, minimally, a post-World War II phenomenon. It also helps explain why ethnic nationalisms often occur in the most backward regions of the welfare state. These are the locales that feel the intrusion of state welfare agencies most directly and yet as most foreign, and where elites who are dissatisfied with state encroachment on their former preserves (or at least who see the opportunities this provides for political access) are most likely to be found.

The latter statement bears amplification because it underscores our interpretation of ethnic nationalisms as political phenomena and provides a means by which to illustrate this contention. As the evolving Western industrial state and, later, welfare state increasingly intrude into locality and community life and increasingly co-opt the older, class bases of political opposition, it gives impetus for local or regional counterelites to utilize inchoate ethnic sentiments for political goals. Although ethnic organizations may and do appear apart from any specific intrusive action by the state—as responses to the perceived cultural, economic, educational, or associational needs of the locality or community—their ultimate success in the prosecution of their goals and the maintenance of their local influence depends on gaining recognition by the state. In earlier, prewelfare state periods, this recognition may consist only of the state's unwillingness or inability to prevent the formation of local power bases by a burgeoning ethnic elite, which organizes the inchoate ethnic collectivity. In later periods, recognition means gaining concessions from the welfare state, in terms of the state's delivery of perquisites and subsidies or its endorsement of a hands-off policy toward ethnic organization and elite control.

Thus, before the full development of the welfare state, elites form ethnic organizations for a variety of local purposes, with a diversity of local goals and activities, and over a spectrum of local power and prestige. However, the ethnic organizations that endure and prevail as the welfare state strengthens and intrudes are those whose form and actions bring them into increasingly direct bargaining for perquisites from the state through the threat or actuality of mobilizing a constituency based on ethnic appeals. Those ethnic elites that cannot mobilize such a following must see their local prominence and autonomy decline as the state successfully intervenes to undercut their previous positions of local influence. Various counter strategies can be employed by ethnic elites to offset their dilemmas of organization and mobilization. If, for example, construction of an ethnic constituency is impeded by the continued salience of class-based ideology, the ethnic leadership can incorporate elements of class ideology into their basically ethnic appeals, and ethnic organizations purposely aimed at specific class interests can be formed. If ethnic mobilization is impeded by an inchoate identity of insufficient prominence the ethnic elite may articulate with the state through primarily cultural demands, aimed at state recognition and subsidy of "cultural" activities and performances. If ethnic mobilization is impeded by extreme state suppression, the ethnic elite may go underground and, through acts of violent protest and sabotage, attempt to mobilize a constituency in the wreckage of the state.

The foregoing emphasizes the importance of leadership from within ethnic populations for the genesis and development of such movements. The common anthropological treatment of ethnic collectivities as basically unstratified or undifferentiated populations obscures that the leadership of ethnic nationalisms is often held by acculturated middle-class professionals who reconstitute their ethnicity and broadcast new symbols of identity and forms of organization to an ethnic following. To the extent that this counterelite, or ethnic elite as we prefer to term them, can create an ideology and organization that link the ethnic collectivity, even though some are wealthier, better educated, and more powerful than others, ethnic nationalisms are set in motion—for political ends that at first are mainly those of the ethnic elite. By showing that ethnic nationalisms are responses to the intrusions of the welfare state and that ethnic elites propagate these ideologies and organizations to protect, define, and/or enlarge their positions at a local or national level, we hope to show these movements as novel responses to the welfare state *and* as basically political activities wielded by dissatisfied elites for power and preferment.

DEVELOPMENTAL PHASES OF ETHNIC NATIONALISM

Five phases are posited in the development of ethnic nationalisms (see fig. 1):

The *incipient phase* is characterized by the existence of an ethnic population, or collectivity, sharing an inchoate or diffuse ethnic identity and (sometimes but not always) an inferior economic and political situation in the society. This collectivity may inhabit a contiguous ethnic "homeland" or may be widely distributed throughout the society, and the degree of territorial nucleation may have important consequences for the ethnic identity felt. There may be intermittent periods of civil disobedience or outright rebellion. However, the ethnic population is not organized around institutions or articulated common symbols, and there is no ethnic elite.

The *formative phase* sees the development of an ethnic elite that organizes into associations, clubs, societies, and other voluntary groups on the basis of shared ethnicity. In the early formative phase, these associations bind together elites at a local level; in the later formative phase, provincial or national associations are developed that define an ethnic elite of much wider compass. This ethnic elite is usually drawn from the most acculturated of the ethnic population, that is those who are able in appropriate situations to dispose of the ethnic markers or diacritica most effectively.

Such ethnic elites, when they achieve successful positions from which to articulate their goals, emerge as brokers in the interstices between the bureaucratic nation-state and the local community and region, either because they develop skills needed by the nation-state as a result of their acculturation or because they claim to represent their ethnic congeners. During this phase, however, ethnic nationalisms are in no sense mass movements. Their associational activities are organized by the elite, and if the state should grant sufficient local authority, the elite may make few attempts to mobilize an ethnic following in actuality. Over the course of the formative phase, the associations created by the ethnic elite often become more secular and the ideology of ethnic mobilization also takes on a more secular cast. Ethnic demands during this phase are in the form of elite political pressure and predominantly for the satisfaction of elite requirements. Co-optation of ethnic leadership by the state or national political institutions is quite common.

The next phase, the *florescent,* has generally occurred in Western industrial states in the wake of World War II and the bureaucratic and technological capabilities it brought such states. The heightened intrusion of the now fully formed welfare state administration and agencies of control threatens the ethnic elite's privileged position or its intermediary role between government and locality that existed in the formative phase. It may also threaten the elite's position within

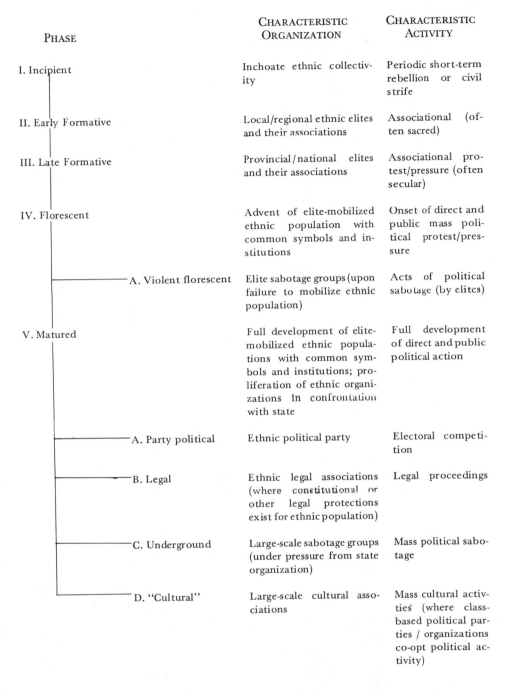

PHASE	CHARACTERISTIC ORGANIZATION	CHARACTERISTIC ACTIVITY
I. Incipient	Inchoate ethnic collectivity	Periodic short-term rebellion or civil strife
II. Early Formative	Local/regional ethnic elites and their associations	Associational (often sacred)
III. Late Formative	Provincial/national elites and their associations	Associational protest/pressure (often secular)
IV. Florescent	Advent of elite-mobilized ethnic population with common symbols and institutions	Onset of direct and public mass political protest/pressure
A. Violent florescent	Elite sabotage groups (upon failure to mobilize ethnic population)	Acts of political sabotage (by elites)
V. Matured	Full development of elite-mobilized ethnic populations with common symbols and institutions; proliferation of ethnic organizations in confrontation with state	Full development of direct and public political action
A. Party political	Ethnic political party	Electoral competition
B. Legal	Ethnic legal associations (where constitutional or other legal protections exist for ethnic population)	Legal proceedings
C. Underground	Large-scale sabotage groups (under pressure from state organization)	Mass political sabotage
D. "Cultural"	Large-scale cultural associations	Mass cultural activities (where class-based political parties / organizations co-opt political activity)

Fig. 1. Developmental Phases of Ethnic Nationalism

the ethnic population by co-opting the services previously offered through the ethnic association. To protect its own position with respect to the government and within the ethnic population, the elite recognizes that it must deal aggressively with the state. In the absence of class-based political groups and political institutions that properly represent ethnic needs, the elite can turn to mass political pressure to guarantee continued privilege. The "depoliticization" of the population and the demise of class ideologies accomplished by the welfare state for the nation as a whole clears the way at the local level for novel attempts at mass mobilization on so-called ascriptive grounds and creates the necessary atmosphere at the national level for acceptance of (or at least response to) this mobilization as a significant and even threatening political movement. The response of the welfare state typically is managerial; it allows the ethnic leaders some of the rewards of the political system, through grants, offices, and other perquisites that, curiously, form the economic base of the ethnic movement and its increasing mobilization (as we shall see in Acadia and Wales).

To apply political pressure effectively so as to guarantee its position and gain perquisites, the ethnic elite *must* mobilize the ethnic population to an extent hitherto unknown, since the threat of ethnic popular dissidence is the only guarantee of state acceptance and reward. If the ethnic elite cannot successfully mobilize the collectivity (usually because of welfare-state repression and/or the continued salience of class-based political organization and ideology), limited (because of lack of following) but strategic acts of sabotage are often undertaken by the elite, as the only means to pressure government into recognition of their demands. However, if mobilization is successful, it sets in motion developments that the ethnic elite often does not foresee and sometimes cannot control, such as new contenders for elite position, often younger and more radical, who may threaten and even successfully challenge the older elite's position or who may push the movement to acts of violence. Both to gain control over the newly mobilized and to magnify their difference from the older ethnic elite, these new contenders for elite position are usually more directly political and institute mass strategies of political confrontation. The ideology they espouse is often more secularized (in keeping with the realities of power politics they see within and outside the movement) than the cultural and sacred demands voiced by the older elite in keeping with its political pressure tactics (compare Eidheim 1969 on the Samish). However much the new contenders secularize the ethnic nationalist movement and admonish the older elite as Uncle Toms and Tomahawks, however much they introduce the rhetoric of radical economic ideology or confrontational tactics, they cannot convert these movements into class oppositions because this would be to abort the basis of mobilization and adherence. It would also make overly transparent the inequalities in wealth, education, and position within the movement. Where class ideology has been introduced into ethnic nationalist movements, it has either been abortive (as in Acadia) or has threatened to factionalize the movement (as in Wales).

The *matured phase* is simply a continuation and further development of the mobilization and politicization of the ethnic population begun in the florescent phase. Ethnic organizations proliferate and specialize to meet the ramifying agencies and activities of the welfare state. Depending on the political framework of the society and historical pattern that linked the ethnic collectivity to the wider society, the increased political and confrontational activity may take the form of ethnic party politics, legal proceedings, mass political sabotage, mass ethnic cultural performances, and both formal and informal citizen groups opposed to specific bureaucratic agencies of the government—or a combination of these.

The developmental phases of ethnic nationalism detailed above represent an ideal sequence, in the sense that ethnic organizational development proceeds "on time" and "in line" with the emergence of the welfare state. This pattern corresponds, therefore, most closely to the genesis and evolution of the most successful and best organized of contemporary ethnic nationalisms. Weaker or less well-organized ethnic nationalisms will depart in greater or lesser degree from this ideal sequence, mainly in the developmental phase obtained at the time the welfare state becomes markedly intrusive. Such departures involve the effectiveness of the ethnic organization as well as the duration of each phase. Although space considerations disallow a full discussion of the variables affecting departures from the ideal sequence, a partial listing will help clarify the case materials on the Acadian, Welsh, and non-Brahman ethnic nationalisms to be discussed below.

Conditions that (at various phases) will create relative weakness or retardation in ethnic nationalism are:

1. Relative geographical dispersal of the ethnic collectivity (incipient phase).

2. Relatively low-level development of a local or regional ethnic elite and organizations at the onset of the welfare state, often because of lack of opportunities provided for such developments by the pre-welfare state (early formative phase).

3. State suppression or nonrecognition of all dissenting organizations (late formative phase).

4. Continued salience of class-based political organizations (florescent or matured phase) (compare the regional variation in the Welsh movement described below).

5. Failure of regional ethnic organization to adapt in competition with the state and ensuing conflict within the ethnic movement (florescent phase) (compare the role of the Catholic church in Acadian ethnic nationalism as described below).

6. Relatively high concentration of power and benefits in the state and a low level of provision of welfare benefits to the ethnic locality. This condition brings the ethnic elite into confrontation with the state more directly and rapidly, but also, since all perquisites depend on state recognition, keeps the movement a predominantly elite phenomenon (late formative) (compare the non-Brahman movement described below).

These developmental phases of ethnic nationalism derive from secondary reserach on many of these movements and primary research in Wales and Acadia (francophone New Brunswick). Space allows only the most cursory review of the developmental pattern in the latter areas as illustration of the general points made above.

WELSH ETHNIC NATIONALISM

Historic reasons for regarding Wales and England as separate nations can be found as early as the Anglo-Saxon invasions of Britain following the departure of the Romans in the fifth century.

Incipient phase. Anglo-Saxon invaders never subdued the Celtic tribes in Wales, nor were the Normans much more successful. In the period following the conquest in 1066, the Norman kings imposed a fairly uniform centralized system of administration on England, but they simply contained the Welsh. They made large grants of land in the Marches on the eastern border of Wales to lords who were given virtual sovereignty if they kept the peace.

Although the Welsh were organized primarily on a tribal basis, they did enjoy a period of political unity and sovereignty in the thirteenth century, which ended with the death of Llywelyn II, the last Prince of Wales, and the conquest of Wales by the English king Edward I. One other brief period of political sovereignty occurred under the "outlaw" Owain Glyn Dwr in the fifteenth century. This very romantic past and the rich literature that was produced were the basis of a distinctive Welsh identity.

Until the passage of the Act of Union in 1536 Wales was treated more or less as a separate, although conquered, country. The act, however completely incorporated Wales into the English administrative and political system (Williams 1960). Further, during this period very close ties developed between the Welsh gentry and the English court under the Tudors, who were Welsh in origin. As a consequence the landowning class became anglicized, but the peasants remained thoroughly Welsh (Coupland 1954, pp. 54-61). An ethnic boundary thus was created in Wales marked by differences in economic and political position, language, manners, and urban orientation.

Formative phase (early). In the eighteenth and early nineteenth centuries an indigenous Welsh elite developed distinct from the anglicized landowning gentry (Coupland 1954, pp. 115-36; Grigg 1973, pp. 17-23). This new elite and the associated Welsh cultural revival were products of the spread of the Nonconformist faiths in Wales. The sectarian nature of Nonconformity and the relative autonomy of individual chapels even within a single denomination made it a weak vehicle organizationally for Welsh unification (Verdery 1976). Nevertheless, several factors made Nonconformity a suitable institutional base for the expression of Welsh identity. The most obvious of these was its use of the Welsh language in services. At the time Anglican ministers were nearly all Englishmen who knew no Welsh, yet their parishioners (aside from the gentry) were virtually all Welsh speaking. In addition, the Nonconformist chapels soon became the centers of village social life. A position of prominence in the democratically organized chapels meant a position of leadership within the Welsh community. Thus, the chapels provided a new status system, not dependent on English social structure, from which came the new Welsh elite. The brokerage role that such a cultural elite performed was primarily to act as spokesman with the gentry on behalf of individuals or of the community.

The earliest concerns that were not strictly local of the new Welsh elite were for the provision of education in Wales and for the nourishment of Welsh culture (primarily in the sense of *Kultur*). In this period many private day schools and literally thousands of Griffith Jones's circulating schools were started (Clement 1960), several Welsh cultural (literary and historical) societies were founded, and the Eisteddfod, a national cultural festival consisting of poetry and music competitions, was revived. The leaders in these activities, although products of the Welsh Nonconformist tradition, very frequently lived outside Wales; often they were prominent members of the London Welsh community (Jenkins and Ramage 1951).

Formative phase (late). With the coming of British electoral reform, starting in the 1860s, the activity of the local cultural elites broadened to encompass politics. Until that time Parliamentary seats had been under the control of the great landed families. Then, in the "great election" of 1868, with Nonconformist leaders campaigning actively as Gladstonian Liberals, Wales returned twenty-one Liberals and only nine Conservatives. This election marked the beginning of half a century of Liberal party dominance in Welsh politics. Besides these new political opportunities at the parliamentary level, the Local Government Act of 1888, which replaced the gentry with popularly elected councils, opened additional career opportunities for the Welsh elite (Morgan 1972, pp. 119-21). The goals of the newly politicized cultural elite remained largely determined by their Nonconformist background: disestablishment, temperance, and education. Their successes included the Welsh Sunday Closing Act of 1881, the Welsh Intermediate Education Act of 1889, and the granting of the charter to the University of Wales in 1893.

For the most part, these leaders acted through the medium of a British political party, specifically the Liberal party. To the extent that they were able to cooperate with one another they formed a moderately effective block of votes within Westminster. Further, the relative security of their seats made them more important to Liberal party leadership than their numbers would suggest, and they were able to influence party policy out of proportion to their voting strength, although they often failed ultimately to secure its implementation. For example, disestablishment for Wales was endorsed by the National Liberal Federation in 1891, but although bills were introduced in 1894 and 1895 they made little progress (Walker 1976, pp. 164-65).

By acting through standard political channels the Welsh leaders obtained a number of concessions (as noted above) for their constituencies and, more important, they established a principle of special legislation for Wales. Yet these political prizes were limited in scope, primarily because at that time the central government really did not have all that much to offer any region in social and economic perquisites. Many of these leaders were more successful in parlaying their position of somewhat disproportionate importance into individual successes in British politics and imperial affairs. Notable among these were Tom Ellis, who became Liberal party whip in 1894, and Lloyd George, who turned increasingly to all-British issues in the late 1890s and became prime minister in 1916.

There was one ultimately unsuccessful attempt to change the political structure itself. In 1887 Cymru Fydd ("Wales to Be") was founded by a few MPs from North Wales. This organization had frankly nationalist goals: a separate legislature and executive for Wales. Lloyd George, then Liberal MP for Caernarvon, in northwest Wales, became its president in 1894, at a time when disillusionment with Gladstone and the Liberal party was high. However, when he tried to bring the industrial areas of South Wales into the organization he failed and Cymru Fydd was defunct by 1898 (Coupland 1954, pp. 227-28, 236; Grigg 1973, pp. 158-160, 200-202).

A major reason for the failure to consolidate an all-Welsh power base was the growing strength of the trade-union movement in South Wales and its increasing importance as an organizational force in that region. Historically, the Nonconformist chapels had held just as central a position in the communities of the South Wales coal fields and industrial valleys as in rural northern and western Wales (Pierce 1960). But with increasing industrialization, Nonconformist concerns, as expressed politically, were being overtaken by economic and related social problems, problems that activity through the existing political channels, dominated now by a Welsh cultural elite, was unlikely even to confront. The newly forming trade-union movement did at least address these problems and offered class-based organization, encompassing all British workers, as the most effective route to their solution, a solution that the movement claimed would ultimately require fundamental transformation of the existing political structure. It is not surprising that the Welsh ethnic elite, by then firmly entrenched in the party political structure and with many among the national leaders essentially co-opted into the British state system, did not welcome such union activity; in fact, many chapels actively opposed unionism and some even denied membership to known trade unionists (Williams 1950, pp. 235-36).

Trade-union organization, as its strength grew, essentially replaced the chapel in industrial areas as the center of community life. The lodge, the local branch of the coal miner's union, was self-governing and permeated all aspects of community life through such auxiliary organizations as its women's committee and welfare committee (cf. Pelling 1965). Where the trade unions were much more effective in developing a power base than the Nonconformists ever had been was in their better organization. All the local unions were linked through their membership in the South Wales Miners Federation, and, further, this regional organization had ties with the British union.

The Labour party, which developed as the political arm of the union movement, began to gain strength in the twentieth century. It held nine Welsh seats after the 1918 election and by 1929 had increased this number to twenty-five, all but two of these in South Wales (Craig 1976). The Labour movement continued to consolidate its position throughout the depression years. After World War II, Labour also began to make inroads in northern Wales, but it has never enjoyed the emotional commitment in the north that existed in much of South Wales, where Labour was almost a religion. When a Labour government came to power in 1945 the party had a solid regional organization in South Wales. In rural northern and western Wales the political leadership continued to come from the old Nonconformist cultural elite, although some of these now gave their political allegiance to the Labour rather than the Liberal party. Thus, the political complexions of the two regions were quite different.

Plaid Cymru (the Welsh Nationalist party) was founded in 1925 by a group of only six people representing two different Welsh societies, from both northern and southern Wales.[4] Initially, its major aims were preservation of the Welsh language and culture (envisaged as the life of the small rural communities centered on the chapel): "It is clear that the Welsh Nationalist Party was at the outset essentially intellectual and moral in outlook, and socially conservative. Its principal concerns were the Welsh language, the Welsh identity, and Christianity in Wales" (Butt Philip 1975, p. 15).

Its areas of strength, although never very great until quite recently, are indicated by the parliamentary seats it contested. Until the 1945 general election the only seats it contested were Caernarvonshire (in northwest Wales) and the University of Wales seat. Through the 1950s Plaid Cymru continued to contest a much greater proportion of the seats in northwest and west Wales than elsewhere (Butt Philip 1975, p. 140). Since 1970 it has put up candidates for all thirty-six parliamentary seats. The existence of a strong class-based political movement in the form of the Labour party diminished the salience and retarded the growth of the Welsh Nationalist party as a viable political movement.

Florescent phase. On July 14, 1966, Plaid Cymru had a dramatic upturn in its fortunes with the victory of its president, Gwynfor Evans, in a parliamentary by-election in Carmarthen. This victory was made possible by a 17 percent swing in the vote from the general election earlier that year. The seat, although it has some industrial pockets, is a predominantly rural and socially conservative constituency. The party lost this seat in the 1970 general election, apparently hurt by the more militant activities of those who were concentrating on the single issue of the preservation of the Welsh language. However, it

4. Jones (1970) gives greater prominence to a third group, the Tair G. However, Hywel Davies, currently completing a historical study of Plaid Cymru in the period of 1925 to 1945, argues that the Tair G was no more than a student society at Bangor and did not play a central role in the formation of Plaid Cymru (personal communication, September 9, 1977). This position was also supported by interviews with relatives of some of the early Plaid Cymru members.

came back strongly in the last two general elections and in 1974 elected first two, then three members to Parliament. The three Plaid MPs are from Caernarvon, Merioneth, and Carmarthen, all predominantly rural, with a high proportion of Welsh speakers.

These sudden successes of Plaid Cymru after over forty years of futile efforts to break into the political arena as a serious political contender have not occurred in a vacuum. Since World War II there has been a burgeoning of organizations proclaiming Wales as their natural constituency, and the recent growth of Plaid Cymru must be explained in this context. These national (that is, Welsh) organizations may be as loosely structured as the Welsh Schools Movement, a series of relatively autonomous parents' groups working at the county level to establish publicly funded schools that use Welsh as the medium of instruction. Or they may be formed within the British state bureaucracy itself, like the Welsh Office and the Welsh National Water Development Agency. But a very common, and revealing, pattern of development is as an offshoot from an all-British organization, the break being precipitated by the feeling that the British organization is not looking out for distinctively Welsh interests in its dealings with the state bureaucracy. Thus, each breakaway group argues that it can more effectively represent its all-Welsh constituency within the bureaucracy than could its British counterpart. Examples of such organizations are the Farmers Union of Wales, the Wales Trades Union Council, and, very recently formed, the Community Councils Association of Wales.

Space permits only a brief discussion of two of these groups, the Welsh Schools Movement and the Farmers Union of Wales (FUW). Even prior to the growth of the Welsh Schools Movement there were primary schools, mainly in the more rural areas of Wales, using Welsh as the medium of instruction simply because all their pupils spoke Welsh as a first language. However, the Aberystwyth Welsh School (Ysgol Gymraeg Aberystwyth) was the first such school established in a self-conscious effort to maintain and revive the language in the face of heavy anglicization. The school was started as a private venture in 1939 by Ifan ab Owen Edwards, who also founded Urdd Gobaith Cymru, a Welsh youth organization. The immediate impetus for the school's creation was the influx of evacuees from Liverpool, whose presence in the area greatly reduced the use of Welsh in the local public schools. Edwards was concerned that his son, just starting school at that time, should receive his education in Welsh and that it be based on Welsh life and culture (Davies 1973, pp. 75-77). The new school was successful academically and by 1945 had grown to seventy-one pupils, but its financial position was uncertain. Even so, it played a central role in the fostering of Welsh-medium schools supported by public funds in other parts of Wales. By 1948 Edwards's youth organization had worked with local parents' groups to obtain Welsh schools at Llanelli, Cardiff, Llandudno, Y Rhyl, Mold, and Holywell; the publication of a highly favorable report on the Aberystwyth Welsh School by the Ministry of Education that same year gave additional impetus and credibility to the movement (Davies 1973, p. 154). The struggle for publicly supported Welsh-medium schools has been based heavily on the 1944 Education Act. This act did not deal explicitly with the language of instruction, but it did guarantee that children would be educated in accordance with the wishes of their parents insofar as practicable. Thus, the central government unknowingly provided a valuable resource that was used by a creative Welsh elite to force local education authorities to provide Welsh-medium schools, not only in Welsh-speaking areas but also in highly anglicized areas where such schools had not existed in the years prior to the act's passage.

The second example, that of the Farmers Union of Wales, provides insight into the process of national "consciousness raising" at the institutional level. The FUW was founded in 1955 by a group of dissidents from the Carmarthen branch of the National Farmers Union, a British organization. The specific issues that stimulated the break were: an afforestation scheme that the central London office of the NFU had accepted without consultation with the Welsh farmers who would be affected by it; and the removal of a government milk subsidy with the consent of the NFU, an act that affected the Welsh hill farmers more adversely than other British farmers. The FUW has from the start presented itself as more responsive than the NFU to the needs of Welsh farmers, who generally have smaller holdings and raise different crops from their English counterparts. It has tried to convince Welsh farmers that the indifference of the London office of the NFU to Welsh farming problems mitigates any advantages it may have in terms of greater influence at the center of the bureaucracy. Furthermore, the FUW has worked to acquire influence for itself within the bureaucracy. At present its leaders can point to regular meetings with the government departments concerned with agricultural policy and to representatives on the important regional panels for northern and for South Wales. They acknowledge that their relations with the bureaucracy are much more important than those with politicians.

In both the above examples, and in others not discussed here, Welsh organizations form in response to (or preexisting organizations are greatly strengthened by their creative use of) resources made available by the central state apparatus. The availability of grants, special consideration in regulatory bodies, and so forth, makes organization along "national" lines worthwhile for a wide variety of groups. The resources that these groups utilize are a result of greater government involvement in everyday life and flow primarily from the bureaucracy, rather than from conventional political sources. Even in the case of the Welsh Schools Movement, where the principal resource was an act of Parliament, it was the interpretation of the act in a way certainly not explicitly anticipated by its framers, a process carried out within the education establishment, that was so crucial to the formation of Welsh-medium schools. Of course, as the example of the Welsh Schools Movement also illustrates, increasingly successful ethnic activity follows such state-level bureaucratic growth only when there is an active, self-conscious elite prepared to recognize the possibilities thereby presented for "national" organization and to respond creatively to them.

While the Welsh organizations described do attempt to secure a fairer share of the bureaucratic "pic" for Wales, most of them are ideologically opposed to increasing encroachments by the state and to bureaucratic centralization. Their very existence implies that a degree of separation brings with it added rewards. Although they themselves seldom carry this argument to its logical separatist conclusion, Plaid Cymru does do so. Thus, these Welsh organizations help create a Welsh constituency for a nationalist political party with a separatist ideology, such as Plaid Cymru. A comparison of Cymru Fydd and Plaid Cymru suggests that in conventional political terms, a Welsh pressure group is most effective when it is itself unified but remains within a British political party. But when the state bureaucracy increasingly provides means for pressure groups to glean rewards for their constituencies outside the purely political process, a separate (and separatist) political party becomes viable. Thus, particularly since World War II, with the growth of the welfare state in Britain, Plaid Cymru and the host of other Welsh organizations trying to represent a national constituency within the bureaucracy have existed in a symbiotic relationship, with the success of any one redounding to the credit of the others.

Plaid Cymru, to develop as a genuinely representative party for all of Wales, must make inroads into the heavily populated areas of the southeast, the traditional Labour stronghold. This it has begun to do, again with almost startling speed. It first became apparent that Plaid Cymru might have considerable strength in these areas in two by-elections (Rhondda West in 1967 and Caerphilly in 1968) in which the nationalists seriously challenged the Labour candidates. The real breakthrough came in local elections in 1976. Plaid Cymru now controls the Merthyr district council, in an area that is almost synonymous with Labour loyalty, and is the largest party on the Rhymni Valley council. Further proof of the party's strength in the area was provided by their creditable performance in county council elections in May 1977, when they captured just over 20 percent of the seats in Mid-Glamorgan. How has this been accomplished? Labour's hegemony in South Wales was not directly undermined by the nationalists, but rather by encroachments of the state under a Labour government. These encroachments were eventually to mean that Socialist ideology ceased to be the amost exclusive property of the Labour party and that the nationalists, offering a Socialist program phrased within a Welsh national context and harking back to an older, pre-Labour radical tradition (cf. Evans in Rees 1975), have been able to move into the area.

Perhaps the most important of the state encroachments in South Wales was the nationalization of the coal fields in 1947. With nationalization of this major industry the government to a great extent absorbed the South Wales union structure into itself. The union came to be in a similar position to that of the nineteenth-century Welsh MPs in the Liberal party. They had considerable power, because of the party's heavy dependence on the South Wales seats, yet they were closely tied to the government (which now ran the coal industry) and could not easily bring excessive pressure to bear against it. In addition, the decline of the coal industry, with pit closures going on throughout the 1960s, and increasing industrial diversification after World War II, meant that the regional organization, based as it was on the coal miners' union, was not as powerful as formerly.

Thus, by the late 1960s there was a real potential for some other organizational basis in South Wales. At this time large numbers of young people from the area, who considered themselves Socialists but felt that Labour had betrayed the cause of socialism began to turn to nationalism and Plaid Cymru. They have had a profound effect on the nationalist party's ideological stance, forcing it to develop more realistic positions on socioeconomic questions and moving it definitely to the left ideologically. Plaid Cymru presents itself in the South Wales valleys as the only radical Socialist alternative to Labour. Of course, it also advocates self-government for Wales. However, in political contests at present it does not emphasize this aspect of its ideology. Stress is put, instead, on the claim that Plaid is the only party in Wales that will truly represent the cause of socialism and the interests of the Welsh working class. However, this stance does not deny the ultimate goal of a self-governing Wales, for nationalists argue that Wales cannot achieve social justice and economic prosperity within an overcentralized British state that is insensitive to the distinctive requirements of peripheral areas. Thus, ideologically, Plaid Cymru accepts Socialist goals but offers a nationalist framework rather than an ideologically "pure" socialism as the means of achieving them.

Many Socialists within Plaid Cymru are acutely conscious of the contradiction implicit in decrying the evils of bureaucratic centralization and yet directing their efforts within the British political system to procuring increased government involvement to solve economic and social problems. They resolve the conflict by saying that some form of state socialism is necessary and for the short term they advocate investment by the London government; but in the long term the British state will prove too unresponsive to Welsh needs and hence they seek eventually a decentralized state socialism under a separate Welsh government.

The ideological stance against bureaucratic centralization also serves to help hold together the strong new leftist element in Plaid Cymru and the normally more conservative cultural nationalists, who retain the earlier primary orientation of the party toward the language and culture. The indifference of the centralized London government can be blamed both for the destruction of traditional Welsh communities (through depopulation and the incursions of the mass media) and for the economic neglect of the industrial areas. Another common theme cementing the party is the sympathy for the cause of the language, which is evident among leaders in anglicized areas; many of them have learned Welsh and others, not Welsh speakers themselves, are yet active champions of the language both within the party and as members of nonpolitical organizations. Thus, although strains within the party leadership are quite evident at times, the ideological stance noted above and the general sympathy for the language has kept the diverse elements fairly harmonious and held them for the most part within a single political organization.

ACADIAN ETHNIC NATIONALISM

Acadian ethnic nationalism is another political movement at the florescent phase of development, but it is somewhat less politically developed than that of the Welsh, not only in its degree and extent of public mobilization, but also in the limits to the pressure it applies to the central government. This lesser development of Acadian nationalism may result in part from the great upheaval in personnel, ideology, and organization brought on as the major vehicle for ethnic goals and interests changed from the Catholic church to secular interest groups; in part it may result from the great success of the Acadian elite in pursuing its own and the larger ethnic collectivity's interests without large-scale popular organization or constant active political confrontation. Another difference from the Welsh movement is the Acadian lack of success in bonding a radical economic argument of deprivation to the Acadian ethnic movement, and yet the inability of a class-based political movement to gain success on its own. The latter point implies that the elite sees no advantage in such an ideology, which suggests that the Acadian elite's rewards from government are sufficient to make further organizational development unattractive at the present, especially given the recent divisiveness within the movement.

Incipient Phase. The Acadians (francophones) of New Brunswick, one of the Maritime provinces of Canada, are the descendants of the early French colony of Acadie.[5] After expelling all French speakers in 1755, the British allowed them to return (or come out of hiding) in 1763. However, Acadian nationalism has its roots in the middle to late nineteenth century.

An Acadian elite initially emerged in conditions of relative isolation and deprivation. The Acadian section was not involved with the development of the New Brunswick polity and was not integrated into the system of local administration in New Brunswick until the latter third of the nineteenth century (cf. MacNutt 1963, pp. 169-70). Community organization in Acadian New Brunswick was dependent on the activities of Quebec missionary priests. By 1800 they had established parishes in seven centers across the Acadian sector; by 1860 the number increased to twenty-five (Michaud 1967, passim). These were both religious and civil units; each parish became a center of community organization and decision making.

Until 1860 the Acadian economy was purely subsistence oriented (Mailhot 1973, 1976), but after 1860 it was increasingly penetrated by capitalist enterprises in the fishing and timber trades. This gave rise to a condition Wolpe (1975) has defined as internal colonialism. As a result there was little economic development while more and more Acadians became engaged in part-time capitalist enterprises. Relative Acadian economic deprivation became increasingly evident. Several scholars (Baudry 1966; Mailhot 1973, 1976; Rumilly 1955) have described the general social conditions in midcentury as oppressive. Thorburn (1961, p. 23) is typical: "During the century after the expul-

5. The counties of Westmoreland, Kent, Northumberland, Gloucester, Restigouche, Madawaska, and Victoria in New Brunswick make up the Acadian sector. In 1871 they accounted for 94.5 percent of the French-origin population of New Brunswick; in 1971, for 88.7 percent.

sion, the Acadians lived in New Brunswick; yet they played virtually no part in the life of the community. Communications were so poor that many had no contact with English-speaking communities during their entire lives.

"As Catholics they were excluded from politics by the requirement of an oath of nonbelief in transubstantiation. . . . As a result there were virtually no Acadians in commerce or industry, and practically none with either capital or learning; they lived apart by farming and fishing."

Formative Phase (early). One goal of the Quebec missionaries had been to train an indigenous Acadian leadership to carry out their work as community organizers. They made four attempts to establish a classical college. The last, Collège St. Joseph, was successful (Cormier 1975, pp. 4-7). This became the recruiting ground for a largely clerical Acadian elite. Because of the high levels of illiteracy, the low levels of social organization, and the presence of a tradition according the priest the highest place in the social order, the Acadian priests became the leaders and organizers within the communities to which they were assigned (Bernard 1945, p. 132; Mailhot 1973, pp. 445, 451; Poirier 1898, p. x). They took over parishes from Quebec priests and established some new ones. Mailhot (1975, pp. 447-48) states that after 1875 the church increasingly became entrenched as the basis of local social organization.

Provincial legislation in the 1870s provided one important basis for the development of the parish structure of the Catholic church as a center of secular leadership and decision making. The provincial legislature passed the Common Schools Act in 1871 and the Municipalities Act in 1877; both defined specific responsibilities to be fulfilled by provincially created local administrative units. However, since the parish structure had been the only effective form of community organization in the Acadian sector since the deportation, the effect of the provincial legislation was to reinforce the status of the church as a center of local administration. Both acts created a new local political arena into which the church could expand. The priest supervised most of the local activity; organized bazaars and festivals; looked after the construction of schools, hospitals, and convents; supervised public works; and looked after the infirm and poor. Mailhot (1973, p. 448) asserts that [the church] "was the sole institution able to assert itself in an organizing role in the rural milieu, long without communication with the exterior. A good part of the savings that it amassed were distributed to the people in terms of educational services, construction of mills, etc." (trans. by author).

In 1880, sixteen years after the foundation of Collège St. Joseph,

Acadian leaders from all parts of the Maritimes came together as a single group for the first time at the National Congress of the St. Jean Baptiste Society in Quebec. This convention is the first evidence of the formation of supralocal elite institutions, but a more firmly grounded elite institutional structure was to follow. A separate Acadian convention for Memramcook was organized the following year. That convention and others following it[6] codified Acadian nationalist ideology. The French clergy dominated the conventions even if laymen led them. Priests were ex-officio delegates and often presided over the study groups. Their ideology can be summarized as follows:

Acadian society is initially depicted as a rural utopia. Harmonious agricultural communities, carved from virgin forests, enjoyed the bounties of nature. The ancestors are lauded for their gentility, pioneering spirit, perseverence, and humility. The expulsion by the British, Le Grand Dérangement, abruptly ended this golden age. A century of misery and untold hardship followed, during which the Acadians were a martyred people, tenaciously clinging to their faith and their language, "la plus belle langue du monde." Emulation of the ancestors is the proposed means of restoring Acadian society to its original condition. Acadians must be devoted to their religion, best sustained by keeping the French language. They must be committed to education to produce the priests, doctors, lawyers, and merchants the new Acadian society will need. Finally, they must return to the economic pattern of their ancestors, agriculture. If these are done a united French, and Catholic, Acadia would emerge from the abyss into which Acadian society had fallen. In further elaborations of the ideology this last phrase is termed La Renaissance (see Robidoux 1907 for ideology and Hautecoeur 1975 for analysis).

Formative Phase (late). Acadian nationalism had progressed considerably by 1900, as evidenced by the appearance of two newspapers and two new colleges. Sixty Acadian priests, their numbers buttressed by many more from Quebec, were active in the Maritimes. They attracted a number of religious communities and major convents had been established. A patriotic organization, Société de l'Assomption, organized major congresses from time to time.

By the late 1890s a clear pattern of power relationships that brought the Acadian clerics into competition with the Irish ecclesiastical establishment had emerged. First, an essentially French Catholic parish structure developed across the Acadian landscape. This was

6. Ten major conventions were held between 1881 and 1937. After that the national society remained dormant until 1957 when it was established as the Société Nationale des Acadiens.

initiated by the Quebec missionaries, then elaborated and intensified by an indigenous Acadian clergy. Almost simultaneously Irish control over a higher level of the church hierarchy had been extended from Halifax. Third, the provincial legislation of the 1870s and the system of provincial-municipal relations it established inadvertently reinforced the position of the church in the Acadian sector as a center of decision making.

As a result of this pattern Acadian leadership was constrained by the presence of the Irish ecclesiastical establishment. The nationalist assertions of the Acadian elite threatened the security of the Irish bishops because, in effect, the elite had established itself by use of the parish structure and by an ideology that radically distinguished French from Irish Catholics. This resulted in the growing disdain of the Irish leaders of the church for the Acadian nationalists. The bishops had various means to control the activities of the Acadian priests. It was in the bishop's power to assign priests in his diocese, to create new parishes, to invite or exclude religious communities, to deny temporarily the priest's right to celebrate Mass and administer the sacraments.

Tensions mounted between the priests and prelates when the Acadian priests tried to put nationalist ideology into practice in the areas of education and agricultural development. Each time the priest asserted his role as an *Acadian* leader by establishing a French school or requesting the creation of a new agricultural settlement, he necessarily (but perhaps unintentionally) called into question the authority of the Irish bishop. He did not act simply as the curate of the bishop, but as an Acadian leader and potential rival of the bishop. Therefore, as the Acadian leadership developed so too did episcopal hostility toward Acadian nationalism. This ultimately led to a struggle for Acadian control of the ecclesiastical structure.

The bitter struggle consumed the first two decades of this century (Doucet 1973, pp. 201-42; Rumilly 1955, pp. 915-17; Savoie 1976; pp. 83-98). By 1920 Acadians controlled both the diocese and a new parish in Moncton, which in 1936 became the center of a new ecclesiastical province with an Acadian archbishop; the Acadians gained complete control over the Catholic church, and the Acadian elite enjoyed a permanent institutional structure at a supralocal level.

Between 1920 and 1960, with the 1930s and 1940s representing the peak, the Acadian leadership and other institutions became firmly grounded around this ecclesiastical structure. Ideology was elaborated to the point where there existed no distinction between "French" and "Catholic." La Société l'Assomption Mutuelle (not to be confused with the patriotic society mentioned above) developed as a fraternal mutual aid society through a network of lodges. The clergy enthusiastically supported membership in the society, which became a focal point of village life. The society set up a special scholarship fund to send students to the classical colleges. The church also supported the Caisses Populaires (credit unions) springing up after 1936 because no other savings institutions existed then. Both these organizations have become major financial institutions and both represent implementations of the ideology emphasizing indigenous development under the guidance of the church. These organizations represent the earliest economic and political mobilization of the Acadian population by the ethnic elite.

At the local level the priest remained the most prominent leader in the village, followed in prestige by the doctor, lawyer, and male teachers. A village would most likely have a small convent and nuns engaged in teaching, hospital services, and domestic services for the priests. Teaching brothers established schools in some of the larger settlements, but they were never as ubiquitous as the nuns or priests. In the eyes of the local population the church, not the municipal authorities or the representatives of the provincial authorities, provided basic education and health services.

The Catholic church had been the first locus of Acadian nationalist struggle precisely because it was a powerful institution that controlled education, provided "welfare" and health services, and formed the structure of local leadership. The church maintained its position because of the poverty in the Acadian sector (see Mailhot 1976 for a discussion of its historical basis and Even 1970 for a summary description in the mid 1960s). The municipalities never had the means to provide services without dependence upon church resources: its organizational capacity and its supply of "cheap labor" in the form of nuns very active in education and health services.

Florescent Phase. The church maintained its integral position until the early 1960s, but the factors bringing about its decline were set in motion before then. In the 1940s the province began to assert a more active interest in education. It promoted the creation of a rural secondary school system. To this end it encouraged school consolidation, placed school finance on a country-wide basis, and made funds available for capital construction (Whalen 1963, pp. 66-70). As the 1950s progressed the financing of education became increasingly burdensome for all New Brunswick county municipalities because of the new provincial demands for educational services. However the situation was especially severe in the Acadian sector because it had the lowest fiscal capacity. The provincial grants were based on a per capita or percentage of cost basis, and therefore could not equalize the growing economic disparity resulting from uneven urbanization and industrialization. The new provincial demands in education had two effects in the Acadian sector—it increased reliance on church resources because of the poverty in the enclave and it drew the elite into some competition at the provincial level to secure provincial funds for education as municipal finances were strained to the breaking point. The Association Acadienne d'Education (AAE), a church-related education service organization, repeatedly sought greater provincial financial participation in the late 1950s even though fifteen years earlier it resisted provincial attempts at rural school consolidation and county unit financing.

Concern over the mounting costs of education was not confined to the Acadian sector. In 1955 a Royal Commission on school finance recommended greater provincial participation in financing education by making the equalization principle the basis of provincial grants. By 1960 most New Brunswick political observers clearly saw that the province would have to share a greater percentage of not only education costs, but costs for other social services as well (Whalen 1963, pp. 59 ff.).

New Brunswick politics received a jolt in 1960 when Louis J. Robichaud was elected the first Acadian premier. Perhaps the most charismatic New Brunswick politician of the century, Robichaud won the election on the strength of personality and political acumen. Neither ethnicity nor Acadian rights were mentioned in the campaign, but Robichaud was also a member in good standing of the Acadian establishment. He had been a member of the AAE and wrote a major detailed brief on the economic hardship of the French and some rural English counties and determined that the province would help. He appointed a Royal Commission to investigate provincial-municipal relations and propose solutions. The commission's report recommended a drastic overhaul of municipal government and the elimination of all county-level municipalities. The commission argued that education, health, welfare, and the administration of justice have a beneficial effect for the entire province and therefore are general services for which the province should assume complete financial and administrative responsibility. The commission further reasoned that only at the provincial level could a competent bureaucracy be formed. A uniform province-wide property tax based on real market value was the cornerstone of the commission's program. Considerable opposition to this program as drawn up by the Robichaud government existed, but none of it was expressed on an ethnic basis even though the Acadian sector was the most obvious beneficiary. In 1967 the legislative package was proclaimed provincial law.

The Robichaud government moved on a number of other fronts

to improve the quality of life in backward areas. In 1963 the government established Université de Moncton to which the three classical colleges then in existence in New Brunswick were affiliated. In 1966 the province entered into a substantial agreement with the federal government to develop northeastern New Brunswick (overwhelmingly French). The Fund for Rural Economic Development (FRED) poured approximately sixty-seven million dollars into the area by 1972 (Northeast New Brunswick Federal Provincial Rural Development Agreement, 1966; Northeast New Brunswick Federal Provincial Rural Development Agreement as Amended to September 5, 1972, 1972). The money went into the construction of schools, technical and vocational training, and infrastuctural development. In 1967 the province embarked upon an ambitious school-construction program in addition to the schools built with FRED funds. In 1968 the Robichaud government passed the Official Languages Act, modeled after the Federal Act, which committed the government to providing services in both official languages.

Although the Acadian elite took satisfaction in the Robichaud reforms, this intrusive provincial welfare program threatened to pre-empt the primary status of the church and to undercut the elite's authority. For almost one hundred years the church had maintained a financially shaky, but still French Catholic, school system. Robichaud replaced that with secular schools, an expanded educational bureaucracy, and a professional teaching corps, trained after 1968 at a French teacher's college. For ninety-nine years the church had had exclusive control over higher education; Robichaud replaced that with a provincially funded university. The church expressed interest in economic development by strong moral support of the Assumption and Caisses Populaires. The FRED program towered over their financial abilities to make improvements. Robichaud had accomplished much of what the Acadian elite wanted done but only by making the province rather than the church the responsible agent and in the process, making the elite realize they would have to bargain aggressively within the political structure if they wished to guarantee their positions.

In the late 1960s a number of events occurred that culminated in the formation of the Société des Acadiens du Nouveau Brunswick (SANB) in 1973. The province's ambitious school program, coupled with its assumption of complete financial responsibility, directed elite ethnic pressure onto the provincial bureaucracy.

The assertion of provincial responsibility in the 1960s precipitated a major reorganization of Acadian ethnic institutions and ideology for increased Acadian competition at the provincial level. This was not achieved without significant dislocation within the Acadian elite, which by 1960 sensed the growing disparity between a nationalist ideology that valued preeminently a closed society around the church and increasing Acadian participation in the economic and political sectors of the wider society, but it was unwilling to abandon completely a religious definition of Acadian nationalism. Neither did the elite see a necessity for mounting new political protest at the provincial level because Robichaud, a member of the elite, was the premier.

If the elite found religious ideology somewhat obsolete in the 1950s its protégés in the classical colleges found it more so. They completely abandoned a relgious nationalism and wanted to organize for competition at the provincial level. The new militants appeared on the scene at precisely the time the ideology was perceived as obsolete, even to the established elite, and when the provincial programs pre-empted the basis of organization around the church. The young people had been mobilized in the classical colleges to think in terms of service to Acadie; they inculcated in the students a sense of ethnic purpose. They also taught them to think of themselves as the future leaders of Acadie. However, they were leaving the colleges at a time when positions developed around the parish structure of the church no longer could be used effectively in service to Acadie, nor were they offered any substantial leadership positions. Instead of the church the province was making the significant decisions, and positions for the younger Acadian leaders were opening up in the expanded public sector. The elite, therefore, could not effectively discipline the new recruits it had mobilized.

The young militants mounted ethnic political protest in those areas where the province asserted responsibility: the implementation of the FRED program, levels of provincial support for Université de Moncton, location of the new schools, creation of unilingual school districts. The activities of the militants between 1966 and 1970 laid the basis for a new form of ethnic association around a political lobby that had no relationship with the Catholic church. They also laid the basis for a new ideology that stressed the linguistic and economic rights of Acadians and the failure or unwillingness of the government to guarantee them.

The younger Acadian leaders looked upon their elders as an Old Guard, caught up in a conservative, religious philosophy, and afraid to assert Acadian rights in the provincial political arena. Correspondingly the established elite looked with increasing contempt at the new militant political actions. They felt the young people were undisciplined, irresponsible, and were more of an embarrassment to the Acadian cause than a help. The established elite abhorred the complete rejection of the religious symbols and the abandonment of organization around the church.

At this point the actions of the federal government become significant to the struggle of the younger Acadians to reorganize Acadian institutions for sustained competition in the provincial political arena. As part of its effort to thwart Quebec separatism, the government made money available for the creation of official language minority associations in each province. The Société Nationale des Acadiens (SNA), the major Acadian organization and a direct descendant of the patriotic society that organized the Acadian conventions, started receiving federal funds in 1969. The new source of funding pre-empted any ability the established elite may have had to direct the nationalist movement. The federal money revived youthful interest in the SNA. They wanted to transform it into a province-wide political association for Acadians.

The SNA comprised Acadians from all three Maritime provinces. The federal government preferred to deal with provincially based organization. By 1970 Nova Scotia and Prince Edward Island Acadians established their own organizations that received federal support. The establishment of a provincial organization in New Brunswick was not so easily accomplished. For nearly three years the young militants clashed among themselves and with the Old Guard over the structures for the new association. In June 1973, the Société des Acadians du Nouveau-Brunswick (SANB) emerged as a provincial pressure group led by the more pragmatic of the new leaders. The Old Guard withdrew from the forefront of Acadian nationalism in 1973 and a new, more politically oriented leadership took over.

Since 1973 the SANB has established itself as an integral component of a new, ethnic, political organization. All of the major Acadian institutions, as well as two thousand individuals, most of them students and middle-class professionals, are members. The new ethnic ideology is a derivative of a bilingualism/biculturalism program focusing on the disparity between the "inherent" rights of French-speaking Canadians to governmental services in their language and the actual domination of English in the New Brunswick civil services. The SANB has successfully lobbied for a French division of the Department of Education, a French grammar school in St. John, and a law school at Université de Moncton. Various other linguistic issues are pending.

While the SANB is recognized as the political voice of the Acadians, it has not been without opposition. Part of the youthful cadre who opposed the Old Guard displayed a greater interest in economic issues, particularly regional underdevelopment in the northeast, than did the SANB leaders. At the same time the SANB was being organized, they formed the Parti Acadien (PA), centered in northeastern New Brunswick. The PA espoused a nationalist ideology derived not from bilingualism/biculturalism, but from a presumed ethnic division of labor (cf. Hechter 1975, pp. 31-43) whereby Acadian labor and resources are integrated into an externally controlled system of production and distribution. Hence, PA concentrated on economic issues for which it emphasized the necessity of Acadian control of resources through some kind of cooperative system.

Since its development, the PA has moved steadily leftward, until in 1975 it formally declared itself a Socialist party, first, and a nationalist party, second. While not all members of the PA were happy with the new Socialist orientation (some, in fact, left the party) a leftist ideology crystallized around a central premise that capitalist development inherently caused regional underdevelopment on a global scale. The PA thus came to develop a critique of multinationals, government, and the Acadian "bourgeoisie"; all were conceived as part of the capitalist system and, therefore in conflict with the political-economic order desired by the PA. Some condemned government development programs in particular, charging that their effect was to keep the population in perpetual subservience because they maintain a surplus labor force, divide the working and unemployed population by defining the latter as "welfare bums," impede class consciousness, co-opt the potential leadership by making them administrators, and support multinational exploitation by offering tax incentives and subsidies to companies to locate in underdeveloped areas under the pretext of easing unemployment.

The PA could not easily reconcile socialism and nationalism. Its Socialist critique led it to condemn the SANB and especially the Assumption, cooperatives, and credit unions as agents of a capitalist (i.e., evil) political-economic system while simultaneously leading it to acknowledge that small, anglophone, primary producers were in the same position vis-à-vis large multinational processors as the francophone producers. One former PA vice-president worked on the organization of fishermen of New Brunswick and Nova Scotia so they might be better able to bargain with the large companies over prices. This attempt at organization necessarily involved anglophones and followed directly from the critique of multinationals.

The PA has little basis of popular support. Most of the support it does have comes from the intellectual community and various of the *animateurs* involved in years of government "development" programs and convinced of their utter futility. Other than this, it is alienated from the remainder of the Acadian population and institutions. In 1974 provincial elections, before the PA formally annnounced its Socialist ideology, it made a very poor showing. Of the thirteen constituencies in the Acadian region of New Brunswick in which it fielded candidates, it affected the race in only two. In nine constituencies it received less than 4 percent of the vote; in three others it received between 4 and 7 percent; and in one it received nearly 19 percent (Dumont 1975, p. 24). The PA thus contrasts sharply with the SANB, which pressed specific linguistic issues on narrow linguistic grounds and achieved a fair amount of success.

A small but vocal minority of the SANB membership support the leftist position of PA. Because the SANB is publicly funded and is supposed to reflect the diversity of Acadian opinion, and because it likes to avoid public Acadian disunity, the SANB has sometimes made minor concessions to the leftists. Several of its own *animateurs* are members of the PA, and the SANB has partially funded *l'Acaven*, a left-leaning journal published by PA intimates, which features articles on capitalist exploitation, and the complicity of government and the nationalist "bourgeoisie" in the process. However, the SANB leadership admits privately that the Socialist position carries little weight in its programs. The leftists regularly condemn the SANB, but remain in it, in large measure because they have no viable, alternative organization of their own.

ETHNIC NATIONALISM IN COLONIAL SOCIETIES

If politicized ethnic movements are an outcome of a particular form of the state, then we should naturally expect to find such movements wherever similar forms of the state exist. Although the term *welfare state* has been used to refer to the state form associated with ethnic nationalism in Wales and Acadia, we have emphasized certain characteristics as most pertinent to the mobilization of ethnicity: the highly bureaucratic nature of such states and their intrusion on and regulation of many aspects of individual and community life; the weakening of class-based ideologies and organization among the political elite and masses and their replacement with a managerial orientation; and the presence of an active ethnic elite, partly thrust up by state intrusion, that organizes protest against the state to maintain or aggrandize its power.

The governments introduced by Western states into their colonial possessions often show these same qualities or evidence somewhat different qualities with, however, similar political results—even though they could hardly be called welfare states by the standards of participatory democracy and equalitarian redistribution of wealth and social services. This section suggests some of the similarities that link political developments in certain colonial societies (British India will serve as an example) with welfare states; it also proposes a somewhat similar course of development (around an elite) for ethnic nationalisms. The following section illustrates these assertions by adducing a developmental pattern for the South Indian non-Brahman movement that is similar to the one followed in Wales and Acadia.

Colonial government was highly bureaucratic and intrusive in British India and perhaps wherever administration was direct and land revenue or taxed crops along with military manpower represented the major sources of wealth extraction practiced by the metropolitan country (compare Seal 1970, pp. 2, 6). For example, the British raj intervened in and transformed South Asian land tenures and land values, proprietorship and tenancy, inheritance laws and family forms, judicial codes, social statuses, caste rankings and organization, language usage, and many other practices—often ostensibly in the name of preserving the "native" system. In fact, the colonial state intrusion may be much greater than that politically advantageous or even feasible in the home country. The costs of the heavy bureaucratic burden are borne by the colonized population, who have little power and no legitimate institutions through which to protest it. The imposed bureaucracy becomes a significant way to extract indigenous wealth for the home population. Further, there are few countervailing legitimate institutions or powerholders—recalcitrant nobility or free peasant— to resist the intrusions of the fully formed bureaucratic state introduced by the colonizing Europeans. We are *not* saying that the Western nation-state was built on consensus while the colonial state was dependent on suppression and conquest. Both states suppressed alternative powerholders, local autonomy, and individual independence that threatened their hegemony (see Tilly 1975, p. 37). But by the time European states colonized other parts of the world and linked them effectively with the home country, the bureaucratic forms and centralized power of the nation-state were fully developed. It had reached its majority in the political upheavals of the sixteenth through eighteenth centuries, with many failures and a few successes before the form was perfected. Transplanted to new ground—that is, released from the restraints that had accompanied its rise in the West—it grew quickly to achieve a maturity and size it was only later to develop in the West. Indians are still proud of the civil services institutions and traditions bequeathed to them under the British raj and are often unaware that nothing comparable in size and competence existed in the British Isles until after its creation in South Asia.

The very bureaucratic efficiency and extension of these colonial states provided the basis for the development of disaffected native elites, just as happened later in the West. These colonial states required sizable cadres of low-level officials, necessarily drawn from the indigenous population. As Riggs (1964) has noted, such state employment became the major vehicle for mobility among the native population, especially if, as in British India, the state subsidized educational programs to insure an abundant number of properly socialized indigenous civil servants. Seal echoes this analysis when he writes that "in societies with an autocratic constitution and backward economy, the will and working of government is the main-spring of enterprise" (1970, p. 115). But the colonial state often risked producing competition for access to these positions, a situation in which Western-educated elites could change from "collaborators to critics" (Seal 1970, p. 22). Seal argues that the early political consciousness of South Asia, including the founding of the Indian National Congress, was developed by the Western-educated indigenous elite to protect or enlarge their preferment within the British colonial administration. The following section argues similarly that the formation of the non-Brahman nationalist movement was at the behest of disaffected members of the English-educated elite, disaffected by their inferior access to state employment (and later, political office), who formulated and propagated a non-Brahman ideology in the furtherance of their interests. Therefore, ethnic nationalism in these colonial societies should follow the developmental course of its ilk in Western welfare states.

Yet one obvious difference separates ethnic nationalist development in colonial states from its sibling in the "postindustrial" world: separates developmentally but links organizationally. If ethnic nationalisms in welfare states represent new forms of political activity alongside class forms then ethnic political movements in colonial states reflect new ways of political mobilization in the absence of class ideology and organization. But the important determinant is the nature of the state, not some invariant, unilinear sequence of political development. Although in the West there is a prior developmental phase of class-based politics and in the developing world, there often is not, the organizational outcome, in the form of ethnic politics, is the same. Some scholars suggest that the present ethnic politics of developing nations will give way to class-based interest groups and political competition, presumably as existed in nineteenth-century Western societies (Hardgrave 1965, p. 6). Yet the very course of contemporary Western development brands this as fanciful, an extravagant notion of "lagging emulation" that depends on unilinear ideas about political evolution derived from modernization theories.

NON-BRAHMAN ETHNIC NATIONALISM

Non-Brahman ethnic nationalism, an early twentieth-century

development, rests on an ethnic identity and political organization created by a disaffected south Indian elite wanting better access to civil service employment.

Incipient Phase. The fourfold varna scheme of the Vedic scripture represents an elite classification of the many casts *(jati)* found throughout India. However, the traditional varna ranking of Brahman, Kshatriya, Vaisya (the Twice-Born "castes"), and Sudra was not applied in southern India, even as a simplifying classificatory scheme by the literati. Only Brahmans, Sudras, and untouchables were said to exist in the south. The Sudra varna, the basis of non-Brahman ethnic identity, contained many different castes, caste categories, and subregional varna categories (for these terms see Fox 1959) as well as populations speaking several Dravidian languages (Irschick 1969, pp. 12-13). Their common description as Sudras or the later self-identification as non-Brahmans gave them an inchoate ethnic identity.

Formative Phase (early). In south India, as well as in most parts of the subcontinent, the various castes or caste categories attributed Brahman varna status were the earliest to take up English education, the first to enter government service, and consequently the initial native elite to organize politically for gaining further concessions from the raj. The situation was especially disproportionate in south India, where in the 1890s 97 percent of the population was non-Brahman, yet 72 percent of the graduates of the University of Madras was; the distribution of government jobs was equivalently unbalanced. As early as 1851 the government of Madras had tried to equalize matters, but as late as the first decade of the twentieth century the superior qualifications and nepotism of the Brahmans led to situations such as the one district that supported forty-nine "friends and relations" of one Brahman official (ibid., p. 220). Although ostensibly "casteless" and in some cases even secular, the early political associations in Bengal, Madras, and Bombay and the later "all-India" associations were heavily dominated by Brahmans and their Vedic ideology (compare Seal 1970). The non-Brahman movement in Tamilnad and the Muslim movement in the United Provinces and Punjab grew up around local elites protesting the disproportionate representation of Brahmans in the civil service, requesting separate communal electorates for the legislative assemblies introduced by the British, and fearing the Indian National Congress's agitation for home rule and later total independence as the ultimate Brahman or Hindu conspiracy. Consequently, the British favored the non-Brahman movement as a counterweight to the Home Rule Movement organized by Besant and the Brahmans (Irschick 1969, pp. 351-53).

The early years of the twentieth century saw the literacy rate among non-Brahmans rise sharply, but with no equivalent increase in access to government service (ibid., p. 17). In 1916 Dr. T. M. Nair, a highly educated and anglicized physician (ibid., pp. 86-87) formed the South Indian People's Association to further the position of non-Brahmans in education and government service. Its ideology exalted Dravidian culture as against that of the Aryan Brahman (ibid., p. 74; see also Barnett 1974, p. 245). The association published an English-language paper, *Justice,* and less influential ones in vernacular languages. In 1917 the South Indian Liberal Federation was formed as the political arm of the People's Association and soon became known as the Justice party, a basically conservative organization that aimed for Madras provincial autonomy while proclaiming its loyalty to the British raj (Hardgrave 1965, pp. 14-15).

The Justice party was an elitist association of wealthy rural land-owners and educated middle-class urbanites (mainly from Madras city) (Irschick 1969, pp. 176-77; Hardgrave 1965, p. 16). It never attempted mass mobilization; from its beginnings in the late teens through its triumphs in the late 1920s to its desuetude in the 1930s, the Justice party worked for the improvement of non-Brahman *elite* interests through pressures applied to the colonial administration. Of its early period, Hardgrave writes, "Despite its many publications, its highly articulate propaganda, and its numerous conferences, the [Justice party] made no attempt to draw the mass following of a popular movement. . . . Its demands were formulated not so much to attract a following, as to influence the official policy of the British in Madras Presidency" (1965, p. 16). Of its later period, Irschick notes: "The aim of the Justice party was to enable these [relatively well-off, landed, educated] non-Brahmans to supplant the Brahmans, while keeping the untouchables at a good . . . distance . . . the party [changed] from the idealistic reform association which Dr. Nair had intended it to be into a mere political mechanism, a broker for government jobs for a few select non-Brahman caste Hindus" (1969, pp. 192-93).

Barnett (1974, pp. 246-47) has challenged this interpretation of the non-Brahman movement as motivated by self-interest alone and argues that the debilitating aspects of Sudra status was an important component. Yet, she also points to a sense of "relative deprivation" experienced by newly urbanized non-Brahmans, cutting away from their traditional precedence in village life yet cut off from status-conferring employment in the civil service. Her own points appear to confirm the self-interest of the non-Brahman elite as a major motivation for political organization.

Formative Phase (late). The legislative council elections, based on a restricted electorate, that the raj introduced after 1920 permitted the Justice party to confirm an effective regional elite presence with the Madras administration. Its electoral success from 1920 to 1926 and again in 1930 depended on the Congress party boycott of electoral competition in these years. In 1926 and with finality in 1934 and 1937, when the Congress (or Congress Swaraj) contested the council elections, the Justice party was thoroughly defeated. But in 1922, during its ascendancy, the non-Brahman elite had pressured the Madras government into officially granting its major demand: priority in government appointment to non-Brahmans and other "backward" groups (Irschick 1969, p. 219).

Partly because its main objective had been gained in the early 1920s and partly because many dissatisfied Justice party office seekers had become Congressites (in pursuit of greater rewards from this more successful political organization?), the non-Brahman party fell on hard times in the 1930s (Hardgrave 1965, pp. 23-24). The Congress had clearly gained control of the political institutions introduced by the British, and Gandhi's leadership and ideology had strengthened its Brahmanical orientation. An effective non-Brahman opposition needed the character of a popular movement, such as the Justice party elite had always disavowed. It therefore required new leadership.

Florescent Phase. The new leaders that transformed the non-Brahman movement came from the Congress rather than the Justice party. They had learned confrontation politics and popular agitation in the Congress noncooperation movement of the 1920s. E. V. Ramaswami Naicker, who was not English educated, bolted the Congress in 1925 over the issues of communal representation and what he regarded as the Brahman sympathies of the Gandhian program. S. Ramanathan, college educated, left the Congress in 1927 over the same matters. These men joined in the Self-Respect Movement of the late 1920s, which attempted to mobilize a non-Brahman popular political movement along secular lines. Naicker also worked within the Justice party, although he criticized it for its disinterest in social reform (Irschick 1969, p. 337). The Self-Respect Movement addressed poorer non-Brahmans, untouchables, and women and rose to prominence in the anti-Hindi agitation of 1937 (a response to the 1935 Congress program for the introduction of Hindi). Naicker became president of the Justice party in 1938 (while in prison) and began its conversion into a mass political organization apace.

The Justice party under Naicker put forth a demand for the separate state of Dravidanad in 1941. In 1944 the party was renamed the Dravida Kazagham (DK) (ibid., pp. 346-47) and in 1945 a flag and a model of grassroots party organization was propounded (Hardgrave 1965, pp. 28-29). The ideology projected by the DK was anti-religious and against caste, and it favored widow and intercaste marriages as part of its secular and anti-Brahmanical program. The extent of its opposition to Brahmans, Hindi, and northern India in general is best gauged by the recension of the Ramayana it developed, one in which the southern "demon" Ravanna becomes a martyr to Brahman North Indian aggression, as personified in the cowardly agent of Dravidian suppression, the no-longer god-hero Rama (ibid.; Barnett 1974, p. 253).

The DK not only propounded a popular and more aggressive non-Brahman identity, it also employed popular means of communication to convey its message. Dramatic troupes, songs and literature in the vernacular, and youth groups were all employed to convey its program in a fashion the older Justice party had never contemplated. By Independence in 1947, the DK may have remained similar to the Justice party in serving as a vehicle of social mobility for its leaders (Hardgrave 1965, p. 33), but it was fundamentally different in organization and audience, as well as in the social antecedents of its leaders.

Matured Phase. In 1949, shortly before the first elections in independent India, C. N. Annadurai broke away from the DK to form the Dravida Munetra Kazagham (DMK). The ostensible reason for the break was the autocratic control exercised by Naicker within the DK and the need for a more democratic leadership (which evidently meant better access to positions of leadership for younger members). Ideologically, the two parties were very similar, and both continued to be politically active under the banner of non-Brahman identity and an independent south India. However, the DK continued to appeal, although not exclusively as had the Justice party, to landowners and other established non-Brahmans. The DMK strove for an even more widely based constituency, including poorer non-Brahman caste Hindus, untouchables, college students, and the educated urban unemployed (ibid., p. 35). The DMK also effectively introduced the political use of mass communcation by employing the cinema and the new culture heroes it threw up for Dravidian consciousness raising (ibid., p. 34; Barnett 1974, p. 254).

The competition that ensued throughout the 1950s between the DMK and the DK saw the former develop into a potent regional party while the latter declined . The DK took on the role of a "spoiler," contriving alliances variously with the Communists or Kamaraj Nader's Congress or perpetrating acts of symbolic violence like flag burning—in other words, an alternation between playing "smoke-filled room" politics and raising the ante for popular mobilization by extremist acts. The DMK incorporated more regional economic issues into its program as it became a party of legitimate opposition within independent India and even dropped its demand for a separate south Indian state. Perhaps this will be the course followed by the Acadian and Welsh ethnic elites as they achieve greater rewards from and involvement in the political process, but since they (and the DMK) now have a popular movement behind them, they will, unlike their precursors in the formative period, have to satisfy their ethnic congeners as well as themselves.

CONCLUSION

This paper has argued that political movements termed ethnic nationalisms occur under certain conditions of state organization and follow a similar pattern of development, dependent on the actions of a self-conscious elite. The bureaucratic intrusion of the welfare state and its managerial orientation exported from elite to masses lead to a weakening of class-based ideology and political organization in the most developed welfare states. Elites, disaffected by the failure of rewards from the supposedly omnipotent but in fact fallible welfare state turn to mobilization of so-called ascriptive collectivities, including ethnic ones, as new constituencies in these postindustrial states. Yet similar developments, we believe, can be found in certain formerly colonial nations—those that suffered the introduction of the fully developed Western state bureaucratic apparatus superimposed on a basically peripheral economy and society.

Obvious differences exist between these colonial states and Western welfare states, even though our presentation has emphasized the similarities of state intrusiveness and of developmental phases followed by ethnic nationalism. Such states do not have the history of class-based ideologies that are weakened or dislodged by the welfare state. They do not enjoy the great economic prosperity that allows the managerial orientation of the welfare state elite to become widespread in the population. Indeed, until recently they had not politically mobilized a significant proportion of their populations.

Rather than invalidating the comparison, however, these differences may help explain the greater importance and more compressed development of ethnic politics in parts of the colonial world. Because the colonial state is an introduced form and therefore has no indigenous competitors and because the economic system is colonialized and of low productivity, the colonial administration becomes the major source of power and economic preferment. That is why the non-Brahman elite enters into much more immediate political discourse with the state administration than do their compeers in Acadia and

Wales, who originally worked through local and regional institutions to define or confirm their precedence and gain status. The greater weight of ethnic nationalism in these colonial states is an obvious function of the absence of preexisting class political alignments to serve as a base for mobile elites. Finally, the compressed quality of ethnic nationalism in the colonial situation is a response to the very late mobilization of the population, a mobilization often induced by the colonial power as a farewell, or more likely, Parthian shot, or by international pressures and expectations (compare Rokkan 1975, pp. 572-73 for a somewhat similar notion of the temporal compression of challenges to the new states, as compared to their earlier European counterparts).

Should we speculate, then, that the class-based politics of the West in the eighteenth and nineteenth centuries was a condition of the pristine industrial order, not to be followed elsewhere and in future time, just as it had few, if any, precursors in the political evolution of human cultures? Perhaps, although colonies such as those in Latin America that were directly attached (albeit in an unequal manner) to Western industrial productivity showed early on clearly formed and vital class politics. We may suggest, however, that looking to the past development of the West for understanding future change in (some part of) the former colonial world may be unwise—not only because conditions have altered so that the third world cannot recapitulate the Western pattern, but also because third-world patterns (such as ethnic nationalism) may presage Western developments. The dependency theorists and world-systems analysts have sensitized us to how the development of export economies in certain colonial economies channeled their development into a skewed version of Western industrialism. Surely the export of the Western nation-state to other of these colonies may have produced an earlier, more intense, and more rapid development of politicized ethnicity that we only recently and with perplexity recognize as developing in our own, Western, midst.

REFERENCES

Barnett, Marguerite Ross
  1974 "Creating Political Identity: The Emergent South Indian Tamils." *Ethnicity* 1:237-60.
Baudry, René
  1966 "Les Acadiens d'aujourd'hui: Rapport de recherche préparé pour la Commission royale d'enquête sur le bilinguisme et le biculturalism." Manuscript. Centre d'Etudes Acadiennes, University of Moncton.
Bell, Daniel
  1962 *The End of Ideology: On the Exhaustion of Political Ideas in the Fifties.* New York: Free Press.
  1975 "Ethnicity and Social Change." In *Ethnicity, Theory, and Experience,* ed. Nathan Glazer and Daniel P. Moynihan, pp. 141-77. Cambridge, Mass.: Harvard University Press.
Bensman, Arthur, and Vidich, Charles:
  1958 *Small Town in Mass Society.* Princeton, N. J.: Princeton University Press.
Bernard, Antoine
  1945 *L'Acadie Vivante.* Montreal: Edition du Devoir.
Butt Philip, Alan
  1975 *The Welsh Question: Nationalism in Welsh Politics, 1945-1970.* Cardiff: University of Wales Press.
Clement, Mary
  1960 "The Campaign Against Illiteracy." In *Wales Through the Ages,* vol. 2, ed. A. J. Roderick. Swansea: Christopher Davies.
Cormier, Clement
  1975 "Université de Moncton." Manuscript. Centre d'Etudes Acadiennes, Université de Moncton.
Coupland, Sir Reginald
  1954 *Welsh and Scottish Nationalism.* London: Collins.
Craig, F.W.S.
  1976 *British Electoral Facts, 1885-1975.* London: Macmillan and Co.
Davies, Gwennant
  1973 *The Story of the Urdd, 1922-1972.* Aberystwyth: Cwmni Urdd Gobaith Cymru.
Doucet, Camille-Antonio
  1973 *Un étoile s'est levée en Acadie: Marcel Francois Richard.* Les Editions du Renouveau.
Dumont, André
  1975 "Statistique des dernières élections." *L'Acayen* 2, no. 6:24.

Eidheim, Harald
1969 "When Ethnic Identity Is a Social Stigma." In *Ethnic Groups and Boundaries,* ed. Fredrik Barth, pp. 39-57. Boston: Little, Brown.

Evans, Gwynfor
1975 "Foreword." In *The Welsh Political Tradition,* pp. 3-10. Cardiff: Plaid Cymru.

Even, Alain
1970 "Le territoire pilote du Nouveau-Brunswick ou les blocages culturels au dévelloppement économique. Contribution à une analyse socio-économique du développement." Ph.D. dissertation, Faculté de Droit et des Sciences Economiques, Université de Rennes.

Field, G. Lowell, and Highley, John
1972 *Elites in Developed Societies: Theoretical Reflections on an Initial Stage in Norway.* Sage Professional Papers in Political Science, no. 3. Beverly Hills, Calif.: Sage.

Fox, Richard G.
1969 "Varna Schemes and Ideological Integration in Indian Society." *Comparative Studies in Society and History* 11:27-45.

Gouldner, Alvin
1970 *The Coming Crisis of Western Sociology.* New York: Basic Books.

Grigg, John
1973 *The Young Lloyd-George.* Berkeley: University of California Press.

Hardgrave, Robert L., Jr.
1965 *The Dravidian Movement.* Bombay: Popular Prakashan.

Hautecoeur, Jean-Paul
1975 *L'Acadie du Discours.* Quebec: Les Presses de l'Université Laval.

Hechter, Michael
1975 *Internal Colonialism: The Celtic Fringe in British National Development, 1536-1966.* Berkeley: University of California Press.

Irschick, Eugene F.
1969 *Politics and Social Conflict in South India: The Non-Brahman Movement and Tamil Separatism, 1916-1929.* Berkeley: University of California Press.

Janowitz, Morris
1976 *Social Control of the Welfare State.* New York: Elsevier.

Jenkins, R. T., and Ramage, Helen M.
1951 *A History of the Honourable Society of Cymmrodorion and*

of the Gwyneddigion and Cymreigyddion Societies (1751-1951). London: The Honourable Society of Cymmrodorion.

Jones, J.E.
1970 *Tros Gymru. J. E. a'r Blaid*. Abertawe: Gwasg John Penry.

Kirchheimer, Otto.
1957 "The Waning of Opposition in Parliamentary Regimes." *Social Research* 24:127-56.

Lane, Robert E.
1965 "The Politics of Consensus in an Age of Affluence." *American Political Science Review* 59:874-95.

Lipset, Seymour Martin
1960 *Political Man*. Garden City, N.Y.: Doubleday.
1977 "The End of Ideology and the Ideology of the Intellectuals." In *Culture and Its Creators*, ed. Joseph Ben-David and Terry Nichols Clark, pp. 15-42. Chicago: University of Chicago Press.

MacNutt, W. S.
1963 *New Brunswick, a History: 1784-1867*. Toronto: Macmillan of Canada.

Mailhot, Raymond
1973 "Prise de conscience collective au Nouveau-Brunswick, 1860-1890, et comportment de la majorité anglophone." Ph.D. dissertation, Université de Montreal.
1976 "Quelques elements d'histoire économique de la prise de conscience acadienne, 1850-1891." *Société Historique Acadienne, Cahiers* 7, no. 2:49-74.

Michaud, Marguerite
1967 *Les Acadiens des Provinces Maritimes, guide historique et touristique*. Commission du Centenaire.

Morgan, Kenneth O.
1972 "Welsh Politics, Cymru Fydd to Crowther." In *Anatomy of Wales*, ed. R. Brinley Jones, pp. 117-44. Peterston-super-Ely, Glamorgan, Wales: Gwerin Publications.

New Brunswick
1963 *Report of the Royal Commission on Finance and Municipal Taxation in New Brunswick, Fredericton*.

Pelling, Henry
1965 *Origins of the Labour Party*. 2nd ed. London: Oxford University Press.

Pierce, G. O.
1960 "Nonconformity and Politics." In *Wales Through the Ages*, vol. 2, ed. A. J. Roderick, pp. 168-76. Swansea: Christopher Davies.

Poirier, Pascal
  1898 *Le Peye le Febure et l'Acadie.* Montreal: C. O. Beauchemin et fils.
Reiter, Rayna R.
  1972 "Modernization in the South of France: The Village and Beyond." *Anthropological Quarterly* 45, no. 1:35-53.
Riggs, Fred W.
  1964 *Administration in Developing Countries: The Theory of Prismatic Society.* Boston: Houghton Mifflin.
Robidoux, Ferdinand
  1907 Conventions nationales des Acadiens, recueil des travaux et délibérations des six premiers conventions. Vol. 1. Shediac, New Brunswick: Le Moniteur Acadien.
Rokkan, Stein
  1975 "Dimensions of State Formation and Nation-Building: A Possible Paradigm for Research on Variations within Europe." In *The Formation of National States in Western Europe,* ed. Charles Tilly, pp. 562-600. Princeton, N. J.: Princeton University Press.
Rumilly, Robert
  1955 *Histoire des Acadiens.* Montreal: Fides.
Savoie, Alexandre-J.
  1976 *Une demi-siècle d'histoire Acadienne.* Montreal: l'Imprimerie Gagneltée.
Seal, Anil
  1970 *The Emergence of Indian Nationalism: Competition and Collaboration in the Later Nineteenth Century.* Cambridge: At the University Press.
Thoenes, Piet
  1966 *The Elite in the Welfare State.* New York: Free Press.
Thorburn, Hugh G.
  1961 *Politics in New Brunswick.* Toronto: University of Toronto Press.
Tilly, Charles
  1975 "Reflections on the History of European State-Making." In *The Formation of National States in Western Europe,* ed. Charles Tilly, pp. 3-83. Princeton, N. J.: Princeton University Press.
Torgerson, Ulf
  1962 "The Trend Towards Political Consensus: The Case of Norway." *Acta Sociologica* 6:159-72.
Verdery, Katherine
  1976 "Ethnicity and Local Systems: The Religious Organization of

Welshness." In *Regional Analysis,* vol. 2, *Social Systems,* ed. Carol A. Smith, pp. 191-228. New York: Academic Press.

Walker, David

1976 "Disestablishment and Independence." In *A History of the Church in Wales,* ed. David Walker, pp. 161-67. Woodland Place, Penarth, South Glamorgan: Church in Wales Publications Education and Communications Centre.

Waxman, Chaim I.

1968 *The End of Ideology Debate.* New York: Funk and Wagnalls.

Whalen, H. J.

1963 *The Development of Local Government in New Brunswick.* Fredericton, N.B.

Williams, David

1950 *A History of Modern Wales.* London: John Murray.

Williams, W. Ogwen

1960 "The Union of England and Wales." In *Wales Through the Ages,* vol. 2, ed. A. J. Roderick, pp. 16-23. Swansea: Christopher Davies.

Wolpe, Harald

1975 "The Theory of Internal Colonialism." In *Beyond the Sociology of Development: Economy and Society in Latin America and Africa,* ed. Ivar Oxaal, Tony Barnett, and David Booth, pp. 229-52. Boston: Routledge and Kegan Paul.

Trosper undertakes in his paper to identify the factors that have led to the ethnic change manifest in the emergence of a new pan-Indian nationalist movement in the United States. He argues that while American Indians have roots in many different groups, many Indians today claim to share a common identity on the basis of having a common mythlike "charter." The central element of this charter is the historical experience of the breaking of a treaty relationship between Indians and the United States government. Trosper shows how such a charter has been forged through a historical process of frontier expansion by the dominant White American society. This process moved through a succession of stages following initial contact between Whites and Indians. As Whites became dominant, treaties formed with Indians during the contact stage were abrogated, ignored, or violated, and Indians were forcibly removed from part or all of their homelands. Some Indians were then accorded autonomy on reservations, but many other Indians were forced into welfare dependency upon the United States government. It was this welfare situation that stimulated the emergence of an Indian nationalist movement with members mobilized through appeals to the charter. A major goal of the Indian nationalist movement is the recognition by the United States government of political autonomy for Indians as Indians. This goal, Trosper also observes, runs counter to the commitment to individual, as distinct from group, rights embedded in American law and institutions. The conflict between Indian nationalist goals and prevailing American notions regarding individual rights remains unresolved.

RONALD L. TROSPER

American Indian Nationalism
and Frontier Expansion

IT is the thesis of this paper that American Indians have transformed themselves from a diverse people with little common identity into an ethnic group. They have done so by mobilizing, with respect to a charter, the shared history of broken treaties. I define a charter[1] as a historical event, or series of similar historical events, that, when used in three ways, aid ethnic mobilization. First, the event is "primordialized"—it becomes a characteristic symbolizing the cultural givens of a group. Indians, for instance, are distinct because they share descent from those people who originally inhabited North America. Although the Indian cultures were very different in pre-contact times, all shared a treaty or a treatylike event; this common element has

1. My definition of a charter differs from those of Nagata and Trottier in this volume. I intend to use "primordial" as Keyes (1976) suggests, following Geertz (1963).

become a myth that defines cultural parts of pan-Indian identity. Second, a charter defines the boundaries of a group. In this case, Indians are those people claiming descent from those who signed treaties. Third, a charter provides a guide to action. Indians use broken treaties to justify claims to the right of self-government and full payment for land unfairly taken. Thus, for me, the use of a charter combines both the cultural and social dimensions of ethnicity. Cultural factors are closely tied to kinship and descent. Social factors reflect the particular political and economic position of a group in the general society.

Defining a charter in this manner allows one to approach the process of ethnic change with some presuppositions. One expects that ethnic mobilization, to be successful, requires a charter combining all three elements. Since the charter must be a historical event, people whose circumstances suggest they share common interests cannot call into play the powerful emotions of ethnicity if history provides them with no such event. A full explanation of ethnicity should, therefore, provide an explanation for the historical event and the characteristics that make it a potential charter. This paper attempts such an explanation.

As the United States expanded westward, relations between Indians and Whites on the frontier passed through a number of typical configurations. One of these configurations almost invariably produced a treaty, while another invariably broke the previous agreement. Consequently, even though Indians are culturally different, and even though details of the encounter between them and Europeans vary, the experience is sufficiently similar that most Indians can claim they share it.

In this paper I will first show that Indian ethnic mobilization exists and, considering the circumstances, has achieved notable success in stating concrete political demands that follow from the charter. I will then examine the manner in which broken treaties provide the other two characteristics of a charter, boundary definition and primordial identification. Finally, I will present a model of frontier expansion that explains why so many Indian groups share this experience, therefore allowing leadership to mobilize with this particular charter.

THE SUCCESS OF PAN-INDIAN MOBILIZATION

The development of a pan-Indian political movement began with the establishment of the National Congress of American Indians (NCAI) in 1944. The NCAI gained strength among American Indians with its successful opposition to what was known as the termination policy. This policy in the 1950s sought to assimilate Indians individually into American society through eliminating reservations and tribal government. The NCAI remains the preeminent pan-Indian political organization today. President Carter included its president and executive director in the list of persons considered for commissioner of Indian affairs, although he appointed neither. Other pan-Indian political activities have attracted attention during the 1960s and 1970s. The occupations of Alcatraz, the headquarters of the Bureau of Indian Affairs, and Wounded Knee, South Dakota, received significant attention in the media. Although some observers have concluded that Indian activism originated in the late 1960s, these symbolic actions have complemented rather than conflicted with the less dramatic actions of the National Congress of American Indians and its affiliated regional Indian organizations.

By the early 1970s, such activism led to a formal disavowal of ultimate assimilation as the goal of federal policy. The president and Congress agreed to return Blue Lake to the Taos Pueblo and to restore the Menominee Indian Reservation to federal trust status. Such recognition of Indian land rights and support for tribal organization were inconsistent with accepted assimilationist policy. Yet many statutes and the mission of the Bureau of Indian Affairs were based upon that policy. The resulting confusion induced the chairmen of Indian Affairs subcommittees in the House and Senate to sponsor a special congressional study. In March 1975, the American Indian Policy Review Commission, consisting of three senators, three congressmen, and five Indians, began work.

The commission had eleven task forces predominantly staffed by Indians. Each task force published a report, and the commission published its final report in 1977. The report proposed that Indian tribes exercise sovereign powers within their reservations and that the federal government protect Indians from outside attacks on their governments and their property. The federal government should also provide services to individual Indians (1977, pp. 4-9).

The commission's interpretation of Indian treaties forms the basis of their program. They write:

> It is generally believed, mistakenly, that the Federal Government owes the American Indian the obligation of its trusteeship because of the Indians' poverty, or because of the Government's wrongdoing in the past. Certainly American Indians are stricken with poverty, and without question the Government has abused the trust given it by the Indian people. But what is not generally known, nor understood, is that within the federal system the Government's relationship with the Indian people and their sovereign rights are of the highest legal standing, established

through solemn treaties, and by layers of judicial and legislative actions. [Ibid., p. 1]

Indian treaties are an important foundation of all of Indian law. Most early court cases involved treaty tribes. Policy changed, however, and the United States began to deal with Indian tribes by other means, such as Executive orders, agreements, and statutes. When those non-treaty tribes came into court, treaty law was applied.

While this discussion has focused on treaty law, any discussion of treaties would be incomplete without mention of the symbolic and moral significance to the Indian people. Unlike almost all other documents in Anglo-American law, treaties are seen as moral statements which represent the "word of the nation" and the "sanctity of the public faith." An Indian treaty is "a bulwark against State encroachment. . . . It is a monument to past guilt; and efforts to change the law include, in themselves, evidences of continued uneasiness."

This Commission, in hearing after hearing, has seen that American Indians rightfully expect that this Nation will continue to abide by the solemn promises made in these old laws: The Constitution is an old law, too. Thus, while treaties can legally be broken by Congress, such extreme action must be truly a last resort. As Justice Hugo Black put it: "Great Nations, like great men, should keep their word." Indian treaties are among the very few laws in our society which raise those kinds of issues. [Ibid., pp. 111-12 (citations omitted)]

The commission uses treaties to redefine the federal government's "trust responsibility." The old policy had the federal government, through the Bureau of Indian Affairs, acting as a trustee in managing Indian property until Indians learned how to manage it themselves. Until that occasion, the federal government also provided services such as health and education to Indians, based on their need, and supported tribal government as a means to educate Indian leaders. The commission's proposals redefine trust responsibility as indefinite protection of tribal self-government without the educative rationale. According to the commission, tribal governments retain inherent sovereignty that should be recognized by Congress, the courts, and the executive branch. Tribal governments are another type of local government, separate from state jurisdiction. The federal government has a duty to protect tribal powers and control over land, but only its courts have legitimate power to review the actions of tribal government. In particular, the Bureau of Indian Affairs should not be able to overrule tribal actions unilaterally, as it usually can do now. It should be removed from the Department of the Interior and the statutes governing its control of Indian affairs should be rewritten to reduce its power.

Indian tribes should retain the right to determine membership based on principles of descent, while the scope of government will be territorial. Tribes, unlike states, could exclude from voting reservation residents who are not tribal members. Other political rights, such as rights to due process, would be protected, although litigation would begin in tribal courts. Federal expenditures for the physical well-being of Indians should be continued, and extended to off-reservation residents. Tribal efforts to develop an economic base should also receive federal support.

Because they support policies contradicting widely held views of federal structure, the commission presents a constitutional challenge. Tribal governments possess inherent sovereignty equal to that of states, which the federal government should protect. The body of the report, especially its third chapter, cites legal and historical precedents for such an interpretation.

Congressman Lloyd Meeds, a sponsor and then vice-chairman of the commission, in dissenting from the commission's final report, provides an alternative explanation for federal policy. He maintains the commission provided "a document encompassing a tribal view of the future of American Indian law and policy," to which he responds:

> The blunt fact of the matter is that American Indian tribes are not a third set of governments in the American federal system. They are not sovereigns. The Congress of the United States has permitted them to be self-governing entities but not entities which would govern others. American Indian tribal self-government has meant that the Congress permits Indian tribes to make their own laws and be ruled by them. The erroneous view adopted by the Commission's report is that American Indian tribal self-government is territorial in nature. On the contrary, American Indian tribal self-government is purposive. The Congress has permitted Indian tribes to govern themselves for the purpose of maintaining tribal integrity and identity. But this does not mean that the Congress has permitted them to exercise general governmental powers of the lands they occupy. This is the crucial distinction which the Commission report fails to make. . . .
>
> In addition, the Commission has failed to make the distinction between the power of American Indian tribes to govern themselves on the lands they occupy, and their proprietary interest in those lands. Mere ownership of lands in these United States does not give rise to governmental powers. Governmental powers have as their source the State and Federal constitutions. [Ibid., pp. 573-74]

I do not wish here to assess the objectivity of either the commission's report or Meeds's dissent. Such significant issues as the distribution of tax revenues between states and tribes, control of water in the West, and regulation of land use depend upon the extent of tribal power. An interesting point, however, is that the commission's recommendations and the Indian claims upon which these recommendations are based are predicated upon a separatist position that is inconsistent with individualism as defined by most Americans. Unlike other minorities, Indians are not demanding equality based on equal citizenship. They lay claim to equality based on equal sovereignty of their governments. Meeds claims such a goal is politically infeasible: "As a legislator, I must say that many of the recommendations have absolutely no chance of being enacted into law. That is because they are oblivious to political reality. The combined effect of a number of recommendations and findings constitutes a degree of separatism which this country is totally unprepared to assume. Some of the recommendations and findings are inimical to concepts we hold sacred as American citizens" (ibid., p. 612). As a consequence, he argues, implementation of the recommendations would lead either to a "backlash" or to close congressional supervision of tribal governments to prevent the exercise of Indian power over non-Indians residing on Indian reservations.

Pan-Indian leaders, in disagreeing with Meeds's argument, use the American Indian Policy Review Commission to present a separatist political and economic program. They do so for several reasons. First, mobilization of Indians required the use of symbols they all share, and treaties provide such a symbol. Second, since treaties define relationships between government, this charter fits well with Indians looking to tribal governments to defend their interests. Third, this position is strengthened because the same events that created broken treaties also reduced the appeal of individualist policies and led to the power of the Bureau of Indian Affairs over Indian property and government. All these factors explain why the Indian program conflicts so much with what Meeds refers to as sacred American principles.

Returning to the main line of the argument, we have seen that the shared historical experience of a broken treaty has provided Indians with a plan of action and a set of demands. Thus one of the three components of a charter is present. A charter also provides a definition of an ethnic group's boundary. Because the set of demands defends tribal governments, Indians are those people whom tribal governments recognize. The American Indian Policy Review Commission answers the question, "Who is an Indian?" with "In most circumstances . . . a person is an Indian if that person's tribe recognizes him or her as an Indian" (ibid., p. 108). Finally, a charter provides a myth to explain and justify a group's distinctiveness. By "primordializing" a shared characteristic, a group is able to use the emotional value of kinship and a sense of shared descent to define an identity and mobilize for action.

Although treaty content varies across tribes, and also varies by time within a tribe's history, certain treaties are similar enough to support the claim that all Indian groups have had the same experience.

Since treaties recognized or guaranteed Indian ownership of land, this charter emphasizes that Indians originally shared the whole continent. The rhetoric of pan-Indian nationalism reinforces this point by referring to land as "mother Earth." In this kinship idiom, all Indians claim to share the same origin and are therefore brothers. Although each treaty protected different land, such land can be seen as belonging to a common Indian earth. The emotional appeal of this metaphor is increased by other cultural and social practices that Indian groups have in common, and by the use of pan-Indian symbols, many of which originated with Plains Indians (See Trottier, below, pp. 278, 290-93).

The occupation of Alcatraz illustrates the invocation of the charter. The occupation is an important event in recent Indian activism (Kickingbird and Ducheneaux 1973, pp. 211-18; Spencer, Jennings et al. 1977, p. 519; Deloria 1974, p. 38). When the government abandoned Alcatraz as a prison, the belief that a treaty promised the return of unused federal property and the need for a new Indian center after an old one had burned down provided the impetus for a dramatic occupation of the island with extensive media coverage. The government eventually evicted the occupiers after their numbers dwindled and world attention waned. Subsequently, a group of the occupiers distinguished between land and treaty-breaking in reporting their view of what happened:

Alcatraz was born a mountain, surrounded by the waters of a great salt sea. By hands of hate this island transformed into a symbol of fear and oppression. For too short a time this same island was held in trust by Indians of all tribes, who sang its praise as a part of mother earth, and who cleansed the evil with the sacred tobacco.

Alcatraz is again the hateful symbol of oppression. Our Indian people have been removed from sacred ground, our children have felt guns at their heads. Steel fences are again being put up. All approaches to the island are being guarded and patrolled. Armed with weapons of war and the sterile theories of law, they try desperately to keep out the Indian spirit. We send out our voices to that desolate rock, and are gifted with echoes which resound our strength.

Alcatraz, the idea, lives. We can only pray the Great Spirit that all brothers and sisters who can understand our song join us. [Bluecloud 1972, p. 13]

The occupation drama here becomes a metaphor for the treaty-breaking process; it includes these elements: land sacred to Indians that rightfully is theirs, Indian unity in occupying the land, and forceful eviction. Omission of a treaty in this case is skirted through a play on words that Indians held the land in "trust." Although the event itself seems to have led to no concrete action, it emphasizes the pan-Indian appeal of broken treaties. Indians with land to reclaim support the rhetoric. The Alcatraz occupation also marked the formal beginning of the appelation "Indians of All Tribes" for urban Indians in many different cities (Kickingbird and Ducheneaux 1973, p. 216). Similar occupations of abandoned government land were staged subsequently. Some of them, such as in Seattle, led to tangible results for urban Indians.

Thus, the charter has provided a program, a boundary definition, and an emotional basis for unity. The history of broken treaties has other advantages. The larger society recognizes it as a legitimate organizing principle. Indians hit a vulnerable point in the American conscience when discussing broken treaties: breaking a contract is dishonest. Treaties consummated an exchange between the United States and individual tribes; in return for a cession of land for a guarantee of peace, the United States recognized Indian rights. The United States also created a special bureau to handle Indian affairs, making Indians a recognized ethnic group.

The Bureau of Indian Affairs dispenses services, supervises Indian land use, and oversees tribal governments. Indians could organize as welfare recipients do; but a "welfare-rights" principle cannot serve the multiple functions of a treaty charter. In particular, welfare-rights movements cannot utilize the appeal of a shared historical event and kinship defined in terms of that event; nor can a welfare-rights movement draw upon the legitimacy of negotiated exchange, a treaty. It remains to explain why each tribe has a broken treaty.

THE DIALECTICS OF FRONTIER EXPANSION

Keyes suggests in his introduction to this volume that ethnic change is a dialectical process. The relations between Indians and Europeans during and after frontier expansion in the United States provides an example of such a process, and Indian mobilization behind the banner of broken treaties emerges as a result of such a process. There seem to be four configurations defining relations between Indian and European settlers and their descendants. I label these *contact, removal, autonomy,* and *welfare.* While all four patterns occurred in a few historical sequences, in other cases, only two or three of the patterns appeared. Most tribes experienced the sequence of contact-removal-welfare, a sequence that was most likely, I argue, to lead to the development of pan-Indian nationalism. All these tribes share the experience that treaties made during contact were violated during removal, leaving the Indians with far fewer resources than they had expected. These same tribes then found themselves subjects of a powerful but rather inept bureaucracy, the Bureau of Indian Affairs. Sharing similar experiences and dealing with similar problems, these tribes predictably began to develop the movement I have already discussed. I will argue that the program proposed by the American Indian Policy Review Commission is one that seeks to recreate autonomy.

Before describing the four patterns at greater length, I want to remark on the term *dialectic*. Although I agree with Keyes that the process of ethnic change is dialectical, I do not want to assume that changes are inevitable. Each of the four configurations is distinct and carries in it both elements that can cause change and elements that promote stability. For instance, during a contact period, growth of the non-Indian population is a destabilizing factor that can bring on removal. The degree of destabilization is directly related to the size of the non-Indian population. Indian political and economic development, however, increases Indian ability to resist removal and blunts the effects of non-Indian population growth. Such population growth may vary in different regions. For instance, Indians from Ohio, Indiana, and Illinois were removed earlier than were southern Indians, in part because non-Indian population pressure was greater and in part because southern Indians gave greater resistance (Abel 1908, p. 295). Settlers may attempt removal before their strength is great enough, suffer military defeat or prospective defeat, and have to wait before trying again. For instance, Cherokee force prevented removal in 1817. When the Tennessee militia was called out to take a census in preparation for removal, the Cherokee "met menace with menace" (ibid., p. 284). In 1819, the Cherokee agreed to a treaty that ended removal possibilities for ten years (ibid.). In the United States, such setbacks did not lead settlers to change their ultimate goals, however; for that reason the historical sequences look, in retrospect, rather inevitable.

Table I shows the four patterns, identifying the main characteristics and the stabilizing and destabilizing elements of each. I maintain that one of several combinations of these patterns affected and still affects every Indian group, although the timing varies.

The first configuration, contact, holds while settlers and Indian relations are governed by treaties of friendship that serve to regulate trade, cession of land to settlers, and other matters. Through military force and economic incentive, the settlers establish a foothold on the area dominated by Indians. Indians do not strongly resist this settlement because they find trade and intercourse with the invaders to be beneficial. Settlers do not have the strength to remove the Indians and find trade with them economically useful. Because of this mutually advantageous relationship, settlers and Indians enter into treaties that serve them both. When settlers come from many countries or represent different corporate groups from the same country, they find alliance with Indians aids competition with other Europeans. Similarly, Indians find alliance with Europeans serves their competitive positions versus other Indians.

RONALD L. TROSPER   255

Table 1

PATTERNS OF FRONTIER EXPANSION

Period	Main Characteristics	Destabilizing Elements	Stabilizing Elements
Contact	Indian population relatively equal to colonists' population Economic specialization by relative cost of production Treaties used to transfer land, secure peace and trade, and to settle colonists' claims among one another Stereotypes focus on differences	Non-Indian population growth relative to growth of Indian population	Indian economic, military strength
Removal	Indians removed from land through expropriation or forced sale Colonists' population greater than Indian population Stereotypes focus on Indian inferiority	Indian poverty causes humanitarian concern for Indian rights	Continued Indian possession of land desired by colonists
Welfare	Bureau of Indian Affairs dominates relations Oscillation between termination and self-determination as means of "assimilation" Stereotypes remain those stressing Indian inferiority	Indian mobilization as an ethnic group	Resident non-Indians The Bureau of Indian Affairs
Autonomy	Tribal jurisdiction and control within reservation boundaries Federal representation is an "agent" rather than "superintendent" Stereotypes focus on Indian advancement, e.g., "Five Civilized Tribes"	Non-Indians resident within reservation	Indian political & economic power

The relationship between Indians and settlers varies with the external conditions influencing the frontier. The fur trade in the seventeenth and eighteenth centuries is a good instance of a contact relationship. Jennings (1975, pp. 85-104) provides an excellent discussion. During the colonial period, Indians hunted furs and processed them for transoceanic shipment: "When the merchant packed peltry for shipment to Europe, it was already a semimanufactured product that had been handled and treated many times" (ibid., p. 90). During the early colonial period, Indians provided wampum as a medium of exchange. Coastal Indians such as the Narragansetts and Indians on Long Island specialized in wampum manufacture in the seventeenth century (ibid., p. 93).

During contact, Indians are a resource for settlers from several points of view. They know the territory and possess superior technology for extracting the traditional fruits of the land. Until the settler adopts or improves upon that technology, the Indian can provide goods at a lower price than can the settler. Indian-settler relations in Puget Sound in the late nineteenth century are an example of this contact stage. Indians specialized in providing fish and were not displaced from this activity until after 1890 (*U.S.* v. *State of Washington,* 384 F. Supp. 312 (1974) at p. 352). Indians can be a resource in other, unsuspected ways, as when they justified construction of a fort in Fort Missoula, Montana. The fort proved to be a good growth stimulus in the 1880s; long after demanding protection from "hostile" Indians, the businessmen ignored them and concentrated on feeding the soldiers (Carroll 1959, pp. 116-17, 186).

Trade with settlers could strengthen Indian society and material living standards, making Indians more potent enemies than they initially were, but two factors militated against this possibility. Indians may suffer from new diseases introduced by the settlers; and they may be dependent on a resource, such as the buffalo, that becomes rapidly depleted. When these factors do not intervene, Indians become stronger, as shown by the Five Civilized Tribes (Young 1971).

Contact is a period of rapid economic change for both Indians and Whites. Since Indians are a resource, it is easier to be objective about them, and to respect their abilities and their virtues. Few studies of non-Indian attitudes emphasize the difference engendered by the changing periods. Carroll found in western Montana that newspaper reports about Indians changed significantly when Indians ceased to be a resource and became an obstacle to expansion (1959, pp. 138-40, 169, 183). The image of the noble savage dates from the period of colonial contact with Indians (Jacobs 1972, pp. 107-25). This point is worth emphasizing, for recent stereotypes of Indians stress Indian inferiority—drunkenness, laziness, low levels of education, reliance on hunting rather than farming. These negative stereotypes, I argue, originate during periods of removal, to which I now turn.

Removal occurs when settlers become sufficiently numerous and economically developed to mount successful military campaigns against Indians. The two national periods of removal, apart from those in colonial days, were (1) the 1820s and 1830s, when most eastern tribes were forced to move west, and (2) from 1887 to 1920, when individual Indians were assigned plots of land on western reservations and the remaining "surplus" land was opened to homesteaders.

The two periods were different in two important respects. First, in the early period, Indians could resettle or be forced to resettle in western lands—in what is now Oklahoma and in other states such as Kansas. Second, in the earlier period, the states had a larger role in supervising the transfer of title from Indians to Whites. Between 1887 and 1920, there was no place for Indians to go. The Department of the Interior and the Bureau of Indian Affairs conducted the surveys, issued title to Indians, and supervised the transfer of title from individual Indians to non-Indians. The consequence was that in the second period, a federal bureaucracy was created. The existence of this bureaucracy made it much easier for the nation to begin to take care of Indians, the typical pattern of welfare, rather than to allow the Indians to establish new governments to conduct their own internal affairs, the typical pattern of autonomy.

Although there were differences, the two removal periods had similarities. At the start of a removal period, Whites tried to obtain a treaty in which the Indians would voluntarily give up their land and move. The Indians would not agree. Then, either with or without a fraudulent treaty—one signed by some Indians against the wishes of the rest—removal would begin. A common technique was to give Indians with homes and farms title to their holdings. These lands were then called allotments. Indians not occupying land were also assigned allotments on the reservations, from either occupied or unoccupied land. Remaining land could then be opened for settlement by non-Indians. The Indians were then induced to sell their allotments. Some individuals obtained a fair price; others did not. The tribe as a whole usually received a low price for nonallotted land that was sold. In the first period, between 1820 and 1840, many Indians left the eastern states and settled in Indian territory. A few stayed behind. There are still Cherokee in North Carolina and Iroquois in New York State, for instance. In the second period, between 1887 and 1920, Indians lost land on their reservations, but did not leave in great numbers. The reservations that were allotted became checkerboards of Indian-owned and non-Indian-owned land.

Removal occupied considerable time; not only did Indians resist, but Whites competed with one another to obtain the land, causing confusion and delays while title could be determined. The early period had more of this problem than did the later one, for example, the sale of Creek allotments in Alabama between 1832 and 1839. Speculators obtained contracts to purchase Indian allotments, by such fraudulent means as the use of Indians to impersonate true owners. This led to several federal investigations to determine which contracts were valid and which were not (Young 1961, pp. 73-96). The question of possible fraudulent acquisition of federally granted title was avoided on Cherokee land in Georgia. Georgia prohibited Indians from testifying in court, allowing individual Whites to claim ownership fraudulently, perhaps for payment of a debt. In addition, Georgia seized land and distributed it by lottery (Foreman 1972, pp. 238-39, 251-52).

Removal ended in the first period when most Indians had moved west. In the second period, it ended when much of the good agricultural land had been taken and some Whites became concerned about the resulting Indian poverty (Downes 1971). The early removal period led to autonomy, especially for tribes that settled in Oklahoma; the second removal led to welfare.

Autonomy has the following characteristics: Indians are self-governing within the boundaries of their land. They recognize the right of the United States to conduct Indian relations with other nations. Indians have some power over the terms on which Whites live under their jurisdiction. Chief Justice Marshall described this relationship in *Worcester* v. *Georgia* in 1832: "The Cherokee nation, then, is a distinct community, occupying its own territory, with boundaries accurately described, in which the laws of Georgia can have no force, and which the citizens of Georgia have no right to enter, but with the assent of the Cherokees themselves, or in conformity with treaties, and with the acts of Congress" (Prucha 1975, p. 61). Had the Supreme Court view been accepted by President Jackson and by Georgia, the Cherokee would have remained on their land in Georgia and Tennessee and would have made the transition from contact to autonomy. The Supreme Court did not prevail, however, and the Cherokee were forced to move west.

After moving west, the Cherokee created the relationship between them and the United States that Marshall had identified in the Worcester case. The fifth article of the Treaty of 1835 governing this relationship read as follows:

The United States hereby covenant and agree, that the lands ceded to the Cherokee nation, in the foregoing article, shall, in no future time, without their consent, be included within the jurisdiction of any State or Territory. But they shall secure to the Cherokee nation the right, by their national councils, to make and carry into effect all such laws as they may deem necessary for the government and protection of the persons and property within their own country, belonging to their people, or such persons as have connected themselves with them: Provided always, that they shall not be inconsistent with the Constitution of the United States. . . . [United States Statues 7:478]

The Supreme Court in *Worcester* v. *Georgia* and its predecessor, *Cherokee Nation* v. *Georgia,* had created the legal opening for the Cherokee to move into an autonomy relationship. Contact and autonomy configurations are similar because in both cases Indians are self governing.

During early contact periods Indians had relations with European nations in competition with the United States—England, France, and Spain. Under autonomy, however, such relations are not allowed, for the federal government places itself between Indians and foreign states, and between Indians and the various states of the United States. But the federal government does not use this position to interfere with internal self-government by Indians.

The presence of non-Indians within Indian reserves destabilizes the autonomy configuration. The Five Civilized Tribes—the Cherokee, Choctaw, Creek, Chickasaw, and Seminole—although internally divided, had sided with the South in the Civil War. When the South lost, they had to renegotiate their treaties. These treaties ceded western Indian Territory for use for other Indians and opened the door to non-Indian settlement in the eastern part, through provisions permitting the construction of railroads. In 1889 Oklahoma Territory was created, leaving only the eastern part of the present Oklahoma as Indian Territory.

In 1890, the federal census showed that, according to physical appearance, there were 109,400 Whites, 18,600 Negroes, and 50,100 Indians in Indian Territory (Debo 1940, p. 13). Tribal governments did not have jurisdiction over United States citizens, and the federal government did not create a court system of its own until 1895 (ibid., p. 18). Consequently, settlers who were not citizens of the Indian tribes had little civil or criminal law to govern them; in addition, reports Debo,

. . . the large white population was living under conditions never before encountered by any considerable body of United States citizens. Thousands of children were growing up with no educational opportunities of any kind, a large body of tenants were cultivating land to which they could never secure title, and the proud and self-assertive white Americans were paying taxes to support a government in which they had no voice and a school system from which they received no benefits. The inhabitants of this fierce frontier did not even consider the fact that the Indian tenure rested upon the most solemn commitments by the Federal Government, and that by settling in the Indian Territory they had voluntarily subjected themselves to these conditions; and they set up a constant clamor for the abolition of the tribal governments. . . . [Ibid., pp. 19-20]

The Cherokees asked to have intruders removed, and when the federal government did not do so, a Cherokee delegation to Washington in 1895 wrote its chief that the intruders were like the contents of the wooden horse at Troy (ibid., p. 29). Indeed, within a few years, as the delegation predicted, Congress abolished tribal governments, allotted Indian land, and created the state of Oklahoma.

A national consensus supported the allotment policy begun with the Dawes Act in 1877; friends and enemies of the Indian agreed on the wisdom of offering backward Indians the benefits of private property. Indian policy subsequently has been viewed as a single entity. It is useful, therefore, to point out that during the previous thirty years many different policies coexisted. Depending upon the area of the country, tribes were in the midst of one of three configurations: contact, autonomy, or removal, and federal policy varied accordingly.

Tribes in the present states of Montana, Idaho, and Oregon signed a series of treaties in 1855 ceding land and creating reservations for themselves. The Sioux won some battles and in 1868 signed the Treaty of Fort Laramie, in which they agreed not to attack the new railroad and other settlements to the south of a large reservation. In return, the federal government agreed not to open the Bozeman Trail through the newly created Sioux reservation (Prucha 1975, pp. 110-14). The occupiers of Alcatraz used this treaty to justify their action because it had also included promise of future allotments of land.

Although Whites signing these treaties knew from their experience that the arrangements were temporary, Indians appear to have regarded them as permanent. Although many of these treaties, including the Treaty of Laramie, provided for future allotment, a contact pattern prevailed for many years. As is typical of contact, Indian economies changed and started to grow. In Puget Sound, Indians specialized as fishermen when settlers began to arrive. In other parts, such as the Yakima and Flathead reservations, Indians began to add farming and ranching to hunting and gathering (Fitch 1974, pp. 75-85; Trosper 1974, pp. 144-82).

Meanwhile, in Kansas, Indians were facing removal (see Paul Gates's [1954] excellent book on the subject). Indian Commissioner Manypenny signed a series of treaties in 1854 with Indians in Kansas, providing for allotments. A territorial and subsequently a state government were created. Lands were opened to settlers even before Indian allotments were identified. The process was disorderly and confusing, with many multiple claimants to particular parcels.

The conflict over land in Kansas continued after the Civil War, and led to the end of Indian treaty-making in 1871. Treaties were being used by the Department of the Interior and the Senate to dispose of Indian lands to their friends, predominantly to railroads. The House forced an end to this practice because it wished to participate in public land policy, in particular to allow settlers rather than railroads to purchase former Osage lands (Gates 1954, pp. 210, 221).

Meanwhile, other tribes were under autonomy. Each of the Five Civilized Tribes was conducting its own internal affairs. Indians in New York State are seldom mentioned at all after the frontier moved west of the Mississippi. Various bands of Iroquois had resisted complete removal and preserved small reserves under the jurisdiction of New York state rather than the federal government. Except for Whites occupying the village of Salamanca, the Indians did not allow non-Indians to settle on their small reserves and have managed to remain self-governing since the middle of the nineteenth century. In such a situation, the autonomy configuration can be stable. It existed between 1860 and 1890 in New York and remains today, although water projects have taken land from the Tuscarora and Allegheny reservations.

But the situation was not stable in the west. The General Allotment Act of 1887 started the opening of reservations to non-Indian settlement. The Curtis Act of 1898 started allotment in Indian Territory. The most recent removal process had begun, and it proceeded in an orderly manner, compared to removal in the South or Kansas (Carlson 1977, pp. 49-132).

While removal in 1820 to 1840 led to autonomy for some tribes, removal under the allotment policy in 1887 to 1920 led to welfare. In welfare, government officials believe they are preparing Indians for eventual assimilation, caring for Indians needs in the meantime.

The Indian stereotype of the removal period supports the caretaker mission of the Bureau of Indian Affairs. Indians' incapability partly justifies taking their property, and also justifies Indian education. In 1928, Indian poverty had moved national leaders into looking for ways to improve the situation. The Meriam Report diagnosed the problem as follows: "The fundamental requirement is that the task of the Indian Service be recognized as primarily educational, in the broadest sense of that word, and that it be made an efficient educational agency, devoting its main energies to the social and economic advancement of the Indians, so that they may be absorbed into the prevailing civilization or be fitted to live in the presence of that civilization at least in accordance with a minimum standard of health and decency" (Prucha 1975, p. 219). The stereotype of removal thus provides a new definition of the purposes of the Indian service: rather than forcing assimilation through the imposition of private property through allotments, educational means will be used to reach the same goal.

One choice is to allow Indians self-government to learn how to run their own affairs. Indians are to use one of several models from non-Indian society. One of these is a democratically elected government under a constitution. Another is a corporation in which Indians, as shareholders, elect a board of directors to undertake their business affairs. In both cases, however, an interim tutorial period is required. The result is that true self-government, though promised, does not arrive, as operation of both the Indian Reorganization Act of 1934 and the Indian Self-Determination and Education Act of 1975 shows. Under the Indian Reorganization Act, the secretary of the interior had to approve all new tribal constitutions. This power was used to create clauses requiring the secretary or his representative to review and approve significant actions by tribal governments (Price 1973, pp. 717-31). Similarly, under Title I of the Indian Self-Determination and Education Act of 1875, the Bureau of Indian Affairs retains the right to review the spending of federal money (Barsh and Trosper 1975). With all of its major decisions reviewed by federal officials, tribal government is not independent.

The Indian bureau has a similar tutorial role with individual Indians: Indian use of allotments is subject to the control of federal officials; an Indian wishing to lease his allotment must have the Bureau of Indian Affairs recognize his lease; Indian boarding schools and scholarship programs are federally operated.

Another characteristic of the welfare period is that incentives are set up in such a way that individual Indians consider the option of political and economic assimilation as a real alternative. Although they might find life in the general society not as good as it would be under Indian systems in autonomy, they are burdened by bureaucratic controls. An individual Indian is inclined to sell his allotment and "assimilate" in a political sense: his land and property become taxable by the state, he has state citizenship, and in an extreme case he would cut off all ties with the Indian government. Some migrate to cities as part of this decision. Whether they completely assimilate into American society is more problematic, because relatives still live on the reservation and ethnic mobilization can occur. Urban Indians led the Alcatraz occupation, for instance.

This pattern results in great federal bureaucratic power. Several publications have described the problems that arise, for the federal role has several inherent conflicts of interest. First, the mission of the Bureau of Indian Affairs places its employees in the position of eliminating their own jobs; once Indians no longer need help, the bureau will no longer be necessary. Second, the executive branch may wish to see Indian land used in ways inconsistent with the best use from an Indian point of view. If the federal government takes Indian property—water, for instance—it then becomes the defendant in litigation as well as the potential lawyer for the plaintiff, its Indian "ward." Third, members of Congress represent states that have an interest in Indian property, while these same members of Congress are responsible for caring for Indian needs. Such conflicts lead to abuses, as Cohen (1953), Cahn (1969), and Chambers (1971) show with numerous examples.

These abuses naturally lead Indians to recognize common interests, which in themselves would cause at least some pan-Indian political action. I would argue, however, that several factors would undermine such action. First, bureaucratic power can be used to divide and conquer. The decentralized BIA structure that Cohen decried in 1953 allows such tactics to be used routinely at regional levels. Also, each tribal structure has special qualities. One reason for this is that state jurisdiction over Indians varies from state to state, and even tribe to tribe within states. Sutton (1975, p. 153) provides a map that describes variation between states; he has six different categories of state-Indian relationships, one of which is "other." Another reason is that the amount of checkerboarding with non-Indian landowners also varies, depending upon the timing and the thoroughness of allotment.

The development of Indian nationalism counteracts these forces. Indian response to government policy is conditioned by the experience of contact and removal. Since removal involves "individualizing" tribal property through allotment, followed by forced sale and even expropriation, Indians resist similar assimilation efforts and also seek to obtain compensation for losses. A typical tribal strategy in the 1920s and 1930s was to cooperate with government policies conditional upon the resolution of tribal claims. Many congressmen saw the Indian Claims Commission Act of 1946 as a way to solve incessant Indian petitions for compensation that were then preventing final resolution of the "Indian problem" (Price 1973, p. 472; Lurie 1968b, p. 81).

In retrospect, we can see that such tribal claims were a part of the development of a national movement. In 1964, having recognized that something was happening, Nancy Lurie solicited opinions from a number of people active in Indian affairs. She described what she felt was "a real and discernible social movement on the part of Indian people at the present time, whatever it may be called" (1968a, p. 315). She called the movement an "American Indian Renascence" and asked if the respondents agreed. Respondents agreed there was a movement, but felt that, rather than a rebirth, it should be called "a logical point in a historical trend of adaptations and adjustments to changing circumstances," a point she accepted (ibid., p. 311). In other words, a dialectical process of change was occurring. Lurie thought the movement had origins in the late nineteenth century at pow-wows and other intertribal events (ibid., p. 297); she also saw evidence of it in the following testy statement in the Meriam Report: "The disturbing influence of outside agitators seeking personal emoluments, and the conviction in the Indian mind that justice is being denied, renders extremely difficult any cooperation between the government and its Indian wards" (ibid., p. 298, citing Meriam 1928, p. 805). She calls this attitude a "treaty ideology."

Although in the mid-1960s the nature and future developments of this movement were unclear, Lurie identified its main features. Among these, she said,

Indian distinctiveness is stressed culturally and historically; emphasis on treaties rather than judicial recourse in obtaining perceived rights of Indians; ineffable attachment to the land; attitude that all other Americans are "immigrants" and that Indians as "First Americans" deserve special consideration; or that it isn't really special consideration but that the nation as a whole permits and at times even protects cultural pluralism of other ethnic minorities such as Jews, Amish, etc., and it is only that whites find it hard to accept the distinctive criteria of Indian ethnicity; and, the nation still "owes" the Indians something for taking their land. [1968a, pp. 308-9]

Subsequent developments have shown this emphasis to be correct. I argue that the report of the American Indian Policy Review Commission represents an outcome of this movement. The five Indian commissioners, perhaps in response to Lloyd Meeds's separate view, also provided a separate statement of their own. They said,

As an experience in policy formulation, our tenure on the Commission has been enlightening for us all. Yet, despite the legal complexities and the confusing range of issues, we have found that the cornerstone of Federal-Indian policy can be stated simply and clearly. From the very beginning of this country, the law has recognized that the Native people in this country possess a right to exist as separate tribal groups with inherent authority to rule themselves and their territory. Although the United States necessarily exercises predominant power, it has time and again bound itself to respect this basic Indian right and has assumed the responsibility to protect the Indian people in the possession of their lands and in the exercise of their rights. Consequently, self-government (i.e., sovereignty) in conjunction with the trust relationship is truly the inheritance of Indian people. Although times and conditions change, the United States' adherence to a policy of continuing to keep faith with the Indians on this fundamental level will always remain the foundation of Federal-Indian policy. [American Indian Policy Review Commission 1977, p. 622]

As with all statements of the treaty charter, the commissioners omit reference to removal treaties and removal laws. The federal government has bound itself to protect Indians during contact periods, and Indians naturally stress this. Opponents of this view, such as Congressman Meeds, refer only to removal policies. Both precedents exist because frontier expansion required both. Because removal could not be carried out completely, due to sympathy for Indian poverty, the government undertook to care for Indians, creating the trust relationship and presenting Indians the opportunity to mobilize as an ethnic group. Such are the dialectics of frontier expansion.

CONCLUSION

Of the four configurations, contact, removal, autonomy, and welfare, the proposals of the American Indian Policy Review Commission show that Indians prefer autonomy. Congressman Meeds's objection to the commission's *Final Report* was that Americans would not tolerate Indian jurisdiction over non-Indians. Although he did not do so, he could have cited Indian Territory in the 1880s and 1890s as evidence. The Five Civilized Tribes were self-governing but could not exclude Americans. As the Cherokee delegation predicted, non-Indians living within their boundaries were in fact a major cause of the abolition of their governments and the allotment of their lands. This cause can operate in reverse: if a reservation has non-Indian residents, the federal government cannot agree to tribal autonomy. In welfare, a destabilizing factor, Indian nationalism, is offset by a stabilizing factor, residential integration.

In spite of this stalemate, Indian mobilization with respect to a treaty charter has shifted debate away from one of the welfare dilemmas: Indian status, and therefore land ownership, is dependent upon Indian poverty. Indians desire less poverty and also wish to retain their property. An increase in Indian sovereign powers, such as taxation and land-use regulation, even if these powers are not as complete as under autonomy, simultaneously decreases poverty and protects property ownership. But considerable inconsistency remains. Although ethnic change is dialectical, we cannot always judge beforehand whether stabilizing or destabilizing forces will predominate.

REFERENCES

Abel, Annie H.
1908 "The History of Events Resulting in Indian Consolidation West of the Mississippi." *Annual Report,* American Historical Association, 1906, 1:233-450.

American Indian Policy Review Commission
1977 *Final Report.* U.S. Government Printing Office, Washington.

Barsh, Russel L. and Trosper, Ronald L.
1975 "Title I of the Indian Self-Determination and Education Assistance Act of 1975." *American Indian Law Review* 3:361-95.

Bluecloud, Peter, ed.
1972 *Alcatraz is Not an Island.* Berkeley: Wingbow Press.

Cahn, Edgar S., ed.
1969 *Our Brother's Keeper: The Indian in White America.* New York and Cleveland: World Publishing Co.

Carlson, Leonard A.
1977 "The Dawes Act and the Decline of Indian Farming." Ph.D. dissertation, Stanford University.

Carroll, James William
1959 "Flathead and Whites: A Study of Conflict." Ph.D. dissertation. Berkeley: University of California.

Chambers, Reid Peyton
1971 *A Study of Administrative Conflicts of Interest in the Protection of Indian Natural Resources.* Washington: U.S. Government Printing Office, Committee print, Subcommittee on Administrative Practice and Procedure, Committee on the Judiciary, United States Senate, 91st Congress, 2nd session.

Cohen, Felix
1953 "Erosion of Indian Rights, 1950-1953: A Case Study in Bureaucracy." *Yale Law Journal* 62:348-90.

1972 *Handbook of Federal Indian Law.* 1942. Albuquerque: University of New Mexico Press.

Debo, Angie
1940 *And Still the Waters Run.* Princeton, N. J.: Princeton University Press.

Deloria, Vine, Jr.
1969 *Custer Died for Your Sins: An Indian Manifesto.* London: Macmillan and Co.

1973 *God Is Red.* New York: Dell.

1974 *Behind the Trail of Broken Treaties: An Indian Declaration of Independence.* New York: Dell.

Downes, Randolph C.
  1971 "A Crusade of Indian Reform, 1922-1934." Reprinted in
    The American Indian: Past and Present, ed. Roger L. Nichols
    and George R. Adams, pp. 230-42. New York: John Wiley
    and Sons.
Fitch, James B.
  1974 "Economic Development in a Minority Enclave: The Case of
    the Yakima Indian Nation, Washington." Ph.D. dissertation,
    Stanford University.
Foreman, Grant
  1972 *Indian Removal: The Emigration of the Five Civilized Tribes.*
    1932. Norman: University of Oklahoma Press.
Gates, Paul Wallace
  1954 *Fifty Million Acres: Conflicts over Kansas Land Policy,
    1854-1890.* Ithaca: Cornell University Press.
Geertz, Clifford
  1963 "The Integrative Revolution: Primordial Sentiments and
    Civil Politics in the New States." In *Old Societies and New
    States,* pp. 103-57. New York: Free Press.
Hertzberg, Hazel W.
  1971 *The Search for an American Indian Identity: Modern Pan-
    Indian Movements.* Syracuse: Syracuse University Press.
Jacobs, Wilbur R.
  1972 *Dispossessing the American Indian: Indians and Whites on
    the Colonial Frontier.* New York: Charles Scribner's Sons.
Jennings, Francis
  1975 *The Invasion of America: Indians, Colonialism, and the
    Cant of Conquest.* New York: W. W. Norton.
Josephy, A.
  1971 *Red Power: The American Indian's Fight for Freedom.*
    New York: American Heritage.
Keyes, Charles F.
  1976 "Towards a New Formulation of the Concept of Ethnic
    Group." *Ethnicity* 3:202-13.
Kickingbird, Kirke, and Ducheneaux, Karen
  1973 *One Hundred Million Acres.* New York: Macmillan.
Levine, Stuart, and Nancy O. Lurie, eds.
  1968 *The American Indian Today.* Baltimore: Penguin Books.
Lurie, Nancy Oestreich
  1968a "An American Indian Renascence?" In *The American Indian
    Today,* ed. Levine and Lurie, pp. 295-337. Baltimore:
    Penguin Books.
  1968b "Historical Background." In *The American Indian Today,*

ed. Levine and Lurie, pp. 49-81. Baltimore: Penguin Books.

McNickle, D'Arcy

    1973 *Native American Tribalism: Indian Survivals and Renewals.* London: Oxford University Press.

Meeds, Lloyd

    1977 "Separate Dissenting Views of Congressman Lloyd Meeds, D-Wash., Vice Chairman of the American Indian Policy Review Commission." In *American Indian Policy Review Commission* 1977: 567-612.

Meriam, Lewis C.

    1928 *The Problem of Indian Administration.* Baltimore: Brookings Institution.

Otis, D. S.

    1973 *The Dawes Act and the Allotment of Indian Lands.* Norman: University of Oklahoma Press.

Price, Monroe E.

    1973 *Law and the American Indian: Readings, Notes, and Cases.* Indianapolis: Bobbs-Merrill Co. Inc.

Prucha, Francis Paul, ed.

    1975 *Documents of United States Indian Policy.* Lincoln: University of Nebraska Press.

Spicer, Edward H.

    1969 *A Short History of the Indians of the United States.* New York: D. Van Nostrand.

Spencer, Robert F.; Jennings, Jesse P., et al.

    1977 *The Native Americans.* 2nd ed. New York: Harper and Row.

Steiner, Stan

    1968 *The New Indians.* New York: Dell.

Sutton, Imre

    1975 *Indian Land Tenure: Bibliographical Essays and a Guide to the Literature.* New York: Clearwater.

Thomas, Robert K.

    1968 "Pan-Indianism." In *The American Indian Today,* ed. Levine and Lurie, pp. 128-40. Baltimore: Penguin Books.

Trosper, Ronald L.

    1974 "The Economic Impact of the Allotment Policy on the Flathead Indian Reservation." Ph.D. dissertation, Harvard University.

Wax, Murray L.

    1971 *Indian Americans: Unity and Diversity.* Englewood Cliffs, N. J.: Prentice-Hall.

Young, Mary Elizabeth

    1961 *Redskins, Ruffleshirts, and Rednecks: Indian Allotments in*

Alabama and Mississippi 1830-1860. Norman: University of Oklahoma Press.

1971 "Indian Removal and Land Allotment: The Civilized Tribes and Jacksonian Justice." In *The American Indian: Past and Present,* ed. Roger L. Nichols and George R. Adams, pp. 132-45. New York: John Wiley and Sons.

Like Trosper, Trottier also considers the type of ethnic change that comes about when peoples from diverse backgrounds are mobilized into unified ethnic nationalist movements. Trottier compares the efforts to forge new ethnic nationalist movements among American Indians and Asian-Americans. He assumes that such efforts have been stimulated by changes in the political-economic context of the United States. While he does not explore these changes to any great extent, he does point out that the interests of those of American Indian and Asian-American backgrounds have not been well served by the ethnic divisions within these populations that have obtained in the past nor by piecemeal assimilation into American society. Given this (and, it might be added with reference to arguments advanced in other papers, given the increasing intrusion of welfare bureaucracy into the lives of many American Indians and Asian-Americans), leaders have emerged who have attempted to formulate and use charters of panethnic identity that elicit sentiments in support of panethnic movements. Trottier demonstrates, thereby collaborating the argument presented in Trosper's paper, that American Indian leaders have been fairly successful in mobilizing a pan-Indian movement. Trottier argues that the ethnic charter of this movement is built around the unifying symbolism of common origin and of a shared relationship with the land in America. This latter symbol is connected with ideas about treaty breaking as discussed in Trosper's paper. In contrast to the American Indians, Asian-American leaders have only been able to draw upon a vague idea of commonality, based on the recognition that Asian-Americans are the same because they have been treated the same in the past by White Americans. This idea does not appear to hold greater appeal than do the more particularized symbols that underlie identities with diverse Asian backgrounds. Trottier concludes that the Asian-American movement remains merely an interest group and that the use of Asian-American identity as a charter for the movement continues, at least for the present, to be no more than a matter of political expediency for a small segment of the total Asian-American population.

RICHARD W. TROTTIER

Charters of Panethnic Identity:

Indigenous American Indians

and Immigrant Asian-Americans

THE intrusion of Europeans upon the indigenous tribes of North America and the subsequent and continuing arrival of immigrants from various parts of the world have given rise not so much to the American "melting pot" of popular and scholarly ideology as to an aggregation of interacting, shifting, and redefined sociocultural identites. Faced with the often devastating effects of contact with White Americans, members of the indigenous tribes and various non-White immigrant communities have responded in several strikingly different ways. Two major adaptive strategies pursued by non-White minorities at various times are what we might broadly term "traditionalism"—the attempt to

My thanks go to Charles F. Keyes for suggesting a comparison of indigenous Indian and immigrant Asian identiy, and, along with Marilyn Bentz, Carter Bentley, Ronald Trosper, C. Stevan Harrell, and Simon Ottenberg, for advice, encouragement, and stimulating critiques of an earlier draft of this paper.

preserve traditional culture and socioeconomic prerogatives in the face of White dominance, and "assimilation"—the attempt to become directly involved in White society by adopting, to whatever extent possible, the customs, attitudes, and appearance of Whites.[1] A third strategy, and one that has gained considerable impetus in recent years, is the attempt to unite people within newly defined panethnic identities.

In this paper I am concerned with this third alternative—with attempts to bring about panethnic unification. A panethnic identity, for the purposes of the present discussion, is one that comprises two or more distinct, existing ethnic identities. I will examine attempts to unite people within two panethnic identities that have developed in the context of the United States, and which may be called for the moment "American Indian" and "Asian-American." Each involves the assertion that the panethnic identity is more significant, for certain purposes, than tribal affiliation or national origin, while at the same time maintaining that the ethnic and panethnic identities are implicit in each other.

The question of identities is here distinguished from the parallel and closely interrelated question of ethnic and panethnic groups. We may regard a social group as comprising individuals who interact recurrently on a basis of interconnected roles (Keesing 1976, p. 231).[2] For ethnic and panethnic groups (as well as for many others) the "interconnected roles" are defined in a sense of collective identity. This characterization, however, refers to existing groups, while in addressing the topic of panethnic identity formation we are concerned with an aspect of group formation. The establishment of a meaningful group identity is presumably facilitated by prior recurrent interaction. Once the identity is well established it might in turn facilitate further interaction, specifically in the form that concerns us here: political mobilization. This is to say that part of the means of effecting unity among people is the formulation of a suitable "charter" of iden-

1. Wallace (1972, p. 202) reports for the Iroquois in the late 1700s: "In response to the dilemma of civilization two points of view developed among the Iroquois, one advocating the assimilation of white culture and the other the preservation of Indian ways." In his study of a Chinese community in California, Weiss (1974, pp. 151-54) refers in a similar vein to what he calls "traditionist" and "modernist" associations among the Chinese (cf. Kitano and Sue 1973, p. 7). For both Indians and Asians the traditionalist view, as opposed to the assimilationist one, generally denies the appropriateness of European or White American culture for the non-European members of tribes and other minorities, and suggests that minority cultures should be preserved to benefit not only their immediate participants, but "to enrich the culture of each nation and of the world and contribute to the energy of the nations" (Leon-Portilla, quoted in Collier 1972, p. 138).

2. I would like to thank Carter Bentley for pointing out the relevance of this definition of group to my argument.

tity, in the sense suggested by Nagata (this volume). By manipulating the symbols of group identity, political leaders can inspire sentiments conducive to collective action. The charter, as an expression of the group identity, also provides the social scientist with valuable insights into the actors' own view of their sociopolitical situation.

This brings us to two major questions that will be addressed in the following discussion: (1) how is a panethnic identity such as "American Indian" or "Asian-American" expressed by those who wish to unify people for collective action; and (2) what difference does it make, if any, that the people in question are in the one case indigenous to the context of their proposed unification and in the other case immigrant to it? The first question asks what it is that proponents of panethnic unity have found will effectively mobilize people. In another sense I am asking what it means, at the present time, to be an American Indian or an Asian-American. These identities both continually change in response to changing circumstances, and political leaders can be expected to keep in touch with relevant trends. Another way to put the questions posed above is to ask what is the symbolic content of such an identity, what are the sources of the symbols that compose it and the concepts they represent, and how is the difference in the nature of the contact situation for indigenous Indians and immigrant Asians related to the availability of *meaningful* symbols of panethnic identity? This difference, I will argue, has direct significance for the possibility of defining the panethnic identity as itself ethnic.

Panethnic unity is not easily accomplished, though the political and economic rewards may be substantial. Some of the divisive factors to which panethnic proponents respond in constructing the charter of a panethnic identity will be brought out in the following pages. Charters of group identity, however, reflect not only obstacles to unity, but factors that are recognized as potential sources of unifying sentiment as well. These unifying influences can be grouped into two broad categories: common interests—expressed as the need to unify for mutual benefit, and common identity as the basis for doing so. When political leaders succeed in establishing the two as closely interlinked the charter may be particularly effective.

COMMON INTERESTS: THE NEED FOR PANETHNIC UNITY

American Indian and Asian-American views on the need for panethnic unity find their roots in a number of factors. For many the polar alternatives of traditionalism and assimilation—both still pursued—have proved unsatisfactory as adaptive responses to contact with Whites. Traditionalism is generally pursued on a tribal or ethnic basis, and assimilation is usually a matter of individual relocation and education. The disadvantages of both approaches provide much of the common experience among Indians and among Asians, and thus speak to the potential benefits of unification.

Some Indians and Asians have found that the retention of traditional values and behavior puts them at a disadvantage in dealing with White society, and some have been convinced that, with the small size of Indian and Asian populations and with their political and economic subordination, they were not self-sufficient and therefore could not avoid contact with Whites (Hicks and Kertzer 1972, pp. 2-3; Sue and Sue 1971, pp. 38-39). Furthermore, since the beginnings of contact, White missionaries and various colonial, state, and national governments have encouraged, coerced, and even forced Indians to assimilate culturally and socially (McNickle 1972, p. 86; Wallace 1972, pp. 217 ff.). In an effort to merge Indians into non-Indian society, the Bureau of Indian Affairs and the U.S. government have since the 1930s pursued a policy of relocating reservation Indians in cities. In the 1950s the rate of relocation, both formally sponsored and informal, increased dramatically, giving rise to substantial communities of Indians in certain urban centers (Svensson 1973, pp. 34-35). Cut off from federal assistance that was available only to reservation dwellers, and inadequately prepared to cope with the urban environment, many of these Indians found themselves in rather dire straits (ibid.). Asians, by contrast, were assumed for a long time to be unassimilable, and on this basis were excluded from participating in White educational, social, political, and economic institutions (Nee and Nee 1972, pp. 30-46, 60-63; Weiss 1974, pp. 31-43). Only since the end of World War II have federal and state governments begun to encourage the social and cultural assimilation of Asians (LaGumina and Cavaioli 1974, p. 98).

In any event, the view that adopting White culture was the only way to acquire the apparent benefits of full participation in American society and that traditional ways were an impediment to progress came to enjoy much preeminence among Indians and Asians as well as Whites (Manners 1972, pp. 141-42; McNickle 1972, p. 86; Nee and Nee 1972, pp. 152-53; Sue and Sue 1971, p. 40), and in recent years increasing numbers of Asians and Indians have voluntarily left their home communities to take part in the larger society—Indians from reservations to the cities (Price 1972) and Asians to urban and suburban residences outside of Chinatowns, Little Tokyos, and so forth (Nee and Nee 1972). The assimilationist assumption is that if people of Indian or Asian descent learn the American way of life they should be able to participate fully in it, just as do Americanized people of, for example, English, French, or Italian descent. They would still be Comanche, Sioux, Japanese, Chinese, and so forth, but that identity would be submerged much of the time in favor of their identity as Americans.

Assimilation involves more than the acquisition of the instrumental features of American culture: language, technical skills, and so forth; it means adopting the traits associated with Anglo-American identity as well. Hicks and Kertzer (1972) describe how the Monhegans[3] had adopted White dress, language, and religion after the official dissolution of their tribe in the late 1800s (see also Chadwick and Stauss 1975). Weiss (1974, p. 152) describes similar efforts to assimilate among Chinese "modernists," who are "citizens of Chinese descent residing in America who consciously and conspicuously pursue an American life-style and who willingly embrace their American heritage." Assimilation, like traditionalist preservation, however, has its shortcomings, for even the most "acculturated" Indians and Asians, willingly or unwillingly, remain tied to their origins in a number of ways. In pursuing the ideal of full participation in the American system through cultural assimilation and emphasis of American identity, many have come up against the reality of racism—invoked by law in the early years of contact (Chun-Hoon 1975, pp. 43-49; Deloria, Jr. 1974, pp. 59-69; Nee and Nee 1972, pp. 30-38), and continuing to the present in both institutional and interpersonal relations (Cash and Hoover 1971, pp. 192-95; Chadwick and Stauss 1975, p. 365; Chun-Hoon 1975; Nee and Nee 1972, pp. 246, 330-31). Indeed, it has been suggested that those non-Whites who are the most "American" are likely to be the most sensitive to real or imagined racial discrimination (Kitano and Sue 1973, p.9).

The occurrence of significant numbers of interracial marriages—since the early years of contact between Indians and Whites (Hicks and Kertzer 1972, p. 4; Trosper 1976, p. 256), and more recently between Asians and Whites (Tinker 1973)—has provided a potential entree to White identity for some of the children and later descendants of such marriages, but there are still many who find it impossible or undesirable to "become White" (Chadwick and Stauss 1975, pp. 364-66). Exposure to White society can lead some to feel, perhaps for the first time, that they are fundamentally different from Whites (Ablon 1972, p. 726), and in recent years some highly educated Indians and Asians have expressed a profound resentment at the implications of even cultural "Americanization": the notion that Indian, Asian, or any other minority cultural traditions are somehow inferior to European ones and therefore should be abandoned, and that stereo-

3. "Monhegan" is a pseudonym for a New England Tribe.

typical or personal characteristics that connect one with a non-American background are deplorable and indicative of one's inferiority (Ablon 1972, pp. 725-27; Nee and Nee 1972, pp. 359-60, 377 ff).

One result has been a back-to-the-community trend—a re-emphasis of traditional identity and concerns, especially among college-age young people (Nee and Nee 1972, p. 355; Svensson 1973, p. 40). This neotraditionalism, however, is an entirely different prospect for Americanized Indians and Asians in the twentieth century than traditionalism was for members of Indian tribes and immigrant Asian groups in the early years of contact. When Monhegans, for example, responded to the Indian Reorganization Act of 1934 by reasserting Monhegan identity and seeking legal status as a tribe, there was no longer a traditional Monhegan way of life to preserve; the Monhegan language had been extinct for a hundred and fifty years and in appearance and behavior Monhegans were indistinguishable from their non-Indian neighbors (Hicks and Kertzer 1972, p. 5; cf. Boissevain 1972, p. 446).

Educated Indians and Asians whose traditional communities still exist may find that their experiences on the outside have produced in them marked changes in values, expectations, and goals, and some who have expressed disillusionment with their supposed Americanization nevertheless feel alienated from traditional ways as well (Schusky 1965, p. 23; Sue and Sue 1971, p. 42; Weiss 1974, pp. 69-80). Furthermore, the poverty and lack of opportunities on reservations, in Chinatowns, and so forth, are often not very inviting to those accustomed to a secure income on the outside (Thomas 1972, p. 743; Yanagisako 1975, pp. 206 ff.). Politically sophisticated Indians and Asians likewise may be frustrated with conditions in the home community. Indian leaders find tribal councils slow and ineffective (Schusky 1965, p. 23), while young Asians are dismayed at what they see as the jaded and self-serving attitudes of traditional community leaders (Weiss 1974, p. 69), and both may thus be inclined to focus their energies elsewhere. They are mindful of the benefits achieved by Blacks and other minorities through political activism, yet they are caught between the usual two alternatives of preservation and assimilation, unable to identify fully with either the traditional group or the larger White society. While communication with their traditionalist and conservative fellows has decreased they are interacting more with other Asians and Indians, and this has resulted in an increasing awareness of common problems and goals that transcend parochial interests. While they may be greatly concerned with conditions in the traditional community, the expression of common interests has been shunted to a higher level. As a result, many have come to reassess the meaning of their identity as Asian or Indian in light of changing circumstances and have turned to the alternative strategy of panethnic unification.

In 1969 a group of Indian college students in the San Francisco area began looking for a way to draw attention to the problems of urban Indians. Four years earlier a suit had been filed to acquire Alcatraz Island in San Francisco Bay for Indians under the Sioux Treaty of 1868, which provided that Indians would have first claim to any government land that was declared surplus, but the suit was unsuccessful. In light of increasingly trying circumstances (see Kickingbird and Ducheneaux 1973, pp. 211-15) the students planned a more dramatic effort to establish the island as a symbol of Indian grievances. From November 20, 1969, to June 11, 1971, the island was occupied by a group calling itself the Indians of All Tribes. In 1972 the Indians of All Tribes produced a volume (edited by Peter Bluecloud) entitled *Alcatraz Is Not An Island,* a collection of "documents and thoughts concerning the occupation of Alcatraz" presented "in the hope that better understanding may be reached between peoples of various cultural backgrounds and traditions" (1972, p. 11).[4]

The purpose of the Alcatraz occupation was to "unite our people and show the world that the Indian spirit would live forever" (ibid., p. 13). It brought together people from many tribes to work for a common purpose, not only on the basis of shared interests, but of shared identity as well:

We join the dance and feel the magic which is passing from hand to hand. All tribes and unity are the words of the drum and all tribes in unity are the dancers. The

4. In focusing on the Alcatraz occupation I do not claim that it is the most significant example of current pan-Indian activism, though some attribute to it that distinction. Kickingbird and Ducheneaux (1973, p. 215) argue that the primary significance of the Alcatraz occupation

> lay in awakening the Indian people, particularly the urban Indians, to what was happening on the national scene. It focused the concern of various city administrations on the problems of the Indian community as no other event could have done. And it gave birth to numerous other invasions of federal property in areas in which there was a desperate need by the local Indian people for services and programs. Most of all, Alcatraz gave birth to the idea among Indian people that no more Indian lands should be surrendered to the federal government. In this sense, Alcatraz became the most important event in the twentieth century for American Indian people.

I chose Alcatraz among all the other examples of pan-Indian activism simply because the publication of *Alcatraz Is Not An Island* provides us with a uniquely detailed documentation of the social drama from the actors' point of view, and because the self-avowed primary goal of the movement was to further the cause of pan-Indian unification.

vast distances separating our many tribes is [sic] forgotten, as are the man-made boundaries. Indians from Alaska to South America are here to dance as brothers and sisters. The ancient dream of Indian unity is begun.

We dance on our turtle island and draw strength from one another and from the past. Isolated, we will learn unity and learn to speak out our demands to a deaf government. This temporary isolation is necessary. We must build our strength. Self-determination is our goal. We must forever survive as Indians. [Ibid., pp. 20-21].

Similar sentiments have been expressed by Asian-Americans—of a need for unity in purpose and identity for people from different backgrounds—though as yet not in so militant a fashion as the Indian occupation of Alcatraz. A leading proponent of Asian activism, Warren Furutani,[5] in attempting to define the "Asian Movement," suggested that "almost anything that is going on in the Asian community in terms of dealing with progressive change is a part of the Movement" (*Amerasia* Staff 1971, p. 70). He feels that the events that signal the progress of the movement are spontaneous rather than directed, "and this means that everybody is starting to feel the need for an Asian Movement" (ibid.). The main "issue" now faced by the movement is "to redefine things. . . . We're redefining the Asian Experience within the United States and we're redefining it as *Amerasia* . . . a whole new interpretation of what we're doing" (ibid.). He suggests, therefore, that the impetus for an organized movement, "the beginning point, a point that's going to turn people on, something that is going to get people excited about the movement" is the reeducation campaign being carried out by the Asian-American studies programs at various universities (ibid., p. 74).

The Contemporary Asian Studies Division, University of California, Berkeley (1973), in an article entitled "Curriculum Philosophy for Asian American Studies," sums up the problems that Asians see themselves as facing in addressing "the present oppressive situation of Asian-American communities" (1973, p. 35). They point out that

Throughout much of America's history, Asians in this country have been the victims of contempt and exploitation. Often they were singled out as scapegoats in periods of severe economic depression, such as the nation-wide anti-Chinese agitations and riots of the 1870's and 1880's, and Asian Americans were regarded as enemies during times of international conflicts, particularly the Second World War and the Korean War. Anti-Asian racism expressed itself in local, state and federal legislation calculated to exclude Asians from major areas of employment, education, housing, business, and ownership of property. [Ibid.]

These problems still exist for contemporary Asian Americans: "Today,

5. Warren Furutani is the national community involvement coordinator of the Japanese American Citizens League in Los Angeles, California.

in spite of recent efforts to promote civil rights and equal employment opportunity for the minority population in the United States, Asians are largely ignored by governmental agencies, educational institutions, and private corporations; and in many cases, Asian-Americans continue to be outrightly excluded" (ibid., p. 36).

The Contemporary Asian Studies Division also cites "a recent study" that reveals that racist sentiments were preventing Asian-Americans from entering decision-making positions in corporations. They claim that "ghetto existence and chronic poverty conditions remain the only way of life for a substantial number of Asians in this country, especially among the elderly and immigrant population" (ibid.). Furthermore, they blame the universities for contributing to "the wide-spread ignorance and misconceptions of Asians," claiming that "biased and limited information about Asians has helped to shape adverse public opinions and discriminatory public policies against Asians . . ." (ibid., p. 37). They accuse the universities of "playing an assimilationist role for a few individual Asians and leaving the masses of Asians behind in their poverty and isolation, which has actually reinforced and intensified the disintegration and distress afflicting the Asian community" (ibid., p. 38). Contemporary Asian Studies therefore proposes "to help students seek self-knowledge or self-awareness, to know who they are as Asian-Americans," and to cultivate "involvement in all aspects of Asian community life" (ibid.).

Panethnic unity no doubt means different things to different Indians and Asians, and it may speak to a variety of needs and purposes. To proponents of pan-Indianism and pan-Asianism it is seen as a proper and effective reaction to pervasive White racism and as a means of achieving equality on their own terms while retaining pride in their traditional identity and cultural background. Whatever incentives had inspired earlier efforts to assimilate to White society may still exist for these people, but through panethnic unity they can pursue these goals without a denial of ethnic distinctiveness.

Activist Asians and Indians, however, comprise but a fraction of their respective minority groups. Efforts to unify and mobilize people under such rubrics as "American Indian" and "Asian-American" must appeal to a broad spectrum of Indians and Asians. Despite the political advantages of unity, pan-Indian and pan-Asian movements have drawn criticism from all sides. Tribal councils and Asian community leaders object to "unbecoming militancy" and "boat-rocking activism" as more typical of Blacks and other minorities than of Asians or Indians (Hirabayashi 1975, p. 125; Svensson 1973, p. 36; Weiss 1974, p. 239). Others who might actively work to improve community conditions are nevertheless reluctant to engage in the close cooperation and interaction with members of other tribes or nationalities that panethnic unity entails (Thomas 1972, p. 743; Weiss 1974, pp. 234-35). Older generations of Japanese and Chinese, for example, remember too well the mutual animosity between their mother countries, and some harbor resentments based on experiences in the United States as well (Weiss 1974, p. 123).[6]

Another objection is that "Indian" and "Asian" are largely stereo-typical categories that fail to reflect the diversity of the groups they subsume. They are the inventions of outsiders—of Europeans, and while they attend to gross notions of racial similarity and geographical contiguity, they do not express the true identities of those so labeled. Filipinos find it difficult to identify closely with "Oriental" East Asians, and even Koreans at times have strenuously resisted "amalgamation" with Chinese and Japanese (LaGumina and Cavaioli 1974, pp. 99-100; Shin 1971, pp. 35-36). The supposed homogeneity of these pan-ethnic categories has been confirmed in the minds of outsiders through the attribution to their members of a variety of stereotypical characteristics, which are often the presumed traits of a prominent subgroup attributed by Whites to the category as a whole.

Some stereotypes that are current among Whites may be used by minority group members themselves to maintain their position, as in the use of Plains Indian traits and practices to distinguish Indians from Blacks (Hicks and Kertzer 1972) and "typical" Indian racial characteristics to distinguish them from Whites (Trosper 1976, p. 257).[7] Even seemingly favorable stereotypes can be detrimental, however, and the "model minority" stereotype of Asian-Americans is now under

6. Weiss (1974, p. 123) cites two interview responses:

Mr. K., a Japanese-American citizen, has lived in the central area all of his life, but he still remembers when his family was relocated during World War II. "I had to sell my home to the Chinese grocer for next-to-nothing. Since then I have had little to do with the Chinese."

Mr. T., a long-time resident and a family association leader, claims: "The Japanese may say they are my friends but I know that when they invaded my home in China they took our land and put me in a prison camp. I am friendly when I shop in their stores but I have never invited them to my home."

7. Trosper (1976, p. 257) has suggested that the special relationship reservation Indians have with the federal government and the special rights they enjoy despite being ordinary citizens in fact depends on stereotypes for survival. The tribal leaders of the Flathead Reservation had learned in defending their land from White encroachment that "successfully to defeat confiscation attempts by congress, they had to adopt their conquerors' idea of what an 'Indian' is," and thus avoid "appearing White" and losing their special rights to land. In part this is accomplished through the use of blood criteria for tribal membership.

attack by Asians themselves as masking discrimination, poverty, and oppression, and preventing the society at large from recognizing that these problems still exist for many Asians (Tong 1971, pp. 19-20; Kitano and Sue 1973, pp. 1-3). Many stereotypes are of course less subtly objectionable. Particularly annoying to Asians is the habit of many Whites of classifying even a fifth-generation Asian-American as "foreign" (Nee and Nee 1972, p. 359). The implication that only Whites are fully American has enticed many young Asians to pursue the "Anglo-conformity" that pan-Asian activists now denigrate in favor of non-White alternatives (Tong 1971, pp. 21-24).[8]

COMMON IDENTITY: ETHNICITY AS THE BASIS OF PANETHNIC UNITY

Bringing people from diverse ethnic groups together within a common identity is no mean task. Those relatively few Indians and Asians who see panethnic unity as a likely means of achieving desired goals must redefine the stereotypical category as a valid identity in terms that are meaningful to those they wish to attract and mobilize. In addition to pointing out the need to unify for political efficacy, they might further accomplish this feat by establishing the panethnic identity as itself ethnic.

In recent years social scientists have come to devote increasing attention on the one had to the role of ethnicity in people's responses to changing political and economic conditions, and on the other to the primordial nature of ethnicity as a charter for defining a group's identity in opposition to other groups (Nagata, this volume). Ethnic change, whether in ethnic consciousness, group definition, the policing of ethnic boundaries, or in changes of personnel from one ethnic group to another (or from one identity to another), can be viewed as adaptive response to changes in political economy that accompany the changing circumstances of contact between groups of people. The assumption here is that in manipulating ethnicity in day-to-day interaction, people are looking out for what they see as their own welfare. In this sense an ethnic group is a type of interest group, and ethnicity serves as a peculiarly effective organizing principle.

An ethnic identity, like any other identity, is an abstraction. The set of symbols that make up a group's charter serves in the first place to objectify the identity of the group—to give it reality in people's minds and to define and express the distinctiveness of its members. Once an identity is so established, the group's charter serves two

8. Ben Tong reports a growing preference among young Asian-Americans for Black heroes and social models over both White and Asian alternatives.

further important functions. One is to attract and unify the prospective members of the group for collective action. Political leaders may see clearly the advantages—for themselves and for their followers—of cooperation and mobilization, but people generally see their interests in terms of individual or family concerns. The group charter will therefore be formulated in such a way as to suggest to people that their interests lie inextricably with those of the group. The second major function is to protect group prerogatives by stating what those prerogatives are and by excluding all but genuine members of the group, however defined.

In the formation of panethnic identities it is the unifying function that is of major importance. As a result of Indian-White intermarriage the exclusion of Caucasian-looking people and so-called "instant Indians" seeking the material benefits intended for "real" Indians presents some problems. Since for the purposes of allotting benefits, however, Indian identity is by law a function of tribal affiliation, this boundary maintenance problem can be dealt with at the tribal level. Tribal charters therefore show greater concern with exclusiveness (e.g., using "blood" criteria, way-of-life, etc.) than with the unity of the group. Among Asian-Americans, by contrast, exclusion has not been a problem, though it might conceivably become so in future years if intermarriage occurs and there are group prerogatives to protect.

We might expect that a panethnic charter would reflect a greater concern with unification than with exclusion of outsiders. What distinguishes ethnicity from other principles of group identity is the means by which this unifying function is accomplished. The unique potential of ethnicity for mobilizing people as an interest group stems from its appeal to sentiments of common origin, from its ability to arouse emotions and loyalties founded on people's early experiences of fundamental human ties (Geertz 1963; Keyes 1976). An ethnic charter, like any effective charter, is therefore not arbitrarily composed. It includes symbols closely associated with such early experiences: symbols of kinship, locality, religion, language, and whatever else may be viewed as the essential components of the cultural milieu into which one is born—especially the features of that environment that symbolize the human relationships within it.

In the formulation of a panethnic charter the problem arises as to what symbols can be found that will appeal in this fashion to members of different ethnic groups, and yet not include unwanted outsiders. For American Indians and Asian-Americans the question is to what extent the panethnic *category* can be redefined as a valid *identity*. While the mobilizing potential of ethnicity may be recognized by the politically minded leaders of any ethnic group, it may not always be possible to formulate a meaningful *ethnic* charter for bringing about unification.

What this suggests is that an ethnic group is not merely a collectivity of persons having some set of cultural or physical traits in common, though indeed they may; nor is it merely an association of individuals whose common interests bring them together in cooperation and symbolic unity. An ethnic group is an interest group with something extra: the belief by its members in their mutual relationship of shared descent—in being fundamentally the same people. The feature of ethnicity that is essential for this discussion is the notion that one is born to one's ethnic characteristics, that one cannot come by them easily in adult life through mere study. One's ethnic identity is seen as a given, and if one has—at different times or simultaneously—more than one ethnic identity, then that too is a given, a result of the circumstances of one's birth and early socialization.

The important point for those attempting to formulate a panethnic identity as an inclusive ethnic identity is that symbolic means must be found to suggest to people not that they are members of a group merely because they have common interests, but rather that they unavoidably have common interests because they are all the same people. From this perspective an attack on one subgroup or individual is seen as an example of the relationship of the entire group to outsiders—"it could happen to any of us"—rather than as something that distinguishes one subgroup from other subgroups. It is the distinctively primordial character of ethnicity that at the same time makes it so effective in this respect and yet so difficult to achieve panethnically.

SOURCES AND ORIGINS OF PANETHNIC IDENTITY

The question before us now is how categories for people have developed into identities held by people. That American Indian and Asian-American now represent, at least for some people and at some times, more than mere terms applied for the sake of convenience by outsiders is demonstrated by the participation of Indians from different tribes and Asians of different nationalities in such pan-Indian and pan-Asian organizations as the National Congress of American Indians and the Asian Law Collective in Los Angeles, and in such issue-oriented movements as the Alcatraz occupation and the Fort Lawton movement in Seattle, among many others. The concept of panethnic identity is also expressed, explicitly or implicitly, in such publications by Indians and Asian-Americans as Vine Deloria's

The Indian Affair (1974) and the UCLA Asian American Studies Center's *Amerasia Journal.*[9]

For Indians the development of panethnic identity can be traced in the history of a long series of attempts to organize pan-Indian confederations, beginning with the League of the Hodenosaunee, or Iroquois, which preceded contact with Whites, and continuing with such later incorporations as the Creek Confederacy of the 1600s, Pueblo unification in 1680, and others (Witt 1970, pp. 94-95). Proposals for greater all-Indian confederacies were advanced by Joseph Brant during the Revolutionary War and later by Tecumseh. Witt (ibid., p. 94) observes, however, that despite these early efforts "confederation among American Indian tribes was the exception rather than the rule throughout traditional and recorded history." And to this day, despite the efforts of the National Congress of American Indians, the American Indian Movement, and other pan-Indian organizations, pantribal identity is by no means universally accepted among Indians. The development of Asian-American unity and identity has a much shorter history and has yet to reach the level of popularity and influence that the pan-Indian movement enjoys among Indians. While examples of White oppression of different Asian immigrant groups stretch back over a century, the current pan-Asian response seems to date from the Third World strike in San Francisco and Los Angeles in 1968 (Endo 1973, p. 281), and its major proponents seem to be organizing the movement almost solely within Asian studies programs on university campuses.

In attempting to popularize unity, panethnic proponents among Indians and Asians have called upon unifying principles that are clearly products of the circumstances of contact with Whites. It frequently has been observed that the stratagems employed in ethnic boundary maintenance change according to the conditions of interethnic contact. The members of a group define themselves in opposition to particular outsiders. As the outsiders change or differ so do the principles by which nonmembers of the group in question are filtered out. The primordial, unifying principles of ethnic identity also reflect the changing characteristics of the contact situation. In part, the developing definitions of "American Indian" and "Asian-American" reveal a growing self-awareness that is itself stimulated by contact with Whites

9. Other examples include *Roots: An Asian American Reader*, by the UCLA Asian American Studies Center (1971), *Aiiieeeee! An Anthology of Asian-American Writers*, ed. Frank Chin et al., and *To Be An Indian: An Oral History*, edited by Cash and Hoover (1971).

and other outsiders. In more subtle ways these changing definitions also reflect the tenor of the times and the attitudes and assumptions prevalent in the dominant White society, either to oppose and undermine them or to exploit them.

Thomas (1972, pp. 739-40) has suggested that "at contact, most American Indians lived in small closed tribal groups. . . . They conceived of those outside of their group as a different order of being, almost a different species." Some tribes did seem to be widening their conception of who they were in relation to others after contact with Whites, but

Although tribal groups in the East were coming to define others outside their groups as human beings, there was as yet no conception of "Indian." To the Cherokee, Englishmen and Creeks were, although human beings, simply different kinds of outsiders. As one examines the historical record in the 1700s, it is clear that tribal groups in the East were beginning to see themselves as having something in common together as opposed to the Europeans. In speeches chiefs would comment on the general style of life in common among tribal groups in that area as opposed to Europeans, and more Indians began to have a common interest in opposing the white man. [Ibid.]

The way Indians and Asians view themselves has been significantly influenced by the way otusiders view them and relate to them. The same ethnocentric "myopia" that led White Americans to lump Indians and Asians into broad categories also formed much of the formal and informal dealings Whites have had with these peoples. Kunstadter (1979, p. 160), in speaking of a similar stereotypical panethnic category, "hill tribe," in northern Thailand, has pointed out that "large, centralized bureaucratic systems seem unable to cope with local cultural and ecological variations except through use of standardized, uniform policies." In the United States, both Asians and Indians have been collectively subjected to a long series of policies, laws, and violent and nonviolent attacks.[10] Being treated as if they were the same can lead at least some people to feel that they are indeed the same with respect to their mutual antagonists.

Wallace (1972, p. 198) cites an early pan-Indian response to White racist attacks on Indian culture and social position: "When the western confederacy met in 1786, for instance, the proposal was made that *all* the nations of our color unite and be of one mind. There it was argued, 'Let us then have a just sense of our own value and if after that the great spirit wills that other colors should subdue us let it be so.'"

10. See, for example, Tong's (1971) and Shin's (1971) accounts of the treatment of Asian-Americans at the hands of Whites, and of U.S. government policies and laws relating to Indians in Svensson (1973).

Joseph Brant, a Mohawk who advocated pan-Indian unity in response to White intrusion, gave Indian commonality a territorial dimension: "Brother: We are of the same opinion with the people of the United States: you consider yourselves as independent people; we, as the original inhabitants of this country, and sovereigns of the soil, look upon ourselves as equally independent, and free as any other nation or nations. This country was given to us by the Great Spirit above; we wish to enjoy it. . ." (Vanderwerth 1971, p. 53, from a speech delivered in 1794).

Tecumseh, a Shawnee, was also moved by White attacks on his people to propose a pan-Indian solution. Witt (1970, p. 98) observes that like others before him, "Tecumseh's wisdom lay in his conception of himself as an Indian first and a Shawnee second. Like Brant, he fought for more than resistance to encroachment; he propounded a design for an Indian state built on national consciousness above and beyond tribal consciousness." Tecumseh again stressed the newly understood bases of pantribal commonality in calling other tribes to join his resistance and ". . . assist in the just cause of liberating our race from the grasp of our faithless invaders and heartless oppressors. The white usurpation in *our common country* must be stopped, or we, its rightful owners, be forever destroyed and wiped out *as a race of people*" (Vanderwerth 1971, p. 64, from a speech delivered in 1811; emphasis added).

He exhorted the Choctaws and Chickasaws to recognize their common interest and mutual obligation with the Shawnee based on a principle of shared descent: "Then haste to the relief of our common cause, as by consanguinity of blood you are bound; lest the day be not far distant when you will be left single-handed and alone to the cruel mercy of our most inveterate foe" (ibid., p. 66).

These efforts at confederation were pursued at a time when Indians could still contemplate, however unrealistically, the final military defeat of White intruders by a unified Indian nation. Depopulation, relocation, and the loss of vastly more territory through the 1800s drove some Indians to the final desperation of the Ghost Dance, while others came to assess Indian strategy in more realistic terms.[11] For the politically minded, preservation was no longer a matter of military victories, but of legal ones, and the arenas of conflict shifted gradually from battlefields to courtrooms and legislatures.

11. Vanderwerth (1971) relates how Black Hawk, an untiring military opponent of Whites, was shown the cities in the east "to impress upon him the strength and greatness of the nation. He finally realized he had come up against an immovable force, and that he could no longer stay the white horde."

The idiom of Indian commonality also underwent some changes. By the 1900s the concept of "race" had grown less popular as a unifier, due in part perhaps to connotations of inferiority it had come to evoke. Hertzberg (1971, pp. 307-8) suggests that in the early 1900s pan-Indians emphasized general Indian characteristics that were common to the tribes: "dignity, fidelity to one's word, love and reverence for nature, cooperation, artistic expression, respect for age and wisdom, bravery, belief in a higher being, an aversion to crass materialism, independence, self-respect, pride, and other such aboriginal virtues." These virtues, she goes on to say, are the ones that happened to be highly respected by White society. Other common Indian characteristics that were less popular, "such as common ownership of land or devotion to traditional ways, were quite understandably neglected. These would be left for a time later in the century when more Americans admired them" (ibid.).

In recent times, as larger numbers of Indians not only interact with one another across tribal boundaries but find themselves in fact isolated from tribal life in urban environments, pan-Indian unity has begun to move ahead. It is in this context that the Alcatraz occupation took place.

THE ALCATRAZ OCCUPATION AND THE
EXPRESSION OF A PANETHNIC CHARTER

The occupation of Alcatraz Island by the Indians of All Tribes and the subsequent publication of *Alcatraz Is Not An Island* (Bluecloud 1972) were explicitly directed toward unifying Indians in their own minds as well as reasserting their distinctiveness in the eyes of other Americans and the government. The occupation carried a message: that the Indians still exist and that they have real grievances, for the typical response they credited to Whites was, "Indians invade Alcatraz, can you imagine? We didn't even know there were any Indians left. . . . What is it they want and what are they trying to prove?" (ibid., p. 28).

Although both Indians and non-Indians contributed to the volume, a few common themes run through all their writings. The occupation was embarked upon in pursuit of certain goals, they say, these goals to be achieved by the occupiers *as Indians* (ibid., pp. 21, 43). Their purpose was to achieve Indian self-determination (ibid., pp. 21, 29), to obtain clear deed to the island (ibid., p. 15), and to build upon it an Indian Cultural Center, consisting of a Center for Native American Studies, an American Indian Spiritual Center, an Indian Center of Ecology, a Great Indian Training School, and an American Indian Museum (ibid., pp. 41-42). These facilities were to be designed and operated by Indians and for Indians (ibid., p. 68).

As might be expected, the occupation met with considerable resistance. The Indians were repeatedly warned by "government representatives" that "the island is dangerous and unsuitable for living upon" (ibid., p. 29), and that they were present there as trespassers (ibid., p. 59). The proposals for an Indian Cultural Center were met with a government counterproposal for a "master park plan for the Island," having a "maximal Indian quality" to be created as "an outstanding recreation resource within reach of millions of urban dwellers." This park, to be developed by the Department of the Interior, would have an Indian name, monuments to Indian heroes, a museum for teaching non-Indians about Indians, and some Indian park rangers trained by the park service (ibid., p. 65).

The Indians saw this as a denial of Indian self-determination, as simply another intrusion by the government upon Indian life. Having no wish to become tourist attractions, as they put it, they refused the government's proposal. Opposition to the Indian cause also took the form of unfavorable media coverage, and eventually the cutting off of electricity and water to the island (ibid., pp. 68, 69).

To pursue their goals in the face of an unheeding public and a hostile government, the Indians had to transcend tribal differences and attract as much unified support as possible among Indians. The occupation and the island itself were designated both as symbols of Indian unity and as means of achieving that unity (ibid., pp. 21, 77). To isolate themselves and thereby emphasize their commonality, only Indians were permitted on the island. Indian identity was stressed, but tribal identity was upheld as well. New arrivals were greeted with the warning, "Indians only. If you aren't Indians, please keep going and don't try to land," and, upon landing, with "Welcome! What tribe you from?" (ibid., p. 19). Boundary maintenance was thereby effected at the level of tribal identity, upon which Indian identity clearly depends and through which it is validated. Throughout the book mention is made of participating tribes: Navajo, Sioux, Winnebago, Blackfeet, Iroquois, Pomo, Paiute, and many others.

The distinctiveness of Indian identity is expressed partly through stereotypical symbols that refer to no single tribe, though many are of Plains Indian origin: the Great Spirit, a peace-pipe ceremony, tipis, feathers (in the cover design), sacred healing ceremonies, and "the universal eagle symbol." These stereotypical symbols, directed largely at Whites, may also appeal to an Indian sense of shared identity, but the major focus of Indian commonality and unity—one that can appeal to all Indians regardless of their tribal or individual experiences—is their unique relationship to the land. It is in this sense that "Alcatraz is not an island." The occupation was carried out on a theme reminiscent of Brant and Tecumseh. As Svensson has recently reiterated,

"American Indians as a group share a unique relationship to the land mass known as North America and a formal association with the United States based in treaty law. While moral and legal arguements as to the sanctity and appropriateness of both the above concepts as applied to Indians have frequently raged, they remain the cornerstones of the *Indian* perspective on their relationship to American government and society . . . " (1973, p. 1).

A wealth of symbolism grows out of this conception of unique Indian sovereignty in *Alcatraz Is Not An Island*. Arrivals to Alcatraz were greeted with "Welcome to Indian land" (1972, p. 19), and a huge sign stating "You are on Indian land" (Bluecloud, 1972, pp. 25, 42; see also pp. 23, 40, 54, and 60). In a "Proclamation To The Great Father And All His People" the Indians of All Tribes echo White principles and rationalizations regarding land ownership in announcing that "We, the native Americans, reclaim the land known as Alcatraz Island in the name of all American Indians by right of discovery" (ibid., p. 40). While the proclamation is a mockery of White behavior in relation to the land and to Indians, the Indians are serious about the validity of their own claims. These are justified, and the Indians expect the government to concur, they said, because "after all, hadn't the whole continent been taken from us?" (ibid., p. 30). Raymond Lego's contribution emphasizes this point:

> Don't feel you're a stranger here.
> This is your land, this is my land.
> This is Indian country.
> My ancestors lived here;
> The Great Spirit put them here,
> Just like he did the oak trees and the water.
> Feel Welcome. Let your spirit be free.
>
> [Ibid., p. 82]

The sentiments of common origin based on mutual relationship to the land are further developed through the use of a kinship idiom—both for Indians among themselves and vis-à-vis the land. The kinship theme appears first in the opening paragraph of the Introduction (ibid., p. 11): "Each person upon this earth had ancestors who lived in close harmony with all of nature. For too many this basic tie between man, spirit and creation has been forgotten. The spirit, the very blood cries out for us to re-examine ourselves in relation to our environment and to one another. Our privilege as people is the care and protection of our earth mother."

"People" in the last sentence refers to all people, not only to Indians, but for Indians in particular "our earth mother" refers specifically to North America. Thus the occupation was not an "invasion," but a homecoming: "Unwanted and unknown by the strangers who now lived upon all parts of our continent, we had come home. Our earth mother wanted us here, for we are of the land" (ibid., p. 28). The resistance of Indians to the alienation of their land is likewise articulated in terms of kinship. When, in the 1950s, the U.S. government offered the Indian tribes of California forty-five cents an acre for the land they had earlier lost, "The Pit River Indians, still living on parts of their ancestral lands, said simply, no! They didn't want money, no matter how much, for their Mother Earth. They wanted and still want, the return of their lands, their mother" (ibid., p. 90). That the kinship idiom was intended to inspire a sense of unity is further demonstrated by the invitation extended to Indians from all tribes to "join your brothers and sisters," for together they are all "earth children" (ibid., pp. 19, 37).

The contradictions inherent in the combination of massive White intrusion upon Indian land with the concepts of property rights contained in law and in the numerous Indian treaties have given rise to a long series of incidents and tragedies between Whites and Indians. While officially serving as the protector of Indians and their property, the U.S. government has at the same time been the primary agent of the alienation of Indian land (Schusky 1965, pp. vi-vii and passim). The Indians of All Tribes suggest that the return of Alcatraz to Indian ownership "is but little to ask from a government which has systematically stolen our lands, destroyed a once-beautiful and natural landscape, killed-off the creatures of nature, polluted air and water, ripped open the very bowels of our earth in senseless greed; and instituted a program to annihilate the many Indian Tribes of this land by outright murder which even now continues by the methods of theft, suppression, prejudice, termination, and so-called re-location and assimilation (Bluecloud, 1972, p. 43). In depriving Indians of their land base the government undermined the basis of Indian identity. While the Indians had made Alcatraz a symbol of unity, after removing them from the island the government again made it "the hateful symbol of oppression" (ibid., p. 13).

Indians therefore see themselves as having a unique relationship not only to the land, but to the government as well. To protect their land, the Indians must try to preserve the protector function of the government, but at the same time government control of Indian affairs is seen as illegitimate, for Indians have a claim to sovereignty. In this light, whatever misfortune befalls any particular tribe at the hands of the government, or of Whites generally, is simply evidence of the overall relationship of Indians and Whites to the land and hence to each other. A recounting of each such incident therefore serves to remind

Indians both of their common uniqueness and of what the battle is all about as well. The position of pan-Indianists is that the problem involves all of them and so must the solution. unification is even more than a matter of political efficacy; it stands as the basis of an Indian understanding of their plight and of any progress toward relieving it, and the rallying point for unity is the Indian land base.

In one way or another, each of the adverse experiences of Indians that are recounted in *Alcatraz* involves the relationship of Indians to land. The Indians of All Tribes report, for example, that Indians in Seattle invaded Fort Lawton "to press for their right to occupy lands about to be declared surplus" (ibid., p. 56). The California Indian Legal Services, in a section entitled "How California Was Taken From the Indians," suggest that the land was taken in two ways: through decimation of people and by means of the law, leaving "over two thirds of the more than 40,000 native California Indians . . . without a land base . . . ." And the Pit River Nation made a number of attempts to reclaim their lands in northern California through peaceful occupation (ibid., pp. 83, 85, 89-96).

In addition to stealing Indian land, the Indians say, the Whites have also desecrated it; they have polluted and destroyed not only the stolen lands but even those the Indians still hold. The Pomo Indians of California are watching the destruction of their sacred Clear Lake, "polluted from the wastes of the thousands of homes, resorts and new sub-divisions," and the surrounding countryside has been bulldozed for new housing and stripped for gravel and mercury. And the Paiutes at Pyramid Lake, Nevada, look on helplessly as the lake dries up, its water supply cut off by dams on the Truckee River that divert the water to "prosperous ranches and farms in the Fallon, Nevada area" (ibid., pp. 62, 86).

Again, the idiom of kinship serves to emphasize Indian identity with the land and Indian outrage at its desecration. Their response to this destruction is of a different kind than the mere "mouthings of environmentalists/ecologists." The return of Indians to Alcatraz was to challenge the White invader "for desecrating the mother earth" (ibid., p. 15). The suggestion, credited to Whites, that Indians should develop their land as Whites do theirs is met with astonishment: "Do you rape your mother? Must you tear her apart and cover her exposed bowels with chemicals and force feed her into a two-crop a year existence?" The Indians of All Tribes propose that Alcatraz Island be allowed to return to a natural state, that native animals and plants be restored to the island and that Indians make only one ceremonial visit a year. This sanctuary amidst the overcrowded coastal area is to be dedicated to "our earth mother" (ibid., pp. 62, 79).

In summary, the redefinition of Indian identity put forward here emphasizes the conceptual unity of all Indians, and seeks to invest that unity with emotional import through the use of kinship metaphors, especially mother-child relationships. The goals of the movement—Indian self-determination and the protection of Indian land—are closely tied in with the fundamental defining feature of pan-Indian identity: their unique relationship to the land. In so far as this relationship is regarded as a given that is prior to contact with Whites, it forms the basis of an *ethnic* identity. While the U.S. government ceased officially to acknowledge Indian sovereignty over the land when it stopped writing treaties and began manipulating Indians and Indian land through acts of Congress after 1871, to the Indians their claim to a land base is still an essential part of Indian identity. The problems of adverse relationships with Whites and with the government are approached as correlates of this relationship to the land.

THE ASIAN-AMERICAN MOVEMENT

Though the Asian-American movement as yet boasts no dramatic public episodes to compare with the occupation of Alcatraz Island, it bears important resemblance to the pan-Indian movement in other respects. Both involve attempts to unify members of a number of non-White ethnic groups within a panethnic identity, and in both cases that identity arose first as a stereotypic category invented as a result of contact with Whites in North America.

A major issue addressed by Asian-American activists is the need to replace the various stereotypes of Asians now current among Whites and among Asians as well. Negative stereotypes often lead to harassment of Asians, a point maintained by the Asian Law Collective in their discussion of the trial of Esther Lau. She is "a Chinese woman who was propositioned and sexually molested by a California Highway Patrol officer and then, amazingly, charged with battery and resisting arrest . . ." (1974, p. 12). The Asian Law Collective tried to indicate during the trial that there were certain "underlying sexist and racist stereotypes which led the officer to attempt such an outrage: the Asian woman has often been portrayed as a bar girl or prostitute (the Suzie Wong image) or as submissive and passive (the Geisha girl), and the G.I. experience in Asia has reinforced these ideas" (ibid., pp. 12-13).[12] Others have argued that whether a particular stereotype is favorable or unfavorable, it is racist and therefore anathema to Asians:

White racism enforces white supremacy. White supremacy is a system of order

12. See Wong (1975) for a detailed account of the Esther Lau trial.

and a way of perceiving reality. Its purpose is to keep whites on top and set them free. Colored minorities in white reality are stereotypes. Each racial stereotype comes in two models, the acceptable model and the unacceptable model. The unacceptable, hostile black stud has his acceptable counterpart in the form of Stepin Fetchit. For the savage, kill-crazy Geronimo, there is Tonto and the Hollywood version of Cochise. . . . For Fu Manchu and the Yellow Peril, there is Charlie Chan and his Number One Son. The unacceptable model is unacceptable because he cannot be controlled by whites. The acceptable model is acceptable because he is tractable. There is racist hate and racist love. [Chin and Chan 1972, p. 65]

Asians have images of themselves, it is further suggested, that must also be overcome in the interest of improving the lot of all Asians. The "quiet" Nisei,[13] and Asian passivity in general must be replaced by a more vocal activism—to the benefit of both Asians and Whites (Hirabayashi 1975, pp. 126-27; Hosokawa 1969, p. 172). The Oriental Student Association on a university campus recently observed:

We realize that almost 95% of the Orientals on campus have used or are still using the term Oriental to describe themselves as a racial group. To most American people, this term has stereotype images—e.g., the sexy Susie Wong, the wily Charlie Chan, and the evil Fu Manchu. To many of us in the Oriental community, we have our own interpretations which differ markedly from that which the majority of the Americans believe. To us an Oriental signifies the quiet, studious, hard-working, generally intelligent individual but who has group apathy. He doesn't care about making waves even though he may be right. He blames the "establishment" or American society in a subtle way—he resigns himself and accepts his fate—no questions asked. [Quoted in Weiss 1974, p. 234]

The disadvantages suffered by Asian-Americans as a result of White racism cannot be eradicated by the achievements of a relative few who succeed and leave the majority behind in poverty and degradation, they argue. Nor can Asian-American problems be solved by mere appeal to White indulgence and charity. The pan-Asian program includes redefining their identity in Asian-American terms, and in uniting among themselves to achieve the political efficacy required in demanding their rights and improving community life. The activists do battle with Anglo-conformity among Asians by replacing it with Asian pride, and by taking the management of Asian affairs into Asian hands wherever White control of Asian life has proved detrimental.

In addition to the obstacles also faced by pan-Indian activists— the inaccuracy of stereotypic definitions of the panethnic category and the objections of both traditionalists and assimilationists to the activists' position—there are some that are rather unique to pan-Asianists. The level of educational and occupational achievement among Asians is not only much higher than among Indians, but is among the highest

13. "Nisei" refers to second-generation Japanese-Americans.

of any ethnic group in the country. The result, often lamented by activists, is an immovable complacency on the part of Asian-Americans who have "made it" and don't want to get involved in anything controversial (e.g., Weiss 1974, p. 239).[14]

A more fundamental problem, perhaps, stems from Asians being immigrants rather than indigenous people. The various Asian homelands still exist and their citizenry and great cultural traditions can remind Asians in America of the depth of their diversity. Furthermore, the U. S. government has treated the various Asian groups in the United States differently, depending on its current relationship with the country of origin. While Japanese were interned during World War II the Chinese enjoyed freedom and relative prosperity; and because their country was a U.S. territory, Filipinos have been treated differently with respect to immigration and naturalization (LaGumina and Cavaioli 1974, p. 99).

The influx of new immigrants from Asian countries since the relaxation of the immigration laws in 1965 has had two important effects that are relevant to pan-Asianism in a different way. For one thing, the immigrants bring with them a pride in being Chinese, Japanese, and so forth that many "assimilated" Asians had forgotten, and which has inspired the reaction against Anglo-conformity that has been a first step toward pan-Asian consciousness for some of the Asian-American leaders (Nee and Nee 1972, pp. 378-79).[15] At the

---

14. After addressing a Chinese Civic Club an Asian-American activist leader gave the following impressions (quoted in Weiss 1974, p. 239):

We were politely received and, because everyone understood English, they listened. I could sense, though, a feeling of tension in the air. It was as if they really did not want to hear some of the things we said. Like when we talked about the struggle of all minority peoples, they wanted to separate the Chinese from everyone else. When I mentioned that we Chinese had, in the past, profited from exploiting Chinese immigrants, they didn't want to believe it, although they knew it had been true. I don't know if they really understand what ethnic studies are all about. Some of them think that we should study Chinese culture and learn the language but that we should keep out of politics.

15. In Nee and Nee (1972, pp. 378-79), Frank Chin tells of a Chinese teacher he once had, a new immigrant, who had strong feelings about Chinese-Americans:

There was one thing that he always said that shook everybody up, it was like a theme of his, and it was that the Chinese-Americans, the Chinese in America, weren't worth shit. He said that they all capitulated to white supremacy, that they were morally bankrupt, and that their language betrayed that. He said, "Why do you want to be called Chinese-Americans? Because you don't want to be called Chinamen, because that's

same time, the more traditional attitudes and customs of the immigrants stand in stark contrast to those of the Asian-Americans and remind the latter of how little they have in common with their fellows in Asia and how much with other Asian-Americans (ibid., pp. 331-32).

Another significant implication of the immigrant origins of Asian-Americans that relates directly to the question of ethnicity is that not only was their commonality first defined as a result of contact with Whites in North America, but that from their own perspective there is no other basis for Asian commonality. Unlike the Indians, they have no symbolic referent of common identity within the North American context that is also prior to and independent of contact with Whites. To put it another way, it is difficult for Asian-Americans to find symbols of common identity that are independent of White stereotypes and that appeal to all Asian-Americans. No Indian or White would deny that Indians were present in North America before Whites; whether to Whites or the government that fact has any moral or legal significance in itself is another matter. To Indians it is very meaningful. But no comparable feature of Asian-American identity presents itself. How, then, do Asian-Americans redefine their identity to give it a unifying validity that the stereotypical lacks?

A number of tactics have been used in pursuit of the twin goals of replacing Anglo-conformity with Asian pride and ethnic diversity with panethnic unity. Just as "Black" replaced "Negro" to signal a new ingredient of defiant pride, so is "Oriental" to be displaced by "Asian-American" in the activist vocabulary:

An Asian-American is an Oriental born or raised exclusively in America—but with one difference. He gives a damn about his life, his work, his beliefs, and is willing to do almost anything to help Orientals become Asian-Americans. In recent years, the term Asian-Americans has been connected with the Third World Liberation Front, Black Student Union, Asian-American Political Association, and other militant organizations that justify violence—things that are against most Orientals' concept of morality. We also believe in non-violence and to date we have followed this principle. We hope you can be proud some day of the term Asian American. [From the *Bulletin* of the Oriental Student Association, quoted in Weiss 1974, p. 234]

---

what they called your grandfathers and your great-grandfathers who were the miners." He said, "What did they do to be bad guys? They mined gold, they dug out the tunnels, they carved the way for the railroad, what's so bad about that? The only thing that was bad was that the white man looked on them with contempt and called them Chinamen. And all we can remember is that they looked on them with contempt, you know. And we think its all our fault, but it isn't, it's the white man's fault that Chinaman is a bad word. And you should never forget that, you should call yourselves Chinamen, not Chinese-Americans.

Images of "yellow Americans" as "humble, meek, self-sufficient, supplicating, gracious, obedient, effete," and scholarly explanations of these character traits as the product of Confucian orthodoxy and imported clan institutions, and indeed, the entire interpretation of the experiences of Asians in America, are to be overturned through a review of the history of Asians—both in Asia and America—from an Asian-American perspective.[16] Ben Tong, for example, in arguing against the "meek and mild" images of "asexual" Chinese, speaks of "such uniquely Cantonese traditions as peasant rebellions, local wars and actively anti-establishment secret societies" and "a worldly, rebellious and emotional lot who were known to articulate the ferociously masculine models from such heroic literature as *The Romance of the Three Kingdoms* and *The Water Margin*," and he cites "the history of a universe of experience that spawned the first Chinamen who busted up the Old West and fought to stay here" (Tong 1974, pp. 182-86).

Others point out that White Americans regard Asian-American culture and identity as Asian, thinking that because it is not White it is not American. In this way Asians are defined as perpetual foreigners (Chin et al 1975, p. xi). Thus another important goal of the re-study of Asian-American history is to demonstrate that Asian culture and identity are equally as American as those of any White community. Nee and Nee (1972, p. 359) cite the efforts of the "cultural radicals" in the Asian-American movement, who "see a new exploration of their ethnic tradition and its deep roots in American soil as essential to the restoration of [their] integrity and dignity. . . ."

Numerous studies and reinterpretations of Asian history in the United States have been undertaken in an effort to unify Asian-Americans—to bring out that which is uniquely Asian about American life and experience and what Asian-Americans have in common that transcends ethnic boundaries. It is an attempt to build unity through self-respect as part of a living tradition. Carlos Bulosan's autobiography, *America Is in the Heart*, an account of his experiences as a farm laborer and union organizer, is described as reflecting "the collective life experience of thousands of Filipino immigrants who were attracted to this country by its legendary promises of a better life or who were recruited for employment here" (McWilliams, quoted in Osumi 1975, p. 1). Furthermore, "the book as well as Bulosan himself symbolizes the struggle for Filipino and other Asian workers against racism and exploitation, for equality, social justice and human dignity" (ibid.).

16. As, for example, in Bulosan (1973), Ichioka (1971), Okihiro (1973), Shin (1971), and Tong (1971).

Lowell Chun-Hoon, in pursuing "an Asian-American perspective on Asian-American history" (1975, p. 43), recounts the various discriminatory laws and informal acts perpetrated against Chinese, Korean, Filipino, and Japanese immigrants and the cynical exploitation of Asian labor, and concludes:

The significance of this exploitation does not lie in the mere fact that Asian immigrants were underpaid and abused, for early European immigrants often endured equal hardships and equal forms of oppression. What is significant is that all of these varied Asian groups, each representing a separate country and unique culture, encountered a similar or identical pattern of racial oppression and economic exploitation. Just as all groups were utilized as a supply of cheap labor for the demands of the rapidly expanding western economy, so were all of the groups effectively excluded from the United States by law. [Ibid., p. 47]

In discussing the "uniqueness of Asian-Americans," Kalish and Moriwaki (1973, pp. 202-3) argue that while other minorities also faced prejudice and discrimination in America,

The Asians were unique, however, in that they were visibly different from the general population and thus regarded as unassimilable. Further, they suffered from discrimination that was codified in law and that explicitly listed them as the victims of the overtly discriminatory laws. The Alien Land Acts, the Alien Exclusion Act, miscegenation laws, the World War II treatment of the Japanese Americans are the most conspicuous of these laws and regulations. . . .
    Not until 1952 could first-generation Asians become citizens. They were thus unable to vote or exert any but the most marginal political influence. Moreover, they were left in legal jeopardy since they could readily be deported.

In addition to recounting past experiences, pan-Asian proponents invite Asians to examine their everyday encounters with White society. Here too they will find evidence of the common Asian-American condition and the need for unity among Asian-Americans to solve their problems. In summing up the experience of a summer's legal work against police harassment in Chinatown, the Asian Law Collective concludes: "The summer experience had a number of positive results. During that period, a basis of unity began to develop among some of the youth and other community people. It became clearer that unity and organization were necessary in order to fight harassment and other community problems and that a total perspective of the American social and economic system had to be developed" (1974, p. 6).

The task of redefining Asian-American identity in terms that are at once attractive and meaningful to all Asian-Americans is undertaken in systematic fashion by the various Asian-American studies programs. Course offerings reveal a similar pattern at different universities. While encouraging relevant studies in other departments, the Contemporary Asian Studies Division at Berkeley, for example, provides three broad categories of courses within its own program. One category deals with the skills needed for successful Asian studies, including reading, composition, and various Asian language courses, especially "community" languages (1973, pp. 40-42). A second category concentrates on the as yet poorly documented history of Asians in the United States, with separate courses for Chinese, Japanese, and Filipino-American history, plus more general courses on Asian women, racism in America, and Asian-American history (ibid., p. 41). The final category of "Community and Institution" courses puts students to work on contemporary problems and has a strong emphasis on field experience and the practical application of research and other skills in meeting the needs of the community.

The Asian American Studies program at the University of Washington also offers courses in the history and culture of various Asian-American "subcultures" (1977, p. 1), as well as on contemporary issues. A recent course-description flyer listed three courses on history and culture and five that focused on contemporary experience. Special attention is given to the "wide range of ideas, attitudes and concerns of citizens of Asian ancestry whose experience in the United States has been significantly affected by their own unique position in this society." Students are expected to have field experience "in a broad range of community settings and agencies dealing with Asian Americans," and to submit "an in-depth analysis of the experience upon termination of the internship" (ibid.). Seminars are also offered that consist of "weekly small group discussions centering on experience," with each student required to research and conduct one such session (ibid., p. 2).

CONCLUSION

It is evident from the foregoing discussion that the major burden of defining Asian-American commonality and of inspiring Asian-Americans to unify for collective community action falls upon their historical and contemporary experiences in the United States. Adverse experience with Whites also serves this function for pan-Indian identity, but for the Indians this experience is built upon the unifying symbolism of common origin and identity. Asian-Americans, by contrast, have only the commonality that results from being treated *as if* they were the same people by White Americans.

While for the Indians it was perhaps their experiences with Whites that first led them to see their commonality, that stage is now long past. For present-day Indians, as I have argued above, it is because of their common identity that the experiences of one tribe with Whites can be seen to exemplify the position of all Indians vis-à-vis Whites. All Indians were indigenous to the land and all therefore suffer from the effects of White intrusion upon it or are susceptible to such intrusion if it in fact has not occurred.

Indian problems are not fundamentally predicated on negative stereotypes, but on their unique relationship to the land. As Trosper (this volume) points out, negative stereotypes of Indians first arose only when the increasingly numerous Whites began to covet their land, not during the period of initial contact. As with the Indians, the stereotypes of Asians varied as Whites saw them as either a source of economic competition or as an exploitable resource. As Nee and Nee (1972) have amply demonstrated, anti-Asian legislation in California and elsewhere grew directly out of agitation by labor leaders and political opportunists who presented Asians as unfair competition for White jobs and as scapegoats for economic ills. Only when coolie labor was needed to build the railroads, or when World War II brought a huge demand for labor and industrial skills were legal and extralegal barriers relaxed and Asians employed in any numbers. But the special talent for austere living and cramped quarters that Whites saw as the essence of Oriental competitiveness can hardly form the basis of a modern Asian-American identity, and the more recent stereotypes are similarly unappealing.

In contrast to the pan-Indian position, then, the pan-Asian one is that "we get treated all the same, so we are all the same," rather than "we are the same and so we all get treated the same." While the Indians are an interest group because they are, fundamentally, an ethnic group, the Asians are merely an interest group, and the use of Asian identity is, at least for the time being, no more than a matter of political expediency.[17]

It seems likely that the task of making commonality more salient than diversity among potential members of a panethnic interest group will be easier where the peoples in question are indigenous rather than immigrant, other things being equal. This would be especially so if the common interests of indigenous peoples are focused on the very feature that defines their uniqueness, to wit: the land. Where the appeal is merely to group interests, those individuals who are economically successful will most likely see their individual or family interests as more important. Where the appeal is to group identity

17. I have heard this view openly expressed by pan-Asian sympathizers. In tacit acknowledgment of this fact a speaker at a recent Asian Students Association meeting at the University of Washington suggested that the association should try "to answer to needs other than political ones."

and primordial sentiments, people can see their interests as lying with the group even when they are not personally affected by mistreatment.

Another result of the Indian relationship to the land is that the pan-Indian movement has a strong element of separatist nationalism, while the pan-Asian movement is more assimilationist, though on a melting-pot and equalitarian basis rather than through Anglo-conformity. In comparing the Black and Indian "civil rights" movements, Svensson suggests that "where the Black goal has seemed to be equal participation in the benefits and privileges of American society, the fundamental Indian objective is best summed up as the right not to have to participate and still maintain an autonomous Indian identity, legally rooted in the historic treaty relationship and the traditional land base" (1973, p. 39). There are of course variations in the Black movement as well as in the Asian one, but by and large the point holds true. Without a distinct land base, or any claim to such, the Asian movement can hardly be nationalist. It is, fundamentally, American rather than Asian. The Asian-American activists are saying that "America consists of us too!"

An interesting question then is to what extent the points brought out above can be generalized to other indigenous and immigrant peoples who find a need to form panethnic identities in opposition to a dominant "other." How do other factors such as religion, language, or race serve the function for immigrants that land can serve for indigenous peoples in defining their panethnic identity? The answer to these and other questions awaits further study into the formulation of panethnic charters in a variety of contexts.[18]

18. A question relevant to a comparison of the actual extent of interaction and unity among Indians and Asians, but one that seems not to have been researched at all for the Asian case, is the rate of intermarriage among the various subgroups. Asian students have suggested to me that they would first prefer to marry another member of their own ethnic group (e.g., Japanese); failing that another Asian, and only then a White. In fact, however, studies such as those by Burma (1963), Kikumura and Kitano (1973), and Tinker (1973), while focusing on White/non-White intermarriage, imply that Asian intramarriage is uncommon. For Indians this question has been studied (e.g., Walker 1972).

REFERENCES ───────────────────────────────────

Ablon, Joan
  1972 "Relocated American Indians in the San Francisco Bay Area." In *The Emergent Native Americans,* ed. Deward E. Walker, Jr., pp. 712-27. Boston: Little, Brown.
Amerasia Staff
  1971 "An Interview with Warren Furutani, National Community Involvement Coordinator, The Japanese American Citizens League (Los Angeles, California)." *Amerasia Journal* 1, no. 1:70-76.
Asian Law Collective
  1974 "Past and Present: Asian Law Collective." *Amerasia Journal* 2, no. 2:1-15.
Boissevan, Ethel
  1972 "The Detribalizaton of the Narrangansett Indians: A Case Study." In *The Emergent Native Americans,* ed. Deward E. Walker, Jr., pp. 435-46. Boston: Little, Brown.
Bulosan, Carlos
  1973 *America Is in the Heart.* Seattle: University of Washington Press.
Burma, J. H.
  1963 "Interethnic Marriage in Los Angeles, 1948-1959." *Social Forces* 42:156-65.
Cash, Joseph H., and Hoover, Herbert T., eds.
  1971 *To Be an Indian: An Oral History.* Chicago: Holt, Rinehart and Winston.
Chadwick, Bruce A., and Stauss, Joseph H.
  1975 "The Assimilation of American Indians into Urban Society: The Seattle Case." *Human Organization* 34, no. 4:359-69.
Chin, Frank, and Chan, Jeffrey Paul
  1972 "Racist Love." In *Seeing Through Shuck,* ed. R. Kostelanetz. New York: Ballantine Books.
Chin, Frank; Chan, Jeffrey Paul; Inada, Lawson Fusao; and Wong, Shawn, eds.
  1975 *Aiiieeeee! An Anthology of Asian-American Writers.* New York: Doubleday, Anchor Press.
Chun-Hoon, Lowell
  1975 "Teaching the Asian-American Experience: Alternative to the Neglect and Racism in Textbooks." *Amerasia Journal* 3, no. 1:40-59.
Collier, John
  1972 "John Collier Comments on the Essay of Robert A. Manners."

In *The Emergent Native Americans,* ed. Deward E. Walker, Jr., pp. 135-38. Boston: Little, Brown.

Deloria, Vine, Jr.
1974 *The Indian Affair.* New York: Friendship Press.

Endo, Russell
1973 "Whither Ethnic Studies: A Re-examination of Some Issues." In *Asian-Americans: Psychological Perspectives,* ed. Stanley Sue and Nathaniel N. Wagner. Palo Alto, Calif.: Science & Behavior Books.

Geertz, Clifford
1963 "The Integrative Revolution." In *Old Societies and New States,* ed. Clifford Geertz. New York: Free Press of Glencoe.

Hertzberg, Hazel W.
1971 *The Search for an American Indian Identity: Modern Pan-Indian Movements.* Syracuse: Syracuse University Press.

Hicks, George L., and Kerzer, David I.
1972 "Making a Middle Way: Problems of Monhegan Identity." *Southwestern Journal of Anthropology* 28, no. 1:1-24.

Hirabayashi, James
1975 "Nisei: The Quiet American?—a Re-evaluation." *Amerasia Journal* 3, no. 1:114-29.

Hosokawa, Bill
1969 *Nisei: The Quiet Americans.* New York: William Morrow.

Ichioka, Yuji
1971 "A Buried Past: Early Issei Socialists and the Japanese Community." *Amerasia Journal* 1, no. 2:1-25.

Indians of All Tribes
1972 *Alcatraz Is Not An Island,* ed. Peter Bluecloud. Berkeley, Calif.: Wingbow Press.

Kalish, Richard A., and Moriwaki, Sharon
1973 "The World of the Elderly Asian American." *Journal of Social Issues* 26, no. 2: 187-210.

Keesing, Roger M.
1976 *Cultural Anthropology: A Contemporary Perspective.* New York: Holt, Rinehart and Winston.

Keyes, Charles F.
1976 "Towards a New Formulation of the Concept of Ethnic Group." *Ethnicity* 3:202-13.

Kickingbird, Kirke, and Ducheneau, Karen
1973 *One Hundred Million Acres.* New York: Macmillan.

Kikumura, Akeni, and Kitano, Harry H. L.
1973 "Interracial Marriage: A Picture of the Japanese Americans." *Journal of Social Issues* 29, no. 2:67-82.

Kitano, Harry H. L., and Sue, Stanley
  1973 "The Model Minorities." *Journal of Social Issues* 29, no. 2:1-
    10.
Kunstadter, Peter
  1979 "Ethnic Group, Category, and Identity: Karen in Northern
    Thailand." In *Ethnic Adaptation and Identity: The Karen
    on the Thai Frontier with Burma,* ed. Charles F. Keyes,
    pp. 119-64. Philadelphia: Institute for the Study of Human
    Issues.
LaGumina, Salvatore J., and Cavaioli, Frank J.
  1974 *The Ethnic Dimension in American Society.* Boston: Hol-
    brook Press.
Manners, Robert A.
  1972 "Robert A. Manners Answers John Collier's Comments
    on His Article." In *The Emergent Native Americans,* ed.
    Deward E. Walker, Jr., pp. 75-86. Boston: Little, Brown.
Nee, Victor G., and Nee, Brett DeBary
  1972 *Longtime Californ': A Documentary Study of an American
    · Chinatown.* Boston: Houghton Mifflin.
Okihiro, Gary Y.
  1973 "Japanese Resistance in America's Concentration Camps:
    A Re-evaluation." *Amerasia Journal* 2:20-34.
Osumi, Megum Dick
  1975 "Editor's Introduction to *America Is in the Heart,* An
    Excerpt, by Carlos Bulosan." *Amerasia Journal* 3, no. 1:
    1-15.
Price, John A.
  1972 "The Migration and Adaptation of American Indians to
    Los Angeles." In *The Emergent Native Americans,* ed.
    Deward E. Walker, Jr., pp. 728-38. Boston: Little, Brown.
Schusky, Ernest L.
  1965 *The Right To Be Indian.* Board of National Missions of the
    United Presbyterian Church in cooperation with the Institute
    of Indian Studies, State University of South Dakota.
Shin, Linda
  1971 "Koreans in America, 1903-1945." *Amerasia Journal* 1,
    no. 3:32-39.
Sue, Stanley, and Sue, Derald
  1971 "Chinese-American Personality and Mental Health." *Amer-
    asia Journal* 1, no. 2:36-49.
Svensson, Frances
  1975 *The Ethnics in American Politics: American Indians.* Minne-
    apolis: Burgess Publishing.

Thomas, Robert K.

    1972 "Pan-Indianism." In *The Emergent Native Americans,* ed. Deward E. Walker, Jr., pp. 739-46. Boston: Little, Brown.

Tinker, John N.

    1973 "Intermarriage and Ethnic Boundaries: The Japanese American Case." *Journal of Social Issues* 29, no. 2:49-66.

Tong, Ben

    1971 "The Ghetto of the Mind: Notes on the Historical Psychology of Chinese America." *Amerasia Journal* 1, no. 3:1-31.

    1974 "A Living Death Defended as the Legacy of a Superior Culture." *Amerasia Journal* 2:178-202.

Trosper, Ronald L.

    1976 "Native American Boundary Maintenance: The Flathead Indian Reservation, Montana, 1860-1970." *Ethnicity* 3:256-74.

University of California, Contemporary Asian Studies Division, Berkeley

    1973 "Curriculum Philosophy for Asian American Studies." *Amerasia Journal* 2:35-46.

University of California, Asian American Studies Center, Los Angeles

    1971 *Roots: An Asian American Studies Reader.* Los Angeles: UCLA, Asian American Studies Center.

University of Washington, Asian American Studies

    1977 Course descriptions.

Vanderweth, W. C., ed.

    1971 *Indian Oratory.* Norman, Okla.: University of Oklahoma

Walker, Deward E., Jr.

    1972 "Measures of Nez Perce Outbreeding and the Analysis of Cultural Change." In *The Emergent Native Americans,* ed. Walker, pp. 235-50. Boston: Little, Brown.

Wallace, Anthony F. C.

    1972 *The Death and Rebirth of the Seneca.* N.Y.: Vintage Books.

Weiss, Melford S.

    1974 *Valley City: A Chinese Community in America.* Cambridge, Mass.: Schenkman.

Witt, Shirley Hill

    1970 "Nationalistic Trends Among American Indians." In *The American Indian Today,* ed. Stuart Levine and Nancy O. Lurie, pp. 93-127. Baltimore: Penguin Books.

Wong, Linda

    1975 "The Esther Lau Trial: A Case Study of Oppression and Sexism." *Amerasia Journal* 3, no. 1:16-27.

Yanagisako, Sylvia Junko

    1975 "Two Processes of Change in Japanese-American Kinship." *Journal of Anthropological Research* 31, no. 3:196-224.

For Cohen, an ethnic group is a collectivity of people who share some interests in common and who, in interaction with other collectivities, coordinate their activities in advancing and defending these interests by means of a communal organization, manipulating in the process such cultural forms as kinship, religion, myths of origin, and ceremonials of all sorts. In this sense ethnicity can be treated as a variable in three major ways. First, it varies in degree, depending on the magnitude of the interests of the group and on the pressure on its members imposed by other groups in the society. Second, assuming that that degree is constant, it varies in the type of organizational articulation developed by the group, between the associative organization at the one end and the communal on the other, with most groups combining these two forms in different proportions. Third, assuming both degree and form of organization to be constant, it varies in the cultural forms exploited by the group in the articulation of its organization, in some cases using a major cultural form, such as kinship or religion, in others using different combinations of a variety of forms. Ethnic groups may differ in any and every one of these ways, making a comparative study complex and difficult, due to differences in social systems, cultural forms, scale, and other circumstances. To overcome some of these methodological difficulties, Cohen devotes the first half of the paper to a comparative study of six different stages in the history of one collectivity—the Creoles of Sierra Leone. The second half of the paper presents a more detailed cross-cultural analysis of these three major variables.

ABNER COHEN

Variables in Ethnicity

INTRODUCTION

Ethnicity has already become the subject of such an extensive literature that there can hardly be any conceptual formulation about it not made by someone before. The debate about definitions, hypotheses, and ideas will and should, of course, go on, but we must prevent the concept from becoming a fetish. At present so much is subsumed under it that the term is in danger of becoming a screen, hiding from our view important sociocultural processes.

One way in which further theoretical development can be made is to break the complexity of ethnic phenomena into separate sociocultural factors and to subject each of these to more rigorous analysis. This can be done meaningfully only with more intensive and detailed monographic studies, within a cumulative perspective of well-documented ethnographic cases. Many writers have indeed been working along these lines; what is needed very badly is a more systematic and methodical procedure.

I shall attempt in this paper to explore some of the ways in which ethnicity can be treated as a sociocultural variable. An ethnic group is a collectivity of people who share some interests in common and who, in interaction with other collectivities, coordinate their activities in advancing and defending these interests by means of a communal type of organization, manipulating in the process such cultural forms as kinship, myths of origin, and rites and ceremonies. In this sense ethnicity can be treated as a variable in three major ways. Firstly, it varies in *degree,* depending on the importance of the interest of the group and on the pressure on the members of that group imposed by other groups in the society. Second, assuming that degree is constant, it varies in the type of *organizational articulation* developed by the group, between the associative organization at the one end and the communal organization at the other, with most groups combining these two forms in different proportions. Third, assuming both degree and pattern of organization to be constant, it varies in the *cultural forms* exploited by the group in the articulation of its organization, in some cases using a major cultural form, such as kinship or religion, in others using different combinations of a variety of forms.

Ethnic groups may differ widely in any and every one of the ways and this makes their comparative study complex and difficult, due to wider differences in social systems, cultural forms, scale, and other circumstances. Some of the methodological difficulties can be effectively overcome if we study one collectivity in historical perspective to analyze variations along the dimensions mentioned above.

I shall therefore explore these theoretical issues in analyzing different stages in the history of one such collectivity—the Creoles of Sierra Leone who, over a century and a half, have undergone dramatic sociocultural metamorphoses in response to cataclysmic changes in their fortunes and in the structure of the political systems within which they have been encapsulated.

THE CREOLES OF SIERRA LEONE

The Creoles are said to be the descendants of slaves who were emancipated by the British, mainly during the first half of the nineteenth century, and duly settled in what came to be known as the "Province of Freedom" (see Fyfe 1962; Porter 1963; Peterson 1969) in the Freetown Peninsula. Today they number 41,783, of whom 27,730 live in Freetown city and most of the others in nearby villages. They are thus essentially metropolitan. (For census details see Government of Sierra Leone 1965). They are nearly all literate, many of them highly educated and occupationally differentiated. Although they comprise only 1.9 percent of the population of the country, they dominate the top positions of the civil service, the judiciary, and the other major professions, including medicine, law, engineering, and teaching, even though they have little executive power or military force.

Until now the Creoles have seen themselves, and were often seen by others, as a discrete ethnic group, with a distinct culture, style of life, common origin, and history. What is more, they are still legally defined as "nonnative." This, however, is to a large extent a false picture. Among many other things, it assumes a strict observance of a rigid principle of descent, tracing clear geneaological link between the living and the original immigrants, and assuming continuous self recruitment. But the Creoles are bilateral and a man will often include within what he calls his "family" patrilateral and matrilateral affines, as well as friends. Throughout their history, men and women of native descent were creolized through various processes (see Banton 1957; Porter 1963). On the other hand, there have been processes in the opposite direction, by which Creole became natives and identified themselves with one or another of the sixteen ethnic groups in the country. More recently, some Creoles have publicly renounced their British names, assumed African names, and advocated complete integration with the natives. Creole men today declare publicly that they are opposed to "tribalism" and try to play down their distinctive identity as Creoles as far as they can go under the circumstances. Creoledom has over the generations passed through different phases, changing socially and culturally, and it will be sociologically instructive to look briefly at the general configurations of these phases.

A NEGATIVELY DEFINED CATEGORY (1787-1849)

In his critique of my introduction to *Urban Ethnicity* (Cohen 1974) Freedman (1975) argued that to conceive ethnicity as the manipulation of cultural tradition for politicoeconomic ends assumes the prior existence of ethnic identities and hence cannot explain ethnicity as such. The Creole case will, however, show how ethnic identity itself is shaped under the impact of politicoeconomic circumstances, for at the beginning there had been no identifiable group called the "Creoles." The history of the group to be known later by that name begins with the settlement of three different small groups of immigrants. In 1787, about 400 Black poor, who had been surviving precariously in England from begging, were taken to Sierra Leone. They were unprepared for the harsh climate and when the rainy season came they were decimated by disease, and the few who remained alive fled in different directions when their settlement was destroyed by a native chief. In 1792 a second group of immigrants came, consisting of about 1100 ex-slaves who had been loyal to the British, had fought on their side in the American War of Independence, and withdrawn with them to Nova Scotia. They were soon joined by the remnants of the Black poor when these heard of their arrival. In 1800, about 500 ex-slaves, known as the Maroons, were brought from Jamaica to join the other settlers (for details see Fyfe 1962; Porter 1963; Peterson 1969). In 1808, Britain assumed control of the Freetown Settlement, making it a colony to which emancipated slaves were brought.

The three small groups of original immigrants came to be known as "Settlers" to distinguish them from the steady flow of liberated Africans, or Recaptives, during the first half of the nineteenth century. These had been captured as slaves from different parts of the coast of West Africa and were being transported across the Atlantic when the British navy, acting under antislavery laws, intercepted their boats and, instead of returning them to their original homelands, took them to Freetown to join the Settlers. Tens of thousands of men and women came to Freetown in this way.

The Settlers, having been exposed to Western culture and having, during displacement and dispersal, become detribalized, looked down on the Recaptives, who had only recently come from their tribal homes and carried with them their tribal traditions. A cleavage developed between the two groups.

During this period the immigrants were only a category, not a group. Even the Settlers themselves were divided by enmity, particularly between the Maroons and the Nova Scotians. The main economic activity was agriculture, which involved little need for collective cooperation, and there was no pressure from outside that drew them together. They had no unified association and no corporate leaders; by no stretch of the sociological imagination could they be described as an ethnic group. They were a category of people who were defined negatively as "nonnative."

A STATUS GROUP (1850-1898)

Within a remarkably short time, the heterogeneous immigrant population of the early decades of the nineteenth century evolved into a fairly homogeneous, sophisticated status group. The Recaptives in particular underwent a spectacular transformation. They worked hard, amassed money, married into the Settlers' groups, and adopted their values and ways of life. Most of them became Christians and the

For Cohen, an ethnic group is a collectivity of people who share some interests in common and who, in interaction with other collectivities, coordinate their activities in advancing and defending these interests by means of a communal organization, manipulating in the process such cultural forms as kinship, religion, myths of origin, and ceremonials of all sorts. In this sense ethnicity can be treated as a variable in three major ways. First, it varies in degree, depending on the magnitude of the interests of the group and on the pressure on its members imposed by other groups in the society. Second, assuming that that degree is constant, it varies in the type of organizational articulation developed by the group, between the associative organization at the one end and the communal on the other, with most groups combining these two forms in different proportions. Third, assuming both degree and form of organization to be constant, it varies in the cultural forms exploited by the group in the articulation of its organization, in some cases using a major cultural form, such as kinship or religion, in others using different combinations of a variety of forms. Ethnic groups may differ in any and every one of these ways, making a comparative study complex and difficult, due to differences in social systems, cultural forms, scale, and other circumstances. To overcome some of these methodological difficulties, Cohen devotes the first half of the paper to a comparative study of six different stages in the history of one collectivity—the Creoles of Sierra Leone. The second half of the paper presents a more detailed cross-cultural analysis of these three major variables.

whole immigrant population embarked on efforts at upward social mobility. Western education was imparted on a grand scale by the many schools founded by missions in Freetown. Fourah Bay College was already established in 1848 under the supervision of Durham University and began training African clergymen to bring the gospel to the interior of Sierra Leone as well as to other parts of West Africa.

The immigrants were still regarded as nonnatives, but this negative definition of identity was superseded by a positive identity, that of "Black Englishmen." They did not form a corporate political body, but were, nevertheless, a status group consisting of families that shared the same values, norms, and ambitions. They were divided internally on class lines, but the majority aspired to reach the highest status in the hierarchy. They did not develop a novel identity but simply tried to become British. Indeed they were officially regarded as British subjects. British civil servants and other colonial officers lived in the same parts of Freetown with them, worshipped in the same churches, frequented the same clubs, and even married immigrant women. A number of Creole men were appointed to senior positions in the colonial administration. Most Creoles regarded themselves as British and were so regarded by the natives in the tribal hinterland of what came to be known as the Protectorate, that is, an indirectly ruled territory over which Britain assumed authority in the last decade of the nineteenth century. The pressure from the natives was not yet felt. Indeed, the Creoles were regarded as a "reference group" by many native families who even gave their own children to be fostered by Creole families in Freetown under an institution known as the "ward system." For many decades this system became a source of recruitment to Creoledom after the drying up of the inflow of the Recaptives. Many of the wards acquired Western education, became Christian, and adopted the names of their fostering Creole families. Although Christianity was associated with Western education, enlightenment, and "civilization," a small group of immigrants formed an influential Muslim community. Some of these had been Muslims before they were captured as slaves; others became Muslim after settlement in Sierra Leone. Whatever its origin among this group, Islam became closely interconnected with the organization of indigenous long-distance trade in which this group was seriously involved. As I argue elsewhere (Cohen 1971b) the whole network of communities engaged in that trade was organized under the beliefs and institutions of Islam. To partake in that trade, it was necessary to be, or to become, a Muslim. This group came to be known as the "Aku." They were in many ways interrelated with the Christian Creoles and sometimes even intermarried with them. There was no cleavage between the two religious communities at that time.

Thus towards the end of the century the immigrants were a status group with different classes and groupings, without corporate organization or leadership. They were regarded as British subjects and the different sections within the group aspired to become more and more Westernized. They were in many ways distinct from the natives, but not homogeneous enough in their culture or corporate in their organization to be called an ethnic group.

AN ESTRANGED COLLECTIVITY (1899-1946)

The next half-century was in many respects tragic for the Creoles. In 1898 the Hut Tax War flared up in the Protectorate and hundreds of Creole traders, missionaries, and others were massacred. During the following decades the Creoles lost their hold on business and were replaced by British, Lebanese, and Indian concerns. A greater calamity was the dramatic change in British policy towards them. British officials in Freetown moved to live separately from the Creoles and improved health conditions made it possible for them to bring their wives and families with them. British writers and officials ridiculed the attempts by Creoles to "ape" the British style of life and poured scorn on Creole "rubbishy culture." More significantly, they stopped the appointment of Creoles to senior positions in the colonial administration and, as existing Creole personnel in those positions died or retired, they were replaced by Britons. The Creoles were certain that it was an intended British policy to encourage the immigration of Lebanese and Indians to push the Creoles out of business. Creole doctors were discriminated against, were paid less than British doctors, and on the whole treated as second-class professionals.

Many Creole missionaries, professionals, traders, and civil servants sought work in other parts of Africa. The number of professionals was steadily increasing as businessmen had invested a great deal of money in university education for their children.

During the Second World War there was a marked improvement in Creole fortunes as a large number of them were employed by the British army in a variety of jobs. Until then, there had been a sharp class difference within Creoledom between a few "aristocratic families" who enjoyed large estates and had some important positions in public life, at the top, and the major part, who were relatively poor, at the bottom. The employment of a large number of these in relatively well-paid jobs during the war created a Creole middle class and the disparity between those at the top and those below them was greatly reduced. In successive decades, Western education and "civilization" became an integral part of Creole life. With more money obtained during

the war, more Creole young men and women were sent for university education abroad.

Sociologically, however, the Creoles continued during that period to be only a status group, without corporate leadership and, under the umbrella of British colonial power, did not have to unite against the natives, even if the latter continued to immigrate into the Creole "homeland" in the Freetown Peninsula to become the majority.

CHALLENGE OF THE NATIVES AND THE EMERGENCE OF CORPORATE CONSCIOUSNESS (1947-1957)

The following decade proved to be the most traumatic in the history of the Creoles. In 1947, the British government proposed constitutional reforms in Sierra Leone, with the aim of unifying the Colony (Freetown and the peninsula) and the Protectorate and setting the whole country on the path to independence. Among other things, the proposals stipulated that the fourteen African members of the new Legislative Council should be elected by the people on the basis of one man, one vote. Although this may not sound a revolutionary change for the country as a whole, it virtually meant the beginning of the end of Creole political influence, even within what they regarded hitherto as their own home: the Colony.

Their reaction was frantic, and within a short time all major Creole associations combined in a struggle to stop the British from going ahead with their constitutional reforms. A major confrontation developed between the Creoles and the natives. The sixteen ethnic groups into which the native population was divided united within one party, the Sierra Leone People's party (SLPP), against the Creoles. There were bitter exchanges between the two sides. The Creole political leader at the time, Dr. Bankole Bright, described the Creoles and the natives as "two mountains that can never meet." When the Creoles failed to stop the franchise they directed their effort at persuading the British to give them independence within the Colony, that is, within the territory of the Freetown Peninsula. But even within that area, indeed even within Freetown itself, the Creoles had become a minority.

While this went on, an equally dramatic development in Creole fortunes, but in an inverse direction, occurred. In their determination to leave Sierra Leone, the British began a consistent Africanization of the administration. This entailed the replacement of British officials by Africans, and as few natives were educated enough to qualify, it was inevitable that most of the new recruits would come from among the Creoles, who were thus appointed to senior positions in the administration. The Creoles also made great gains from their land and housing

estates, when the value of those rose sharply with the increasing demand both by natives and by foreigners. In general, the Creoles stood to gain a great deal of power and privilege, even if they were formally losing politically. This meant that they would lose everything if they persisted in standing as an associatively organized political bloc within the new state structure; with their hopelessly small numbers, they would not gain any seats in the Assembly. On the other hand, if they cooperated with the natives in the maintenance of a liberal regime on the basis of equality they would gain a great deal, in view of their superiority in education, cultural sophistication, and experience in administration.

Those Creoles who thought along those lines eventually cooperated with the native-dominated government headed by Sir Milton Margai. Milton Margai, who was a shrewd politician, knew that he could not establish a government without the Creoles and also recognized the immense contribution the Creoles had made and could still make to develop the country. He therefore included many Creoles in his party's representation and retained Creole men in key government positions. In the election of 1957, the Creole party, headed by Bankole Bright, suffered a dismal defeat and the leader died shortly afterwards.

The party failed so badly because the overwhelming majority of the Creoles realized that it would be disastrous for them to stand as a formally organized group. Any official institutionalization of their distinctiveness would inevitably lead the opposition to argue that the Creoles should get, say, scholarships and appointments to the bureaucracy in proportion to their number within the population, that is, less than 2 percent. The debacle of the 1957 election was the last attempt by the Creoles to organize themselves associatively within Sierra Leone. (For details on political events during this and the next phase, see Kilson 1967; Cartwright 1970).

THE DEVELOPMENT OF COMMUNAL ORGANIZATION (1957-1967)

But the 1957 failure did not mean lack of unity among the Creoles. They were indeed for the first time in their history united in their stand. It was also for the first time that they sought to develop a corporate organization with a corporate leadership. When these could not be achieved by means of overt organization, a covert organization soon developed. Largely without conscious policy or design, the major Creole institutions were intensified and manipulated to articulate different organizational functions. The loosely knit network of kinship relationships became closely knit and its ceremonials became more intensive and more exclusive than ever before. As the danger and

challenge to Creole privileged position and power continued in different forms, the need for greater cooperation among the Creoles and closer coordination of their activities increased. They particularly felt the need for a unified leadership, which they had never had. During the colonial period, the natives had their own tribal chiefs and paramount chiefs as part of British indirect rule. The Creoles, however, were British subjects and, theoretically, the British governors were their centralized authority, but with independence, the Creoles had no acknowledged leaders of their own. Creole politicians who had conducted the political struggle in the previous decade did not enjoy the trust and approval of the majority of the Creoles.

This gap in Creole corporate organization was now filled significantly by the ritual hierarchy within the Freemasonic order within which increasing numbers of Creole men became affiliated. The number of Masonic lodges increased from six in 1947 to seventeen in 1970, with an estimated membership of between 1500 and 2000 men, overwhelmingly Creole. Senior civil servants and professionals of all sorts, they were also the patrons, the heads of the extended families, and of the overlapping networks of cousinhood, of Creoledom. These men could not develop in their secular life a unified authority structure as they were divided into different occupational, social, and denominational groupings, and within each of these groupings there was intense competition for promotion into higher positions and perpetual tension between superior and subordinate. But within the Masonic order they became integrated by an all-encompassing authority structure in which members from the higher positions of the different secular hierarchies were included. The different types and bases of power within those groupings were "translated" into the uniform symbols and ideology of Freemasonry. (For a more detailed account see Cohen 1971a.) In many respects this resort to a secret ritual society was in response to a similar strategy adopted extensively by the natives, who had frequently used their traditional men's secret societies, the Poro (see Little 1965, 1966; Kilson 1967), to mobilize votes and support in elections, often against the Creoles themselves.

During this period ethnicity emerged on a national scale within Sierra Leone. During the 1947-57 period the sixteen tribes of the hinterland were united supertribally in one front against the Creoles. Of those tribes, the largest were the Temne and the Mende, each comprising about 30 percent of the population. The government was formed under the Mendes, not because these were slightly greater in number than the Temnes, but, having been nearer to Freetown than the Temnes and having greater access to education, were more sophisticated and had a larger number of educated men who were capable

of forming and running a modern government. The Temne were given a few posts in that government.

In 1964 Sir Milton Margai died and was replaced by his brother Albert. During the following three years there were enough changes to indicate that the new leader was planning to have a Mende hegemony: by increasing the Mendization of the bureaucracy, by proposing to opt out for a one-party state, and by turning the country into a republic. When Sir Milton died, the Temne had hoped that their leader, Karefa Smart, would succeed him. They were taken aback when this did not happen. Throughout the years of the alliance, the Temne had hoped their province would be developed to compensate them for decades of negligence during the colonial period. Those hopes did not materialize. Furthermore, Sir Albert systematically replaced Temne ministers with Mendes; he even carried the Mendization process to the army, where more than 60 percent of the commissioned officers were Mende. Thus by the middle of the 1960s the ruling SLPP came to be identified with the Mende. The Temne and other opposition elements came to be identified with the All Peoples' Congress (APC).

There was thus a sharp polarization in the country into Mende- and Temne- led camps. The Creoles joined and in many ways supported the Temne camp for two main reasons. The first was particularistic. The Mendization of the civil service began to threaten the hold of the Creoles over the bureaucracy and indeed endangered the whole Creole establishment in the country. The second was universalistic. The Creoles genuinely upheld the principles of a liberal democracy with an independent bureaucracy and judiciary and free opposition, and they sought to prevent Sir Albert Margai's alarming proposals for a one-party state at any cost.

Creole heads of trade unions, clergymen, lawyers, doctors, teachers, and university students used every shred of influence they had to bring about the downfall of Albert Margai. Particularly crucial was the action taken by Creole professionals, and Albert Margai began an ominous attack on "the doctors, lawyers, and lecturers of Freetown" who were refusing to see the blessings of the one-party system. The conflict came to a head in the election of 1967, when the Mende-led SLPP, despite its strategic hold over the government at the time, was defeated by a narrow majority. Historians of the period, as well as political scientists who analyzed the election, are unanimous in their belief that it was Creole active support and meticulous organization that brought about the collapse of the Mende regime. The conduct of the campaign by the opposition indicated a remarkable coordination between the different groups and factions that the loosely formed APC party was not capable of achieving and there is no doubt that

it was Creole corporate organization that spearheaded and marshalled the opposition. This was indeed the Creoles' finest hour.

ETHNIC GROUP–STATE ELITE

By 1970, when the major part of my field study was carried out, the Creole establishment was more powerful than ever before. The Mende menace had been stopped. What is more, Creoles replaced Mendes in many senior positions in the bureaucracy, when these were sent to prison as a result of their involvement in a coup after the SLPP defeat in the election of 1967. The Sierra Leone polity evolved into a "segmentary system," consisting of two major fronts, each associated with one of the two major tribes, with the Creoles being pushed, and partly maneuvering themselves, into the role of "the stranger," maintaining the unity, stability, and continuity of the polity. Their cultural distinctiveness and corporate exclusiveness enhanced that role. As most Creoles work for the state as civil servants and professionals of various sorts, their exclusiveness was that of the state bureaucracy in many other state systems. Marx and others have pointed out that everywhere bureaucracy tends to be autonomous and secretive. Indeed for the Creoles, bureaucracy is very much a way of life, one that has conditioned their culture and the very structure of their kinship organization.

Members of state elites (for the concept, see Miliband 1973) are supposed to be individuals who achieve their status by merit and who conduct their jobs in accordance with the written blueprint of the bureaucracy. But everywhere bureaucrats tend to develop a normative culture of their own to serve as an informal mechanism for coordinating their activities in their various positions. This is why some students of elites (see Meisel 1958) state that an elite can perform its task and survive to the extent of its success in developing three basic C's: consciousness, cohesion, and conspiracy. Thus by 1970 Creole culture was doubly exclusive, serving as an informal organizational mechanism for both particularistic and universalistic purposes.

DEGREES OF ETHNICITY

From this brief outline of the sociocultural history of the Creoles in its six different phases, it will be possible to draw some analytical formulations about using the concept of ethnicity as a variable. Ethnicity is always two-dimensional, consisting of both a cultural and an organizational factor. When we talk of ethnic groups, we are by definition talking about *groups in interaction* with other groups within a

common political system. There is no point in referring to isolated, independent societies, like nations within their own boundaries, as ethnic groups. Also by definition, ethnic groups are culture groups, that is, groups that are distinct from other groups in patterns of normative symbols or in their institutions. Interaction with other ethnic groups within one political system can take the form of either alliance or conflict. Alliance is bound to lead to integration, first political and later cultural, between the groups involved, that is, it will lead to the disappearance of ethnic differences between them. Conflict, on the other hand, is bound to sharpen the cultural differences between groups and to develop corporate organization in each in order to conduct the struggle effectively.

In the account given above, the Creoles were considered as a group operating in interaction with other groups within the Sierra Leone polity. This is partly a projection from the present into the past because Sierra Leone as a geopolitical entity did not emerge until recent decades. During the 1787-1850 phase, the Creoles did not form one homogeneous culture group with distinct political interests; they were a conglomeration of different splinter groups thrown together by historical circumstances. They were in fact divided among themselves into Settlers and Recaptives and each of these was duly divided on different lines. But they soon began to share a common experience, that of ex-slaves helped by a foreign power to settle in a new land. During the next phase, 1850-98, they began to integrate within a class system institutionalized by the British within the Colony, that is, the Freetown Peninsula. Class lines cut across past cultural differences among the immigrants and a great deal of cultural homogenization took place. The 1899-1946 phase was uneventful as far as Creoles ethnicity was concerned; it was the period when the British rejected them as partners in their political ascendancy and culture and when many Creoles emigrated, temporarily or permanently, to other parts of Africa.

Creole ethnicity came to its own during the 1947-57 phase, when for the first time they faced a cataclysmic challenge to their hitherto privileged position, at times to their very livelihood and to their possessions. This challenge continued in different episodes at different times from 1958 to 1967. During these two periods Creole cultural definition and distinctiveness was intensified through different processes. The Aku, who until about 1947 regarded themselves as Creoles, were no longer ready to be so identified. The majority of the natives were Muslims and when executive political power in the whole country was inherited from the British by the natives, it was folly for the Aku to maintain affinity with the hated Christian Creoles. Indeed the Aku, being more educated and sophisticated than most of the natives,

became the reference group for most of the Muslims of the county. Similarly, many of the former wards who had adopted the names of their Creole foster families and accepted Christianity reverted to their original names and religious affiliation. On their side, the Creoles highlighted their own cultural distinctiveness by intensifying their family ceremonials and hence the bonds of cousinhood and of the network of amity based on it. This inevitably meant that they were left with less time to spend on cultivating relationships outside of Creole boundaries. They also greatly intensified their cult of the dead, which strengthened the links across whatever class differentiation that existed within the extended families and within the Creole community as a whole. The cult also inhibited the alienation of land through sale of Creole estates to non-Creoles.

This cultural distinctiveness was further enhanced with the development of a unified informal Creole authority structure articulated through the Freemasonic order. This led to greater unity and coordination of corporate action. In the course of two decades, Masonry became institutionalized in the Creole home, extended family, and the Creole cousinhood as a whole. Men came under pressure to join the order, and the order developed into a "brotherhood," and thus deepening the relationships of amity within the Creole cousinhood (see Cohen 1971a). Added to all this, and in many ways interconnected with it, was the life style, the cult of decorum, expressed in patterns of dress, etiquette, manners, and conventions, which the Creoles cultivated in their functioning as a state elite in manning the bureaucracy and as professionals, as state-employed doctors, lawyers, engineers, and teachers. Family cult, cult of the dead, church cult, cult of secrecy, and cult of decorum, all became integrated within the personal and social life of Creole men and women and heightened their social and cultural distinctiveness.

There is thus a fundamental difference in degree between this kind of sociocultural distinctiveness and that manifested by the Creoles in earlier phases of their history. And here we come to a significant lesson in the analysis of ethnicity. As van den Berghe (1965) once put it, ethnicity is a matter of degree. There is ethnicity and ethnicity. In some cases ethnicity manifests itself in violence and bloodshed, as in northern Ireland or in postindependence Ruwanda and Burundi, where literally tens of thousands of Tutsi and Hutu were massacred. In other cases ethnicity manifests itself only in some rather superficial manner, such as the wearing of a special style of dress or the holding of an occasional dance attended by a fraction of the membership of an ethnic collectivity, or the exchange of jokes between the members of different ethnic groups at the bizarre customs of one another. This is not to dismiss the significance of this latter type of ethnicity, but only to point out that it differs radically from that of the first type. Most of the ethnicity reported in the literature falls on a continuum between these two extreme types. We should nevertheless pose the question whether it is heuristically helpful to treat all ethnicity, the strongest and the weakest, as one phenomenon, characterized in terms of one criterion, such as identity. Can we meaningfully and operationally distinguish between a strong identity and a weak identity? Barth (1969, p. 14) conceived of ethnicity as a vessel that is always there, whether it is relevant to behavior or not. This can of course be a helpful metaphorical statement, but what it does not convey, indeed what it hides, is that it is not just the contents of the vessel that vary, but the vessel itself, so to speak. When for a long time the vessel is not used, it atrophies and withers away and the people who were contained in it become involved in different, stronger vessels.

Again, many scholars have defined ethnicity in terms of origin, real or putative. Thus Weber defined ethnic groups as those human groups that entertain a subjective belief in their common descent. Similarly, Barth (ibid.) defined them by classifying persons by what he called their "basic most general identity," as determined by their origin and background. More recently, Keyes (1976) has carried this view to its logical end by describing ethnic groups as descent groups that have the potential of forming segmentary hierarchies.

The analogy of descent is indeed very appropriate here. Some years ago, a controversy arose among social anthropologists about the definition of lineage. Distinction has been made between, for example, strong partriliny and weak patriliny. The question was, how weak would patriliny have to be to cease being patriliny, or to be at all useful as an analytical tool? If a group of related families in contemporary United States kept a record of descent, tracing their common ancestry in one line for many generations, do we describe them as a lineage, in the same sense in which the term is used to describe lineages among the Zulu and the Tallensi? Some of the protagonists advocated a minimal definition, a simple common denominator that applies extensively to a wide variety of collectivities, but many others—among them E. Evans-Pritchard, M. Fortes, E. Leach, M. Gluckman, and E. Peters—restricted the term to groups that are exogamous, corporate, internally segmented, localized, and externally forming part of an autonomous political system.

Do we have to develop a similar stand on the use of the term "ethnicity"? We may not be in a position to do so yet, but we can and should develop criteria by which we can mark different degrees of ethnicity, to treat ethnicity as a variable.

The Subjective Factor

There are different senses in which ethnicity can be described as a variable, depending on what factors one is considering. One of these factors refers to the intensity of subjectively experienced attitudes, feelings, and sentiments—conscious or unconscious—held by a collectivity of people in relation to other collectivities. Some anthropologists describe this subjective factor as the *cognitive* dimension and have tried to devise techniques for measuring it. Thus, Mitchell (1974) sought to measure what he called the cognition of "social distance," by administering a formal, self-completed questionnaire, among 329 senior-grade schoolboys in what today is Zambia. The boys were asked whether they would willingly admit members from twenty different ethnic categories into close relationships with them by marriage, work, commensality, visiting at home, and so forth. The answers were tabulated, statistically processed, and the results were projected in a diagram showing "hierarchical clustering of perceptions of social distance between categories" (ibid., p. 6). The methodological techniques he used were ingenious but the value of the evidence is highly questionable and Mitchell himself was aware of this. Even amongst mature adults, subjective experience is vague, shifty, changeable, and very largely unconscious. This must be even more so among teenage boys who are not yet directly involved in the networks of economic, political, and social relationships. The evidence added little to Mitchell's final analysis or to our understanding of the situation he discussed, which is why he had to combine it with evidence from what he called "behavioral ethnicity."

During my study among the Creoles in Sierra Leone the majority of the men and women with whom I talked strongly objected to tribalism and played down their identity as Creoles. People who proved later to be "diehard Creoles" told me during our first meeting that categorization in ethnic terms was a remnant of the colonial period, that now all were Sierra Leoneans, and they were vehement in demonstrating from their own genealogies that there was a great deal of "mixed blood" in them. In the course of a year, I often heard the same person expressing different, often contradictory, views about Creoledom and about the various ethnic groups in the country. If there was any one pattern in the statements I heard, it was that those Creoles who were employed in the public sector or students hoping to be so employed, refrained from stressing their identity as Creoles, at least during our first meeting. Unemployed women, retired men, and self-employed persons, on the other had, were not inhibited from expressing strong ethnic sentiments or from expressing antagonistic views against the natives. In most cases, however, the views expressed seemed to be genuinely felt and any fieldworker would know how shaky an evidence are attitudes and their "measurement." It is not that informants attempt to mislead the sociologist, although this may happen sometimes. The views are often given honestly as persons hold them or feel them at the time.

What we must realize is that the patterns of behavior that we call ethnicity are not the products of the idiosyncrasies of individuals, but the collective representations of a group. They are certainly rooted in psychic processes, in individual motives, values, and interests that are subjectively experienced. But the symbolic formations in which they are expressed—mythologies of origin and descent, slogans, stereotypes, and ideologies—are social constructions that are impressed on the minds of members through continuous socialization. They might have originated in the mind of one individual, a leader, artist, or prophet, but once they are externalized and adopted by a group they become collective and objective, assume an existence of their own, so to speak, and confront the individual from the outside, constraining him, giving expression to his uncertain feelings, and exerting pressure on him to conform. Often it is these objective and collective representations that generate the subjective experience of ethnicity, not the other way round. A group "ideology" is concrete, empirically observable, and needs no depth psychology for understanding its social import. The subjective factor in ethnicity is significant for sociological analysis only in its objective manifestations. Its variation is related to variations in the intensity and ubiquity of the group's ceremonials, their magnitude in cost of time, energy, and resources, and their exclusiveness.

The Power (Economic-Political) Factor

Everywhere, in both industrial and preindustrial societies, ethnicity is directly involved in the struggle for power and privilege between individuals and groups. People do not resort to violence against one another because they differ culturally; but if they do resort to such violence it is almost always because their cultural differences articulate opposing economic and political interests. We have seen this clearly in the dramatic emergence of Creole ethnicity from 1947 onwards. When different cultural groups share the same interests and align themselves in opposition to other interest groups, their cultural differences tend to become weaker and insignificant as time passes. In the process they may borrow customs from one another, intermarry, develop a common language and a common life style. Again, this is clearly demonstrated by the Creoles when the different groups of immigrants, Settlers, and Recaptives, hailing from different places with different patterns of culture, evolved a homogeneous culture. Until about 1947 there had still been some differences between some immigrant groups as expressed in the persistence of Settlers' associations and the practice of hypergamy between them, but these differences quickly disappeared when the Creoles confronted the natives after 1947. On the other hand, when the members of one culture group become seriously divided into opposing interest groups they will tend to articulate their opposition in cultural cleavage of some sort, such as that on the basis of religious denominationalism.

The bloody series of massacres by Hutu against Tutsi in Ruwanda and by Tutsi against Hutu in Burundi after independence were the result of a deep class cleavage between the two groups. The struggle was over land, political office, taxation, funds, scholarships, and privileges in general, not over cultural symbols. Similar issues are at the roots of the Catholic-Protestant cleavage in Northern Ireland. On the other hand, when formerly conflicting ethnic groups cooperated on class lines within a new situation, they began to shed their cultural differences. This is clearly shown in the now classic case reported by Epstein (1958) for the copper belt in what is now Zambia, where the dominant power cleavage was between White employers and a multiethnic Black labor force. During the struggle, laborers thwarted sustained efforts by employers to deal with them through mediation by tribal elders. They set aside their traditional tribal enmities and developed a common ideology and an effective, formally organized union that pursued the struggle for higher wages and better working conditions. A great deal of cultural homogenization developed and some forms of institutionalized "joking relationships" evolved between the members of tribes that had been at war in the past.

The economic-political factor varies in its seriousness from one case to another and it is possible to conceive of a continuum from the least to the most serious.

The Organizational Factor

In its efforts to advance or consolidate its privileges, an interest group tends to develop some basic organizational functions: distinctiveness, communication, decision making, authority structure. The most effective way of achieving this is for the group to develop what Weber (1974, pp. 136–39) called an associative organization, in which the aims of the group are clearly and precisely stated and the different organizational functions arranged rationally on bureaucratic lines. As many sociologists have shown, this is the most economical way of articulating the organization of a group. Among other advantages, it is segmental, for a member is involved in it in only one role, thus releasing the rest of the total person to engage in other tasks and its demands on the time and resources of the members are kept to the minimum. This was clearly demonstrated in the 1947-57 period, when the Creoles sought, through organization in an official political party and in official negotiations with the British government, first to thwart the franchise, then, when this did not succeed, to gain independence for the Colony.

There are, however, some social and political conditions under which an interest group cannot develop any or most of its organizational functions through a formal association. The Creoles, with the independence of the country, realized that it would be disastrous for their interests to organize themselves overtly in a formal political association, as then the natives would have insisted that the Creoles' share of such privileges as scholarships, appointments, and the like should be no more than their 1.9 percent ratio of the population. Also, an elite cannot organize as a corporate group in a formal association, as its members are not formally related to one another; they are meritocrats who achieve their status through training and competition. But as many writers have shown, an elite tends to develop into largely "invisible" sociocultural groups, to cooperate more effectively and to ensure the recruitment of their own children to the same status.

Under such conditions, the group will resort to an organization that is developed through communal relationships, like those of kinship, friendship, godparenthood, and a host of other primary relationships that are developed between men and women. While associative relationships are segmental, involving only part of the person, communal relationships are total, involving the whole personality. Associative relationships are manipulative, utilitarian, nonmoral, in which one person uses another person as a means to an end. Communal relationships, on the other hand, are moral, nonutilitarian, in which persons use one another as ends in themselves. In the words of the philosopher Immanuel Kant, associative relationships are governed by a hypothetical imperative, which says, for example, if you want to earn money, you *must* do such and such a job. Communal relationships on the other hand are governed by a categorical imperative that simply says you *ought* to respect your father, love God, and help your friend.

Few relationships are purely communal or associative; most combine the two, though in different proportions. Similarly, most organizations are both associative and communal, with some being more so of the one type than of the other. The organization of religious groupings in the United States is a case in point. In some cases, a group would articulate some of its organizational functions in associative relationships, and other functions in communal relationships.

A communal organization has no specifically stated aims, except in the most vague and ambiguous terms, and is not rationally arranged. As an organization, it is clumsy, wasteful of the time and resources of its members, and highly inefficient. For example, a formal medical association would discuss an issue by circulating an invitation to its members to attend a formal meeting, with a fixed time, date, and agenda. At the meeting, the issue is discussed squarely, decisions are taken, the meeting comes to an end, and the members disperse. A communally organized group, on the other hand, would meet to celebrate an occasion, such as the birth of a saint or the wedding of a member, would engage in many symbolic activities that have nothing to do with the issue, and would discuss the issue only informally and sporadically in the course of what for the issue are highly irrelevant activities.

Ethnicity is a communal organization that is manipulated by an interest group in its struggle to develop and maintain its power. In the articulation of their organization, ethnic groups vary on a continuum from the most associative, least communal, at the one end, to the most communal, least associative, at the other. In analysis, we can refer to this variable as the *organizational factor*. Change along this variable can be seen clearly in the case of the Creoles by observing the differences between the 1947-57 phase, characterized by attempts at associative organization, and the 1958-67 phase, characterized by the development of a predominantly communal organization. The difference in strategies is of course not hard and fast. The resort to communal organization went along with the associative type during the 1947-57 phase. From the beginning of this period some Creoles saw the dangers of associative organization and did not support it and many of these joined the Freemasonic order. Many other men struggled for formal autonomy in the Colony and for organization within an official political party. The election of 1957 demonstrated the futility of this policy and ushered in the period of "going invisible" on the part of the Creoles, renouncing formal distinctiveness and organization but intensifying the formally nonpolitical communal organization. During this latter phase, we find elements of associative organization combined with a great deal of communal organization. The difference in organizational strategy between the two periods is relative, a matter of degree.

The Cultural Factor

If we are to analyze and comprehend the nature of ethnicity, we have to isolate sharply its organizational aspects from both the subjective factor and the power (economic-political) factor. We must also analytically separate it from the cultural factor. To do so, we have to distinguish between cultural forms and cultural functions. The same organizational function, such as distinctiveness, can be effected through different cultural forms, such as a mythology of descent, forming a separate religious denomination, or having an exclusive network of kinship and affinity relationships. In small-scale preindustrial societies an entire political system may be articulated in terms of either kinship or ritualized relationships, though many polities combine these two major cultural forms in articulating different organizational functions. Thus, if we conceive of a number of ethnic groups that are developed on the basis of similar politicoeconomic interests that are equal in size and are all organized on a predominantly communal basis, these groups may articulate *the same basic organizational* functions in *a variety of* cultural forms, under different traditions. Different types of communal relationships, of ritual, ceremony, manners, etiquette, and a host of other symbolic activities, are differently manipulated by different groups to solve the same basic organizational functions. Which symbolic form will be adopted by a group will depend on circumstances.

In the Creoles' case, an observer in 1947 might have predicted that religion would be an obvious choice in the articulation of a corporate communal organization. Until then the Christian church had provided the framework within which Creole social life developed. The Creoles had always been devout Christians, organized within local churches with elaborate hierarchies of leadership. Indeed, Christianity had endowed the Creoles with their most precious basis of excellence and privilege—education and a Western style of life generally. But what has actually happened after 1947 was different, if not the opposite, for a number of reasons. First, although most of the Christians in Sierra Leone were Creoles, many of the native elites were also Christians, though affiliated with different churches. Second, the Christian churches were organized in denominations and those were affiliated within world-wide organizations that would not have approved of the politicization of religion in the interests of a narrow section of the population of the country. Third, and more important than the first two reasons, there were well over a million Muslims in the country and any politicization of Christianity as such would have inevitably led to the politicization of Islam with unfavorable results. Fourth, there were the Muslim Akus who had shared with the Creoles a good deal of experience and interests as immigrants, living with them in the Colony. While it is not possible to single out any of these factors as being crucial in inhibiting the Creoles from using religion as a basis for corporate organization, their combined effect can be well understood. Instead of Christianity, the Creoles intensified other symbolic activities, such as their cult of the dead, and adopted new ones, such as that of Freemasonry.

The discussion of religion here raises a significant issue in the analysis of ethnicity. The interest in ethnicity may be relatively recent, but the articulation of group organizations in communal relationships generally has been recognized in sociology, political philosophy, and anthropology for a very long time. For example, the role of religious beliefs and practices in the organization of sectarian interests, of states, or of whole empires has been discussed extensively by a succession of writers. Here we arrive at probably the most crucial issue in the definition of ethnicity. Ethnicity, as I have pointed out, is essentially a type of communal organization. But how do we distinguish it from other types? Is such a distinction possible? Is it sociologically important?

In what respects is ethnicity, *as an organizational strategy,* different from that of religion? The answer may be that while ethnicity tends to embrace the total way of life of the members of the group, religion embraces only a segment of that way of life. But of course, not always: it is common to find cases where the claims of religion on the totality of the person and on his way of life are far greater than those of ethnicity. It is also well known that under some circumstances, some ethnic groups transform themselves into religious communities and there are well-documented case studies of such transformation from both industrial countries (including the United States), and preindustrial countries (see for example Glazer and Moynihan 1965; Cohen 1969). Thus religion and ethnicity can be adopted interchangeably, as articulating principles of group organization. And there are groups, such as the Jews, that are referred to indiscriminately as either ethnic or religious, or both.

A more serious attempt at distinguishing ethnicity from other communal organizations is that which associates ethnicity with an ideology of common origin and descent. If the term *descent* will be used here loosely, in the sense of bilateral descent, for collectivities that have practiced a high degree of endogamy over a long time, then the distinction will be a valid one, but it will apply to nearly all communal groupings. If, on the other hand, the term is used in a more strict sense, it will be equally valid, but will hold for very few cases. The issue at stake here is a matter of description, not of analysis or theory. It is a question of categorization and classification of groups.

The question is not if the distinction is valid, but how useful it is in analysis, and this depends on the theoretical preoccupations of the student. If one is interested in the analysis of the role of communal relationships in the articulation of organizational functions under various politicoeconomic conditions and following various cultural forms and traditions, then the restrictive use of the concept of descent will narrow the comparative perspective and will limit the range and possibilities of the analysis. If, on the other hand, one is interested specifically in the analysis of the potentialities of ideologies of descent in the organization of interest groups, then the restrictive definition will certainly lead to more rigorous analysis, but the enterprise will eventually become the study of descent groups generally and will thus merge with, perhaps become identical with, the now well-established tradition of social anthropology of the study of small-scale descent groups. It will probably cease to be a study of what is loosely called by many students today ethnicity.

What should, however, be clear to us is that controversy about whether ethnicity is to be discussed in terms of descent concerns only the cultural factor in ethnicity, not the organizational nor the power (economic-political) factors. Even within the cultural factor, it concerns cultural forms, not cultural functions.

The State System as a Factor

In all of our discussion of ethnicity, we seem to assume that wherever and whenever collectivities choose to organize themselves as ethnic groups, they have the freedom to do so. Yet state systems differ greatly in their policies in this respect. Some allow the formation of both associative and communal organizations. Others allow only communal organizations, but prohibit associative organizations. Yet others allow no sectional organizations of either kind. The same population may pass in time from one state system to another, thus bringing about a change in the fortunes of interest groups within it. In many African states, independence ushered in some dramatic changes of this nature. In those countries formerly ruled by Britain, ethnic divisions were the very basis of colonial administration; some writers claim that it was colonialism that created "tribes" for its own convenience. But upon independence, ethnicity was declared "enemy number one" of the new nation-state and horizontal political parties that cut across ethnic divisions were developed for a while. In many of these countries, this phase lasted for only a few years, eventually giving way to either one-party rule or to a military regime. In these circumstances, participation in the political process reverted once more to communal organizations, including ethnicity. For it has been difficult for those regimes to suppress the development of primary interpersonal relationships and symbolic patterns of activities generally, and it is these very relationships and activities, and the beliefs and ceremonials that go with them, that can serve as bases for communal organizations. In developed totalitarian states, the organizational potentialities of ethnicity, religiosity, or other types of communal activities for articulating sectional interests are fully understood by the central authorities and attempts to develop groups based on them are severely suppressed. The question should therefore be posed: If we want to analyze ethnicity cross-culturally on an international scale, how do we take the systemic factor into account?

Part of the answer to this question was implicit in discussing the organizational factor above, where the systemic factor was partly referred to when discussing "circumstances" that prevent a group from articulating its organization formally in an associative form. But as has just been stated, some systems do not allow any sectional organization, associative or communal. The sociological significance of the systemic factor in the comparative study of ethnicity can be assessed if we pose the question differently: Is the absence of ethnic groupings in a state system due to suppression or to the absence of the other circumstances that usually bring about the phenomena of ethnicity?

I have probably posed more questions in this article than provided answers. What I have tried to point out is that we cannot study ethnic change without first isolating the major factors involved in ethnicity. Ethnicity is not one variable, but a number of variables combined in different ways under different circumstances. Ethnic change can be due to change in the power (economic-political) factor, or in the organizational factor, or in the cultural factor, or in the systemic factor, or in more than one of these factors. Any one of these can serve as a basis for comparison and hence for the study of ethnic change. But these different factors are dynamically interrelated and a paradigm for the analysis of ethnic change should assign a place for every one of them and at the same time treat the whole as a system made up of interdependent parts.

REFERENCES

Banton, M.
    1957 *West African City*. London: Oxford University Pesss.
Barth, Fredrik
    1969 Introduction. In *Ethnic Groups and Boundaries,* ed. F. Barth, pp. 9-38. London: George Allen & Unwin.

Cartwright, J.R.

    1970 *Politics in Sierra Leone 1947-1967.* Toronto: University Press.

Cohen, A.

    1969 *Custom and Politics in Urban Africa.* Berkeley and Los Angeles: University of California Press; London: Routledge and Kegan Paul.

    1971a "The Politics of Ritual Secrecy." *Man* 6: 427-48.

    1971b "Cultural Strategies in the Organisation of Trading Diasporas." In *The Development of Indigenous Trade and Markets in West Africa,* ed. C. Meillassoux, pp. 266-81. London: Oxford University Press.

    1974 *Urban Ethnicity,* ed. A. Cohen. London: Tavistock Publications.

Epstein, A. L.

    1958 *Politics in an Urban African Community.* Manchester: Manchester University Press.

Freedman, M.

    1975 "Ethnic Puzzles." *The Jewish Journal of Sociology* 17: 55-66.

Fyfe, C.

    1962 *A History of Sierra Leone.* London: Oxford University Press.

Glazer, N. and Moynihan, D.

    1965 *Beyond the Melting Pot.* Cambridge, Mass.: Massachusetts Institute of Technology Press.

Government of Sierra Leone

    1965 *1963 Population Census of Sierra Leone.* Freetown: Central Statistics Office.

Keyes, C. F.

    1976 "Towards a New Formulation of the Concept of Ethnic Group." *Ethnicity* 3: 202-13.

Kilson, M.

    1967 *Political Change in a West African State.* Cambridge, Mass.: Harvard University Press.

Little, K.

    1965 "The Political Functions of the Poro." *Africa* 35: 349-
    & 1966 65; 36: 62-72.

Meisel, J. H.

    1958 *The Myth of the Ruling Class.* Ann Arbor: University of Michigan Press.

Miliband, R.

    1973 *The State in Capitalist Society.* London: Quartet Books.

Mitchell, J.C.
   1974 "Perceptions of Ethnicity and Ethnic Behaviour: An Empirical Exploration." In *Urban Ethnicity,* ed. A. Cohen.
Peterson, J.
   1961 *Province of Freedom.* London: Faber & Faber.
Porter, A.
   1963 *Creoledom: A Study of the Development of Freetown Society.* London: Oxford University Press.
van den Berghe, P. L.
   1965 *Africa: Social Problems and Conflict.* San Francisco: Chandler Publishing Co.
Weber, M.
   1947 *The Theory of Social and Economic Organisation.* Glencoe, Ill.: Free Press.

Contributors

Aull, Charlotte H., Ph.D. in Anthropology from Duke University and currently engaged in postdoctoral work at the Centre for Development Studies, University of Wales, under a grant from the Social Science Research Council

Banton, Michael, Professor of Sociology, University of Bristol, Bristol, England

Bentley, G. Carter, Ph.D. candidate in Anthropology, University of Washington, Seattle, Washington

Cimino, Louis F., Ph.D. in anthropology from Duke University and currently Director of Programs at the American Anthropological Association, Washington, D.C.

Cohen, Abner, Professor of Anthropology, School of Oriental and African Studies, London, England

Fox, Richard, Professor of Anthropology, Duke University, Durham,

North Carolina

Keyes, Charles F., Professor of Anthropology, University of Washington, Seattle, Washington

Light, Ivan, Associate Professor of Sociology, University of California, Los Angeles, California

Nagata, Judith, Associate Professor of Anthropology, York University, Downsview, Ontario, Canada

Tessler, Mark A., Professor of Political Science, University of Wisconsin-Milwaukee, Milwaukee, Wisconsin

Trosper, Ronald L., Assistant Professor of Economics, Boston College, Chestnut Hill, Massachusetts

Trottier, Richard, Ph.D. candidate in Anthropology, University of Washington, Seattle, Washington

SCHOOL OF INTERNATIONAL STUDIES
PUBLICATIONS ON
ETHNICITY AND NATIONALITY

1. M. Nazif Mohib Shahrani. *The Kirghiz and Wakhi of Afghanistan: Adaptation to Closed Frontiers.* 264 pp., biblio., index, maps, illus. 1979.
2. Charles F. Keyes, ed. *Ethnic Change.* 334 pp. 1981.
3. G. Carter Bentley. *Ethnicity and Nationality: A Bibliographic Guide.* Forthcoming.